Global Development Finance

The Development Potential of Surging Capital Flows

I: Review, Analysis, and Outlook

Global Development Finance

The Development Potential of Surging Capital Flows

I: REVIEW, ANALYSIS, AND OUTLOOK   2006

THE WORLD BANK

Cover photo: Dennis Degnan/Corbis.
Cover design: Drew Fasick.

ISBN-10: 0-8213-5990-8
ISBN-13: 978-0-8213-5990-7
eISBN-10: 0-8213-6480-4
eISBN-13: 978-0-8213-6480-2
DOI: 10.1596/978-0-8213-5990-7
ISSN: 1020-5454

The cutoff date for data used in this report was May 17, 2006. Dollars are current U.S. dollars unless otherwise specified.

Table of Contents

Tables

Figures

Boxes

Foreword

ROBUST GLOBAL GROWTH AND A favorable financing environment provided the context for a record expansion of private capital flows to developing countries in 2005. These conditions now provide a unique opportunity for the international policy community to place development finance on a firmer footing before the tightening of global liquidity closes the window of opportunity.

Most of the record $491 billion in net private capital bound for the developing world in 2005 went to a small group of middle-income countries. Many of those countries took advantage of the growing inflows to improve their external debt profiles and accumulate large holdings of official foreign exchange reserves.

By contrast, many low-income countries still have little or no access to international private capital, and instead depend largely on official finance from bilateral and multilateral creditors to support their development objectives. With a decade remaining to attain the Millennium Development Goals (MDGs), expectations of a "big push" in development assistance escalated during 2005. Donors enhanced their efforts by scaling up aid volumes and reallocating them to the poorest countries, particularly those in Sub-Saharan Africa. In addition, the Multilateral Debt Reduction Initiative (MDRI) will provide additional debt relief to qualifying heavily indebted poor countries (HIPCs), reducing debt service and freeing up more fiscal resources for the MDGs.

At the same time, the development finance landscape is being transformed. A growing number of countries are issuing longer-term maturities in international capital markets, in some cases even denominated in local currencies. Domestic debt markets have become a major source of finance in some countries, attracting international investors in search of higher yields and potential gains from currency appreciation. Structured financial instruments such as credit default swaps allow investors to better manage exposure to

credit risks associated with emerging market external debt portfolios. Financial integration among developing countries continues to deepen with capital flows between developing countries (so-called South–South flows) playing a prominent role. The role of the euro has evolved, gaining importance both as an international reserve currency and for debt issuance by governments and the corporate sector in developing countries. The emerging market asset class has matured far beyond the earlier dominance of U.S. dollar-denominated, high-yield, sovereign-debt instruments—indeed the Brady bonds issued in the 1980s that once exemplified this category have all but disappeared.

Global growth has remained surprisingly resilient to the rise in world oil prices over the past few years. Developing countries led the way with GDP growth in 2005 of 6.4 percent, more than twice the rate of high-income countries (2.8 percent). While inflation has, on the whole, remained subdued, there are signs of a pickup in several rapidly growing countries, which raises the possibility of overheating and the need for a tightening of macroeconomic policies. More generally, current account balances in oil-importing countries have deteriorated significantly, leaving them more vulnerable to subsequent adverse shocks.

Looking forward, while many of the external factors that have supported strong developing-country growth are projected to weaken, economic growth is expected to remain relatively strong. However, downside risks predominate. Persistent global imbalances, elevated current account deficits in some developing countries, and asset price over valuation are potential sources of risks to growth prospects in developing countries. In addition, a sharp supply shock could send oil prices even higher, with serious consequences for the most energy-dependent developing economies. A fall in non-oil commodity prices could have similar consequences for some of the poorest countries, which have benefited from higher metals and mineral prices. Finally, the Doha Round stands at a critical juncture; governments need to agree on the key elements of a deal by mid-2006, but positions on the central issue of market access for agricultural and nonagricultural goods remain far apart.

A key priority for developing countries going forward is to pursue policies that strengthen their capacity to weather whatever global storms may be brewing. Continued macroeconomic stability is vital to ensure effective management of capital flows to advance long-term investment and growth. Countries must preserve sound financial management, with monetary and fiscal policies working in tandem to maintain debt sustainability and price stability. They must also build a system of risk management robust enough to respond to the needs of a more flexible exchange rate and open capital markets. Regulators in developing countries need to build their capacity to monitor credit default swap transactions and define a clear line of responsibility and necessary expertise to better manage the associated risks. Oil exporters face the special challenges of managing the risks surrounding volatile export revenues and using those revenues productively.

All countries would be affected by a disorderly unwinding of global imbalances, which would destabilize international financial markets and curtail global growth. But developing countries would suffer disproportionately, particularly if the imbalances were to foster a backlash of trade protectionism. With deepening economic and financial integration, all countries share responsibil-

ity for ensuring that policies are pursued that permit imbalances to unwind in an orderly and timely manner. This requires cooperation. The key policy prescriptions are well-known—the challenge is to make meaningful progress in implementing those policies. Policy makers in the major economies understand the importance of a coordinated approach and therefore have endorsed the proposal for the International Monetary Fund to play a more prominent role in coordinating the required collective action.

Global Development Finance is the World Bank's annual review of global financial conditions facing developing countries. The current volume provides analysis of key trends and prospects, including coverage of capital originating from developing countries themselves. A separate volume contains detailed standardized external debt statistics for 135 countries as well as summary data for regions and income groups. More information on the analysis, including additional material, sources, background papers, and a platform for interactive dialogue on the key issues can be found at www.worldbank.org/prospects. A companion online publication, Prospects for the Global Economy, is available in English, French, and Spanish at www.worldbank.org/globaloutlook.

François Bourguignon
Chief Economist and Senior Vice President
The World Bank

Acknowledgments

THIS REPORT WAS PREPARED BY THE International Finance Team of the World Bank's Development Prospects Group (DECPG). Substantial support was also provided by staff from other parts of the Development Economics Vice Presidency, World Bank operational regions and networks, the International Finance Corporation, and the Multilateral Investment Guarantee Agency.

The principal author was Mansoor Dailami, with direction by Uri Dadush. The report was prepared under the general guidance of François Bourguignon, World Bank Chief Economist and Senior Vice President. The principal authors of each chapter were:

Overview	Mansoor Dailami, with contributions from the International Finance Team and William Shaw
Chapter 1	Andrew Burns
Chapter 2	Mansoor Dailami, Ismail Dalla, Dilek Aykut, Eung Ju Kim
Chapter 3	Douglas Hostland, William Shaw, and Gholam Azarbayejani
Chapter 4	William Shaw, Dilek Aykut, Jacqueline Irving, and Neeltje Van Horen
Chapter 5	Mansoor Dailami, Johanna Francis, and Eung Ju Kim

Preparation of the commercial and official debt restructuring appendixes was managed by Eung Ju Kim, with inputs from Haocong Ren and Gholam Azarbayejani. The financial flow, debt estimates and the statistical appendix were developed in a collaborative effort between DECPG and the Financial Data Team of the Development Data Group (DECDG), led by Ibrahim Levent and including Nevin Fahmy, Shelly Fu, and Gloria R. Moreno. Background notes and papers were prepared by Paul Masson (University of Toronto), Michael Pomerleano (Operations and Policy Department of the Bank's Financial Sector), and Ivan Zelenko (Banking, Capital Markets, and Financial Engineering of the Bank's Treasury). The main macroeconomic forecasts were prepared by the Global Trends Team of DECPG, led by Hans Timmer and including John Baffes, Andrew Burns, Carolina Diaz-Bonilla, Maurizio Bussolo, Betty Dow, Annette de Kleine, Fernando Martel Garcia, Don Mitchell, Mick Riordan, Cristina Savescu, Shane Streifel, and Dominique van der Mensbrugghe. Gauresh Rajadhyaksha managed and maintained the modeling and data systems. Mombert Hoppe, Denis Medvedev, Sebnem Sahin, and Shuo Tan provided research assistance and technical support.

Contributors to regional outlooks included Milan Brahmbhatt (East Asia and Pacific); Asad Alam, Cheryl Gray, and Ali Mansoor (Europe and Central Asia); Ernesto May and Guillermo Perry (Latin America and the Caribbean); Mustapha Nabli (Middle East and North Africa); Ejaz Syed Ghani (South Asia); and Delfin Go (Sub-Saharan Africa).

The online companion publication, Prospects for the Global Economy, was prepared by Andrew Burns, Sarah Crow, Cristina Savescu and Shuo Tan with the assistance of Roula Yazigi and Shunalini Sarkar and the Global Trends team. Technical help in the production of that Web site was provided by Reza Farivari, Sarubh Gupta, David Hobbs, Shahin Outadi, Raja Reddy Komati Reddy, Malarvizhi Veerappan, Cherin Verghese, and Kavita Watsa.

The report also benefited from the comments of the Bank's Executive Directors, given at an informal board meeting on May 4, 2006.

Many others provided inputs, comments, guidance, and support at various stages of the report's preparation. Charles Collyns (International Monetary Fund), Ishrat Husain (Former Governor, State Bank of Pakistan), Mark Sundberg, Michael Klein, and Stijin Claessens were discussants at the Bankwide review. In addition, within the Bank, comments and help were provided by Alan Gelb, Alan Winters, Ali Mansoor, Asli Demirguc-Kunt, Barbara Mierau-Klein, Anderson

Caputo Silva, Angela Gentile (MIGA), Brian Pinto, Cheryl Gray, Dan Goldblum, Deepak Bhattasali, Doris Herrera-Pol, Ekaterina Vostroknutova, Ellis Juan, Eric Swanson, Francis Jean-Francois Perrault, Frannie Leautier, Gianni Zanini, Jeffrey Lewis, Joseph Battat (IFC), Marilou Uy, Muthukumaras Mani, Punam Chuhan, Sergio Schmukler Shahrokh Fardoust, Sona Varma, Ulrich Zachau, and Vikram Nehru.

Outside the Bank, several people contributed through meetings and correspondence on issues addressed in the report. These include Hiro Ito (Portland State University), Boubacar Trore (African Development Bank), Joyce Chang (JPMorgan Chase Bank), and William Cline (Institute for International Economics).

Steven Kennedy edited the report. Maria Amparo Gamboa provided assistance to the team. Araceli Jimeno and Dorota Agata Nowak managed the production of the report, while communication guidance and support for the report were provided by Christopher Neal and Cynthia Carol Case McMahon. Book design, editing, production, and printing were coordinated by Susan Graham and Andres Méneses of the World Bank Office of the Publisher.

Selected Abbreviations

ABF	Asian Bond Finance
ABMI	Asian Bond Market Inititative
ADB	Asian Development Bank
ADRs	American Depositary Receipts
AfDF	African Development Fund
ASEAN	Association of Southeast Asian Nations
ASW	asset swap
BIS	Bank for International Settlements
CDS	credit default swap
CPIA	Country Policy and Institutional Assessment
DAC	Development Assistance Committee (OECD)
DRC	Democratic Republic of Congo
DSF	Debt Sustainability Framework
EBRD	European Bank for Reconstruction and Development
ELMI	Emerging Local Markets Index
EMBI	Emerging Markets Bond Index
EMBIG	Emerging Markets Bond Index Global
EMCDS	emerging market credit default swap
EMEAP	Executives' Meeting of East Asia and Pacific Central Banks
EU	European Union
FDI	foreign direct investment
FLIRBs	Front-Loaded Interest Reduction Bonds
FoBF	Fund of Bond Funds
G-3	Group of Three (European Union, Japan, United States)
G-7	Group of Seven (Canada, France, Germany, Italy, Japan, United Kingdom, United States)
G-8	Group of Eight (G-7 plus Russian Federation)
G-90	Group of Ninety (developing countries)
GDF	*Global Development Finance* (World Bank)
GDP	gross domestic product
GEP	*Global Economic Prospects* (World Bank)
GNI	gross national income
HIPCs	heavily indebted poor countries
IABs	interest arrears bonds
IDA	International Development Association (World Bank Group)
IDB	Inter-American Development Bank
IMF	International Monetary Fund
IPO	initial public offering
LDCs	least developed countries
mbpd	million barrels per day
MDGs	Millennium Development Goals
MDRI	Multilateral Debt Reduction Initiative
MERCOSUR	Southern Cone Common Market (Mercado Común del Sur)
MIGA	Multilateral Investment Guarantee Agency
NAFTA	North American Free Trade Agreement
NDF	nondeliverable foreign exchange forward market
ODA	official development assistance
OECD	Organisation for Economic Co-operation and Development
OPEC	Organization of Petroleum-Exporting Countries
PAIF	Pan-Asian Bond Index Fund
PPP	purchasing power parity
ROSCs	reports on the observance of standards and codes (IMF and World Bank)
SAARC	South Asian Association for Regional Cooperation
SADC	Southern African Development Community
SBI	State Bank of India
SME	small and medium enterprise
SOE	state-owned enterprise
UAE	United Arab Emirates
UNCTAD	United Nations Conference on Trade and Development
WDI	*World Development Indicators* (World Bank)
WDR	World Development Report (World Bank)
WHO	World Health Organization
WTO	World Trade Organization

Overview and Policy Messages: The Development Potential of Surging Capital Flows

2005 WAS A LANDMARK YEAR IN global development finance, in both the official and private spheres. International private capital flows to developing countries reached a record net level of $491 billion. The increase in private capital flows in 2005 was broad-based, with long-term bond issuance, bank lending, and portfolio equity showing strong gains. A wave of privatizations and cross-border mergers and acquisitions drew substantial foreign direct investment (FDI). Governments and private entities took advantage of favorable financial-market conditions to refinance outstanding debt and fund future borrowing, while local-currency bond markets in Asia and Latin America attracted substantial interest from international investors in search of higher yields and potential gains from currency appreciation. Meanwhile, financial integration among developing countries continued to deepen. Capital flows between developing countries (so-called South–South flows) are now growing more rapidly than North–South flows, particularly FDI. The strong gains in private capital flows have been supported by financial innovations, notably local-currency financing and structured financial instruments, such as credit default swaps and other derivatives, which have improved the ability of investors to manage their exposure to the risks associated with emerging market assets.

Development finance took center stage at a series of major international forums in 2005. With a decade remaining to attain the Millennium Development Goals (MDGs), expectations for a big push in development assistance escalated over the course of the year, with a strong focus on Sub-Saharan Africa, the only region not on track to meet any of the goals. There was broad agreement on the need to scale up aid significantly and to further reduce the debt burdens of heavily indebted poor countries (HIPCs) to provide additional financial resources needed to make progress on the MDGs. In keeping with those objectives, donors have enhanced their aid effort over the past few years and taken steps to improve the allocation of aid by providing more development assistance to the poorest countries, particularly those in Sub-Saharan Africa. Donors also have provided targeted support for trade facilitation and developed a framework for improving the effectiveness of aid. Overall, aid in the form of grants and concessional loans has risen, while net lending by the official sector on nonconcessional terms has declined significantly.

The global economy grew at a robust pace of 3.6 percent in 2005, with the developing world exceeding 5 percent growth for the third year running. Global economic and financial conditions remain favorable, on the whole, despite several potentially destabilizing developments, notably high and volatile oil prices, growing global financial imbalances, and rising short-term policy interest rates in some of the major industrial countries. International financial markets have remained resilient to the test of several major credit events, including the downgrading of two major U.S. automakers and the settlement of backlogged credit derivatives contracts that had come to the attention of U.S. regulatory authorities. The upward trend in private capital flows appears to have continued in the early months of 2006, and the short-run prospects are good. But the external environment could well prove less auspicious in the future than in recent years, depending critically on the course and dynamics of the necessary rebalancing of global savings and investment patterns to underpin the orderly unwinding of large and unsustainable global financial imbalances.

The surge in private capital flows offers national and international policy makers a major opportunity to bolster development efforts if they can successfully meet three challenges. The first is to ensure that more countries, especially poorer ones, enhance their access to developmentally beneficial international capital through improvements in their macroeconomic performance, investment climate, and use of aid. The second is to avoid sudden capital flow reversals by redressing global imbalances through policies that recognize the growing interdependencies between developed and developing countries' financial and exchange rate relations in the determination of global financial liquidity and asset price movements. And the third is to ensure that development finance, both official and private, is managed judiciously to meet the development goals of recipient countries while promoting greater engagement with global financial markets. These are the themes and concerns of this year's edition of *Global Development Finance*.

The broad surge in private capital flows continues

Net capital inflows from official and private sources increased from $418 billion in 2004 to $472 billion in 2005. While net official lending was negative, net flows of private capital to developing countries swelled for the third consecutive year, reaching $491 billion in 2005, the highest level on record (figure 1 and table 1). Demand for emerging market debt and equities remained strong, spurred by improved fundamentals in many developing countries and investors' search for higher yields in an environment where long-term interest rates remain low in major industrial countries, despite higher short-term interest rates. Developing countries' finances also received a boost from workers' remittances, which continued their steady increase of the past decade (box 1).

The increase in private capital flows has been broad-based, extending across most debt and equity components and across most of the developing world. Long-term bond flows (up $19 billion over 2004), medium- and long-term bank lending (up $28 billion), and portfolio equity (up $24 billion) showed the strongest gains. The cost of bond

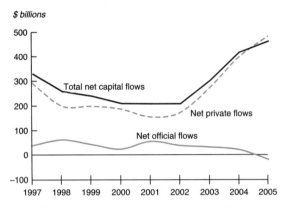

Figure 1 Financial flows to developing countries, 1997–2005

$ billions

Source: World Bank Debtor Reporting System and staff estimates.

issuance has dropped for many developing countries, as long-term interest rates in industrial countries remain low (despite increases in short-term rates in the Euro Area, the United States, and elsewhere) and spreads on emerging market sovereign bonds continue to decline. Those spreads reached a record low of 174 basis points in May 2006 (figure 2). Short-term borrowing remained at approximately the same level as in 2004 and about $14 billion higher than in 2003, in sharp contrast to the negative flows of short-term debt that were seen from 1998 to 2001.

The rise in private flows also was widespread, with all regions experiencing an increase (table 2):

- A surge in flows to the Russian Federation and Turkey helped to boost flows to the Europe and Central Asia region to $192 billion in 2005, up from $160 billion in 2004. The region accounts for 39 percent of developing countries' private flows, almost double the share it commanded in 2001.
- Stronger bond and equity activity increased private flows to Latin America and the Caribbean from $59 billion in 2004 to $94 billion in 2005. But the region's share of private flows to the developing world plummeted from 45 percent in 2000 to 19 percent last year.
- Flows to East Asia and the Pacific increased to $138 billion from $125 billion the year before, despite lower FDI to China. A marked strengthening in flows to several regional economies explains the increase.

Table 1 Net capital flows to developing countries, 1997–2005
$ billions

	1997	1998	1999	2000	2001	2002	2003	2004	2005e
Current account balance	−84.5	−89.4	−4.0	47.1	18.8	69.8	122.3	153.1	248.4
as % GDP	−1.5	−1.6	−0.1	0.8	0.3	1.2	1.8	1.9	2.6
Financial flows:									
Net equity flows	199.3	179.4	195.9	182.9	183.3	166.1	186.8	248.8	298.9
Net FDI inflows	168.7	172.4	183.3	168.8	176.9	160.3	161.6	211.5	237.5
Net portfolio equity inflows	30.6	6.9	12.6	14.1	6.4	5.8	25.2	37.3	61.4
Net debt flows	107.2	54.3	16.3	−1.0	−1.5	10.7	72.8	119.1	120.1
Official creditors	13.1	34.3	13.9	−5.7	27.4	5.2	−12.3	−28.7	−71.4
World Bank	9.2	8.7	8.8	7.9	7.5	−0.2	−0.9	1.3	0.7
IMF	3.4	14.1	−2.2	−10.7	19.5	14.0	2.4	−14.7	−41.1
Others	0.5	11.5	7.3	−2.9	0.4	−8.6	−13.8	−15.4	−31.0
Private creditors	94.1	19.9	2.5	4.7	−28.9	5.5	85.1	147.8	191.6
Net medium- and long-term debt flows	85.0	85.7	22.0	11.5	−6.2	1.2	30.2	77.8	122.3
Bonds	38.4	40.6	30.6	20.5	11.0	10.8	26.4	43.0	61.7
Banks	44.0	50.3	−7.1	−5.2	−10.8	−2.8	9.8	39.4	67.4
Others	2.7	−5.2	−1.5	−3.8	−6.3	−6.8	−5.9	−4.6	−6.7
Net short-term debt flows	9.2	−65.8	−19.6	−6.8	−22.7	4.2	54.9	70.0	69.3
Balancing item[a]	−169.5	−127.8	−175.0	−183.6	−118.8	−74.7	−90.3	−116.2	−274.5
Change in reserves (− = increase)	−52.4	−16.4	−33.2	−45.4	−81.7	−171.9	−291.6	−404.8	−393.0
Memo items:									
Bilateral aid grants (ex technical cooperation grants)	25.3	26.7	28.5	28.7	27.9	32.5	43.7	50.3	52.6
Net private flows (debt+equity)	293.5	199.3	198.4	187.6	154.4	171.5	271.9	396.6	490.5
Net official flows (aid+debt)	38.3	61.1	42.4	23.0	55.3	37.7	31.4	21.6	−18.8
Workers' remittances	71.2	73.1	77.0	85.2	96.4	113.2	141.2	161.1	166.8

Sources: World Bank Debtor Reporting System and staff estimates.
a. Combination of errors and omissions and net acquisition of foreign assets (including FDI) by developing-country private entities.
e = estimate.

Box 1   International migrant remittances

Remittances are the largest source of external financing in many developing countries. According to official statistics, in 2005 remittance flows—defined as the sum of workers' remittances, compensation of employees, and migrant transfers in the balance-of-payments statistics collected by the International Monetary Fund—are estimated to have exceeded $233 billion worldwide, of which developing countries received $167 billion. Unrecorded flows moving through informal channels push the total far higher, as they are conservatively estimated to amount to at least 50 percent of the recorded flows.

Remittances bring substantial benefits to developing countries:

- Household survey evidence, confirmed by cross-country analyses, indicates that remittances can have a significant impact on reducing poverty.
- Remittances are associated with increased household investment in education, entrepreneurship, and health—all of which have a high social return under most circumstances.
- Remittances tend to be countercyclical and thus support economic activity in the face of adverse shocks.

- By generating a steady stream of foreign exchange, remittances can improve a country's creditworthiness and enhance its access to international capital markets.

Recorded remittance flows to developing countries have doubled over the past five years, for several reasons. Increased scrutiny of financial transactions since the terrorist attacks of September 2001 has made remittances more visible. With the growth of competition in the remittance industry, costs have dropped in major corridors, while networks have expanded. Recently, high oil prices have swelled remittance flows from oil-exporting countries. Bahrain, Kazakhstan, Kuwait, Oman, Saudi Arabia, and the Russian Federation have been important sources of remittances to developing countries. The depreciation of the U.S. dollar (which raises the value of remittances denominated in other currencies) and growth in the number of migrants and their incomes have contributed further to the increase.

Source: World Bank, *Global Economic Prospects 2006;* World Bank staff calculations based on various data sources.

Figure 2 Benchmark spreads for emerging markets, 2001–6

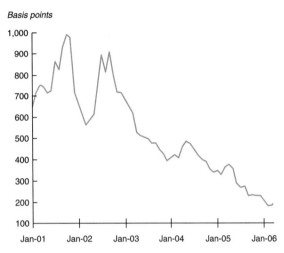

Basis points

Source: JPMorgan Chase.
Note: As of April 7.

The creditworthiness of most developing countries continued to improve in 2005, as upgrades by credit rating agencies handily outpaced downgrades. Moreover, the pace of credit upgrades rose to 46 in 2005, up from 31 in 2004. Many developing countries have taken advantage of the favorable financial conditions by issuing bonds with longer maturities in international markets—in some cases denominated in local currency. Others have been able to buy back existing debt using the proceeds of new bonds issued at lower rates. Also, many countries have pre-funded future financing requirements. Syndicated bank lending to developing countries set records in 2005. Gross bank lending of $198 billion, an increase of 77 percent over 2004, involved 1,261 transactions in a broad range of sectors, dominated by oil-and-gas projects and oil-import financing. Meanwhile, booming stock markets in

emerging market economies boosted portfolio equity flows to a record $61 billion, up from $37 billion in 2004. However, private capital flows remain concentrated in just a few countries. In 2005 about 70 percent of bond financing and syndicated lending went to ten countries; three countries (China, India, and South Africa) accounted for almost two-thirds of all portfolio equity flows.

Rather than fueling domestic investment, the rise in net inflows of private capital in 2005 financed a substantial rise in developing countries' official reserve assets (almost as large as the record increase in 2004) and a very sharp increase in the accumulation of foreign assets by private entities—to $258 billion, again a record level (see figure 3).

The opening of capital accounts in the developing world has increased opportunities for capital outflows, enabling developing-country residents to improve their investment returns and reduce their risks through international diversification.

Global growth has propelled the surge in capital flows, but serious risks remain

Global growth has remained surprisingly resilient to the rise in world oil prices over the past few years. Despite a doubling of oil prices from early 2003 to late 2005, world GDP expanded by a robust 3.6 percent in 2005. Developing countries led the way, with GDP growth of 6.4 percent, more than twice the rate of high-income countries (2.8 percent).

The impact of higher oil prices on economic growth and inflation has been more subdued than in previous episodes. Global growth was down only 0.5 percentage points, and the expansion among developing countries was 0.7 percentage points, slower than in 2004. The reduced impact

Table 2 Net private capital flows to developing countries by region, 1998–2005
$ billions

	1998	1999	2000	2001	2002	2003	2004	2005
East Asia and Pacific	6.5	28.8	28.0	39.2	58.9	81.5	125.4	137.7
Europe and Central Asia	66.7	50.9	51.5	33.1	59.7	101.1	160.2	191.7
Latin America and the Caribbean	98.9	95.8	85.2	59.5	28.2	49.9	59.3	94.4
Middle East and North Africa	8.1	2.6	3.3	4.8	8.3	7.8	8.3	14.6
South Asia	5.3	3.5	9.7	5.8	10.1	15.8	22.7	23.6
Sub-Saharan Africa	13.7	16.7	9.9	12.1	6.3	15.8	20.7	28.4

Sources: World Bank Debtor Reporting System and staff estimates.

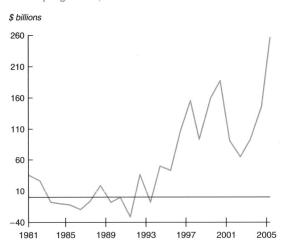

Figure 3 Capital outflows by private entities in the developing world, 1981–2005

$ billions

Sources: International Financial Statistics, IMF; and World Bank staff calculations.
Note: The size of the increase in private assets is hard to judge, since it is calculated as a residual and thus includes errors and omissions from elsewhere in the balance of payments.

reflects several factors, notably lower oil intensities, more flexible product and labor markets, exchange rate flexibility, and more credible monetary policy. Higher nonoil commodity prices have offset the impact of higher oil prices on the terms of trade of some countries.

Higher oil prices have had a major influence on the external and fiscal positions of most developing countries, however. For net oil *exporters*, higher oil prices have meant significant increases in external and fiscal surpluses, and higher foreign exchange reserves. For net oil *importers*, healthy current-account surpluses and ample foreign exchange reserves made it possible to cover the sizable increase in oil-import bills. Considerable increases in foreign aid for some of the poorest countries, particularly those in Sub-Saharan Africa, provided an additional source of foreign currency. But fiscal deficits have risen alarmingly in countries that subsidize domestic energy prices.

Despite high oil prices, growth in developing countries is expected to remain above 5 percent per year during the period 2006–8, well above the performance of the past two decades, and with inflationary pressures in check. The main risks to this relatively benign outlook are broadly unchanged since the last edition of *Global Development Finance*. The possibility that global imbalances might

unwind in a disruptive fashion remains a risk—particular for heavily indebted countries and those with close economic ties to the United States. A second risk is that a sharp supply shock might send oil prices even higher, with potentially serious consequences for the most energy-dependent developing economies. A fall in nonoil commodity prices could have similar consequences for some of the poorest countries, which have benefited from higher metals and mineral prices. There is also a possibility that the current glut of liquidity in global financial markets may have caused investors to underprice the risk of emerging market assets (both debt and equity). Political risk has reemerged as a key concern for investors in several emerging market economies, where elections could portend major changes in policy direction. Finally, there is a risk that avian influenza (bird flu) could mutate into a form that is easily transmitted between humans and for which the population has limited immunity. Depending on the severity of the eventual disease, such a pandemic could kill between 14 million and 70 million people and lower global GDP by between 2 and 5 percent (with the latter number implying a global recession).

Capital flows are being transformed
Financial integration among developing countries

For much of its postwar history, development finance has been characterized as a one-way flow of capital from industrial countries to the developing world. But as developing countries have become more integrated with the global economy, they have emerged as important sources of capital flows in their own right. In the past decade, with rising incomes in developing countries and increasingly open policies toward trade and financial markets, developing countries have become a significant source of FDI, bank lending, and even official development assistance (ODA) to other developing countries.

Overall, growing FDI between developing countries in recent years has sometimes compensated for reductions in FDI flows from high-income countries. But South–South capital flows, in particular, have also opened opportunities for low-income countries, because developing-country investors are often possibly better able to handle the special risks encountered in poor countries. Banks from developing countries play an increasingly prominent role in cross-border lending to low-income countries—borrowers in low-income countries received 17 percent of total South-South cross-border syndicated lending flows in 2005, up from 3 percent in 1985. Moreover, 27 percent of foreign bank assets in low-income countries are held by developing-country banks, compared to just 3 percent in middle-income countries. South–South FDI is significant for many low-income countries, particularly those located close to major investors.

Although South–South capital flows remain relatively small compared to North-South flows, they have the potential to change the landscape of development finance over the next few years, particularly if growth in developing countries continues to outstrip that in advanced countries and the trend toward deeper trade and financial integration persists.

Financial innovations

The market for debt issued by developing countries is expanding beyond the dollar-denominated, high-yield, sovereign debt instruments that had come to define the emerging market asset class, as exemplified by Brady bonds (which will drop to only 6 percent of the original amount outstanding once announced buybacks are completed). Today, the emerging market asset class includes a range of instruments in both local and foreign currency that offer the capacity to tap dollar and euro investors alike and cater to the funding needs of both sovereign and corporate borrowers on both the cash and derivatives sides of the market.

Credit default swaps—derivatives that provide insurance against defaults—are being applied in new ways in emerging markets. This has potentially important implications for the pricing and supply of debt capital to developing countries, offering investors a new way to take on exposure and enhancing the markets' ability to gauge credit risk. By transferring banks' credit risk from lending and trading activities to other market participants, credit derivatives have altered, perhaps fundamentally, the traditional approach to credit risk management and the lending business. While the emergence of this market could improve the ability of financial systems to diversify risk across a greater number of market participants, it remains a relatively immature and potentially vulnerable

market because of infrastructural shortcomings, a lack of regulatory frameworks robust enough to cope with the market's dynamic nature, and the concentrated participation of a small number of dealers in emerging markets, which carries the risk that failure of a single player could have a destabilizing impact on the market.

Domestic debt markets

Local-currency bond markets in developing countries have, since the crises of the 1990s, emerged as a major source of long-term development finance. They are now the fastest-growing segment of emerging market debt. Driven largely by domestic institutional and individual investors, these markets grew from $1.3 trillion at the end of 1997 to $3.5 trillion in September 2005. Their rapid growth has enabled major developing countries to improve debt management by reducing currency and maturity mismatches. Robust domestic bond markets have also improved financial intermediation and contributed to domestic growth, as both the government and corporate sectors have readier access to long-term capital. However, bringing the local-currency bond markets in emerging economies up to the standards of mature markets will require concerted efforts akin to those of the East Asian countries, which have yielded early successes. But local-currency debt markets also present new challenges for policy makers. The development of domestic debt markets requires modern and professional debt management procedures—to manage debt on an integrated basis (that is, both local and international debt)—especially in countries with few capital controls.

The global role of the euro

Since its introduction on January 1, 1999, the euro has assumed an increasingly important international role. It has emerged as a principal issuing currency in the global debt market, as a vehicle for foreign exchange transactions, and as an important reserve currency for official holdings of foreign-exchange reserves. The elimination of exchange risk within the Euro Area has created a pan-European market for euro-denominated securities, attracting both sovereign and private borrowers, not only from Euro Area countries, but also from other countries—among them emerging market economies such as Brazil, Colombia, China, Mexico, and Turkey. Today's euro-denominated bond market rivals the dollar-based fixed-income markets in important respects, including size, depth, and product range.

The euro is used increasingly in debt issuance, because it is the home currency of a large set of investors. It is less popular as a currency of denomination for reserves, owing to the dominance of the dollar as a vehicle for foreign exchange transactions and currency interventions—as well as the greater liquidity of the market for U.S. Treasury securities. Nevertheless, if the deteriorating U.S. current-account deficit sufficiently undermines confidence in the dollar, more official reserve holdings could be moved into euro-denominated assets, with the potential for a period of financial instability if the shift is abrupt.

Net official flows continue to decline
Official lending falling
Net official flows of grants and loans continued to fall in 2005—for the fourth consecutive year—as a sharp decline in net official lending more than offset gains in bilateral aid grants (table 1 and figure 4). Net official lending came to –$71.4 billion in 2005, the third consecutive year of net outflows from developing countries. In three years, developing countries have repaid $112 billion in loans to creditors. This largely reflects repayments of nonconcessional loans mostly by middle-income countries. In contrast, aid (comprised of concessional loans and grants) has increased significantly during this period, particularly for low-income countries.

Figure 4 Net official lending and foreign aid grants to developing countries, 1980–2005

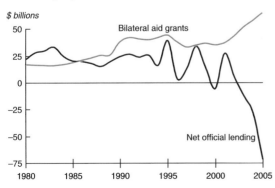

Source: World Bank Debtor Reporting System and staff estimates.

Figure 5 Net official lending, 1997–2005

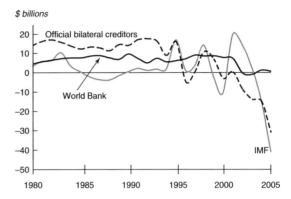

Source: World Bank Debtor Reporting System and staff estimates.

The dramatic decline in net official lending over the past few years reflects, for the most part, large repayments to the International Monetary Fund (IMF) and large prepayments to bilateral official creditors (figure 4). In 2005 net debt *outflows* from developing countries to the IMF totaled $41.1 billion, down from a net debt *inflow* of $19.5 billion in 2001, implying a –$60.6 billion swing in net lending by the IMF over the period 2001–5. The sharp decline is due to large repayments on emergency assistance loans made to Indonesia and the Russian Federation in 1997/8, and to Argentina, Brazil, and Turkey in 2001/2. The sharp decline in 2005 reflects large repayments by Argentina ($2.4 billion), Brazil ($16.8 billion), Indonesia ($1.0 billion), the Russian Federation ($2.3 billion), and Turkey ($4.2 billion). Moreover, gross lending by the IMF has declined from about $30 billion in 2002–3 to only $4 billion in 2005. This reflects the marked improvement in international financial stability, supported by the favorable global economic and financial conditions. The IMF's outstanding credit has declined from special drawing rights (SDR) 71 billion in 2002/3 to SDR 23.5 billion in March 2006. Despite the low level of IMF credit outstanding, net lending by the IMF could continue to decline over the next few years with large scheduled repayments by Indonesia, Turkey, and Uruguay.

Net lending by the official bilateral creditors declined by $27.0 billion in 2005 mainly due to large prepayments to the Paris Club by the Russian Federation ($15 billion), Poland ($5.6 billion) and Peru ($2.0 billion). Russia financed a $15 billion prepayment to the Paris Club using domestic financial resources, as its fiscal revenues increased dramatically in the wake of higher world oil prices. The prepayments by Peru and Poland were financed by borrowing in private capital markets, effectively substituting private debt for official (Paris Club) debt. Large prepayments to the Paris Club are expected to continue into 2006. In May 2006, Algeria and the Russian Federation made offers to prepay all of its remaining Paris Club debt, totaling $22 billion and $8 billion, respectively. Paris Club creditors have indicated their willingness to accept the proposals. Poland has announced its intention to prepay some of its €12.3 billion debt to the Paris Club, which will be due between 2005 and 2009.

More aid for the poorest countries, and more debt relief

Net disbursements of ODA by OECD DAC member countries increased dramatically in 2005, reaching $106.5 billion, up from $79.6 billion in 2004. Expressed as a share of gross national income (GNI) in donor countries, ODA has risen from 0.22 percent in 2001 to 0.33 percent in 2005, just below the 0.34 percent peak reached in the early 1990s. However, most of the record $27 billion increase in 2005 reflects debt relief provided by Paris Club creditors to Iraq (nearly $14 billion) and Nigeria (a little over $5 billion). Nevertheless, even excluding debt relief, ODA rose by 8.7 percent in real terms, up from a 5.6 percent average annual increase over 2002–4.

ODA is likely to decline as a percentage of GNI in 2006–7, as the debt relief component falls to more normal levels, before increasing gradually through the end of the decade. Donors have made commitments to increase ODA by $50 billion by 2010, half of which is targeted to go to Sub-Saharan Africa. Based on those commitments, ODA should reach 0.36 percent of GNI in 2010. Extrapolating this rate of increase would mean that the UN target of 0.7 percent would not be attained until 2030, 15 years after the 2015 deadline set for attaining the MDGs.

The international community made significant progress in 2005 to reduce debt burdens in some of the poorest countries. Debt relief provided under the Heavily Indebted Poor Countries (HIPC) Initiative and the Multilateral Debt Reduction Initiative (MDRI) will significantly reduce the debt burdens of poor countries that qualify. The 18 countries that reached the completion point prior to May 2006, under the HIPC Initiative, will see their total debt stock fall from an average level of 55 percent of GDP (before HIPC debt relief) to 13 percent (after MDRI debt relief).

Debt relief together with other special-purpose grants—for technical cooperation, emergency and disaster relief, and administrative costs—has accounted for a rising portion of ODA over the past few years. The increase in ODA as a share of GNI since 2001 reflects higher special purposes, rather than more flexible forms of funding. Donors have reallocated aid to the poorest countries, particularly those in Africa, and have continued to shift their resources from concessional loans to grants, with the goal of avoiding unsustainable increases in the debt burdens of aid recipients.

To ensure economic stability, developing countries must manage capital flows effectively

The current surge in private capital flows has occurred in the midst of much-improved domestic policies and global financial conditions compared with those that prevailed during the capital flows surge of the 1990s. This time around, governments have so far generally managed to avoid excessive expansion of aggregate demand, large current-account deficits, and sharp appreciations of the real exchange rate. However, the policy agenda for managing capital flows is broad and complex, and considerable challenges remain.

Effective macroeconomic policies

The improved response to the surge in capital flows this time around has been supported by the adoption of more flexible exchange rate regimes and a monetary policy framework that favors price stability. Inflation has fallen dramatically in virtually all developing countries, from a median of 11 percent in the mid-1990s to a median of 4.5 percent during 2002–5. At the same time, the greater autonomy in monetary policy afforded by more flexible exchange rates has allowed authorities to lower local interest rates. Flexible exchange rates and lower interest rates have drastically reduced the incentive to resort to short-term external borrowing, a major vulnerability that contributed to the financial crises of the 1990s. Governments also have taken steps to accelerate development of domestic capital markets (especially local bond markets) to create more diversified financial markets that would be more capable of handling volatile flows in portfolio capital. These developments, along with the shift from debt finance to equity (particularly FDI), have contributed to the marked improvement in developing countries' net external liability position. The ratio of external debt to GNI for developing countries as a whole fell from a peak of 44 percent in 1999 to about 34 percent in 2004, while since the mid-1990s short-term debt has declined in most developing countries relative to long-term debt and foreign exchange reserves.

Progress has been made in simplifying the very complex web of capital controls and exchange rate restrictions imposed by many countries. But the gradual opening of capital accounts must be accompanied by a further strengthening of macroeconomic policies, the development of local capital markets and the institutions needed to regulate them, and the establishment of a system of risk management robust enough to respond to the needs of a more flexible exchange rate and open capital account. Liberalization of the capital account once implemented is difficult to reverse. A return to capital controls should be seen only as a policy of last resort, to be used to dampen excessive exchange rate volatility or to moderate large inflows of capital when other policies, such as interest rates and intervention in foreign exchange markets, prove fruitless.

Despite the considerable improvement in policies in recent years, the surge in capital flows still presents substantial risks to developing countries. Future risks to economic and financial stability will likely take a different form and character than those encountered in the past—and may expose institutional and macroeconomic weaknesses that cannot be anticipated at this juncture. One warning sign of potential troubles has been the surge in portfolio inflows that has been associated with a dramatic escalation of stock market prices and valuations in many developing countries, particularly in Asia, raising the risk of asset price bubbles. Other signs of possible trouble are appreciated exchange rates and current account deficits in some

Eastern European countries. The impact of individual risks could be magnified if several were to occur simultaneously.

Prudent accumulation of reserves

The current account in many developing countries, particularly major oil exporters and emerging Asia, has moved from deficit to sizable surplus, intensifying the demand for reserve accumulation. That many of these countries have accumulated foreign exchange reserves far in excess of the level required for intervention and liquidity purposes partly reflects a desire to self-insure against global financial shocks. As the volume of reserves increases, however, so does the importance of balancing their use for intervention, investment, and insurance purposes against their domestic resource costs. For countries with large holdings of foreign exchange reserves, allowing local institutional investors to diversify their investment portfolio globally—while ensuring their more effective regulation—could provide a viable channel of capital outflow, as well as an opportunity to further diversify risk. This would transfer currency risks, currently concentrated on the books of central banks, to domestic institutional investors with a longer investment horizon and a greater ability to manage such risks. Such an approach is also more desirable for many developing countries than inducing adjustments through the current account as a way of absorbing reserves. In addition to allowing institutional investors greater scope to invest overseas, consideration should be given to enabling local residents to invest in approved international assets, as the Republic of Korea has done.

Careful management of oil-export revenues

Oil-exporting countries face particular challenges in managing volatile export revenues. Although high oil prices are now expected to persist, considerable uncertainty remains, and oil exporters should save a part of the windfall—for example, to reduce debt and make productive physical and social investments. Some countries have put aside a fraction of their oil revenues in a stable portfolio of diversified financial assets (referred to as "funds for the future"), thus reducing the risk of overconsumption of oil revenues and the potential for Dutch disease. Such funds require robust governance and legal frameworks to effectively insulate earmarked oil wealth from political decisions guided by short-term agendas. The government must set and adhere to clear objectives for their investment, protection, and eventual use. Countries that depend heavily on oil revenues should also consider using derivatives to reduce the volatility of future income.

Improvements in standards for the corporate sector

A growing number of developing countries have made considerable efforts to meet international standards for transparency, corporate governance, and the regulation and supervision of financial systems. Although this is a global trend, individual countries take different approaches to adapting international standards to their corporate environment. Some, for example, are issuing codes that set compliance targets in tandem with laws setting minimum compulsory standards, while others are using codes to raise public awareness in advance of upcoming regulatory reform. The adoption of national codes of corporate governance in at least 60 countries by the end of 2005—including all of the Asian crisis countries, plus China, Colombia, Turkey, and Ukraine—underscores the growing recognition of the importance of corporate governance in enhancing investor confidence, a recognition that bolsters the resilience and stability of capital markets globally. Priority must now be given to effectively implementing and enforcing these new domestic policy and institutional reforms at the national level.

Multilateral cooperation is key to resolving global financial imbalances

Developing-country policies must be reinforced by renewed international efforts to promote stability and maintain a financial environment conducive to a balanced expansion and deployment of capital flows in developing countries. One major risk to stability is the growing imbalance in global payments and the associated market anxiety about the possibility of a disorderly adjustment of the imbalance through sudden changes in exchange rates and global interest rates. Such changes could desta-

bilize and disrupt international financial markets, which would cause all countries to suffer.

Although a coordinated policy of intervention in foreign currency markets—similar to the Plaza Agreement of September 1985—is neither desirable nor feasible (given the changes in global financial market conditions and actors over the past two decades); a degree of multilateral cooperation is needed to address the current global imbalances. That approach, based on the mutual interests of deficit and surplus countries, should reflect the structural asymmetry between international reserve currencies and other currencies. At its center must be consensus on a blend of exchange rate and aggregate spending adjustments adequate to rebalance global aggregate demand toward surplus countries without causing a global recession. Ordinarily, policy coordination among key players is unnecessary, because floating exchange rates, accompanying monetary policies (oriented primarily toward domestic targets for inflation and economic activity), and independent central banks do their job to facilitate adjustment to any shocks hitting the world economy. But when the sustainability of the sources of finance for global payment imbalances is in doubt, as it is at present, multilateral cooperation to prevent sudden and disorderly market reactions becomes highly desirable, especially if the growing global imbalances create pressure for protectionist trade policies in some countries.

Developing countries, in particular, have much to gain from multilateral cooperation, and much to lose from its absence, and they would suffer disproportionately if instability were induced and a disorderly unwinding of global financial imbalances ensued. The world economy is moving toward a multipolar international monetary system in which the monetary and financial policies of the United States, Euro Area, Japan, and several key emerging market economies, including China, all exert substantial influence. Policymakers in emerging market economies should therefore strive to strengthen institutions and promote policies and mechanisms that will improve their ability to navigate in a world of increasingly integrated and interdependent financial and production systems.

1

Prospects for the Global Economy

Summary of the outlook

Confronted with capacity constraints in the resource sector, sharp rises in commodity prices, and a tightening of monetary policy among Organisation for Economic Co-operation and Development (OECD) countries, the global economy has slowed from the record pace posted in 2004. Nevertheless growth remains robust, especially among developing countries. Their GDP increased 6.4 percent in 2005 (4.3 percent for oil-importing developing economies, excluding India and China) as compared with 2.8 percent among high-income countries. The resilience of developing countries—which reflects a sustained improvement in the potential growth rate of many developing countries—has been heartening, especially given the magnitude of the oil-price shock. This brisk expansion is projected to continue, but slow towards a more sustainable pace of 5.9 percent by 2008. Such rapid growth argues against a sharp decline in oil prices, which are expected to remain above or close to $60 a barrel through 2008.

This relatively benign soft-landing scenario for developing countries faces both internal and external risks. First, the high growth of the past several years is generating tensions within individual countries. In several East European countries this has taken the form of rising inflation, currency appreciation, and high current-account deficits, while in others it has expressed itself in rising asset prices, inflationary pressure, and growing domestic tensions between fast and slower growing regions and sectors. Second, many of the buffers that permitted countries to absorb higher oil prices with a minimum of disruption have been exhausted, and countries have yet to fully adjust to

higher oil prices. As a result, developing countries are much more vulnerable to potential external shocks, such as a disruptive resolution of global imbalances, a decline in nonoil commodity prices, or a hike in oil prices following a supply shock.

High oil prices have had only a limited impact on global growth

Lower oil intensities, more flexible product and labor markets, exchange rate flexibility, and more credible monetary policy have all reduced the real-side and inflationary impacts of higher oil prices. As a result, and in contrast to past episodes, monetary policy has remained accommodative and interest rates low. This, plus the fact that oil deliveries have continued to increase rapidly (as opposed to the 1970s and 1980s, when supply was cut), helps explain the resilience of output to higher oil prices. An additional factor for developing countries has been the substantial rise in the share of exports in GDP, which has increased the foreign currency inflows available to finance a given increase in the oil bill.

Adjustment was facilitated by solid initial conditions. In particular, many oil-importing developing countries entered the period of high oil prices running current-account surpluses and building up foreign currency reserves. This, plus high nonoil commodity prices and a rapid expansion in trade, meant that finding foreign currency to pay higher oil bills was relatively easy. In addition, foreign currency inflows for the poorest countries were bolstered by increasing aid flows, which in many cases rose by more than 0.5 percent of GDP in 2004 (the last year for which data is available).

While output has remained resilient, developing countries nevertheless have endured a large hit on their incomes. On average, the rise in oil prices between 2003 and 2005 reduced real incomes in oil-importing countries by 3.6 percent and by as much as 10 percent for some low-income oil importers. For developing oil importers the additional expenditure, some $137 billion annually, exceeds by a large margin official development assistance (ODA, $84 billion in 2005 net of additional debt relief) and is about one-half of foreign direct investment (FDI) inflows ($234 billion).

Unsurprisingly, some countries are having difficulty adjusting. Fiscal deficits have risen alarmingly in several countries that subsidize domestic energy prices. In many African countries, utility firms, unable to pay mounting energy bills, have imposed rolling blackouts. Moreover, a few countries appear to be financing their higher oil bill through an unsustainably rapid reduction in international reserves. Finally, rising food and transportation prices have pushed inflation to worrisome levels in several countries in Africa and, to a lesser extent, South Asia. While it is not clear that an inflationary spiral has begun, an eventual economic slowdown appears likely if policy makers are forced to use macro policy measures to bring inflation back under control.

Developing countries face further adjustment challenges over the medium term

While the resilience of output to high oil prices is heartening, the initially comfortable current-account positions that allowed many developing countries to weather higher oil prices have now been absorbed. Moreover, many of the factors that allowed countries to deal with higher oil prices relatively easily in the short run imply that much real-side adjustment has yet to occur.

Adapting to more or less permanently higher prices poses substantial challenges, especially for those countries where high oil prices are already generating economic strain, as evidenced by excessive increases in current-account or fiscal deficits or by unsustainable financing of oil import bills through the depletion of reserves or bank borrowing. Policy makers in these countries must take urgent steps to increase energy efficiency in general and reduce oil dependency in particular. Unwinding energy subsidization programs would simultaneously relieve pressure on government finances and also promote private sector energy conservation. For those countries that have managed the

recent rise in oil prices more easily, similar policy steps would reduce their vulnerability both to further oil shocks and other shocks, including a decline in nonoil commodity prices. For countries benefiting from fixed-price contracts at what are currently below-market prices, policy should encourage energy conservation now before the contracts expire or are renegotiated.

More generally, because higher prices are likely to be a more or less permanent fixture, countries need to take steps to improve their international competitiveness. Policies that stimulate productivity growth and investment in the domestic economy are most likely to be successful. Countries with flexible exchange regimes are likely to have more success in improving their export revenues and diminishing nonoil imports so as to reestablish a comfortable margin on the current account. Trade reform—domestic, behind-the-border reforms to improve competitiveness, accompanied by progress at the multilateral level—could further expand developing-country exports and the base upon which oil and other imports essential to development can be financed.

For oil exporters the challenge will be to use petroleum revenues in a way that minimizes economic distortions and maximizes development gain. Even if oil prices remain high for an extended period, most countries do not have the capacity to absorb these huge inflows immediately. As a result, they should resist the temptation to use oil-related budgetary revenues for programs that are politically popular but developmentally unsound. Instead, they should consider introducing or expanding oil funds by sequestering that part of revenues that cannot be productively placed in the domestic market and investing it abroad, where it will generate a permanent income stream to support development even after current prices ease or oil supplies dwindle. Recent steps by some oil-exporting countries that have unwound structural reforms for short-term political gain are unlikely to be helpful.

Global imbalances may have been exacerbated by high oil prices

The rapid rise in oil prices has contributed to global imbalances by increasing the U.S. current-account deficit by some $125 billion since 2002. It also has changed the nature of those imbalances by inducing a swing in the counterparts to the U.S. deficit away from oil importers and toward oil-exporting countries. Their oil-related export earnings are up some $400 billion since 2002. These are being recycled—partly through increased imports, approximately 65 percent of additional export revenues are being spent as additional imports, and partly via financial flows. As a result, there is little likelihood that an excess in oil exporters' savings will lead to a global slowdown. Rather, increased financial flows—either directly or through third-party intermediaries, are contributing to low interest rates and, both directly and indirectly, to the financing of the U.S. current-account deficit.

Despite the ease with which the U.S. deficit is being financed, the continued accumulation of foreign liabilities is not sustainable. Unwinding these imbalances will almost certainly take a long time. Indeed, given the magnitude of the required adjustment, a gradual approach is to be preferred to an abrupt one. However, the longer significant steps to resolve the issue are delayed the greater will be the tensions implicit in the disequilibrium and the risk that they will be resolved in a disorderly manner. Of particular concern is that some of the temporary factors holding down interest rates (including corporate balance-sheet restructuring and financial flows from oil revenues) will ease, increasing the servicing costs on U.S. liabilities. That would add to the deficit and possibly raise concerns about its sustainability, driving interest rates even higher.

Resolving these imbalances is a common but differentiated responsibility requiring increased private and public savings in the United States, increased demand outside of the United States, and more flexible exchange rate management. Action on all fronts is required, particularly because in the absence of higher U.S. savings, increased foreign demand or exchange rate appreciation is unlikely to have a meaningful impact on imbalances.

The outlook for developing countries carries both internal and external risks

Prospects for a soft landing among developing countries are good, but a hard landing is also possible. In particular, many countries, notably in the Europe and Central Asia region, now have current-account deficits that exceed 5 or 6 percent of GDP. In some instances those deficits are associated with high interest rates, strong capital inflows, and appreciating currencies. The future ability of these economies to finance current levels of consumption and investment is vulnerable to changes in investor confidence or additional external shocks. Elsewhere, rapidly rising incomes may be contributing to asset bubbles in regional real estate and stock markets. In other countries, tensions arising from localized labor market shortages, combined with significant disparity in the degree to which regions or segments of the population are benefiting from growth, could prompt a harder-than-projected landing. These internal risks could generate a hard landing on their own or they could be triggered by and exacerbate an external shock. In particular, growth in several countries in South Asia and a few in Latin America is generating significant inflationary pressures requiring a tightening of macroeconomic policy if an abrupt slowdown in the future is to be avoided.

The principal external risks to the global economy have not changed much since the publication of the last edition of the World Bank's *Global Economic Prospects* (2005). These include the possibility that persistent global imbalances will resolve themselves in a disorderly manner, either through a significant increase in interest rates or a sharp depreciation of the dollar; the possibility that a significant supply shock will send oil prices even higher; and the possibility that nonoil commodity prices will weaken. Should any of these risks be realized, they might reduce global growth by between 1 and 3 percent, depending on the shock, with much of the slowdown borne by developing economies. Even if the impact of the shock is relatively benign at the global level, the increased current-account deficits of many oil-importing developing countries make them vulnerable. For heavily indebted countries, the most serious risk stems from the possibility of higher interest rates. For small oil-importing African countries, the largest risk is that nonoil commodity prices, particularly for metals and minerals, will decline.

The outturn from the Doha trade liberalization round poses a balanced risk to the outlook. The baseline scenario assumes an unambitious accord. However, an ambitious conclusion to the Round, including significant liberalization of trade in agricultural products and on-the-ground progress in the aid-for-trade agenda, could yield substantial benefits for developing countries. More importantly, a failure of Doha could go beyond this agreement by weakening the whole multilateral trade liberalization process—resulting in a more fragmented path forward with fewer benefits for developing countries.

While a remote possibility, an influenza pandemic could have serious consequences

The continued spread of avian influenza (bird flu) among wild birds, with limited bird-to-human transmission, comprises part of the baseline forecast. A serious risk to the global economy is presented by the possibility that avian influenza mutates into a form of the flu that is easily transmitted between humans and to which the population has only limited immunity.

The potential human and economic consequences of such a pandemic are very large. They depend importantly on the nature of the flu that emerges and on the reactions of people as it spreads. Even a relatively moderate flu in terms of transmission and mortality could have serious consequences for the world economy if the global population has limited immunity. Estimates suggest that, depending upon the severity of the eventual disease, a combination of lost output due to illness, additional deaths, absenteeism, and private and public efforts to avoid infection could lower global GDP by between 2 and 5 percent (with the latter number implying a global recession). More important, between 14 and 70 million people could be killed.

Policy makers need to focus simultaneously on two critical tasks: (1) further strengthening efforts to monitor and curtail outbreaks of avian influenza at points (such as domestic poultry flocks) where the likelihood is highest of the disease mutating into a viable human-to-human form; and (2) developing and putting systems in place to minimize the human cost of a pandemic if one does emerge, whether by developing effective containment strategies or improving the world's capacity to rapidly create and distribute vaccines.

Global growth

Despite oil prices that reached $60 a barrel in the second half of the year, the world economy grew by a very robust 3.6 percent in 2005. Developing countries led the way, expanding by 6.4 percent, more than twice as fast as high-income countries (table 1.1).

Outturns and prospects in high-income countries

Growth among industrialized economies in 2005 came in at 2.8 percent, substantially lower than the 3.3 percent recorded the year before. Industrial production and trade flows among these countries were particularly anemic. Industrial production growth declined from more than 5 percent in mid-2004 to less than 1 percent in late spring. Growth has since accelerated, reaching 3 percent (year-over-year) in the first quarter of 2006 (figure 1.1).

High oil prices, rising short-term interest rates, a cooling of the housing market, and an unusually disruptive hurricane season helped slow growth in the United States to 3.5 percent in 2005 as compared with 4.2 percent in 2004. Partly reflecting a bounce-back in activity following a weak fourth quarter, GDP expanded 4.8 percent in the first quarter of 2006. Although inflation

Figure 1.1 Industrial production remains robust

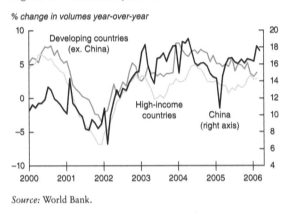

% change in volumes year-over-year

Source: World Bank.

Figure 1.2 Inflation in high-income countries

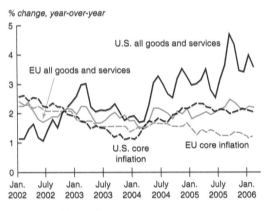

% change, year-over-year

Sources: World Bank, Datastream.

Table 1.1 The global outlook in summary
% change from previous year, except interest rates and oil prices

	2004	2005*	2006**	2007**	2008**
Global conditions					
World trade volume	10.6	7.1	7.6	7.7	7.8
Consumer prices					
G-7 countries[a,b]	2.1	2.6	2.2	1.8	1.8
United States	2.7	3.4	2.9	1.9	2.0
Commodity prices (US$ terms)					
Non-oil commodities	17.5	13.4	5.8	−3.2	−5.8
Oil price (US$ per barrel)[c]	37.7	53.4	64.2	61.0	56.9
Oil price (% change)	30.6	41.5	20.2	−5.0	−6.8
Manufactures unit export value[d]	6.9	0.8	1.6	2.8	1.2
Interest rates					
$, 6-month (%)	1.6	3.6	5.1	5.2	4.9
€, 6-month (%)	2.1	2.2	2.6	3.1	3.9
Real GDP growth[e]					
World	4.1	3.6	3.7	3.5	3.5
Memo item: World (PPP weights)[f]	5.3	4.6	4.6	4.5	4.5
High-income countries	3.3	2.8	3.0	2.8	2.8
OECD Countries	3.2	2.7	2.9	2.7	2.8
Euro Area	2.0	1.4	2.1	2.1	2.2
Japan	2.7	2.8	2.8	2.1	1.8
United States	4.2	3.5	3.5	3.3	3.3
Non-OECD countries	6.2	5.5	5.1	4.7	4.7
Developing countries	7.1	6.4	6.3	6.0	5.9
East Asia and Pacific	9.1	8.8	8.3	8.2	8.1
Europe and Central Asia	7.2	5.7	5.5	5.4	5.1
Latin America and Caribbean	6.0	4.4	4.6	4.0	3.7
Middle East and N. Africa	4.7	4.8	5.3	5.2	5.1
South Asia	6.7	7.7	6.8	6.5	6.2
Sub-Saharan Africa	5.2	5.2	5.4	4.9	5.4
Memorandum items					
Developing countries					
excluding transition countries	7.2	6.6	6.4	6.1	6.0
excluding China and India	6.1	5.0	5.1	4.8	4.5

Source: World Bank.
Note: PPP = purchasing power parity; * = estimate; ** = forecast.
a. Canada, France, Germany, Italy, Japan, the United Kingdom, and the United States.
b. In local currency, aggregated using 2000 GDP Weights.
c. Simple average of Dubai, Brent and West Texas Intermediate.
d. Unit value index of manufactured exports from major economies, expressed in US$.
e. GDP in 2000 constant dollars; 2000 prices and market exchange rates.
f. GDP mesaured at 2000 PPP weights.

spiked following Katrina-related increases in gasoline prices, it has since declined and remains relatively muted at 3.4 percent in March 2006. Core inflation (price changes of goods and services other than energy and food) remains low at 2.1 percent, below the rate recorded in December 2004 (figure 1.2).

The relatively low oil intensity of European economies, significant excess capacity, and a relaxed macroeconomic policy stance limited the slowdown in Europe. For the year as a whole, growth was a relatively weak 1.5 percent (1.4 percent for the Euro Area), but this reflected a fourth-quarter pause in exports following a strong acceleration in the first nine months of the year. Since then economic activity has picked up with GDP in the Euro Area estimated to have increased by around 2.4 percent in the first quarter of 2006.

In Japan, growth has been strong, with industrial production ending the year up 5 percent and unemployment declining to 4.4 percent of the labor force. Overall, GDP increased by 2.8 percent, with both domestic and external demand contributing about equally to the overall result. As a result, both consumer and business confidence have improved.

The increase in oil prices in 2005 and early 2006 are expected to slow growth in high-income countries by about 0.25 of a percentage point in 2006 compared with what it would have been had prices remained stable. In the United States, improved net exports are projected to maintain the pace of growth in 2006, despite weaker consumer demand due to higher interest rates and a cooling of the housing market. For 2007/8, the balance of these forces is expected to reverse somewhat, leading to a moderate easing of growth.

Continued accommodative macroeconomic policy and pent-up investment demand following several years of very weak growth should maintain the recent acceleration of output in Europe during 2006. As a result, GDP is projected to expand by about 2.1 percent in 2006 and to continue growing at close to its potential rate in 2007/8.

In Japan, vigorous growth in developing East Asia, renewed consumer and business confidence, and reduced drag from consolidation are all expected to keep the recovery strong in 2006. While the economy is projected to slow somewhat (partly because of less expansionary monetary and fiscal policies), GDP should expand at or above the economy's potential rate of growth.

Developing economy outturns and prospects
Notwithstanding high oil prices, economies in every developing region continued to grow at above-trend rates in 2005. Overall, the GDP of low- and middle-income countries expanded by an estimated 6.4 percent. The expansion was particularly robust in China and India, where output increased by 9.9 and about 8.0 percent, respectively. Excluding these countries, growth in other oil-importing developing countries came in at an estimated 4.3 percent, down significantly from 5.7 percent in 2004. At the same time, dwindling spare capacity in the petroleum sector caused the expansion of oil-exporting developing economies to ease from 6.6 to 5.7 percent, even though oil revenues continued to rise.

High oil prices, rising interest rates, and building inflationary pressures are expected to restrain growth in most developing regions in 2006/8 (figure 1.3). As a group, however, low- and middle-income countries should again outperform high-income economies by a wide margin. Growth in five of the six developing regions

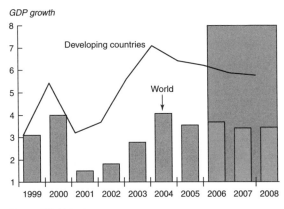

Figure 1.3 Developing-country growth remains robust

GDP growth

Source: World Bank.

is projected to exceed 5 percent through 2008, with the Latin America and Caribbean region projected to expand 4.1 percent on average over the projection period.

Regional outlooks

More detailed descriptions of economic developments in developing regions, including regional forecast summaries, are available at http://www.worldbank.org/globaloutlook.

East Asia and the Pacific[1]
The economies of the East Asia and Pacific region continued to expand rapidly in 2005. Their GDP is estimated to have increased by 8.8 percent, down from 9.1 percent in 2004 (figure 1.4). Growth in China was very strong (9.9 percent), despite a substantial slowing in both private consumption and investment demand, because exports continued to grow rapidly, and imports slowed.

For other countries in the region, output expanded by a more modest 5.3 percent, as the slowdown in Chinese imports, weak global high-tech demand, and elevated oil prices translated into reduced export growth and rapidly rising producer prices. Among larger oil-importing countries in the region, GDP growth slowed relatively sharply in the Philippines and Thailand. Among oil-exporters, growth slowed in Malaysia, but picked up in Vietnam and Indonesia.

Strong exports and weak import demand in China meant that the region's current-account bal-

Figure 1.4 Regional growth trends

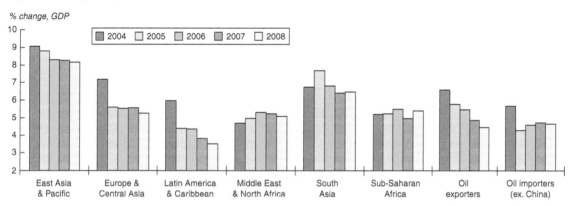

Source: World Bank.

ance improved, reaching a surplus of $143 billion (4.9 percent of GDP). Of the larger economies, only Thailand and Vietnam are running current-account deficits, while the surpluses of China and Malaysia exceed 6 and 15 percent of their respective GDP.

Output in the region continues to feel the effects of endemic bird-to-bird avian influenza. Cambodia, China, Indonesia, Laos, Thailand, and Vietnam are the countries most affected. So far some 200 million domestic birds (less than 1 percent of domestic bird production in the region but rising to 12 percent in Vietnam) have died or been killed to prevent the spread of the disease. As of early May 2006 no new outbreaks have been recorded among birds in Thailand and Vietnam, attesting to the effectiveness of preventive measures. However, new outbreaks have been recorded in China, East Java, Indonesia, Malaysia and Myanmar[2].

While the disease has had only a limited effect on GDP so far (depending on the country, the sector represents between 0.6 to 2 percent of GDP), its impact on incomes has likely been more acute. Poultry accounts for as much as 7 percent of the incomes of the poor.

As higher oil prices take hold, reduced investment growth in China and reduced global liquidity are expected to slow regional growth to around 8.1 percent by 2008. This reflects a modest slowdown in China, as slower export growth is partially offset by stronger domestic demand. Excluding China, growth in the remaining economies in the region is expected to come in at about 5.5 percent in 2006 through 2008. Stronger domestic demand, terms of

trade effects and some currency appreciation are projected to result in about a $25 billion decline in the region's current-account surplus.

Europe and Central Asia
Economic activity in the Europe and Central Asia region grew by a robust 5.7 percent in 2005. High oil prices boosted demand in the region's oil producers, particularly in the Russian Federation, where real GDP increased 6.4 percent. That, in turn, contributed to strong exports for other countries in the region, notably the Baltics and the Commonwealth of Independent States. Turkey and other Central European countries participated in the export boom to a lesser extent, as they reoriented exports away from a still weak European Union.

The region received record capital inflows in 2005, reflecting favorable international credit conditions and the advancing EU accession process for new and candidate members. These flows contributed to rapid credit growth in the Baltics, Bulgaria, Romania, Turkey, and Ukraine, and a significant deterioration in current-account positions. High oil prices, substantial increases in the price paid for imported natural gas in some countries, and lax fiscal policy in the Czech Republic, Hungary, the Kyrgyz Republic, and Poland also boosted current-account deficits.

About half of the region's economies posted current-account deficits equal to or in excess of 5 percent of GDP in 2005. Current-account deficits exceeded 6 percent of GDP in Albania, Bulgaria, Croatia, Estonia, Georgia, Hungary, Latvia, Lithuania, Romania, and Turkey.

At the regional level these deficits were significantly offset by improved external positions of oil exporters, including Azerbaijan, where the deficit shifted from a 30 percent share of GDP in 2004 to 5 percent in 2005, as new oil capacity came on stream. This also propelled Azerbaijan's growth to more than 25 percent.

GDP growth is projected to slow slightly in 2006, coming in at 5.5 percent, as tighter international credit conditions and monetary policy are expected to slow domestic growth in the Commonwealth of Independent States (CIS) subregion. Elevated energy revenues, investment expenditure, and the projected recovery of western European demand are expected to sustain growth at relatively high levels in 2007/8. High fiscal and current-account deficits in a number of countries, including Hungary and Turkey, pose serious risks to the outlook. For regional oil exporters, key challenges include the need to foster greater investment and productive capacity in the nonoil sectors so as to improve economic diversification, control inflation, and prevent excessive exchange rate appreciation.

Latin America and the Caribbean

Economic activity in Latin America and the Caribbean is estimated to have increased by some 4.4 percent during 2005. Outturns were strong throughout the region, reflecting high levels of international liquidity, strong global demand, and high prices for the region's exports. Macroeconomic policy has also played a role. Except in Brazil and Mexico, where rising interest rates contributed to a slowdown in 2005, monetary policy in the region has been generally accommodative. Fiscal policy, in turn, has been relatively neutral. Despite windfall revenues from high international commodity prices and reduced debt servicing charges (due to reduced interest rates and lower debt stocks) most countries, with the notable exception of República Bolivariana de Venezuela, have avoided a significant pro-cyclical surge in spending. As a result, government deficits in the region have declined and "structural" balances actually improved in some countries. Nevertheless, structural rigidities in public expenditures remain an issue in a number of countries.

Increases in coffee, sugar, and metal prices largely offset the effect of higher oil prices and lower agricultural prices (notably soybeans) in many countries. High nonoil commodity prices and strong inflows of remittance prevented most countries in the region from experiencing a significant deterioration in their current-account positions. Indeed, with a few exceptions (Honduras, Nicaragua, Panama, Paraguay, and Uruguay), the current-account balances of most countries in the region have either remained constant or improved since 2002. These favorable external conditions contributed to a general pressure toward exchange rate appreciation that has been checked by accumulation of international reserves.

Looking forward, regional growth is projected to pick up in 2006 as easier monetary policy boosts output in Mexico and Brazil. Growth in most countries in the region is expected to be broadly stable in 2007 and 2008, slowing only somewhat in the face of a modest weakening in commodity prices and a gradual moderation in capital inflows. However, the expansion for the region as a whole is projected to slow toward 3.7 percent in 2008, reflecting a significant slowing in Argentina and República Bolivariana de Venezuela toward more sustainable growth rates.

Growth trends in Central American countries are projected to improve, partly because of the recent Central American Free Trade Agreement. The agreement should boost both trade (the United States is these countries' major trading partner) and investment, thereby lifting longer-term growth prospects. However, to reap the full benefits of this reform, further steps need to be taken towards improving road quality, increasing port and customs efficiency, boosting financial depth, and raising the quality and coverage of education.

A central risk to this forecast remains the possibility that as growth slows and commodity prices ease, government deficits will rise, potentially raising inflation or increasing uncertainty. Either result could lead to higher-than-projected interest rates and slower growth.

Middle East and North Africa[3]

High oil prices and strong oil demand continue to be key drivers for the developing economies of the Middle East and North Africa[4], where GDP is estimated to have increased by 4.8 percent in 2005. A 40 percent increase in oil revenues, to some $250 billion or (66 percent of their GDP), boosted public spending in oil-exporting developing countries in the region, causing their GDP to expand by 5.3

percent. This had spillover effects for the region's oil importers in the form of strong exports, tourism revenues, and inflows of investment and remittances. All of these factors helped to sustain robust growth among regional oil importers (4.2 percent), despite higher oil-import bills and relatively weak demand in Europe.

Looking forward, high oil prices are expected to continue feeding domestic demand in oil-producing countries—outstripping domestic supply and causing imports to continue rising rapidly, even as growth of export revenues slows. As a result, GDP in developing oil-exporting countries should expand by 5.2 percent in 2006 before slowing to around 4.8 percent in 2008. Their current-account surpluses should decline from around 20 percent of GDP in 2005 to about 8 percent of GDP in 2008. In the oil-importing economies, growth is expected to accelerate to about 5.3 percent, supported by stronger European growth, continued exports of goods and services to regional oil exporters, and a weaker negative effect from the reduction in textile and clothing quotas.

Prospects for the region remain clouded by geopolitical developments. For the region as a whole, western investors' risk perceptions have worsened. For the moment, this has been offset by an intraregional recycling of oil revenues, which has contributed to a sharp inflation in asset prices.

South Asia
Strong external demand and private consumption growth, supported by generally accommodative monetary policies, spurred growth in South Asia to a very robust 7.7 percent in 2005, led by India and Pakistan, which both expanded by about 8 percent. Excluding these two countries, regional growth was still a strong 5.3 percent. Robust regional clothing exports following the removal of quotas helped limit the overall deterioration of the current account, the deficit of which is estimated at 2.6 percent of regional GDP in 2005.

Despite some efforts to raise retail energy prices, higher oil prices have not been completely passed through to consumers. Nevertheless, inflationary pressures in the region have been building. Consumer prices rose 9.1 percent in 2005 as compared with 3.6 percent in 2003. To a significant degree, higher inflation reflects fluctuations in food prices. However, rapid growth, particularly strong domestic demand in response to a relaxed

monetary policy stance in both India and Pakistan also played a role.

Because higher oil prices have not been passed through fully, there remains significant latent inflationary pressure from this source. In addition, implicit energy subsidies have raised fiscal deficits by as much as 0.7 percent of GDP between 2002 and 2005, apparently crowding out spending on education and health care in India (Devarajan and Ghani 2006).[5] Moreover, by impeding the price mechanism from restraining energy demand, the pass-through policy (along with robust domestic demand) has contributed to a deterioration equal to 4.0 percent of GDP in the region's current-account balance since 2003.

Growth is projected to weaken to about 6.8 percent in 2006, reflecting continued above trend growth in Pakistan and India. However, domestic capacity constraints and rising inflation are projected to cause growth to decline to a more sustainable 6.2 percent by 2008.

Notwithstanding this cyclical slowdown, growth is projected to remain robust with investment in both India and Pakistan expected to continue to benefit from strong external and domestic interest. This, plus a four-year infrastructure project (Build India) valued at 5 percent of GDP, are projected to augment capacity and support demand over the projection period. The services sector in India is expected to continue expanding rapidly, as a result of strong FDI inflows and outsourcing. Export growth throughout the region should remain strong, despite slower growth in the United States, partly because of increased demand from Europe.

Solid domestic demand should cause the current-account deficit to grow further, reaching around 3.5 percent of GDP in 2006 before improving somewhat as demand slows.

Sub-Saharan Africa
GDP in Sub-Saharan Africa expanded by an estimated 5.2 percent in 2005, bolstered by robust growth in resource-rich countries. Indeed, oil-exporting economies grew an estimated 6.4 percent in 2005, while growth in South Africa came in at 4.9 percent, lifted by high metal prices, strong consumer confidence, and low nominal interest rates. Economic activity in small oil-importing economies expanded by a slower but still robust 4.3 percent, down from 4.7 percent in 2004.

This strong performance marks a sharp departure from the weak and relatively volatile growth recorded by the region in the 1980s and 1990s. 2005 was the fifth year in a row that regional growth was at least 3.5 percent, and ended the first 5 year period since the 1960s that per capita growth remained positive in every year. Hearteningly this improved performance reflects stronger growth by many countries rather than very fast growth by a few. More than half of Sub-Saharan African countries have grown by 4 percent or more on average during the past five years, compared with fewer than one-quarter during the period 1980–95.[6]

Better subsistence and cash crops bolstered agricultural incomes and industrial production in many West African countries, while performance in East Africa was also good, despite drought in some areas. High metal prices bolstered growth in small resource-rich oil-importing economies.

The current-account position of oil exporters improved significantly because of higher oil revenues. However, external balances in many oil-importing countries have come under pressure. Excluding South Africa, the current-account position of oil importers deteriorated by 2.8 percentage points in 2005, reaching 6.4 percent of GDP. In Ghana, for example, the current-account deficit is estimated to have more than doubled to reach 6.8 percent of GDP, while in Tanzania it surged close to 6.2 percent of GDP. In several other countries, a failure to fully pass through higher prices has placed fiscal accounts under serious strain (Madagascar, Mauritius, Rwanda, and Uganda) or forced utilities to ration energy consumption by imposing rolling electrical blackouts (Madagascar, Malawi).

Looking forward, growth in established oil-exporting countries is projected to average more than 6 percent as new oil production is expected to come online in Angola, Republic of Congo, Equatorial Guinea, and Sudan. Moreover, Mauritania and São Tomé and Principe are expected to begin exporting oil in 2006.

Small oil importers are also expected to do well, with growth remaining at about 4.5 percent in 2008 as many countries benefit from debt write-offs and increased aid flows. Madagascar, Tanzania, and Uganda are expected to continue to profit from prudent macroeconomic policies and reforms implemented in previous years. In contrast, growth in sugar and textile producers (Lesotho,

Mauritius, and Swaziland) is expected to weaken as European sugar preferences are withdrawn, while strong competition from low-cost textile producers in China and South Asia will continue to be a drag on regional exports. Continued rapid expansion in South Africa is expected to spill over into the Southern Africa Development Community. A more peaceful and stable sociopolitical environment will serve to accelerate growth in Liberia, Sierra Leone, and several other countries. On the other hand, should low-level conflicts, in places such as Chad, Côte d'Ivoire, Nigeria, and the Sudan escalate, they could bring down regional growth to a significant degree.

Commodity markets
The oil market

The sharp rise in oil prices since 2003,[7] which was driven by strong demand and dwindling spare capacity, showed signs of ending toward the end of 2005. Beginning in September 2005, the trend rise in oil prices marked a pause, with barrel prices fluctuating around $63. However, the market remains tight, and the pricing power of OPEC has increased. As a result, prices are volatile, and sensitive to small changes in perceptions such as concerns over future supply, which sent barrel prices toward the $73 mark in early May 2006, before declining once again (figure 1.5).

Oil demand slowed to 0.5 million barrels per day (mbpd) in the second half of 2005, from 3.5 mbpd in the first half of 2004 (figure 1.6). While slower GDP growth played a role in this decline, the most important factor appears to have been higher oil prices. Econometric models suggest that

Figure 1.5 An end to the trend rise in oil prices?

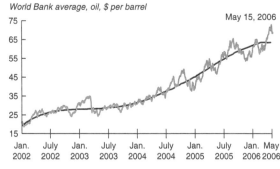

World Bank average, oil, $ per barrel

Sources: Datastream, World Bank.

Figure 1.6 Higher prices slow oil demand

Change in apparent oil demand, millions of barrels of oil per day

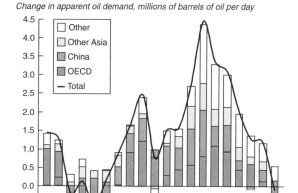

Source: International Energy Agency.

Figure 1.7 A disappointing supply response

Change in global oil deliveries, millions of barrels of oil per day

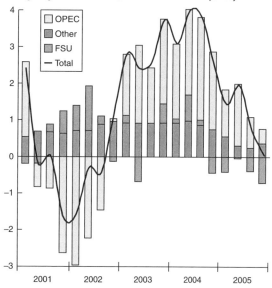

Source: International Energy Agency.

had prices remain unchanged, oil demand would have increased by some 2–2.5 mbpd.[8]

Incremental oil demand declined in all regions. In addition to prices, a number of special factors were at work. In the United States, higher petrol prices in the wake of hurricane Katrina provoked a sharp decline in both vehicle miles and gasoline consumption in the autumn, while a mild winter has also eased demand. In Asia, growth in oil consumption slowed, due in part to subsidy cuts in countries such as Indonesia and Thailand. In China energy demand eased partly because new electrical-generating capacity reduced the use of relatively inefficient diesel-fueled backup power generators.

Notwithstanding some three years of higher prices[9] and the coming on stream of new fields in Africa and elsewhere, there has been no discernible acceleration in aggregate oil supply (figure 1.7).[10] This contrasts with the 1970s and 1980s, when increased output brought substantial new capacity online, helping to reduce prices.[11]

Aggregate supply has failed to respond, despite a sharp increase in investment activity among oil-exporting developing countries. Output from those sources has increased just 2.7 percent, or 0.9 mbpd (4.2 percent, or 0.2 mbpd, for African producers).

A number of factors have contributed to limit the response of aggregate oil supply:

1. Existing fields in the United States and in the North Sea have entered into a period of de-

clining yields and the rate of increase in production of fields in the former Soviet Union has slowed.

2. A deterioration in the investment climate in some developing countries has lowered production levels and reduced investment, despite the existence of ample reserves.

3. Low oil prices during the 1990s limited incentives to explore for new oil. More recently, uncertainty over the durability of higher oil prices led firms to be cautious about investing in new (relatively high-cost) capacity, especially given the long lead times (between three and six years) needed to develop new fields.

4. Low investment in the past has contributed to a lack of skilled labor and equipment, further delaying the supply response.

5. A large share of known reserves is located in countries to which major oil companies do not have access. Major oil firms have been offered service contracts to help countries develop their resources. Thus far, however, oil companies appear to have found share buybacks and increased dividends to be a more profitable use of their earnings. Recent decisions in some developing countries to renounce existing contracts are unlikely to increase firms' willingness to invest further.

Figure 1.8 Spare production capacity remains low

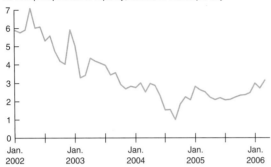

OPEC spare production capacity, millions of barrels per day

Sources: World Bank, International Energy Agency.

The combination of still growing demand and a weak supply response has meant that although spare production capacity has improved, it remains tight (figure 1.8). Looking forward, investments in new productive capacity are increasing (up some 15 percent in 2005). Moreover, continued high prices will increase incentives to adopt more petroleum-efficient technologies and conserve fuel. As a result, demand growth is expected to remain relatively moderate (at about 1.5–2 million barrels per day).

Unless non-OPEC supplies rise much faster than expected (the International Energy Agency, 2005, projects non-OPEC supply to increase by 3 mbpd over the next three years), spare capacity will remain limited and OPEC's pricing power high. The organization has signaled its willingness to reduce output in line with demand.

Prices are expected to remain volatile but should gradually decline, reflecting the countervailing influences of continued strong growth in global output and limited increases in non-OPEC oil on the supply side, and increasing energy efficiency on the demand side. While the precise path to be taken in these conditions is largely unknowable, the forecasts reported in this chapter assume that barrel prices will begin moderating in 2006, averaging $64 for the year and decline gradually towards $57 in 2008.

However, the market remains vulnerable to disruption, whether by natural disasters or geopolitical events.[12] Hence, the possibility of sudden upward spikes in oil prices cannot be ignored, even if the general trend is one of stabilization or slight decline.

Nonoil commodities

The rise in oil prices since 2003 has been accompanied by increasing prices for agricultural goods, metals, and minerals (figure 1.9). Reflecting continued strong growth in global output, metals and minerals prices increased by some 27 percent in 2005 and up an additional 24 percent in the first four months of 2006. Increases in 2005 were concentrated in industrial metals, such as iron ore (up 72 percent), zinc (up 38 percent), and copper (up 21 percent). Prices for other metals and minerals also rose, but by less. Tin, the price of which fell by 13 percent over the year, stands out as an exception.

At the global level, prices of agricultural products have been relatively stable, up 9.3 percent between April 2006 and the same date a year earlier. High prices early in 2005 reflected a poor monsoon season in South Asia and drought conditions in Sub-Saharan Africa. Improved weather conditions, in combination with increased supply in some countries, contributed to an easing in agricultural prices through much of 2005, followed by a modest pickup in prices in the first quarter of 2006. Raw materials are up 11 percent since April 2005.

The recent strength of nonoil commodity prices is primarily a reflection of strong world demand in recent years and low spare capacity brought on by low prices during the 1990s. Prices also have been influenced by strong energy prices, because energy is a major input in the production of many commodities (notably aluminum), and because several commodities are important substitutes for petroleum-based products (such as rubber and sugar used in the production of ethanol). Overall, about one-third of the increase in nonoil

Figure 1.9 Commodity prices

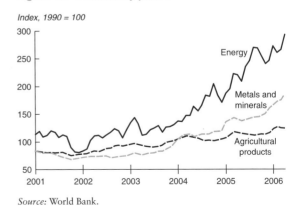

Index, 1990 = 100

Source: World Bank.

commodity prices between 2002 and 2005 was due to higher oil prices (Baffes 2005).[13] Some of the very recent strength in the prices of precious metals may also reflect investor uncertainty in the face of a declining dollar and continued global imbalances.

Improved supply should ease the prices of most agricultural commodities beginning in 2006. However, the prices of close energy substitutes and energy-intensive products are expected to rise further. Overall, agricultural prices are projected to rise by about 10 percent in 2006 before easing by about 3 percent in each of 2007 and 2008. Strong demand from China and other developing economies, low stocks, and high energy prices are projected to push metals and mineral prices up some 25 percent in 2006, before they begin easing by about 5 percent in 2007 and 12 percent in 2008. Demand-driven increases in energy prices represent an upside risk to energy-sensitive non-oil commodities including food stuffs, whose yields depend on energy-intensive fertilizers.

Inflation, interest rates, and global imbalances

Inflation

Perhaps the most critical explanation for the limited impact of higher oil prices on output has been the weak response of inflation to higher oil prices—especially in high-income countries, where world interest rates are determined.

While inflation is up in virtually every region, most of the increase appears to reflect the direct impact of higher oil prices. With perhaps the exception of South Asia and Sub-Saharan Africa (see discussion below), there is little evidence of the rapid price pass-through or the wage–price spirals that characterized the oil shocks of the 1970s and 1980s (figure 1.10). Despite a pickup toward the end of 2005 in the United States, core inflation (the rate of price increase of goods and services, excluding food and energy) has increased relatively little (see figure 1.2). As a result, inflation expectations and interest rates have remained low, eliminating one of the principal mechanisms through which past oil shocks have slowed growth.

Many factors explain this inflationary performance—among them more flexible labor and product markets in high-income countries, lower oil intensities, more credible monetary policy,

Figure 1.10 Moderate increases in inflation

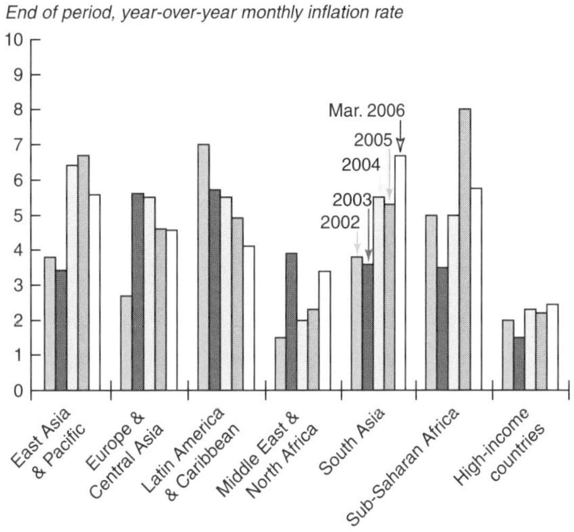

End of period, year-over-year monthly inflation rate

Source: World Bank.

and more prudent fiscal policies. In addition, the rapidly expanding role of Asia and, to a lesser extent, the countries of the former Soviet bloc as low-cost manufacturing centers have served to dampen price inflation in high-income countries, where many of these products are consumed.

The pickup of inflation in Sub-Saharan Africa and South Asia is partly explained by food prices, which increased substantially in both regions during the course of 2005 and should be expected to ease in 2006 as crops improve. However, as is the case in a few Latin American countries, it also likely reflects overheating in those regions, which have been growing at historically high rates.

This possibility is particularly worrisome in the case of Africa, because the credibility of monetary authorities is not yet well entrenched. Should an inflationary spiral develop, it could have serious consequences for macroeconomic stability and affect the ability of those economies to sustain the strong growth of the past several years. In the meantime, continued aid flows to finance improved governance and social and physical infrastructure investments will be essential to raising the trend growth rate that these countries can sustain.

Interest rates

The subdued response of inflation has allowed monetary (and fiscal) policy to remain relatively accommodative. While short-term interest rates are

Figure 1.11 Flattening yield curve

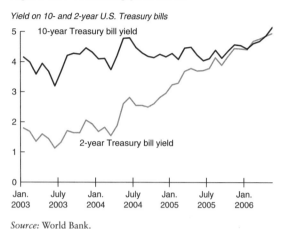

Yield on 10- and 2-year U.S. Treasury bills

Source: World Bank.

Figure 1.12 Changes in real effective exchange rate

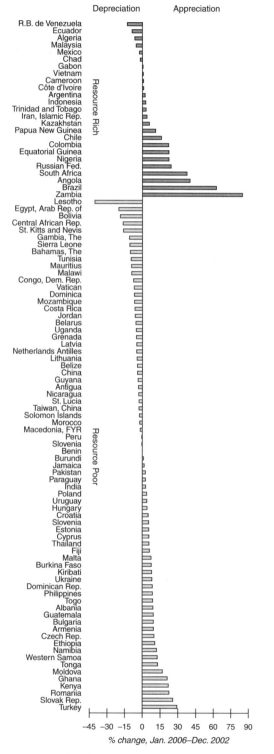

Sources: World Bank, IMF.

rising, they remain low in real terms, and long-term rates have only recently begun rising in high-income countries. As a result, the yield curve has flattened significantly, with short-term bond yields virtually equal to longer term yields.

Indeed, on several occasions during February and March 2006 the yield on two-year U.S. Treasury bonds marginally exceeded that of the 10-year bond (figure 1.11). Such yield-curve "inversion" has historically been a good indicator of a future recession (Estrella 2005).[14] As such, these inversions may signal a slowing of the U.S. economy. However, they were very small and occurred with both short- and long-term real interest rates at low levels. Moreover, while the yield curve remains flat, long-term rates in April and early May were once again higher than short-term rates. In this context, the flattening of the yield curve reflects a broadly positive outlook for global growth, characterized by stable expectations for inflation, significant spare capacity in Europe, and an American economy that continues to expand quickly even as it slows in response to a more neutral monetary policy stance.

Developing economies experienced a similar flattening of the yield curve. Bond spreads continued to decline, reaching a historic low of 174 basis points for sovereign borrowers in May 2006. However, the combination of relatively stable bank spreads (around 100 basis points) and rising rates in high-income countries means that the average interest rate paid by developing countries actually rose over the past 12 months (see chapter 2).[15]

Exchange rates

A further factor limiting the real-side consequences of higher oil prices is the wider adoption of flexible-exchange-rate regimes over the past two decades (see chapter 5). Among oil-importing developing countries that have not benefited from high metals and minerals prices, there was a modest tendency toward depreciation.[16] Unsurprisingly, among developing oil exporters the tendency toward appreciation was much more pronounced, with two-thirds of these countries appreciating by an average of 18 percent.[17] Such exchange rate fluctuations contributed to the resilient response of these economies to higher oil prices by facilitating adjustment to the change in relative prices implied by higher oil prices (figure 1.12). For oil importers, the depreciation transfers the price shock over a wider range of tradable goods and services. Moreover, by making exports more competitive and imports less so, the depreciation increases net exports, reducing the impact on economic output that would otherwise be observed as a result of reduced incomes and lower consumption.

Most developing oil importers have financed higher oil bills successfully

Another factor behind the resilience of growth has been the relative ease with which developing countries were able to finance higher oil bills. Many developing countries entered into this period of higher oil prices with positive or near-zero current-account balances. As a result, despite deteriorations of 2 or more percent of GDP in many cases, current-account positions for most countries remain at levels that should not pose serious financing difficulties (figure 1.13).

In the poorest countries, substantial increases in ODA during 2004 and 2005 provided some of the foreign currency necessary to finance the increase in their oil bills (figure 1.14). For many African countries, the increase in foreign currency earnings from this source amounted to more than 0.5 percent of GDP in 2004 (data for 2005 are not yet available). Simulations suggest that for oil-importing poor countries, increased ODA inflows may have reduced the first-round impact of higher oil prices by as much as two-thirds (Diaz-Bonilla and Savescu, 2006) (figure 1.14).[18]

While some countries may have used the money directly to finance oil consumption, in

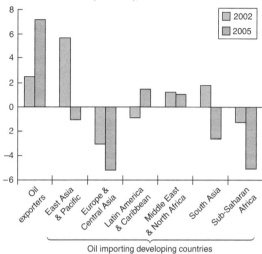

Figure 1.13 Developing countries' current-account balances

Current account balance (% of GDP), 2002 and 2005

Source: World Bank.

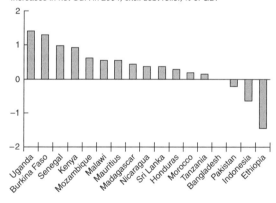

Figure 1.14 Increased aid helped finance oil costs in 2004

Increases in net ODA in 2004, excl. debt relief; % of GDP

Sources: OECD, World Bank.

most instances this was not the case. To the degree that projects financed by this aid had low import intensities, the foreign currency, after conversion to domestic currency, would be available to finance other imports—perhaps, but not necessarily, more expensive oil. Moreover, if there is a positive externality associated with domestic export activity (Frankel and Romer 1999; Ibrahim and

MacPhee 2003), the negative oil shock may actually have improved development prospects by partially offsetting the Dutch-disease effect associated with the increased aid.[19]

Despite these offsetting factors, several countries appear to be encountering difficulties financing their higher oil bills. In Africa, current account deficits among oil-importers (excluding South Africa) have soared and average more than 6 percent of GDP. Current-account deficits have also reached worrisome levels in many European and Central Asian countries. Many countries are experiencing fiscal difficulties because of less-than-complete pass-through. Madagascar, Malawi, and Sierra Leone have been forced to ration electricity consumption through rotating blackouts in an effort to conserve energy, suggesting that they may have met binding current-account constraints and are unable to finance additional oil imports. Several other countries appear to be consuming international reserves at unsustainable rates (Benin, Guinea Bissau, Mali, Tanzania) (figure 1.15). In still others, reserves represent a dangerously low share of monthly import cover (Bangladesh, Madagascar, Namibia, Swaziland). In all of these countries, policy makers will need to take concrete steps, including currency depreciation and energy conservation measures, so that domestic demand and the country's net revenue positions adjust to recent changes in relative prices.

Figure 1.15 Reserves in some countries are falling rapidly or worrisomely low

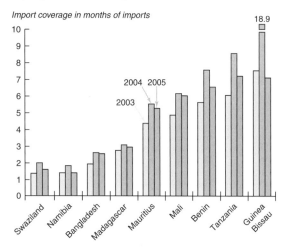

Source: World Bank.

Figure 1.16 Tensions associated with fast growth, the case of Turkey

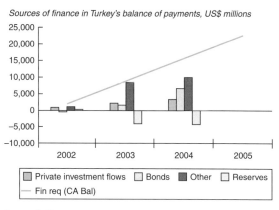

Source: IMF.

Of particular concern are a number of countries that combine high current-account deficits, significant capital inflows, high interest rates, and an appreciating currency, notably Bulgaria, Romania, and Turkey (figure 1.16). These conditions pose serious problems for policy makers, as the capital inflows (initially in the form of direct investments) prompt an appreciation of the currency, increase domestic money supply, and raise inflationary pressures. In each of these countries monetary institutions have responded by raising interest rates, which reduces domestic money supply growth but has also induced additional financial inflows, adding to domestic liquidity and inflationary pressures.[20] While tighter fiscal policy has helped combat these tendencies, external deficits continue to rise and currencies to appreciate in many of these countries. Should capital inflows slow or stop, financing current levels of expenditure could be very difficult, placing these currencies under significant pressure. A sudden depreciation could generate an inflationary push—partially undoing recent achievements in stabilizing currencies and controlling domestic inflation.

More generally, the deterioration in the current-account position of oil-importing developing countries means that they are much more vulnerable now than they were in 2003. An important supply disruption that pushed oil prices even higher, or a decline in nonoil commodity prices, would be much more difficult to finance and could precipitate painful adjustments (see risks section).

Global imbalances persist

The imbalances in global spending patterns that have characterized the world economy over the past five years, with the United States consuming significantly more than it produces and running a large current-account deficit, persisted in 2005 (figure 1.17). High oil prices both exacerbated imbalances and changed their nature, contributing to about 40 percent of the additional deterioration of the U.S. current-account deficit in 2005.[21] At the same time, high oil prices caused the current-account position of almost all oil-importing countries to deteriorate and substantially boosted those of exporters. As a result, whereas in 2002 oil-importers in virtually every region except the United States were running a current-account surplus, now almost all are running deficits—with the notable exceptions China, Japan, Korea, and a few other high-income countries.

The sustainability of these imbalances and their financing is a question of growing concern (IMF 2006; World Bank 2005a, 2005b). Persistent current-account deficits have transformed the United States from being the world's most important creditor nation (with a net international investment position of 13 percent of GDP in 1979) to being the world's largest debtor (with a net asset position of –21 percent of GDP in 2004). Unless savings in the United States increase substantially,

its net asset position is set to deteriorate sharply, reaching between 65 and 48 percent of GDP by 2015 (Higgins, Klitgaard, and Tille 2005).[22]

So far, financing of these deficits has not posed a serious problem for the United States, in part because of low interest rates and because of a generalized willingness of foreigners to hold American assets that yield lower returns than the foreign assets held by Americans.[23] As a result, despite the deterioration of its net asset position, the United States has continued to earn a positive net return on foreign investments.[24] If investor's willingness to continue accumulating such assets changed, U.S. interest rates would rise and the current account balance would deteriorate (by about 0.5 percent of GDP for every 100-basis-point rise in U.S. interest rates relative to foreign rates).[25] Over the past year, short-term interest rates in the United States have risen by about 100 basis points more than in Europe, bringing the overall difference to 220 basis points. The long-term differential is now some 100 basis points (figure 1.18). Although it is certainly too early to tell, this movement (and the decline in emerging-market risk premia against the dollar) could reflect a reassessment of the dollar as a safe haven.

Independent of the reasons for these movements, the course of long-term interest rates continues to be sensitive to the willingness of nonmarket sources of finance (formerly developing-country central banks and now, increasingly, authorities in

Figure 1.17 Global imbalances

Current account balance, $ billions, 2002 and 2005

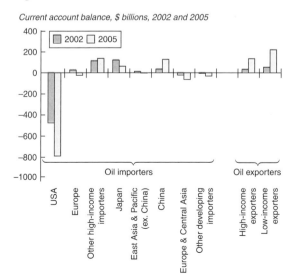

Source: World Bank.

Figure 1.18 Interest rate spreads support the dollar

3-month and 10-year bond yield, %

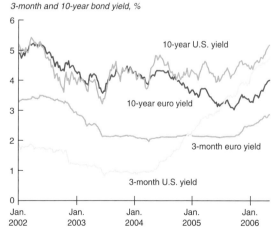

Sources: World Bank, Datastream.

Figure 1.19 Funding the U.S. current account deficit

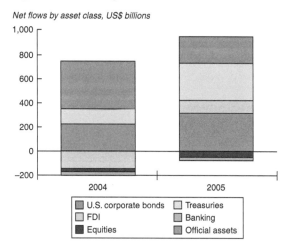

Net flows by asset class, US$ billions

Legend:
- U.S. corporate bonds
- FDI
- Equities
- Treasuries
- Banking
- Official assets

Source: World Bank.

oil-exporting countries) to purchase low-yield dollar-denominated assets. Lower reserve accumulation by oil-importing developing economies translated into a $130 billion decline in their purchases of U.S. Treasury bills and official assets (figure 1.19). This was only partly offset by a $14 billion increase in purchases by oil exporters. The need to meet this (nonmarket) financing shortfall may have been among the factors that pushed up long-term U.S. interest rates.

The tensions implicit in the U.S. current-account deficit are building and need to be addressed. Reducing global imbalances is a shared international responsibility, requiring a tightening of fiscal policy in the United States, increased imports abroad and increased exchange-rate flexibility. Implementation must necessarily be gradual—to avoid excessive disruption, both within the United States as macro policy is tightened and in developed and developing Asia as currencies are allowed to appreciate. However, to be effective and pre-empt market jitters the effort must be credible. In particular, in the absence of increased savings in the United States, increased domestic demand abroad and greater exchange rate flexibility are unlikely to have a significant effect on global imbalances and would likely exacerbate global capacity constraints—reducing the likelihood of a soft landing.

Although in the near term global imbalances are unlikely to provoke the serious currency crisis suggested by some (Roubini and Setser 2005), they do imply that the dollar will face further down-

ward pressure and that U.S. interest rates will continue to exceed those in Europe. Indeed, between January and early May 2006, dollar cross rates have been relatively sensitive to interest rate differentials. During this period, it has depreciated 7 percent against the euro (4 percent against the won and 0.7 percent against the renminbi) and 2.3 percent in real-effective terms. Looking forward these trends are expected to continue and the dollar to depreciate slowly by about 5 percent per year over the projection period.

World trade

Overall, merchandise trade growth slowed somewhat in 2005, expanding by 8.9 percent, as compared with 11.8 percent in 2004 (figure 1.20). Most of the slowdown occurred during the first half of the year and among high-income countries. For 2005 as a whole, their export volumes increased only 6.0 percent, down from 10.2 percent the year before. However, toward the second half of the year and into 2006, outturns have improved, in part because of increased European exports to the Middle East.

In contrast, China's export volume expanded by 27.8 percent in 2005, almost exactly as fast as in 2004. Moreover, despite a slowing in the pace of Chinese foreign sales towards the end of 2005, export volumes have once again picked up—expanding by more than 25 percent during the first

Figure 1.20 Healthy growth in world trade

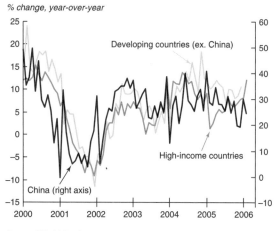

% change, year-over-year

Developing countries (ex. China)

China (right axis)

High-income countries

Source: World Bank.

two months of 2006. Other developing countries also continued to expand their market share. Their export volumes increased 10.3 percent, only somewhat slower than the year before. Here, too, trade growth decelerated early in the second half of 2005 but has since picked up.

Oil revenues of developing-country oil exporters nearly doubled between 2002 and 2005, increasing by some $215 billion. For all oil exporters, the increase was about $400 billion. However, oil exporters have increased their own imports markedly, and more than three-quarters of additional export revenues have been spent on additional imports.

Oil exporters are also recycling petrodollars through financial markets. Between 2002 and 2005, oil-exporting developing countries increased foreign currency reserves by $255 billion (with $117 billion of the increase accounted for by the Russian Federation). In total some $245 billion has flowed into the United States as securities, bonds or bank deposits, while about $50 billion has been placed directly into the European banking sector. Unfortunately, because of the use of third-party intermediaries and reduced reliance on the banking sector (as compared with past episodes of high oil prices) it is particularly difficult to trace the destination of these funds (BIS 2005).

Not all regions shared equally in the recycling of petrodollars. In particular, the share of the United States in the imports of oil-exporting countries fell from 25 to 20 percent during this period.[26] In contrast, most developing countries increased their market share in the imports of oil-exporting countries. However, the increase in their export revenues paled in comparison with the increase in their oil bills.

Can developing countries continue to gain market share at recent rates?

The strong economic performance of low- and middle-income countries over the past several years reflects both rapid growth in world exports (up 90 percent since 1995) and an almost 50 percent increase in the market share of developing economies, up from 20 percent in 1995 to almost 30 percent in 2005. This improvement is due, in large part, to increases in the market share of China. Nevertheless, every developing region (except East Asia excluding China) has seen its global market share increase (figure 1.21).

Figure 1.21 Regional increases in market share

% increase in global market share, 2005, since1995

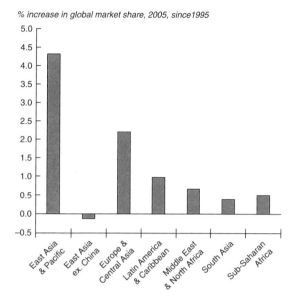

Source: World Bank.

The export boom of China is similar to past booms in a number of countries that are now classified as high income (Israel, Japan, the Republic of Korea, and Taiwan) in that it was mostly driven by an expansion in the range of goods exported. Thus, while technological progress, investment, and labor productivity growth contributed to a 290 percent increase in Chinese sales to the United States of products already on sale in 1992, more than 60 percent of the total increase came from the sale of goods that China did not export to the United States in 1992.[27] This contrasts with Bangladesh, for example (figure 1.22). That country's revenues from exports of traditional products to the United States increased by an impressive 173 percent between 1992 and 2005, but compared with China it managed only to generate one-tenth as much additional revenue from new products.

While not as marked as in China, there is evidence that other developing countries are diversifying the range of goods that they export and moving up the value-added ladder. Today, the revenues of developing countries from exports to high-income countries depend much less on raw materials (figure 1.23) and much more on higher-value-added goods (and services).

The rapid increase in the market share of China and other developing countries resulted from the exploitation of preexisting competitive

Figure 1.22 Increased product range explains most of Chinese export growth

Index of the value of exports to the USA, 1992 = 100

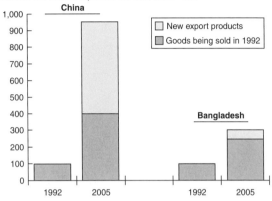

Source: World Bank.

Figure 1.23 Exports of developing countries have diversified

Product shares in exports of developing countries (ex. India & China) to high-income countries, %

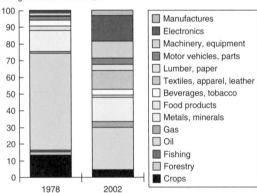

Source: World Bank.

advantages that have been exposed by market liberalization and domestic policy reforms. These include trade liberalization (both multilateral and, importantly, autonomous liberalization [World Bank 2005]), and behind-the-border reforms, such as regulatory reform, liberalization of foreign investment regimes, and improved labor market regulations.[28]

The important role that expanding the range of goods exported has played in China's success suggests that trade expansion need not be bound by increases in productivity or lower wages. Rather, it reflects the exposure of preexisting com-

parative advantages to new markets, the application of lessons learned in existing sectors to new ones, and a widening of the product base.

Long-term prospects for developing economies will depend importantly on their ability to continue increasing market share in this way. For countries and regions that, like Bangladesh, have yet to enjoy an export boom, trade liberalization and facilitation comprise key agendas. For China, the boost in exports associated with accession to the World Trade Organization (WTO) may be easing (accession is estimated to have increased export growth by 12 percentage points). Nevertheless, China's volume of exports can be expected to continue growing at around 18 percent.[29]

More generally, developing countries must establish and maintain low tariffs across the board, minimize administrative burdens associated with trade, and reduce transit times so that markets can be served in a timely manner (Newfarmer 2005). On the multilateral front, efforts need to be concentrated on agriculture, the most heavily protected sector and one where many developing countries enjoy a comparative advantage. Liberalization here would allow these countries to reap the same kind of benefits that have accrued to countries specialized in manufacturing following the liberalization of that sector. Second, countries need to reduce rigidities in product, labor, and financial markets so that firms can react with agility to new opportunities to expand the range of products they produce and sell.

Risks

The relatively benign soft-landing scenario for developing countries that is described above is subject to a number of important downside risks.

Managing fast growth

Internal risks exist on both the upside and downside. Following several years of very fast growth, a number of economies are showing signs of strain, as capacity constraints appear in some sectors or as weaknesses in their infrastructure or institutional frameworks are exposed. In several countries in the Europe and Central Asia region, strong FDI inflows attracted by privatizations and the prospects of accession to the European Union have prompted an appreciation of domestic currencies, high current-account deficits, and domestic monetary expansion. Subsequent increases in domestic interest rates have attracted further financial inflows, exacerbating the current account and exchange rate pressures. While, these pressures are projected to ease in our baseline projection, they carry with them the potential to prompt a currency crisis—possibly resulting in a hard landing—in one or more of these countries.

The rapid expansion of investment and domestic credit in some Asian economies may be overextending the banking sector in these countries in ways that are not yet obvious, potentially resulting in a sharp reversal of fortunes. The rapid rise in stock-market valuations, housing prices, and prices of other assets in several oil-exporting countries may also spur a crisis if conditions change rapidly.

Finally, the real-income shocks that developing countries have been subjected to are large, and adjustment to them remains incomplete. While inflationary pressures in most countries have been contained so far, pressures on wages are being felt in some. Rising inflation in a few countries in Latin America, South Asia, and, perhaps, Sub-Saharan Africa are suggestive of the beginning of an inflationary spiral. Unless fiscal and monetary authorities succeed in slowing growth, inflationary expectations may become engrained requiring a sharper slowdown later on as authorities intervene to contain them.

External risks

The external environment of the past few years has been especially propitious for growth, characterized by ample liquidity, rapidly expanding demand for the exports developing countries. Looking forward, conditions will be less benign. Interest rates are rising, while very high current account deficits in a number of developing countries suggests that many have yet to adjust fully to higher oil prices and that they have become more vulnerable to additional shocks.

The principal external risks facing the global economy have changed little over the past several years. They include: (1) the possibility that a supply shock will cause the price of oil to rise even further; (2) the possibility that interest rates demanded by foreign investors to finance the large U.S. current-account will rise, either gradually, in response to depreciation of the dollar, or more precipitously, because of a change in perceptions or

behavior; and (3) the possibility that nonoil commodity prices will fall significantly.

The effects on output in the global economy, should those risks be realized, have been presented in past editions of *Global Development Finance* and *Global Economic Prospects*. Rather than discuss them at length here (past results are summarized briefly below), this section explores their potential effects on the most vulnerable of low- and middle-income countries, particularly those that have significantly less room for maneuver than they did in 2002 because of the recent increases in oil prices.

Table 1.2 summarizes the results from previous simulations of three hypothetical shocks: (1) a reduction of 2 million barrels per day in oil supply, resulting in a rise in oil prices to $100 a barrel for three months and $80 for a further nine months; (2) a 200-basis-point increase in long-term interest rates and risk premia; and (3) a 15-percent decline in the price of nonoil commodities.

While for analytical clarity these simulations are presented independently, there are likely to be interactions between them. For example, were output to slow following a disruptive resolution of global imbalances both oil and non-oil commodity prices would likely decline. This kind of interaction is accounted for in table 1.2, but not in the more detailed impact analyses presented in tables 1.3–5. Similarly the probabilities of these external shocks differ. The probability of a disruptive resolution of global imbalances is low (but grows the longer corrective steps are not taken), while experts argue that there is a 70 percent chance of a 2 mbpd supply disruption sometime in the next 10 years (Beccue & Huntington, 2005).

In the first scenario, a substantial disruption in global oil supply pushes oil prices to $100 for one quarter and to $80 for a further nine months. As a result, global growth slows by about 0.75 percent a year over two years. The impact is more severe in large low-income and middle-income countries, both because of higher energy intensities and a greater inflationary impact, which requires a larger contraction to eliminate. On average, the current-account position of oil importing countries would deteriorate by about 1.1 percent of GDP.

In the second scenario, concerns over the U.S. current-account deficit push long-term interest rates up by 200 basis points. Heightened insecurity, especially because the dollar—the traditional

Table 1.2 Estimated impact of three risk scenarios

| | GDP (% change from baseline) | | | | First-round impact, % of GDP |
	Year 1	Year 2	Year 3		
Scenario 1: a 2-million-barrels-per-day negative supply shock[a]				**Scenario 3: a 15 percent decline in non-oil commodity prices**	
World	−1.0	−1.5	−1.1	High-income countries	0.0
High-income countries	−0.7	−1.5	−1.3	Low- and middle-income countries	−0.1
Middle-income countries	−1.6	−1.6	−0.1	Low- and middle-income oil exporters	0.0
Large low-income countries	−1.7	−2.8	−1.8	Low- and middle-income other	−0.1
Current-account-constrained				Low-income countries	0.0
low-income countries	−0.3	0.1	0.0	Low-income oil exporters	0.2
				Low-income other	−0.1
Scenario 2: a 200-basis-point increase in interest rates[b]				East Asia & Pacific	0.1
World	−1.7	−2.9	−1.9	Latin America & Caribbean	−0.4
High-income countries	−1.5	−2.7	−2.5	Europe & Central Asia	−0.2
Low- and middle-income countries	−2.4	−3.5	−3.0	Middle East & North Africa	0.5
				South Asia	0.2
				Sub-Saharan Africa	−0.7
				Oil exporters	0.3
				Oil importers	−1.1
				Oil importers less South Africa	−1.1
				HIPC	−0.7
				Oil exporters	0.0
				Other	−1.2

Source: World Bank.
a. For more details see (World Bank 2005b, Table 1.5)
b. For more details see (World Bank 2005b, Table 1.6)

safe haven currency—is the source of disruption, causes developing country risk premia to increase by an additional 200 basis points. World growth slows by about one-half for a period of two years, as higher interest rates cut into investment and consumption demand, both through classic transmission mechanisms and via the impact of interest rates on housing prices and consumer wealth. Slower growth eases inflationary pressure and global tensions, allowing monetary policy to loosen. Growth starts to pick up again.

In the third scenario, a 15 percent fall in nonoil commodity prices affects global growth only marginally. The bulk of the impact is felt by Sub-Saharan African oil-importing countries, which sustain a terms-of-trade loss equal to 1 percent of GDP. In the context of already elevated current-account deficits, this translates into a substantial reduction in domestic demand but only a limited fall in output, because net exports increase as a lack of access to foreign currency forces non-oil import volumes to decline in line with the increased oil bill.

Potential impacts in the most vulnerable countries

For the majority of developing countries, the fundamental improvements (increased globalization in both product and financial markets, improved

credibility of monetary policy, and more flexible labor and product markets) that allowed them to absorb the recent hike in oil prices with limited effects on output should also permit them to deal with the kinds of shocks modeled above without too much difficulty.

For other countries, however, the recent oil price hike caused a substantial deterioration in their current-account position. In addition to the real-side consequences of higher interest rates or a further increase in oil prices, the macroeconomic position of these countries could be placed under serious strain by the shocks assumed here—resulting in significant disruption. In the case of an interest rate shock, heavily indebted countries and middle-income countries would be most vulnerable, while a further increase in oil prices would strike the most oil-intensive economies hardest. A decline in nonoil commodity prices could also have important consequences for countries that are currently benefiting from strong nonoil commodity prices, notably metals and minerals.

Tables 1.3 through 1.5 summarize these sensitivities by highlighting the expected first-round impacts of the three shocks outlined above on the current accounts of developing economies. These simulations are meant to be illustrative—not predicative. Both the likelihood of a shock and its eventual magnitude are very uncertain. As the results presented in these tables are estimates of the first-round impact for a given size shock, they can be scaled up or down to estimate the impact of a smaller or larger shock.

Table 1.3 shows an estimate of the the cumulative impact of a 200-basis-point increase in U.S.

interest rates and a 200-basis-point increase in risk premia for the most vulnerable developing countries[30] (the most heavily indebted and those with high concentrations of short-term and other interest sensitive debt). Such a shock could represent as much as 3.5 percent of these countries' GDP and could send their current-account deficits

Table 1.3 Impact of a 400-basis-point increase in interest rates in selected developing countries
% of GDP

	Increase in debt servicing costs	Interest payments on external debt, 2004		Increase in debt servicing costs	Interest payments on external debt, 2004
Estonia	3.8	3.4	Lithuania	1.4	1.6
Latvia	3.4	2.3	Jordan	1.4	1.6
Kazakhstan	3.0	2.2	São Tomé and Principe	1.3	5.0
Croatia	2.9	3.5	Poland	1.3	1.4
Moldova	2.0	2.4	Romania	1.3	1.5
Argentina	2.0	1.2	Zimbabwe	1.2	0.5
Hungary	1.9	1.8	Mauritius	1.2	1.4
Sudan	1.8	0.4	Turkey	1.2	2.3
Slovak Republic	1.8	2.2	Malaysia	1.1	1.8
Bulgaria	1.8	2.1	Paraguay	1.1	1.9
Chile	1.7	1.5	Nicaragua	1.1	1.0
Uruguay	1.6	3.6	Lebanon	1.1	6.6
Philippines	1.6	4.4	Peru	1.1	2.1
Côte d'Ivoire	1.5	0.7	Panama	1.0	4.8
Czech Republic	1.4	1.3	Colombia	1.0	2.5
Indonesia	1.4	1.8	Jamaica	1.0	3.8

Source: World Bank.

Table 1.4 Impact of a further $30 hike in oil prices in selected developing countries
% of GDP

	Change in current account due to $30 hike in oil price	Current account balance in 2005		Change in current account due to $30 hike in oil price	Current account balance in 2005
Guyana	−8.2	−25.1	Vanuatu	−3.0	−44.4
Mongolia	−6.4	−2.8	Antigua and Barbuda	−3.0	−5.5
Tajikistan	−6.3	−4.2	Ukraine	−2.9	1.3
Lesotho	−5.8	−2.9	Paraguay	−2.9	−0.8
Togo	−5.4	−10.3	Lebanon	−2.8	−16.3
Kiribati	−5.3	−13.6	Mali	−2.7	−8.5
Solomon Islands	−5.2	−14.2	Jordan	−2.7	−5.8
Swaziland	−5.1	1.9	Mozambique	−2.6	−5.1
Tonga	−4.4	−0.5	Malawi	−2.6	−7.1
Cambodia	−4.4	−5.2	Bahamas, The	−2.5	−11.6
Ghana	−4.3	−6.9	Grenada	−2.4	−71.7
Belize	−4.3	−14.2	Gambia, The	−2.3	−12.4
Honduras	−4.0	−4.4	Dominica	−2.2	−26.3
Moldova	−3.8	−25.1	St. Lucia	−2.2	−10.1
Nicaragua	−3.5	−18.6	Nepal	−2.2	−1.3
Samoa	−3.5	−0.3	Pakistan	−2.2	−1.9
Jamaica	−3.3	−11.3	Mauritius	−2.2	−4.8
São Tomé and Principe	−3.3	−32.1	Madagascar	−2.1	−9.1
Macedonia, FYR	−3.2	−6.0	New Caledonia	−2.1	—
Maldives	−3.2	−25.1	Kyrgyz Republic	−2.1	−5.0
Micronesia, Fed. States of	−3.1	—	Lao PDR	−2.1	−7.9
Palau	−3.0	—	Armenia	−2.1	−2.3

Sources: World Bank; IMF.
Note: — = not available.

Table 1.5 Impact of a 15 percent fall in non-oil commodity

% of GDP

	Change in current account balance	Current account balance (2005)
Guyana	–8.3	–25.1
Tajikistan	–7.3	–4.2
Suriname	–7.0	–12.3
Solomon Islands	–4.5	–14.2
Belize	–3.8	–14.2
Mauritania	–3.8	–29.6
Mongolia	–3.7	–2.8
Paraguay	–3.5	–0.8
Papua New Guinea	–3.5	10.0
Kyrgyz Republic	–3.1	–5.0
Mali	–3.0	–8.5
Côte d'Ivoire	–2.9	2.2
Ghana	–2.9	–6.9
Malawi	–2.8	–7.1
Chile	–2.5	–0.9
Zimbabwe	–2.3	46.6
Zambia	–2.2	–10.3
Ukraine	–2.0	1.3
Jamaica	–2.0	–11.3

Source: World Bank; IMF.

to unsustainable levels. Depending on the availability of additional financing, this would require substantial retrenchment in these countries, likely implying large cuts in government spending and reductions in domestic demand that would likely translate into a period of sustained lower growth or a sharp recession. Encouragingly, a number of heavily indebted countries have taken advantage of favorable financing conditions to restructure their debt, reducing their sensitivity to changes in interest rates. As a result, countries that have experienced financial crises in the past, such as Brazil, Mexico and Thailand, appear to be much less vulnerable to a rapid rise in interest rates and do not appear in table 1.3.

On average, for oil-importing low-income countries, the initial terms-of-trade shock of a further $30 hike in oil prices is estimated at 4.1 percent of their GDP. This would translate into a 2.7 percent decline in domestic demand, with potentially serious impacts on poverty. For the most oil-intensive economies, this could amount to as much as 8 percent of GDP (table 1.4). While many countries throughout the developing world would be hard hit, most countries could be expected again to manifest the same resilience they showed during the previous oil hike. Problems are most likely to crop up in those countries that combine a large ex-

pected impact with already large current-account deficits. Such countries are unlikely to be able to find additional financing for their oil bills and, as a result, could be expected to undergo significant real-side adjustments as the volume of domestic demand, as well as oil (and nonoil) imports, would have to be cut in order to finance the higher cost of imported oil.

Table 1.5 reports the expected terms-of-trade impact from a 15 percent reduction in nonoil commodity prices, as well as estimates for the current-account deficit in 2005, for those countries where the impact would be greater than 2 percent of GDP. While countries throughout the developing world would be hard hit, large impacts are concentrated in developing Africa. Indeed, for the region as a whole, the negative impact would be 0.7 percent of GDP, or 1.2 percent of the GDP of heavily indebted poor countries. While many of these countries currently have healthy current-account balances (for example, Côte d'Ivoire, Papua New Guinea, Paraguay, and Ukraine) and can be expected to absorb even such a large shock relatively easily, many others are already in a vulnerable state. For these countries, taking steps now to improve the competitiveness of their export industries and reduce reliance on imports is even more critical.

Avian influenza

The continued spread of the bird-to-bird version of avian influenza (or bird flu, also known by its scientific identifier H5N1), with limited bird-to-human transmission comprises part of the baseline forecast. A serious risk to the global economy stems from the possibility that avian influenza might mutate into a form of flu that is easily transmitted between humans and for which the population has limited immunity.[31] The human and economic consequences of such a pandemic are potentially very large and depend importantly on the nature of the flu that emerges and on the reactions of people as it spreads.

Economic consequences of a further spread of bird-to-bird flu

The principal economic impact of the H5N1 virus so far has come in the rural sectors of several Asian economies in which the disease is endemic.

Table 1.6 Impact of a widening of bird-bird flu
% change in GDP, relative to the baseline

	Bird-bird[a]
World total	–0.1
High-income countries	–0.1
Low- & middle-income countries	–0.4
East Asia & Pacific	–0.4
Europe & Central Asia	–0.4
Latin America & Caribbean	–0.7
Middle East & North Africa	–0.4
South Asia	–0.4
Sub-Saharan Africa	–0.3

Source. World Bank.
a. Assumes that 12 percent of domestic birds in each region die from the disease or are killed in efforts to prevent its spread.

Its appearance in a number of European and African countries suggests that the disease may become as prevalent among the wild birds of these continents as it is currently in Asia.

Table 1.6 reports an effort to estimate the economic impact of such a spreading of the current bird-to-bird flu. The reported results are based on a scenario where bird-to bird flu becomes endemic throughout the world to the degree observed in Vietnam in 2004 (approximately 12 percent of all domestic birds died from the disease or were culled to prevent spread). While direct costs are small (only 0.1 percent of world GDP),[32] differing degrees of international specialization and cost structures suggest that, allowing for interactions with other sectors, regional impacts could be as high as 0.7 percent of GDP.[33] Because the sector is more important in developing countries and relatively labor intensive, job losses could represent about 0.2 percent of the global work force, or some 5 million jobs during the time it takes the global economy to adjust.

Possible economic consequences of a human pandemic

Even a flu with "normal" characteristics in terms of transmissibility and deadliness could have serious consequences for the global economy if the world's population has limited immunity. Estimates suggest that such a flu could infect as much as 35 percent of the world's population (WHO 2005), spreading throughout the world in as few as 180 days (RTI, 2006). As compared with a normal flu season, where some 0.2–1.5 million die (WHO 2003),[34] deaths from even a mild new flu might include an

additional 1.4 million people worldwide. A more virulent form, such as the 1918-9 flu, which was more deadly for healthy adults than a normal flu, could have much more serious consequences, killing as many as 1 in 40 infected individuals (Barry 2005) or some 71 million, with some authors suggesting that as many as 180–260 million could die in a worst-case scenario (Osterholm 2005).

Table 1.7 reports the results of three separate simulations of the economic consequences of a pandemic (McKibbin and Sidorenko 2006). The first (mild) scenario is modeled on the Hong Kong flu of 1968-9; the moderate flu has the characteristics of the 1957 Asian flu; and the severe simulation is benchmarked on the 1918-9 Spanish flu.[35] Each of these scenarios assumes that efforts by individuals and official agencies to limit the spread of the disease are no more effectual than those observed during previous epidemics and reflects differences in population density, poverty, and the quality of health care available. For the world as a whole, a mild pandemic would reduce output by less than 1 percent of GDP, a moderate outbreak by more than 2 percent, and a severe pandemic by almost 5 percent, constituting a major global recession. Generally speaking, developing countries would be hardest hit, because of higher population densities, poverty and weaker health infrastructure.[36] In addition, as modeled, less flexible market mechanisms accentuate the economic impacts in some countries.

Table 1.8 shows an alternative modeling of a pandemic. It is based on a pandemic similar in terms of mortality to the Asian flu epidemic of 1958. This scenario is presented with a view to better understanding the factors driving the aggregate

Table 1.7 Possible economic impacts of flu pandemic
% change in GDP, first-year

	Mild	Moderate	Severe
World	–0.7	–2.0	–4.8
High-income countries	–0.7	–2.0	–4.7
Developing countries	–0.6	–2.1	–5.3
East Asia & Pacific	–0.8	–3.5	–8.7
Europe & Central Asia	–2.1	–4.8	–9.9
Middle-East & North Africa	–0.7	–2.8	–7.0
South Asia	–0.6	–2.1	–4.9
Deaths (millions)	1.4	14.2	71.1

Source: World Bank calculations based on McKibbin & Sidorenko (2006).

Table 1.8 A breakdown of economic impacts of a potential human-to-human pandemic

% of GDP

	Mortality[a]	Impact of illness and absenteeism[b]	Impact of efforts to avoid infection[c]	Total	Total ($ billions)
World total	−0.4	−0.9	−1.9	−3.1	−965.4
High-income countries	−0.3	−0.9	−1.8	−3.0	−744.9
Low- and middle-income countries	−0.6	−0.9	−2.1	−3.6	−220.4
East Asia & Pacific	−0.7	−0.7	−1.2	−2.6	−44.8
Europe & Central Asia	−0.4	−0.7	−2.3	−3.4	−21.7
Latin America & Caribbean	−0.5	−0.9	−2.9	−4.4	−87.3
Middle East & North Africa	−0.7	−1.2	−1.8	−3.7	−32.2
South Asia	−0.6	−0.8	−2.2	−3.6	−22.7
Sub-Saharan Africa	−0.6	−0.9	−2.2	−3.7	−11.8

Source: World Bank.

a. Assumes a human flu pandemic similar to the 1958 Asian flu. Globally 1.08 percent of the world population dies, with regional mortallity rates varying from 0.3 percent in the U.S. to more than 2 percent in some developing countries.

b. Assumes that for every person that dies 3 are seriously ill, requiring hospitalization for a week and absence from work for two weeks, 4 require medical treatment and are absent from work for a week and approximately 27 percent of the population has a mild bout of flu requiring two days absence from work. It assumes that in addition for every sick day another absentee day is registered either because people stay at home to care for a sick person or to avoid illness.

c. Efforts to avoid infection are modelled as a demand shock, reflecting reduced travel, restaurant dining, hotels, tourism and theatre as individuals seek to avoid contact with others.

numbers in such simulations. The first column shows the impact in terms of GDP lost in the first year of the pandemic purely from additional deaths (here roughly equal to McKibbin and Sidorenko's severe scenario). The second column builds in the impact on aggregate productivity resulting from the infection of some 35 percent of the population. Even though individuals are only temporarily unavailable from work, the impact on output here is more than twice as large as from the loss of life, because the affected population is so much larger.

The third column shows the largest impact. Here individuals are assumed to change their behavior in the face of the pandemic by (a) reducing air travel in order to avoid infection in the enclosed space of a plane, (b) avoiding travel to infected destinations, and (c) reducing consumption of services such as restaurant dining, tourism, mass transport, and nonessential retail shopping. The degree to which such reactions would occur is necessarily uncertain. In this scenario it was assumed that for the year as a whole air travel would decline by 20 percent and that tourism, restaurant meals, and consumption of mass transportation services would also decline by 20 percent.

This compares with a peak decline of 75 percent in air travel to Hong Kong during the SARS epidemic and an average decline of 50–60 percent during the four-month period the outbreak was active. Retail sales declined by 15 percent at the peak and by about 9 percent over the four month period—implying about 15 percent decline from trend (Siu and Wong, 2004). Higher declines on an annualized basis are assumed in these simulations because a flu pandemic would likely last more than a year (pandemics are typically experienced in at least two waves with a peak period of infection during the winter).

The total impact of a shock combining all these elements is 3.1 percent for the global economy and ranges from 4.4 percent in Latin America and the Caribbean to 2.6 percent in the East Asia and Pacific region, mainly reflecting the relative importance and labor intensity of tourism and other services in each region.

The modeling attempted to take into account the possibility that the economic effects of an outbreak would be greatest in the country where the human-to-human strain originates, the main factor here being private and public efforts to isolate and contain the disease by avoiding travel and imposing quarantines. However, simulations of an outbreak beginning in Thailand suggest that whatever additional costs the originating country may endure, these would be dominated by secondary effects as the disease spreads to other countries and global economic activity declines.

Given the tremendous uncertainties surrounding the possibility and eventual nature of a pandemic, these simulations must be viewed as purely illustrative. They provide a sense of the overall magnitude of potential costs. Actual costs, both in terms of human lives and economic losses, are likely to be very different.

That said, these simulations serve to underline the importance of mobilizing global efforts to meet this potential crisis. Monitoring outbreaks of bird-to-bird and bird-to-human infections and culling infected flocks appear to be effective strategies to reduce bird-to-human transmission and reduce the likelihood that the disease will mutate into a form that is easily transmissible between humans. The fact that there have been no reported cases of bird flu in Vietnam in the 2005-6 flu season suggests that such preventative efforts can be effective.

However, even with such efforts, an eventual human pandemic at some unknown point in the future is virtually inevitable (WHO, 2004). Because such a pandemic would spread very quickly, substantial efforts need to be put into place to develop effective strategies and contingency plans that could be enacted at short notice. Much more research and coordination at the global level are required.

Notes

1. In addition to the Prospects for the Global Economy web site (http://www.worldbank.org/outlook) the World Bank's East Asia update provides more detailed information on recent developments and prospects for the East Asia and Pacific region (http://www.worldbank.org/eapupdate/).

2. The World Bank's East Asia Update provides additional detail on avian influenza in the region (http://www.worldbank.org/eapupdate/).

3. In addition to the *Prospects for the Global Economy* web site (http://www.worldbank.org/globaloutlook), which provides more detail on the regional forecasts, the World Bank's Middle East and North Africa Region's *Economic Developments and Prospects* (http://www.worldbank.org/mena) provides country-specific analysis of economic developments, projections, and policy priorities.

4. For the purposes of this report, the developing countries of the region are Algeria, Egypt, Jordan, Iran, Morocco, Oman, Syria, Tunisia, and Yemen. A lack of data prevented inclusion of Djibouti, Iraq, Lebanon, and Libya from the projections. Important regional players include the high-income countries of Bahrain, Kuwait, Qatar, Saudi Arabia, and the United Arab Emirates.

5. Fiscal and quasi-fiscal spending increased by 0.7 percent of GDP in Bangladesh, by 0.5 percent of GDP in India, and by significant, though lesser, amounts in other countries of the region.

6. More than one-third grew faster than 5 percent on average between 2000 and 2005, compared with less than 10 percent during the period 1980–1995.

7. While large in percentage terms, the increase in oil prices from around $10 to $20 a barrel between 1999 and 2000 is not considered as part of the oil shock, because it merely reflected the reversal of a similar fall in prices the year before.

8. The short-term price elasticity of oil demand is estimated at between –0.01 and –0.2 percent (Burger 2005), implying that immediately following a 100-percent increase in oil prices, such as observed between 2002 and 2005, oil demand would be expected to decelerate by between 1 and 20 percent. Long-term elasticities are larger (between –0.2 and –0.6 percent), implying that the negative effect of higher prices over the past few years will continue to be felt.

9. The current rise in oil prices began in early 2003.

10. OPEC did increase its deliveries during 2004 by drawing down its spare capacity, but so far investments to increase that capacity have been limited.

11. In the three years following both the 1973 and 1979 oil price hikes, non-OPEC non-former Soviet Union oil producers increased their output by some 3.5 million barrels per day. In contrast, since 2002, production from these sources has actually declined.

12. Beccue and Huntington (2005) estimate the probability of a 2 mbpd supply shock occurring during the next 10 years as 70 percent for one lasting 6 months and 35 percent for one lasting 18 months.

13. Baffes (2005) estimates the elasticity of nonoil commodity prices to oil prices to be 0.15.

14. Normally, the yield curve is upward sloping, implying that bonds of shorter duration yield lower rates of return than longer term bonds. This upward slope is generally thought to reflect individuals' time preference for money, on the one hand, and the increased risk associated with longer term lending.

15. For low- and middle-income countries as a whole, net bank lending actually exceeded bond emissions by a small margin.

16. About as many appreciated as depreciated. Overall, the unweighted average impact was a real effective depreciation of just 1 percent.

17. The unweighted average appreciation of oil and mineral exporters was smaller, at around 9 percent.

18. Simulations using the World Bank's MAMS model (a computable general equilibrium model for studying the impact of aid on achieving the Millennium Development goals) indicate that a negative term-of-trade shock of 1 percent of GDP would reduce import volume growth in the first year by 2 percent. When combined with a 1 percent of GDP increase in aid flows, imports fall by only 0.7 percent.

19. The same simulations suggest that the real appreciation from a permanent increase in aid inflows equal to 1 percent of GDP would reduce exports by about 3 percent in the first year and .66 percent per annum over a 10-year period. When combined with a negative terms-of-trade effect equal to 1 percent of GDP, the appreciation is reduced by half and the impact on export growth rates reduced by 10 percent.

20. In the case of Turkey, the central bank has tightened policy rates, while in Bulgaria the rise in interest rates is an automatic response to capital inflows by the country's currency board system.

21. The current-account deficit of the United States came in at $805 billion or about 6.4 percent of U.S. GDP.

22. These estimates are based on three scenarios. In the first, the current-account deficit is assumed to remain constant at 6 percent of GDP; nominal GDP is projected to increase by 5 percent per annum; and exchange rates and rates of return of U.S. and foreign assets are to remain constant. Because net returns fall to –1.2 percent of GDP, this implies an improvement in the U.S. current-account deficit equal to 1 percent of GDP. A second scenario assumes that the current-account deficit declines to 2.5 percent of GDP, implying a substantial improvement in the U.S. trade balance equal to 0.5 percentage point per year. In the third scenario, the rates of return on U.S. and foreign assets are assumed to equalize, increasing net debt-servicing costs to 2.1 percent of GDP.

23. Empirically, this willingness takes three principal forms. First, foreigners hold a higher share of relatively low-yield dollar-denominated assets than do Americans—reducing the overall earnings on their assets. Secondly, as recorded in the balance of payments, American investments abroad earn a significantly higher rate of return than do foreign investments in the United States (6.9 percent vs. 2.5 percent over the past 10 years). Finally, foreigners hold large quantities of dollars in cash, which earn no return. These three factors, in combination, mean that despite the negative net international asset position of the United States, the country continues to earn a small but positive net income from capital services.

24. Haussman and Sturzenegger (2005), in a controversial article, take this observation to an extreme. They argue that if the United States earns a positive return on its net foreign asset position, in economic terms, it must be positive. They propose to measure it as the net present value of the income stream recorded in the balance of payments. They then redefine the current-account balance as the change in that net asset position (effectively 20 times the annual change in income flow). Finally, they define the difference between this measure and the normal current account of the balance of payments as exports of "dark matter," or know-how services embodied in FDI, insurance services provided by less risky U.S. assets, and liquidity services deriving from the quality of the U.S. dollar as the world reserve currency. On this basis they compute that the net asset position of the United States was actually a small surplus in 2004.

25. Interestingly, such a change in the willingness of investors to hold U.S. assets would cause Haussman and Sturzenegger's (2005) definition of the net international investment position of the United States to deteriorate by 10 percent of GDP, and would imply an equal fall in their estimate of the current account—highlighting the sensitivity of their measures to interest rates and unmeasurable confidence factors.

26. While economic factors certainly have played a role (the erosion of market share among high-income countries mirrors earlier developments), political factors also played a role. In particular, the imports of oil importers from the United States declined substantially in the period 2001/2. While growth rates since then have been on a par with other high-income countries, the lost market share has not been recouped.

27. Between 1972 and 2004, China went from exporting 510 separate goods to 10,199 (Borda and Weinstein 2004).

28. In the case of China, many behind-the-border changes were precipitated by the country's desire to join the World Trade Organization. Similarly, many reforms in the European transition countries were motivated by the desire of those countries to join the European Union.

29. Econometric estimates suggest that over the past three years the underlying trend growth in China was 11.7 percent. WTO accession contributed an additional 12 percent to Chinese export growth. Market growth was worth 6.3 percent. Relative price changes reduced the total by 4.2 percent (Martel Garcia, forthcoming).

30. Only countries where the estimated impact equals or exceeds 1 percent of GDP are shown.

31. There are a number of kinds of avian influenza that are carried by many wild bird species with no apparent harm. Some of these make other bird species, notably domestic poultry, sick. Typically, the birds are mildly sick, but the H5N1 virus that is currently circulating is relatively dangerous for domestic birds. Most forms of avian influenza viruses are highly species-specific and do not normally infect people. However, H5N1 has crossed the species barrier to infect humans on three occasions in recent years—in Hong Kong in 1997 and during the current outbreak, which began in December 2003. While deadly (115 human deaths among 208 confirmed cases as of May 12, 2006), the virus in its current form is not easily transmitted to or between humans (WHO 2006).

32. Direct costs are small. Six percent of the world population of domestic poultry amounts to some 170 million birds. At a retail price of $2 per bird, and assuming (based on the Vietnamese experience) 0.75 cents in costs associated with monitoring and culling infected birds, this would amount to about $760 million worldwide, or about 0.02 percent of world GDP.

33. While the poultry sector represents less than 0.2 percent of the GDP of high-income countries, its share in developing countries is about 1.2 percent of GDP, rising to 2.4 percent of GDP in the East Asia and Pacific region.

34. The World Health Organization (2003) estimates between 200,000 and 500,000 deaths each year. Osterholm (2005) reports a higher death toll of between 1 and 1.5 million people worldwide from influenza infections or related complications, making it the third most deadly infectious disease after AIDS and tuberculosis, but ahead of malaria.

35. McKibbin and Sidorenko also model an "Ultra" flu, which is not based on any known previous pandemic, but has the characteristics of the Spanish flu, plus higher mortality for older people. This simulation is not reported here.

36. McKibbin and Sidorenko's model has relatively limited country coverage: 20 economies. comprised of 10 high-income countries and 1 residual high-income region; 5 low- and middle-income countries in East Asia and one in South Asia; and three additional developing regions. Regional aggregates in table 1.7 are approximations based on the countries and regions modeled.

References

Baffes, John. 2005. "Oil Spills over to Other Commodities." Unpublished paper, World Bank, Washington, DC.

Barry, John M. 2005. *The Great Influenza: The Epic Story of the Deadliest Plague in History*. London: Penguin.

Beccue, Phillip C., and Hillard G. Huntington. 2005. "An Assessment of Oil Market Disruption Risks." Energy Modeling Forum, Stanford University. October. http://www.stanford.edu/group/EMF/publications/doc/EMFSR8.pdf

Billings, Molly. 1997. "The Influenza Pandemic of 1918." Stanford University. http://www.stanford.edu/group/virus/uda/.

Borda, C., and D. C. Weinstein. 2004. "Globalization and the Gains from Variety." NBER Working Paper 10314, National Bureau of Economic Research, Cambridge, MA.

Buiter, Willem. 2006. "Dark Matter or Cold Fusion." Global Economics Paper 136. Goldman Sachs, New York. January.

Cline, William. 2005. *The United States as a Debtor Nation*. Washington, DC: Institute for International Economics.

Devarajan, Shantayanan, and Ejaz Ghani. 2006. "Oil Price Shocks, Fiscal Adjustment, and Poverty Reduction in Asia." Paper presented at the SAARC finance seminar on "Current Oil Price Shock and Its Implications on South Asian Economies," Colombo, Sri Lanka. January.

Diaz-Bonilla, Carolina, and Cristina Savescu. 2006. "Simulations of Economic Impacts of Official Development Assistance and Oil Price Increases: Ethiopia." Unpublished paper, World Bank, Washington, DC.

Estrella, Arturo. 2005. "Why does the yield curve predict output and inflation?" *Economic Journal*. July.

Frankel, Jeffrey A., and David Romer. 1999. "Does Trade Cause Growth?" *American Economic Review* 89 (3): 379–99.

Higgins, Mathew, Thomas Klitgaard, and Cedric Tille. 2005. "The Implications of Rising U.S. International Liabilities." *Current Economic Issues* (Federal Reserve Bank of New York) 11 (5). December.

Hausmann, Ricardo, and Federico Sturzenegger. 2005. "Global Imbalances or Bad Accounting? The Missing Dark Matter in the Wealth of Nations." Unpublished paper, Harvard University.

Hummels, D., and P. J. Klenow. 2004. "The Variety and Quality of a Nation's Exports." Unpublished paper. Purdue University and Stanford University.

Ibrahim, Izani, and Craig MacPhee. 2003. "Export Externalities and Economic Growth." *Journal of International Trade & Economic Development* 12 (3): 257–83.

IMF (International Monetary Fund). 2006. *World Economic Outlook*. IMF: Washington, DC.

Kehoe, T. J., and K. J. Ruhl. 2003. "How Important Is the New Goods Margin in International Trade?" Research Department Staff Report 324, Federal Reserve Bank of Minneapolis.

Laster, David, and Robert N. McCauley. 1994. "Making Sense of the Profits of Foreign Firms in the United States." *Quarterly Review* (Federal Reserve Bank of New York) 19 (2).

Martel Garcia, Fernando. 2006. "Understanding Long Export Booms: The Case of China." Unpublished paper, World Bank, Washington, DC.

Mataloni, Raymond J. 2001. "An Examination of the Low Rates of Return of Foreign-Owned U.S. Companies." *Survey of Current Business* (March): 55–73.

McKibbin, Warwick, and Alexandra Sidorenko. 2006. "Global Macroeconomic Consequences of Pandemic Influenza." Lowy Institute for International Policy, Sydney Australia.

Newfarmer, Richard, ed. 2005. *Trade, Doha, and Development: A Window into the Issues*. World Bank, Washington, DC.

Osterholm, Michael T. 2005. "Preparing for the Next Pandemic." *New England Journal of Medicine* 352 (May): 1839–42.

Roubini, Nouriel, and Brad Setser. 2005. "Will the Bretton Woods 2 Regime Unravel Soon? The Risk of a Hard Landing in 2005–2006." Paper presented at conference on "Revived Bretton Woods System: A New Paradigm for Asian Development," San Francisco, February 4.

Setser, Brad. 2006. "On the Origins of Dark Matter." January http://www.rgemonitor.com/blog/setser/113810.

Siu, Alan, and Y. C. Richard Wong. 2004. "Economic Impact of SARS: The Case of Hong Kong." Hong Kong Institute of Economics and Business Strategy, Working Paper 1084. April.

World Bank. 2005a. *Global Development Finance 2005: Mobilizing Finance and Managing Vulnerability*. World Bank: Washington, DC.

———. 2005b. *Global Economic Prospects 2006: Economic Implications of Remittances and Migration*. Washington, DC.

World Health Organization. 2003. "Influenza." Fact Sheet 211, Geneva. http://www.who.int/mediacentre/factsheets/fs211/en/index.html.

———. 2004. "World Is Ill-Prepared for "Inevitable" Flu Pandemic." *Bulletin of the World Health Organization* 82 (4): 317–18.

———. 2006. "Avian Influenza ("bird flu") Fact Sheet." http://www.who.int/mediacentre/factsheets/avian_influenza/en/index.html. February 2006.

2

The Growth and Transformation of Private Capital Flows

In 2005, global capital flows to developing countries continued to grow at a record pace. Net private flows increased sharply by $94 billion, reaching $491 billion, reinforcing a trend underway since 2002. The sharp rise came despite lingering uncertainty about the impact of higher oil prices, rising global interest rates, and growing global payments imbalances. The flows have been broad-based, with bond issuance, bank lending, foreign direct investment (FDI), and portfolio equity all recording substantial gains (figure 2.1). During the year, governments and private entities took advantage of favorable financial-market conditions to refinance their debt or prefund future borrowing. As a result, foreign currency–denominated bond issuance by governments and the private sector rose to a record gross of $131 billion in 2005. The spread on emerging market debt dropped to historic lows, averaging 306 basis points for 2005, compared with the 2004 average of 423 basis points and the recent high of 832 basis points, recorded in September 2002. Meanwhile, local-currency bond markets in Asia and Latin America attracted substantial interest from international investors in search of higher yields and potential gains from currency appreciation.

Accounting for the growth in recent years have been the policy responses to the financial crises of the 1990s, a favorable environment for mergers and acquisitions, a wave of privatizations, and innovations in the global marketplace. In the aftermath of the financial crises of the 1990s, many major emerging markets adopted more flexible exchange rate policies, while strengthening domestic financial markets and relaxing controls on cross-border financial flows. Several countries, especially in East Asia, made concerted efforts to accumulate precautionary reserves and build their domestic bond markets to better manage risks associated with foreign portfolio flows.

The favorable environment for cross-border mergers and acquisitions and a new wave of privatizations, particularly in the new member countries of the European Union (EU), pushed FDI to an all-time high of $238 billion. The increase raised the share of developing countries in global FDI flows from 13 percent in 2000 to 24 percent in 2005. During the year, share prices quoted on emerging market stock exchanges turned in a stellar performance, receiving record flows of portfolio equity. Stock issuance by emerging market countries in international financial markets also grew substantially.

Figure 2.1 Net private debt flows to developing countries, 1991–2005

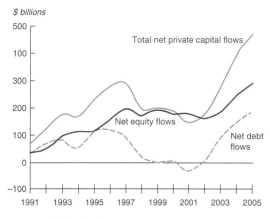

Source: World Bank Debtor Reporting System.

Financial innovations in global financial markets—notably local-currency financing and structured finance instruments—have allowed investors to assume greater exposures in emerging markets. The euro has emerged as a major international reserve currency and as an increasingly important issuing currency for governments and the corporate sector in developing countries.

This chapter provides updates on all types of private capital flows to developing countries, exploring some implications of the increased importance of the euro, the fast-growing credit derivatives markets, and the increasing reliance of many countries on local-currency funding. The key messages emerging from this review are highlighted below.

- Developing countries have benefited from strong economic growth and sounder macroeconomic policies, leading to marked improvements in their external payment positions. Despite the easing of financing conditions, however, developing countries' access to international capital markets remains limited. Private capital flows to the developing world are concentrated in just a few countries. Of the 136 that report to the World Bank, 51 continue to rely primarily or entirely on official sources of cross-border finance. If they are to attract and absorb private capital effectively for long-term growth and development, they will need to, inter alia, further develop their domestic financial markets and institutions.

- Local-currency bond markets in developing countries have, since the crises of the 1990s, emerged as a major source of long-term development finance and are now the fastest growing segment of emerging market debt. Driven largely by domestic institutional and individual investors, these markets grew from $1.3 trillion at the end of 1997 to $3.5 trillion in September 2005. However, bringing the local-currency bond markets in emerging economies up to the standards of mature markets will require concerted efforts. The East Asian countries may provide a case worth watching in this regard, given their early successes. Local-currency debt markets also present new challenges for policy makers. Professionalism in debt management will be needed to manage currency and duration risks associated with

burgeoning government debt denominated in local currencies.

- Credit default swaps (CDSs)—derivatives that provide some insurance to the buyer against defaults and other adverse credit events—are being applied in new ways in emerging securities markets—among them those of Bulgaria, the Republic of Korea, Mexico, Peru, the Philippines, and the Russian Federation. This development has important implications for the pricing and supply of debt capital to developing countries, because it offers investors another way of assuming exposure to emerging market risk and enhances the markets' ability to gauge credit risk. Also, by transferring to other market participants some of the credit risk that banks incur in their lending and trading activities, credit derivatives have altered, perhaps fundamentally, the traditional approach to credit-risk management. Presently, only a few banks engage in CDSs in emerging markets, posing the risk that a failure of a major player could create broader risks. Trading takes place largely in the private over-the-counter market and thus lacks transparency. Regulators in developing countries need to build their capacity to monitor CDS transactions and to define a clear line of regulatory responsibility and expertise so as to better manage the associated risks.

- The strong recovery of FDI in developing countries over the past two years reflects healthy global economic conditions and a better investment climate in developing countries. While increased corporate profits, favorable financing conditions, and higher stock-market valuations fueled cross-border investments globally, many developing countries managed to attract high levels of FDI through privatizations, mergers, and acquisitions. Almost all developing countries experienced higher FDI inflows, but the increase was especially notable in new members of the European Union. In China, liberalization of the financial sector and accession to the World Trade Organization led to several important privatization deals in the banking sector in 2005. Many middle-income countries received high levels of services-related FDI through privatizations, while FDI to low-income countries grew principally because of high commodity prices.

- In the years ahead, policy makers in developing countries will have to remain alert to certain risks and vulnerabilities. The current glut of liquidity in the global financial markets may lead to a buildup of risky exposures, as investors in search of higher yields settle for borrowers of lower creditworthiness. The locus of credit risk in developing countries is shifting as private corporates, rather than sovereigns, are emerging as the main borrowers in global credit markets. Political risk has emerged once again as a key concern for emerging market investors. In several countries, populist candidates will stand for election in 2006, raising the fear of policy changes that could reverse the gains from recent fiscal stabilization and liberalization measures. Meanwhile, the traditional policy discipline and frameworks agreed to with multilateral lenders are becoming less prominent with the dwindling need for official financing. The cumulative risks are particularly pronounced in oil-importing countries like Turkey and the Philippines, which have suffered from recent oil price increases without benefiting from the commodity price boom.

Private debt market developments in 2005

In 2005, net private debt flows to developing countries increased sharply to an estimated $192 billion, up from $148 billion in 2004 and $85 billion in 2003 (table 2.1). The net increase reflected an increase in gross financing through bonds and syndicated loans, which set record highs, with flows 54 percent higher in 2005 than in 2004 (table 2.2). New bank lending was particularly strong, swelling to $198 billion in 2005 from $112 billion the year before. Bank lending now accounts for 60 percent of gross debt flows and more than two-thirds of the increase from 2004 (table 2.2).

Driving the strong upswing in foreign private debt flows are abundant global liquidity, steady improvements in developing-country credit quality, lower yields in developed countries, and continued broadening of the investor base for emerging market assets. Upgrades in credit ratings have outpaced downgrades for eight consecutive quarters, with 46 upgrades and 18 downgrades in

2005. As a result, foreign private debt flows have become more soundly based and resilient to swings in external financing conditions.

Bond issuance set records in 2005

The investment community now accepts emerging market debt as a bona fide asset class that is becoming less volatile. The spread on such debt has dropped to historic lows, with an average of just 306 basis points in 2005, compared with 423 basis points in 2004 (box 2.1). In 2005, developing countries raised a record $131 billion in 367 bond issues, an increase in proceeds of 28 percent from 2004. Net issuance of foreign currency–denominated bonds last year amounted to $62 billion, less than half of the total raised.

Table 2.1 Net private debt flows to developing countries, 2002–5
$ billions

	2002	2003	2004	2005
Total net debt flows	5.5	85.1	144.8	191.6
By region:				
East Asia and Pacific	−2.4	9.3	43.3	45.8
Europe and Central Asia	24.9	64.7	93.7	113.8
Latin America and the Caribbean	−21.4	5.4	−1.0	20.5
Middle East and N. Africa	4.8	2.1	2.3	4.6
South Asia	2.4	2.1	6.7	3.0
Sub-Saharan Africa	−2.8	1.5	2.8	3.8
By component				
Bond financing	10.8	26.4	43.0	61.7
Bank financing	−2.8	9.8	39.4	64.4
Other financing	−6.8	−5.9	−4.6	−6.7
Short-term debt financing	4.2	54.9	70.8	69.3

Source: World Bank Debt Reporting System.

Table 2.2 Gross market-based debt flows to developing countries, 2002–5
$ billions

	2002	2003	2004	2005
Total gross flows	120.8	168.9	214.3	329.1
Bonds	51.7	82.2	102.4	130.9
East Asia and Pacific	12.5	11.6	15.7	20.3
Europe and Central Asia	13.8	26.5	38.2	54.7
Latin America and the Caribbean	21.1	38.8	35.9	43.0
Middle East and N. Africa	2.7	1.0	5.6	5.4
South Asia	0.2	0.5	5.1	5.3
Sub-Saharan Africa	1.5	3.9	2.0	2.3
Bank lending	69.1	86.9	111.8	198.1
East Asia and Pacific	21.5	26.9	19.5	34.5
Europe and Central Asia	16.8	22.2	37.8	77.6
Latin America and the Caribbean	18.5	20.6	29.9	46.3
Middle East and N. Africa	5.8	4.6	9.7	15.7
South Asia	1.7	4.0	7.0	12.2
Sub-Saharan Africa	4.9	8.5	7.9	11.9

Sources: Dealogic Bondware and Loanware and World Bank staff.

Box 2.1   The emerging bond market enters the mainstream

Emerging market debt is heading firmly into the mainstream of global bond trading. The traditionally high idiosyncratic risk associated with emerging market bonds has declined significantly since 2002, a trend reflected in the spreads of such bonds over U.S. Treasuries. Four important features of this transformation are:

- First, emerging market bond spreads are moving increasingly in tandem with U.S. high-yield bonds (see figure at top left). In the midst of uncertainty about the fate of the Brazilian economy in 1998, emerging market spreads were 1,200 basis points. At the end of 2005 they were just over 200 basis points.[a] The decline occurred despite Argentina's default in 2002, a period of tightening of U.S. monetary policy during 2004–5, and turmoil in the U.S. corporate bond market caused by downgrades of car makers.
- Second, volatility in emerging market bond spreads, as measured by the standard deviation of Emerging Market Bond Index (EMBI) spreads, has declined significantly since 1999 (see top right figure on next page).
- Third, emerging bond indices are becoming more strongly correlated with both global and U.S. bond indices (see figure at lower left). The strength of the correlation between emerging market and global bond markets has been increasing for five years.

- Fourth, the extraordinary narrowing of spreads has been accompanied by a parallel move to smaller daily fluctuations—both lower variability and fewer extreme changes (see figure at lower right). The frequency distribution of changes in daily spreads seems to be best characterized as nonnormal, having fatter and asymmetric tails (kurtosis and skewness). A measure of the nonnormality, the Jacques-Bera test,[b] indicates that the distribution became more normal in 2002–2004 because of a decline in excess kurtosis, although non-normality was higher again in 2005 because kurtosis and skewness were both higher. Skewness was significantly negative in several years, including 2005, indicating that longer tails to the left were probably caused by the decline in spreads.[c]

Source: World Bank staff calculations based on various data sources.
a. The EMBIG is affected by the removal of defaulted bonds from the index; adjusting for these changes, however, gives the same picture of a dramatic decline in spreads.
b. The Jacques-Bera test statistic is $(N/6)(.25K^2+S^2)$, where N is the number of observations, K is excess kurtosis, and S is skewness. It is distributed as a chi-square with 2 degrees of freedom, so that a value in excess of 6 indicates rejection of normality at the 5 percent level.
c. The distribution of daily changes in EM bond spreads is becoming more normal, in the sense that the excess kurtosis displayed in changes in spreads has been declining roughly since 2001, although it has increased slightly in the 2004–5 period. The standard deviation has also declined significantly from a high of 21.8 in 2001 to 5.7 in 2005. Over this period, the distribution tended toward a normal distribution, since the Jacques-Bera test statistic has been declining, with the exception of 2005.

Bond issuance was concentrated. Ten countries (Brazil, China, Hungary, India, Indonesia, Mexico, Poland, the Russian Federation, Turkey, and República Bolivariana de Venezuela) accounted for 69 percent of the issuance.[1] Forty developing countries accessed the international bond market, compared with 34 in 2002 and 2003. Countries from Europe and Central Asia accounted for 42 percent of total issuance in 2005, with Poland, the Russian Federation, and Turkey leading the pack. Three of the five largest issues in the region were by Russian firms, including two U.S.-dollar-denominated bonds issued by the financial entity Gazstream SA. In Poland, 13 sovereign issues, totaling $12 billion, were issued to refinance the country's Paris Club debt. Four of these were publicly issued in the euro market, two in the global dollar market, and four in the Swiss franc market.

Latin America and the Caribbean region accounted for about 33 percent of total issuance, with Brazil's government being the most active borrower. In 2005, the Brazilian government exchanged its outstanding C-bonds for U.S.-dollar-denominated global bonds having a face value of $4.5 billion and a maturity of 12 years, retiring a third of its Brady debt. The Southern Copper Corporation carried out a notable transaction in Mexico, issuing two U.S.-dollar-denominated bonds, one with a maturity of 10 years ($200 million), and the other 30 years ($600 million). The average maturity of fixed-rate issues by Latin American firms in 2005 was 13.2 years.

Countries in East Asia and the Pacific issued bonds to borrow $ 20.3 billion, with China being the major issuer through government-owned banks. The Export-Import Bank of China and the China Development Bank each issued $1 billion in

Convergence of emerging market bond spreads with U.S. high-yield bonds, December 1998–December 2005

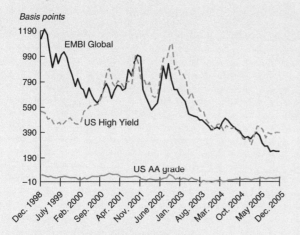

Sources: JPMorgan Chase and Merrill Lynch.

Decline in emerging market bond volatility, 1994–2004

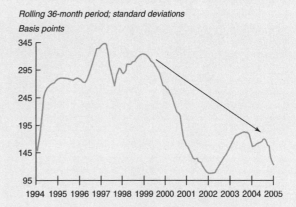

Sources: JPMorgan Chase and World Bank staff calculations.

Correlation of emerging market bond indices with global and U.S. indices, 1998–2005

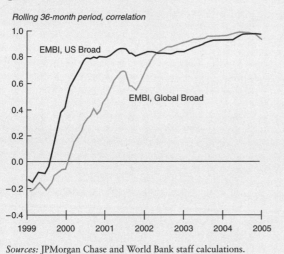

Sources: JPMorgan Chase and World Bank staff calculations.

Distribution of daily changes in emerging market bond spreads

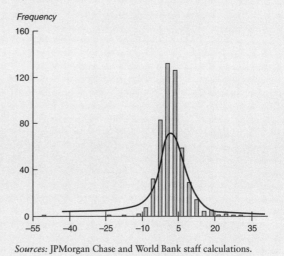

Sources: JPMorgan Chase and World Bank staff calculations.

10-year U.S.-dollar-denominated bonds. In September 2005, the government of the Philippines completed its 2005 funding program by successfully issuing a 10-year U.S.-dollar-denominated bond for $1 billion at a spread of 430 basis points over 10-year U.S. Treasuries.

Sovereign borrowers accounted for 46 percent of total issuance (figure 2.2) in 2005. They took advantage of favorable market conditions to refinance costlier debt and prefund future funding requirements. Private sector issues increased as well, accounting for a third of issuance in 2005. Private

sector issuers were able to borrow on better terms, thanks to the convergence of spreads for private and sovereign issuers since 2003 (figure 2.3).

In 2005, bond issuance covered the entire credit spectrum, but almost half of the *increase* in 2005 was accounted for by borrowers rated below investment grade. Investment-grade-rated borrowers accounted for 36 percent of 2005 issues, compared to about 51 percent in 2002 (figure 2.4).

Since late 2002, the favorable financing environment has reduced the burden of arranging new financing for many borrowers—among them

Figure 2.2 Emerging market bond issuers by type, 2002–5

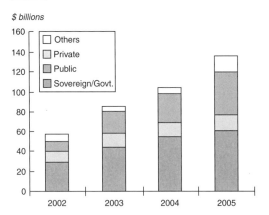

Source: Dealogic Bondware; Bank of International Settlements.

Figure 2.3 Average spreads on new bond issues, 2001–5

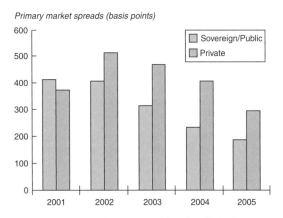

Sources: Dealogic Bondware and World Bank staff calculations.

Brazil, Mexico, the Philippines, and Poland, all of which were able to prefund their 2005 financing needs before mid-year. By late 2005, some sovereigns were well advanced in financing their 2006 and 2007 requirements. Infrequent and first-time borrowers, such as Pakistan and Vietnam, were able to tap international debt markets at attractive rates during 2005. Large institutional investors (such as public pension funds and endowment funds) as well as Asian central banks are now interested in investing in emerging market debt because of fundamental improvements in the economies of major developing countries.

Figure 2.4 Bond market financing by risk category, 2002–5

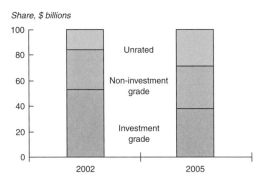

Source: Dealogic Bondware and Loanware.

Syndicated bank loans showed a cyclical recovery

Syndicated bank lending to developing countries set records in 2005. Gross bank lending of $198 billion, an increase of 74 percent over 2004, involved 1,261 transactions in a broad range of sectors, dominated by oil and gas projects and oil import financing. Europe and Central Asia accounted for about 39 percent of the gross flows (table 2.3), followed by Latin America and the Caribbean (23 percent) and East Asia (17 percent). Like FDI and bond issues, lending was highly concentrated, with the top 10 countries (Brazil, Chile, China, India, Mexico, Poland, the Russian Federation, South Africa, Thailand, and Turkey) receiving 70 percent of the total bank lending to developing countries. Average gross flows to the top 10 grew by more than 107 percent, with lending to Thailand increasing by 455 percent in 2005. Sixty-seven countries, mostly low-income countries rated below investment grade or unrated, received no new loans at all.

In 2005, *short-term debt* to developing countries increased by $61.9 billion to $556.7 billion, an increase of 12.5 percent from 2004. China accounted for 41 percent of the increase, with Brazil, Malaysia, the Russian Federation, and Turkey accounting for most of the balance. During 2000–5, short-term loans grew considerably from the $316.4 billion recorded in 2000, with East Asia and Europe and Central Asia accounting for almost all of the increase, while Latin America experienced a drop of 16 percent. (In 2005, short-term lending to Europe and Central Asia increased by 21 percent). Although global short-term debt has risen, its size relative to developing countries' foreign exchange reserves declined from 48 percent in 2000 to around 28 percent at the end of 2005.

The uses of financing raised by syndicated bank loans vary considerably by region. Most lending to the Russian Federation, which accounted for half of all flows to Europe and Central Asia, was for oil and gas transactions, with the Gazprom acquisition ($13.1 billion) accounting for almost two-thirds of the Russian total. In Latin America and the Caribbean, the major borrowers were petroleum companies (Petrobras in Brazil and Pemex in Mexico) seeking to refinance existing loans or to finance trade. In East Asia, China received $18.5 billion (54 percent of the gross flows to East Asia and the Pacific) for a broad range of transactions including oil and gas, property, project finance, and purchase of aircraft. In Thailand, telecommunication companies and utilities were the major borrowers. In South Asia, India received $11 billion, or 91 percent of gross flows to the region. Proceeds, most intermediated through Indian banks, were used for projects such as a new airport in Bangalore and trade financing. In Sub-Saharan Africa, the major borrowers were central banks, which refinanced existing borrowing at more attractive rates. In the Middle East and North Africa, Turkey was the major borrower, with almost all borrowing moving through Turkish banks for use as trade financing.

In several new EU member countries, including Hungary and Slovenia, large financial and nonfinancial borrowers were able to borrow from banks at spreads close to levels paid by their western European counterparts. Most loans were denominated in euros. Banks also invested in euro-denominated debt instruments issued by Poland and Hungary. In Latin America, the oil and cement sectors secured exceptionally cheap loans.

The gap in access to credit persists

Developing countries can be divided into three categories based on their degree and nature of access to global capital markets (table 2.4):

- *Countries with access to bond markets.* These are countries that have issued bonds regularly since 2002. Included in this group are eight countries that are the developing-country "stars" of the bond market—Chile, China, Hungary, Malaysia, Mexico, Poland, the Russ-

Table 2.3 Gross cross-border loan flows, 2005

	No. of loans	Amount US$ millions	Amount %	Avg. loan size US$ millions
Total	1,261	198,135	100.0	158
East Asia and Pacific	215	34,470	17.4	162
Europe and Central Asia	368	77,586	39.2	215
Latin America and the Caribbean	432	46,316	23.4	107
Middle East and N. Africa	89	15,726	7.9	177
South Asia	101	12,151	6.1	121
Sub-Saharan Africa	56	11,887	6.0	203

Source: World Bank staff calculations based on Dealogic Loanware data.

ian Federation, and Thailand. All are rated investment-grade, have significantly lower spreads than the overall developing-country average, and exhibit low volatility in spreads.

- *Countries with access to bank lending only.* This category comprises countries that lack access to bond markets because of inadequate legal and institutional regulations or an unstable macroeconomic environment. Although perceived as posing high credit risks, they can access bank credit because of well-defined revenue streams (such as exports and remittances) or their ability to securitize borrowing (often thanks to the presence of extractive industries).

- *Countries with limited access to capital markets.* These are countries with no access to either bond markets or medium- and long-term bank lending. They may have access to other types of private international finance, such as short-term loans or FDI. Countries in this group rely mainly on official financing for their long-term capital needs.

Some 52 developing countries have accessed the global bond markets each year since 2002. The number has not risen, despite the favorable financing environment. Bond financing is more concentrated than bank financing (figure 2.5). In 2005, 15 countries alone accounted for about 80 percent of bond volume. Non-investment-grade and unrated borrowers, who accounted for some 49 percent of total gross bond flows to emerging markets in 2002, saw their share increase to about 64 percent in 2005. Borrowers in bond markets from 10 major emerging market economies, including Brazil, República Bolivariana de Venezuela, and Turkey accounted for the bulk of the rise in high-risk issuance in 2005.

Table 2.4 Countries' access to international capital markets by intermediaries, 2002–5

Countries with access to bond markets	Credit ratings[a]	Countries with access to bank lending only[b]	Credit ratings[a]	Countries with no access to private debt markets[c]	Credit ratings[a]
Argentina	B3	Albania	NR	Armenia	NR
Barbados	Baa2	Algeria	NR	Benin	B+
Belize	Caa3	Angola	NR	Bhutan	NR
Brazil	Ba3	Azerbaijan	BB	Burundi	NR
Bulgaria	Ba1	Bangladesh	NR	Cambodia	NR
Chile	Baa1	Belarus	NR	Cape Verde	NR
China	A2	Bolivia	B3	Central African Republic	NR
Colombia	Ba2	Bosnia and Herzegovina	B3	Chad	NR
Costa Rica	Ba1	Botswana	A2	Comoros	NR
Croatia	Ba3	Burkina Faso	B	Congo, Dem. Rep.	NR
Czech Republic	A1	Cameroon	B-	Côte d'Ivoire	NR
Dominican Republic	B3	Congo, Rep.	NR	Dominica	NR
Ecuador	Caa1	Djibouti	NR	Eritrea	NR
Egypt, Arab Rep.	Ba1	Equatorial Guinea	NR	Fiji	Ba2
El Salvador	Baa3	Ethiopia	NR	Gambia, The	NR
Estonia	A1	Gabon	NR	Georgia	B+
Grenada	B-	Ghana	B+	Guinea-Bissau	NR
Guatemala	Ba2	Guinea	NR	Guyana	NR
Hungary	A1	Honduras	B2	Haiti	NR
India	Baa3	Kenya	NR	Lesotho	NR
Indonesia	B2	Kyrgyz Republic	NR	Madagascar	B
Iran, Islamic Rep.	B+	Lao PDR	NR	Malawi	NR
Jamaica	B1	Liberia	NR	Mauritania	NR
Jordan	Baa3	Maldives	NR	Moldova	Caa1
Kazakhstan	Baa3	Mali	B	Mongolia	B1
Latvia	A2	Mauritius	Baa2	Myanmar	NR
Lebanon	B3	Mozambique	B	Nepal	NR
Lithuania	A3	Nicaragua	Caa1	Niger	NR
Macedonia, FYR	BB+	Nigeria	BB-	Paraguay	Caa1
Malaysia	A3	Papua New Guinea	B1	Rwanda	NR
Mexico	Baa1	Senegal	B+	Samoa	NR
Morocco	Ba1	Seychelles	NR	São Tomé and Principe	NR
Oman	Baa1	St. Lucia	NR	Sierra Leone	NR
Pakistan	B2	Sudan	NR	Solomon Islands	NR
Panama	Ba1	Tanzania	NR	Somalia	NR
Peru	Ba3	Turkmenistan	B2	St. Kitts and Nevis	NR
Philippines	B1	Uzbekistan	NR	St. Vincent and the Grenadines	NR
Poland	A2	Vanuatu	NR	Swaziland	NR
Romania	Ba1	Yemen, Rep.	NR	Syrian Arab Republic	NR
Russia	Baa2	Zambia	NR	Tajikistan	NR
Serbia and Montenegro	BB-			Togo	NR
Slovak Republic	A2			Tonga	NR
South Africa	Baa1			Uganda	NR
Sri Lanka	BB-			Zimbabwe	NR
Thailand	Baa1				
Trinidad and Tobago	Baa2				
Tunisia	Baa2				
Turkey	Ba3				
Ukraine	B1				
Uruguay	B3				
Venezuela, RB	B2				
Vietnam	Ba3				

Sources: Dealogic Bondware and Loanware, Moody's, S&P and Fitch, and World Bank staff calculations.
Note: This table classifies the 135 countries that report to the World Bank's Debtor Reporting System (DRS) by accessibility to international capital markets across bond and bank segments (based on data cover transactions on international loan syndications and bond issues reported by capital-market sources, including Dealogic Bondware and Loanware). Countries are divided into three main categories: countries with access to bond markets, including all the countries that have issued bonds between 2002 and 2005; countries with access to bank lending only; countries that have no access to either bond or bank lending, including countries that primarily rely on official financing for their financing needs.
a. Long-term sovereign foreign currency debt ratings, as of February 3, 2006. Moody's ratings were used for most of the countries. However, S&P and Fitch ratings were used for countries that are not rated by Moody's, including Benin, Ghana, Grenada, Macedonia, FYR, Mali, Senegal, and Serbia and Montenegro. NR indicates countries that are not rated by either Moody's or S&P.
b. For analytical purposes, bank lending in this table is only referred to as medium- and long-term lending (excluding short-term lending that has less than 1 year of maturity).
c. The use of the term, "no access to capital markets," is not intended to imply that all countries in this category do not have access to other types of international private capital, such as FDI and portfolio equity. International capital defined here only refers to the bond and bank segments of the market.

Figure 2.5 Concentration in bond and bank financing, 1993–2003

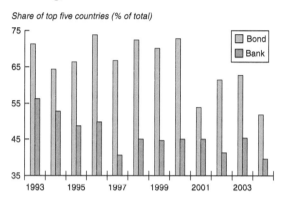

Share of top five countries (% of total)

Source: World Bank staff calculations based on Dealogic Bondware and Loanware data.

The difference between the cost of bond and bank financing narrowed substantially in 2005 due to movements in spreads over benchmark pricing and changes in the benchmark rates (figure 2.6). For *bond financing*, spreads declined to an historic low in 2005, while the underlying benchmark long-term rate (10-year U.S. Treasury bonds) remained depressed despite 10 hikes in short-term rates since June 2004. At the end of December 2005, the long-term rate was about 4.48 percent, compared with 4.72 percent in June 2004, when short-term rates began their rise. These developments caused absolute borrowing costs to drop from 8.8 percent in June 2004 to 6.8 percent in December 2005.

For *bank lending*, the decline in spreads was not as stark as for bond financing, falling only 50

basis points from June 2004 to December 2005. However, the underlying pricing benchmark, usually the six-month Libor rate, rose by almost 285 basis points, in step with the short-term U.S. interest rates. In the end, this led to an increase of about 235 basis points in absolute borrowing costs over the cost in June 2004.

The vast majority of developing countries continue to rely on bank credit for their financing needs, despite rising costs. Information asymmetry is one reason why bank lending is so much more common than bond financing. Because of their close relations with clients and their ability to monitor clients' businesses, banks are better positioned than bond investors to gather information on prospective borrowers, enabling banks to reach out to more borrowers.

Higher-risk borrowers have no alternative to bank financing. Between 2002 and 2005, some 80 percent of bank loans were made to borrowers that had no credit rating or were rated below investment grade. High-risk borrowers use such loans to finance trade or specific projects, refinance debt, and fund day-to-day operations (figure 2.7). Using the bond markets for such core activities is not an option for high-risk borrowers. Since 2002, the share of bank credit attributed to financing core activities has been rising, partly because borrowers that could make the transition to bond financing did so, thereby increasing the share of core financing activities in remaining bank credit.

Although the average cost of bank borrowing has increased, the average maturity of bank loans has grown as well—by about four years since

Figure 2.6 Comparative cost of bond and bank financing, June 2004–December 2005

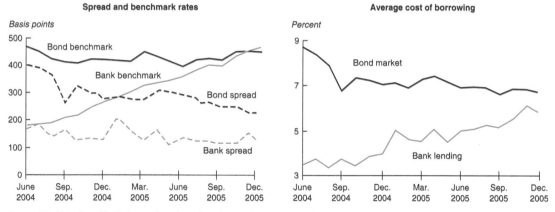

Source: World Bank staff calculations based on Bloomberg and J.P. Morgan Chase data.

Figure 2.7 Bank financing raised for core activities, 2002–5

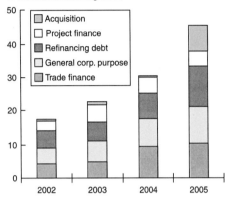

Sources: Dealogic Loanware and World Bank staff calculations.

Figure 2.8 Bank credit for high-risk borrowers: rising rates but longer maturities, 2001–5

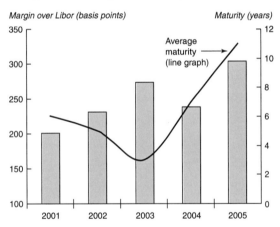

Sources: Dealogic Loanware and World Bank staff calculations.

2004 (figure 2.8). Loan maturities normally shrink as lending rates rise, suggesting that high-risk countries may now be willing to pay higher costs in return for longer maturities.

Developing-country credit continued to improve in 2005, as rating agency upgrades handily outpaced downgrades. Moreover, the pace of credit upgrades is accelerating. Some 46 upgrades occurred in 2005, in contrast to 31 in 2004. Some countries enjoying upgrades are commodity exporters, (for example, Brazil, Mexico, the Russian Federation, and Republica Bolivariana de Venezuela). These economies paid down external debt and built up substantial liquidity with commodity-driven windfall gains. Yet several net oil importers, such as Thailand and South Africa, also earned upgrades through strong growth and improved economic management.

Portfolio equity showed major gains

Portfolio equity flows to developing countries made major gains in 2005. At $61 billion, flows were up sharply from $37 billion in 2004. The record gain was driven by a significant increase in international corporate equity placements in emerging markets and foreign investment in emerging market stocks. The revival of interest in emerging market equity can be traced to fundamental changes in emerging markets and to the growing popularity, among managers of large funds, of separate, actively managed emerging market portfolios.

In 2005, as in the recent past, portfolio equity investments remained concentrated in major emerging markets. The Asia region continued to account for the lion's share (about 63 percent) of total portfolio equity flows, with China, India, and Thailand together making up about 94 percent of the region's total. Notwithstanding the fact that the Chinese stock market performed poorly over the last five years, China continues to attract portfolio equity flows through initial public offerings (IPOs). In 2005, China accounted for about 31 percent of the total equity flows to all developing countries and almost half of those to the Asia region. Greater investor interest in Brazil and Mexico increased the shares of Latin America slightly. Flows to Europe and Central Asia slumped to $2.3 billion from $4.2 billion the previous year, due to outflows from the Czech Republic and the Russian Federation.

The volume of equity placements surged in 2005, as stock markets in emerging markets outpaced those elsewhere (box 2.2). Most of the portfolio equity investment in 2005 took place through international equity placements, which were up about 60 percent over the same period in 2004. After a slow period in the first quarter, issuance continued briskly throughout the year, on the strength of an expanded investor base and attractive valuations. Just 10 percent of the transactions, including a few large IPOs, accounted for 64 percent of the total volume. In 2005, IPOs accounted for about 63 percent of all emerging market equity transactions, up from 47 percent in

Box 2.2   Strong performance of emerging stock markets in 2005

Emerging stock markets performed exceptionally well in 2005. With an increase of about 32 percent in the MSCI Emerging Market Index, these stock markets outperformed most mature markets. However, stock prices were volatile, because of rising concern about inflation and the tightening of monetary policy in the United States and Europe. In 2005, emerging market equity eas-ily outpaced other asset classes, including both bonds and equities. Stellar performers during 2005 included Brazil (43.5 percent), India (40.2 percent), Mexico (38.6 percent), the Russian Federation (69.8 percent), and Turkey (49.2 percent). Expectations of returns from emerging market equities in 2006 are subdued in the face of relatively high valuations.

Performance of global equity markets, 2002–5

Sources: Bloomberg and World Bank staff calculations.

Total returns from global capital markets in 2005

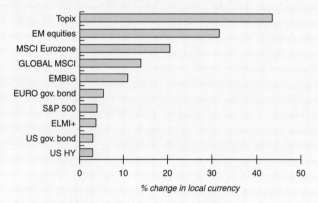

Sources: Bloomberg, JPMorgan Chase, and World Bank staff calculations.

2004. Asian countries accounted for a majority of these transactions. China alone accounted for about 21 percent of global IPO activities in 2005 and almost 61 percent of the total in emerging markets (figure 2.9). Many of these IPOs involved sales of stakes in underperforming state-owned banks and other financial institutions. Among the efforts was a jumbo IPO by China Construction Bank, which raised $9.2 billion.

Revival of interest in local equity placement was evident in Latin America, where more than $5.5 billion was raised on local equity markets in 2005. Issuance volume, although still relatively low, contrasted markedly with the negligible activity in the region's equity markets over the past several years. Issuance in emerging Europe was dominated by the Russian Federation, which accounted for about 64 percent of the regional total. Most equity issues in emerging Europe took the form of depository receipts and IPOs issued by companies in the communications sector, along with a few of-ferings by companies in the oil and gas sector. In Sub-Saharan Africa, only South Africa had equity offerings, where shares of mining companies that are world leaders in their sector were an attractive destination for foreign portfolio investment.

In recent years, major institutional investors in the United States and elsewhere have gradually increased their international stock holdings, including stocks from emerging markets (table 2.5). The trend has accelerated since 2003, with international markets generating higher adjusted returns than the U.S. market. At the end of 2004, financial assets under institutional management (pension, insurance, and mutual funds) totaled $46 trillion,[2] of which the United States accounted for $20.7 trillion. Allocation to international equity ranged from a low of 13 percent in the United States to 40 percent in the Netherlands. Because the United States accounts for such a large share of international financial assets, the recent increase in U.S. managers' allocations to international markets,

Figure 2.9 IPO activities in emerging market
countries 2001–5

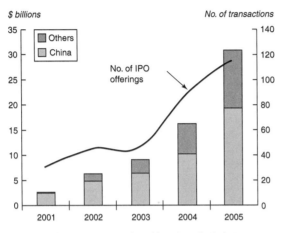

Source: Dealogic Loanware and World Bank staff calculations.

although small in percentage terms,[3] represents a
major increase in flows into emerging market equities. The year also brought a large increase in retail
investments in emerging markets through emerging
market stock funds. The availability of exchange-
traded funds has made it much easier for private individuals to invest in emerging markets

FDI grew through privatizations and expansion of the European Union

FDI flows to developing countries continued to
grow in 2005, reaching a record level of $237.5
billion, or about 2.8 percent of developing countries' aggregate GDP (table 2.6). Much of the momentum derives from the same factors that account
for the strong recovery of FDI at the global level
(which totaled $959.4 billion in 2005, up sharply
from $666.5 billion in 2004).[4] Those factors in-

clude robust global growth, increased corporate
profits, favorable financing conditions, and higher
stock market valuations, which have fueled cross-
border mergers and acquisitions. Factors specific to
developing countries have also been at play:

- Global economic growth has recently been
much more favorable to the developing world,
bringing with it a commodity price boom and
generally higher developing-country growth.
Rapid growth makes developing countries attractive destinations for global FDI, particularly the market-seeking investments that have
become the largest share of global FDI flows
since the late 1990s.
- Corporate profits have risen in developing
countries (UNCTAD 2005). In 2005, income
generated from FDI in developing countries
climbed to $120 billion from $80 billion in
2002. Approximately $45 billion of the 2005
total was reinvested.
- The investment climate in many developing
countries, including low-income countries,
has improved over the years (World Bank
2005). Many countries have revised their policies toward FDI to make them more favorable
(UNCTAD 2004). After a slow down, privatizations and mergers and acquisitions (M&A)
deals gained momentum in 2005, bringing in
large amounts of FDI.

The investment climate improved in many developing countries

A better investment climate in many developing
countries played a role in the recent rapid growth
of FDI. Many low- and middle-income countries
have taken steps, either unilaterally or in compliance with multilateral and regional agreements, to
strengthen their foreign investment policies by easing sectoral restrictions and improving corporate
governance (World Bank 2005; UNCTAD 2004).
At the same time, better macroeconomic conditions, such as higher growth rates, increased openness to trade, lower external debt, and exchange
rate stability made investments in developing countries less risky. Countries with a better investment
climate managed to attract higher levels of FDI
flows as a percentage of their GDP (figure 2.10).

The key policy implications for countries at-
tempting to attract FDI are to create a better in-

Table 2.5 Asset allocation of major international pension funds, 2004
Share of total

Country	Domestic Equity	International equity	Domestic bonds	International bonds	Cash	Other
Australia	31	22	17	5	6	19
Japan	29	16	26	11	11	7
Netherlands	7	40	7	32	4	10
Sweden	21	16	29	26	2	6
Switzerland	13	14	34	10	8	21
United Kingdom	39	28	23	1	2	7
United States	47	13	33	1	1	5

Sources: International Financial Services, London, Fund Management, August 2005.

Table 2.6 Net FDI flows to developing countries, 2000–5
$ billions

	2000	2001	2002	2003	2004	2005ᵉ
Total	**168.8**	**176.9**	**160.3**	**161.6**	**211.5**	**237.5**
East Asia & Pacific	44.3	48.5	57.2	59.8	64.6	65.3
Europe & Central Asia	30.2	32.7	34.9	35.9	62.4	75.6
Latin America & Caribbean	79.3	71.1	48.2	41.1	60.8	61.4
Middle East & North Africa	4.2	3.4	3.7	5.6	5.3	9.1
South Asia	4.4	6.1	6.7	5.7	7.2	8.4
Sub-Saharan Africa	6.5	15.0	9.5	13.6	11.3	17.6
Low-income countries	10.7	12.8	15.0	14.9	17.0	23
Middle-income countries	158.2	164.1	145.3	146.7	194.5	214.4
Global FDI Flows	*1,388.4*	*807.8*	*721.0*	*623.8*	*666.5*	*959.4*

Sources: World Bank, *Global Development Finance*, various years, and World Bank staff estimates for 2005.
Note: Numbers may not add up due to rounding.
e = estimate.

vestment climate by (a) improving access to adequate infrastructural and institutional facilities; (b) providing a stable, consistent, and transparent legal and regulatory framework and decreasing red tape; and (c) engaging in international governance arrangements. More importantly, developing countries should identify and develop those national competitive advantages that are likely to be of particular interest to foreign investors. In this context, countries should promote local skills development and encourage private sector development in order to broaden the opportunities for entrepreneurial activity. Countries also should strengthen their investment-promotion activities by establishing a broad-reaching agency that can list and market investment opportunities as well as provide information about doing business in the country.[5] Countries should focus not only on policies to attract FDI, however, but also on the policies that are necessary for FDI to generate a positive development impact in the recipient country (see chapter 5).

The concentration of FDI has declined in recent years

Although the top 10 countries (China, the Russian Federation, Brazil, Mexico, the Czech Republic, Poland, Chile, South Africa, India, and Malaysia) accounted for almost 65 percent of FDI to developing countries in 2005, that concentration is considerably less than the 75 percent share of the late 1990s. In addition, the share of low-income countries has increased steadily to almost 10 percent, mainly due to increases in resource-seeking FDI. Relative to the size of the economies, the differ-

Figure 2.10 Investment climate and FDI

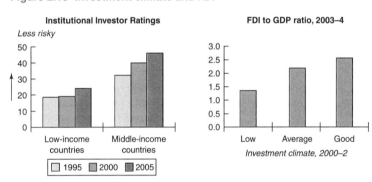

Source: Institutional Investor Magazine, various years; *Global Development Finance*, various years.
Note: Investment climate (Institutional Investor Rating) is the average for the 2000–2 period; FDI to GDP ratio is the weighted average for 2000–4 for 86 countries, excluding major oil exporting countries.

ence between FDI flows to the top 10 recipient countries (2.7 percent of GDP) and other developing countries (2.4 percent in other low-income and 2.3 percent other middle-income countries) declined significantly over the years (figure 2.11).

Regional differences remain important

Europe and Central Asia absorbed much of the increase in FDI in 2005. Investment in the region reached a record $76 billion in 2005, up from the previous record of $62 billion in 2004. High commodity prices encouraged significant increases in FDI in the resource-rich countries of the region, notably the Russian Federation, Azerbaijan, and Kazakhstan, while FDI flows to EU accession countries in the region also rose significantly. Several of the countries in the first wave of the recent

Figure 2.11 The concentration of FDI, 1995–2005

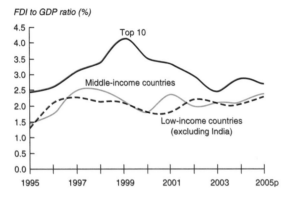

Sources: Global Development Finance, various years; *World Development Indicators,* various years; World Bank staff estimates for 2005.
Note: Top 10 countries include China, Russian Federation, Brazil, Mexico, Czech Republic, Poland, Chile, South Africa, India and Malaysia. Low and Middle Income averages exclude these countries. p = projected.

EU expansion (Czech Republic, Hungary, and Poland) continued to receive high levels of investment due to buoyant corporate profits and substantial reinvested earnings. Romania and Bulgaria, which are expected to join the European Union in 2007, also received large amounts of investment. In Latvia, and the Slovak Republic, FDI levels were stabilized, mainly supported by reinvested earnings. Progress in privatization of the telecom and financial sectors, along with early talks on EU accession, brought FDI flows to Turkey to an all-time high.

FDI in Latin America stabilized at $61.4 billion in 2005. The continuing economic recovery in the United States and resource-seeking investors were the principal forces behind the high level. The impact of improved competitiveness was discernible in the increase in investment in manufacturing, while FDI in services stalled (except in Mexico's financial sector). In Brazil, FDI in manufacturing increased, even as overall FDI decreased slightly because of political problems. Both Brazil and Mexico were among the top developing-country recipients of FDI, absorbing $15 billion and $18 billion respectively. Colombia experienced strong growth in FDI because of investments in coal and the sale of a major beer company.[6]

FDI in East Asia and the Pacific rose only slightly in 2005, in contrast to more vigorous growth in previous years. As expected, FDI flows to China showed their first-ever decline. Although economic growth remains high and income from FDI increased, investors worried about declining profit margins from increased competition (IMF–World Bank Global Investor Survey 2005) and overheating of the economy (A.T. Kearney 2005). Reinvested earnings declined significantly in 2004. FDI in services, particularly in the financial sector, is on the upswing, as China opens up to meet the requirements of WTO membership (box 2.3). The country's financial sector received more than $13 billion in investment in 2005, as banks (including banks from Chile and Brazil) positioned themselves by opening branches or representative offices.[7] In contrast to the situation in China, FDI inflows to other Asian countries increased sharply, with Indonesia receiving $2.3 billon, largely related to the continuing privatization of state assets and acquisitions of private firms. Malaysia and Thailand also received substantial flows.

FDI in South Asia also grew in 2005. In India, investment rose in industries such as cement, sugar, plastics and rubber, and hotels. In Pakistan, as in the countries of the Middle East and North Africa, privatization and resource-related FDI led growth in FDI. Both the Arab Republic of Egypt and Tunisia received significant levels of FDI in energy and energy services. FDI in Sub-Saharan Africa increased significantly in 2005, mainly because of two large acquisitions in South Africa.[8] The other countries in the region that continued to receive high levels of FDI were resource-rich countries, notably Nigeria and Angola.

A new wave of privatizations and cross-border mergers and acquisitions is cresting

An important factor in the recovery of FDI from its low point in 2002–3 has been the growing number of privatizations, mergers, and acquisitions in developing countries (table 2.7). In the late 1990s, FDI flows to developing countries were boosted by such deals, particularly in Latin America and Eastern Europe; similarly, the slowdown in activity since 2000 has been reflected in lower FDI flows. Since 2004, however, several important privatizations have been completed, but their full effect on FDI was not necessarily immediate because of the general lag between approval of the investments and actual implementation of the projects.

Box 2.3   Growing FDI in China's banking sector

Since China joined the World Trade Organization in 2001, foreign banks have been positioning themselves in China's market, where restrictions on local-currency transactions are expected to be removed by December 2006. Foreign banks can enter the market in one of two ways: they may either invest in a domestic bank and hold a minority share (less than 25 percent) or open up fully owned branches. To gain immediate accesses to a large branch network, many foreign banks are increasing their holdings in domestic banks (see table below). They have invested an estimated $17 billion since 2001.

Despite the opportunities that come with such a large and untapped market, investing in the sector is risky. There remains some uncertainty about the financial health of some banks, including high non-performing loans, and credit allocation culture and standards. But foreign banks seem to be striving to replicate the success of Bank of America, which bought shares in China Construction Bank before its very successful public offering in October 2005 in the Hong Kong stock market.

Sources: "Bankable Prospects," *Business China* (October 10, 2005); "Only the Bravest of Bankers Boldly Go to China," *USA Today* (January 19, 2005).

Chinese banks	Date	Foreign investors	Investment (US$ billions)	Stake %
Bank of Communications	Aug. 2004	HSBC	$2.10	20
Bank of China	Aug. 2005	Merrill Lynch, others	$3.10	10
Bank of China	Sept. 2005	Temasek (Singapore Gov. Fund)	$3.10	10
Industrial and Commercial Bank of China	Sept. 2005	Goldman Sachs, American Express, Allianz	$3.00	10
China Construction Bank	Sept. 2005	Bank of America	$3.00	9
Huaxia bank	Oct. 2005	Deutsche Bank	$0.33	10
Bank of China	Oct. 2005	UBS	$0.50	—
China Pacific Life Insurance	Dec. 2005	Carlyle Group	$0.41	25

Sources: JPMorgan Chase Securities (Asia Pacific); *China Economic Review.*
Note: — = not available

Table 2.7 Selected announced privatization and M&A deals in developing countries, 2005

Target (location)		Sector	Buyer (country)	Value (US$ billions)	Date
NBR (Ukraine)	P	Banking	Sberbank (Russia)	$0.12	Jan-06
Texakabanka (Kazakhstan)	P	Banking	Sberbank (Russia)	$0.13	Jan-06
Turk Telekom (Turkey)	P	Telecom	Saudi Oger (Saudi Arabia)	$6.50	Jul-05
Telsim (Turkey)	P	Telecom	Vodafone (UK)	$4.50	Dec-05
BCR (Romania)	P	Banking	Erste Bank (Austria)	$4.20	Dec-05
Cesky Telecom (Czech Republic)	P	Telecom	Telefonica (Spain)	$3.60	Apr-05
PTCL (Pakistan)	P	Telecom	Etisalat (UAE)	$2.60	Jul-05
Mobitel (Bulgaria)	P	Telecom	Austria Telekom	$1.97	Jul-05
Turkcell (Turkey)	P	Telecom	Alfa Telecom (Russia)	$1.60	Dec-05
Disbank (Turkey)		Banking	Fortis (Belgium)	$1.28	May-05
Aval Bank (Ukraine)		Banking	Raiffeisen International (Austria)	$1.03	Oct-05
Varna and Rouse Thermal Power Plant (Bulgaria)	P	Energy	RAO UES (Russia)	$0.97	Dec-05
Al Furat (Syria)		Oil	CNPC (China) & ONCG (India)	$0.57	Dec-05
Garanti Bank (Turkey)		Banking	GE Consumer Finance (U.S.)	$0.25	Aug-05
Jubanka (Serbia)		Banking	Alpha Bank (Greece)	$0.19	Jan-05
Albtelecom (Albania)	P	Telecom	A consortium led by Turk Telekom	$0.17	Jun-05
Telekom Montenegro	P	Telecom	Matav (Hungary)	$0.15	Mar-05
MISR Romaina Bank	P	Banking	Blom Bank (Lebanon)	$0.09	Dec-05
Podgoricka Banka (Montenegro)	P	Banking	Société Générale (France)	$0.02	Oct-05

Sources: Country Reports Economist Intelligence Unit; *Financial Times;* other news media.
P = privatization deals.

Box 2.4 Accession to the European Union and FDI

The recent enlargement of the European Union (EU) has had a salutary effect on FDI flows to Eastern Europe. Seven developing countries (the Czech Republic, Estonia, Hungary, Latvia, Lithuania, Poland, and the Slovak Republic) have joined the European Union; two others (Bulgaria and Romania) are expected to join in 2007. Croatia and Turkey may join in the future.

EU membership requires structural changes in national laws and regulations related to FDI. All member countries are expected to adopt a body of EU law (the *acquis communautaire*). Doing so improves the business environment in accession countries, and thus their attractiveness to investors, but it may also raise the cost of doing business because of higher environmental and labor standards. New EU members are also expected to amend their bilateral and multilateral treaties to comply with EU standards. Arrangements such as special zones and tax incentives must be gradually eased, which may lead some multinationals to decrease their investments.

On the plus side, full membership in the European customs union reduces the cost of trade with the rest of Europe, a significant advantage in terms of attracting investors wishing to produce for the EU market. Adoption of the euro will reduce exchange rate risk, though it may also make the accession countries less cost-competitive. Finally, in some of these countries, privatizations related to the liberalization of the economy can be expected to continue to attract FDI.

The accession countries have access to EU Structural Funds intended for basic infrastructure development, human resources development, competitiveness and enterprise development, rural development, and environmental protection (Kalotay 2006). Use of such funds can be expected to bring significant improvements in the investment climate of these countries. Although implementation of structural changes is at a different stage in each accession country, all are expected to comply eventually with EU standards as highlighted above.

The impact of accession on FDI inflows varies with the degree of implementation of the new policies. FDI surged in Ireland, Portugal, and Spain following their accession, thanks to trade integration, whereas FDI in Greece did not increase (left figure). Despite the adoption of EU standards and improved investment climate, Greece lagged behind the other EU members even after accession.

In newly acceding countries, particularly Romania, as well as candidates (Croatia and Turkey), progress in privatization has been providing opportunities for foreign investors. An example is the sale of the Romanian state bank, the largest privatization deal in the banking sector in 2005. In Turkey, recent privatizations raised the country's FDI to new heights in 2005 (right figure).

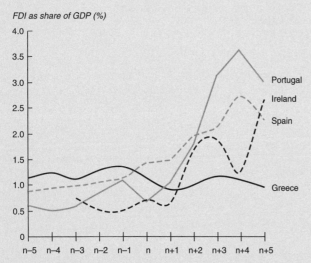

FDI as share of GDP (%)

Source: World Bank Debtor Reporting System.
Note: Accession year (n) = 1973 for Ireland, 1981 for Greece, and 1986 for Portugal and Spain.

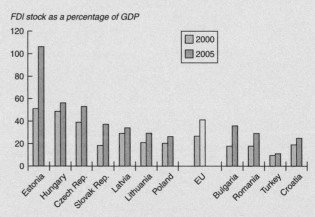

FDI stock as a percentage of GDP

Source: World Bank Debtor Reporting System.

The impact of privatizations on FDI was particularly evident in many eastern European countries, particularly where upcoming or possible EU accession promises better investment climates, investment-related regulations and policies, and trade integration (box 2.4). However, even countries in the region that are not slated to join the European Union received notable levels of privatization-related FDI in 2005.

As in the 1990s, most large privatization deals occurred in banking or telecommunications. The sale of BCR, a Romanian bank, was the largest privatization deal in the banking sector in 2005 and the second-largest cross-border bank merger in a developing country since the Mexican Banamex deal of 2001.

Structural changes in emerging market debt

Emerging market debt markets are evolving. No longer are they dominated by the sort of dollar-denominated, high-yield sovereign debt typified by the Brady bonds of the 1980s. Today, the emerging asset class includes a cluster of instruments in both local and foreign currency that offer the capacity to tap dollar and euro investors alike and cater to the funding needs of both sovereign and corporate borrowers. Active trading is occurring on the cash and derivatives sides of the market. In this section, we take stock of three structural changes that are making emerging debt markets a more diversified, robust, and liquid funding source for both sovereign and corporate borrowers in developing countries. Those forces

are the euro, credit default swap markets, and local-currency bond markets.

The euro's role is growing

Since its introduction on January 1, 1999, the euro has assumed an increasingly important international role. It has emerged as a principal issuing currency in the global debt market, as a vehicle for foreign exchange transactions, and as an important reserve currency for official holdings of foreign-exchange reserves. The elimination of exchange risk within the Euro Area has created a wide European market for euro-denominated securities, attracting both sovereign and private borrowers not only from within the Euro Area but also from other countries—among them emerging market economies such as Brazil, Colombia, China, Mexico, and Turkey. Today's euro-denominated bond market rivals the dollar-based fixed-income markets in several respects, including size, depth, and product range. As of June 30, 2005, outstanding international bonds (debt securities marketed and sold outside a borrower's own country) and notes issued in euros amounted to $6.2 trillion, or 45 percent of outstanding debt obligations (table 2.8). The share of international dollar-denominated bonds and notes, meanwhile, has steadily declined—from 49.4 percent in 1999 to 38.3 percent at the end of June 2005. The popularity of the Japanese yen as an issuing currency has dwindled; its share was only 3.6 percent in June 2005.

Thus far, the major beneficiaries of the rise of the euro bond market have been the new countries of the European Union. But although Poland, Hungary, and the EU accession countries have been especially active in the euro-denominated

Table 2.8 International bonds and notes outstanding, by currency, 1999–2005
$ billions

	1999	2000	2001	2002	2003	2004	2005 (June)
Euro	1,500.1	1,862.1	2,429.1	3,610.5	4,930.3	6,233.3	6,166.4
U.S. dollar	2,610.6	3,243.9	3,870.9	4,202.4	4,709.4	5,020.8	5,199.1
Yen	478.3	417.4	389.3	429.1	508.1	518.7	486.0
Pound sterling	402.3	448.4	503.6	621.6	829.6	1006.3	1019.4
Others	291.5	275.4	302.2	398.2	530.4	662.6	717.3
Total Issues	5,282.8	6,247.2	7,495.1	9,261.8	11,507.8	13,441.7	13,588.2
Euro as % of total	28.4	29.8	32.4	39.0	42.8	46.4	45.4
U.S. dollar as % of total	49.4	51.9	51.6	45.4	40.9	37.4	38.3
Yen as % of total	9.1	6.7	5.2	4.6	4.4	3.9	3.6

Source: Bank for International Settlements Quarterly Review, December 2005, World Bank staff calculations.

Figure 2.12 Euro-denominated international bond issues, by region, 1999–2005

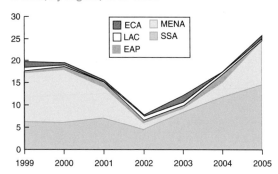

Legend:
- ECA
- LAC
- EAP
- MENA
- SSA

Source: Bank for International Settlements.

market, other developing countries, too, have found it a viable funding alternative. Among the emerging market entities that have issued sizable euro-denominated bonds are Mexico's PEMEX, the Korea Development Bank, and the governments of China and the Republica Bolivariana de Venezuela. In 2005, sovereign and corporate borrowers in emerging markets issued $33.7 billion in euro-denominated bonds in the international market, up from $21.7 billion in 2004 (figure 2.12). Much of the growth came from Argentina's issuance of $9.9 billion in bonds as a part of its debt workout. No euro-denominated issues came from Asia in 2005.

Several factors account for the increase in euro issues. The decision to issue bonds in foreign-currency markets is shaped chiefly by considerations of risk and cost, but also by a desire to diversify funding sources (for example, to match the issuer's trade patterns). Most prudent borrowers wish to match the currency denomination of their bonds to their assets and cash flow over the duration of the bonds. (The risk of a mismatch may also be covered using an appropriate derivative, such as a currency swap.) Borrowing costs are influenced by regulatory requirements (related, for example, to the withholding of tax from payments to investors) and market liquidity. Otherwise, the quantity of bond issues in a given currency is limited only by the funding requirements of borrowers, the preferences of institutional investors, and interest rate differentials or prospective exchange rate trends. The cost of issuing bonds in euros is determined by the cost of the benchmark (10-year Bunds) plus a spread (figure 2.13) over the benchmark.

Emerging market issuers from China, Colombia, Lebanon, Mexico, Philippines, Poland, Turkey, and Ukraine have issued bonds in euros because of lower interest rates on euro-denominated bonds than on comparable U.S.-dollar bonds.[9] Most of the difference is explained by the fact that 10-year euro interest rates have been lower than corresponding dollar rates. Spreads over the benchmarks are about the same for comparable issues in the two currencies.

For eastern European countries, the extent of present and future trade with Euro Area countries, and the prospective adoption of the euro by the accession countries, has undoubtedly played a part in the choice to issue debt in euros. Poland, for example, is part of the Euro Area, and its future assets will be denominated in euros; it trades already primarily with other EU countries. Decisions to issue in euros also depend on the terms of issuance and the liquidity of the market. Underwriting fees are roughly comparable for dollar and euro issues and may in fact be lower for euro issues.[10] Market liquidity for comparably sized issues is also similar. These factors all help to explain the dramatic growth in international debt denominated in euros since 1999.

Credit default swap markets have grown substantially

As anticipated in the 2003 edition of *Global Development Finance*, trading in credit default swaps (CDSs), and especially Emerging Market Credit

Figure 2.13 Yields on U.S. and German 10-year government bonds, 1999–2005

Source: Bloomberg.

Figure 2.14 Comparison of euro-denominated and U.S. dollar-denominated emerging market sovereign bond issues

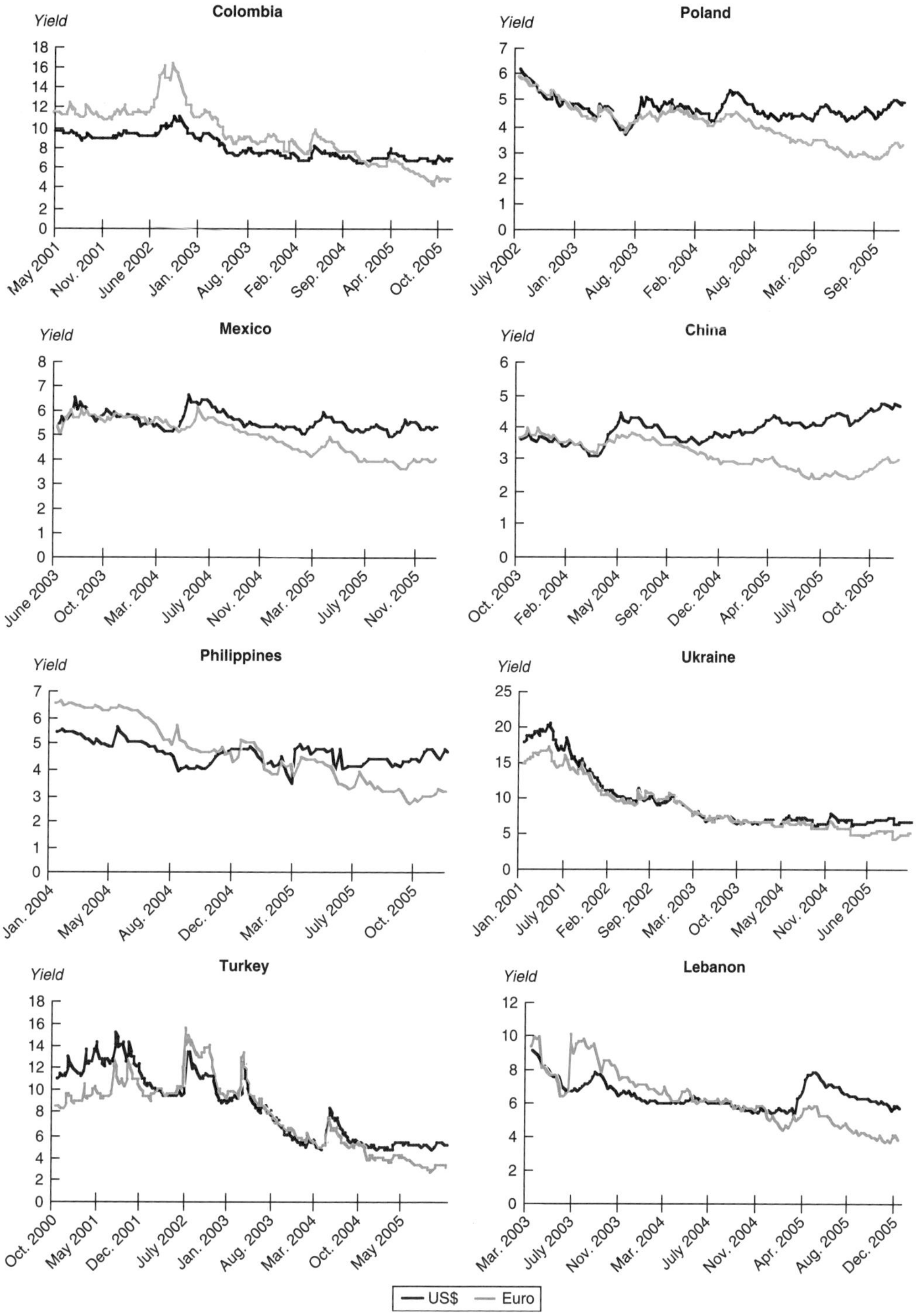

Source: Bloomberg.

Default Swaps (EMCDSs), has grown substantially over the past three years, extending beyond the Republic of Korea, Mexico, and the Russian Federation to several new countries (Bulgaria, Peru, and the Philippines). A CDS contract, like an insurance contract, provides the buyer some protection against a specific risk, namely the risk of default. As a derivative, CDSs, the most popular type of credit derivatives, make it possible to trade credit risks separately from the underlying bonds or loans (box 2.5). They can help diversify risks in financial markets by allowing financial institutions to hedge risks embedded in their loan portfolio by transferring credit risks to other market participants, such as insurance companies and hedge funds. CDSs also enable institutional investors to take a position on a given credit without acquiring underlying assets in the cash market.

The growth of the global credit derivatives market since the early 1990s represents a major story of financial innovation, comparable, in many respects, to the development of the interest rate derivatives markets developed to manage financial risk in the 1980s. At the end of June 2005, the market had a total notional amount outstanding of around $12 trillion, representing an increase of almost 48 percent from $8.42 trillion at the end of 2004 (figure 2.15).

The CDS market is divided into various sectors defined by their underlying credit: corporates, banks, sovereigns, and emerging market sovereigns. A CDS may be based on a single credit or several. So-called single-name CDSs account for 60 percent of the market in credit derivatives. Their outstanding notional value was approximately $7.3 trillion at the end of June 2005 (BIS 2005).

Emerging market credit default swaps (EMCDS) have grown with the global expansion of CDS markets, although at a slower pace. But with a notional outstanding value of $350 billion, the EMCDS market is now larger than the cash segment of the EMBI Global (estimated to be around $250 billion). EMCDSs currently cover a broad range of sovereign credits and are actively traded. In 2003, annual trading volumes in EMCDSs were estimated at almost $200 billion, approximately 5 percent of total trading in emerging market credit (Emerging Market Traders Association 2003). In the same year, three-quarters of the volume of transactions concerned 10 countries: Brazil, Hong Kong (China), Republic of Korea,

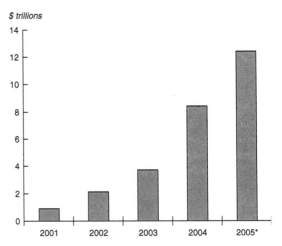

Figure 2.15 The global credit derivatives market in notional terms, 2001–5

$ trillions

Source: International Swaps and Derivatives Association Market Survey, 1987–present.
* = as of end-June 2005.

Malaysia, Mexico, the Philippines, the Russian Federation, Taiwan (China), Turkey, and Uruguay. Quotes are now available on debt issued in more than 29 countries. Dealer banks estimate that trading volumes in EMCDSs now rival those in emerging cash bonds. For some countries, such as Hungary and Lithuania, the amount of outstanding CDSs dwarfs the amount of outstanding cash bonds by a factor of 10.

The growth of the EMCDS market has coincided with the sharp increase in emerging market financing over the 2003–5 period and has been driven largely by the same forces. It has also been aided by standardization of documentation and the development of CDS indices and index-related products that improve liquidity and price transparency (box 2.5). In 1999 and 2003, the International Swaps and Derivatives Association published standard CDS documentation that appears to provide a robust legal framework for the instruments. Although the CDS market has begun to mature, it has not yet been subjected to major stress testing.

Investor demand. The market is presently dominated by institutional investors seeking to invest in emerging markets by selling protection in the CDS market as an alternative to purchasing cash bonds. CDSs are not subject to special features that may affect the yield of a particular bond, and the standardization of CDS contracts makes it easier to compare

Box 2.5   Credit default swaps

A credit default swap (CDS) is a derivative contract transacted using standard documentation developed by the International Swaps and Derivatives Association. In a contract, one party (the protection buyer) pays a periodic fee to another party (the protection seller) in return for a promise of compensation in the event of default (or other adverse credit event) by a specified firm or sovereign, known as the "reference entity," which is not a party to the CDS. The CDS transfers the credit risk of that entity from one party to another. Corporate bond investors generally buy CDSs to insure against default by the issuer of the bond, but these flexible instruments can be used in many ways to customize exposure to corporate credit.

CDSs now exist for more than 1,500 "reference names" in every bond category. Liquidity is provided by the market makers, which include commercial banks, insurance companies, asset managers, and, more recently in a significant manner, hedge funds. Standard trading sizes range from $10–20 million (notional value) for investment-grade credits and $2-5 million for high yield. The most liquid CDS contracts carry a maturity of five years.

The single-name CDS applies to a single entity and is the most common form of this instrument. Other forms include tradable indices, options, first-to-default or tranched basket products, cash collateralized debt obligations (CDOs), and synthetic CDOs. There are two families of tradable CDS indices: the Dow Jones CDX indices for North America and the emerging markets, and the Dow Jones iTraxx for Europe, Japan, and Asia. The first comprises equally weighted CDSs on 125 reference entities.

A CDS transaction depends on a clearly defined credit event and on valuation methodology. The market generally uses three credit events (failure to pay, restructuring, and bankruptcy) as triggers for contractual protection payments. Market practitioners are converging in their views on modeling and valuing single-name CDSs. Pricing techniques currently in use are derived from reduced-form models that apply to defaultable bonds, as presented in Jarrow and Turnbull (1995) and Duffie (1999).

There have been disputes in the past over whether a debt restructuring was to be considered a default. According to definitions provided by ISDA in 2003, a restructuring is deemed a default if the obligations become less favorable to the holders.

credit risk across countries. EMCDSs are also more liquid than emerging market cash bonds. And, since a large segment of emerging market investors tend to buy and hold, investors wishing to enter the market may find it difficult to invest in a specific country's bonds. In the context of buoyant demand, investors can establish a position more quickly by buying EMCDSs than by going through the underlying cash markets. Furthermore, EMCDSs are not subject to withholding or capital gains taxes in the United States. In sum, for actively traded issues, EMCDSs tend to enjoy a status similar to that of emerging economies' benchmark bonds, with a yield curve for maturities up to 10 years. EMCDSs also provide investors with a slightly higher yield than bonds.

Market participants. The chief buyers of protection in CDS markets are major international commercial banks, hedge funds, and other institutional investors seeking to eliminate credit risk from their portfolios (figure 2.16). Commercial banks are attracted by the fact that banking regulators in most developed countries do not require

loans hedged with purchases of CDSs to be fully backed by capital reserves, thus freeing capital for other uses. Institutional investors like the fact that CDSs enable them to take a position on an operation without subjecting themselves to the regulatory restrictions that would govern a cash investment in the underlying credit. The key sellers include most institutional investors such as insurance companies, monoline insurers (financial guarantee companies), hedge funds, and mutual funds.

Liquidity. The top 10 dealers, all large investment banks, account for about 70 percent of CDS sales (Fitch Ratings 2004). Trading in the EMCDS market is influenced by liquidity in the repo markets for the underlying bonds. The market practice is for dealers to intermediate in a two-way market without taking a position and without the need to rely on the cash market to hedge themselves. Advances in credit-risk management have enabled dealers to take selected positions and hedge their position on a portfolio basis, relying heavily on correlations between classes of emerging market issuers. Although there is no direct relation between

Figure 2.16 Credit derivative participants, 2004

Source: British Bankers Association 2003/2004, Credit Derivatives Survey.

prices in cash markets and the prices of CDSs, the underlying bond prices provide essential references for the determination of EMCDS premiums.

Liquidity in EMCDS markets is driven by the large and growing number of participants—hedge funds in particular. Liquidity has been improving over the past two years for CDSs based on issues in a broad range of countries.

There are now 29 names in the liquid EM.CDX Diversified CDS index, a good indication of the number of names that are particularly easy to trade. The bid–ask spread is typically around 10 basis points, with a transaction size in the range of $10 to $20 million. For liquid names such as the Republic of Korea, Mexico, and the Russian Federation, the spread narrows to 5 basis points; it can reach 20 to 30 basis points for less traded names such as Chile, Morocco, and the Philippines.

Price discovery. EMCDS and bond prices tend to move in tandem, although they can deviate for short periods (figure 2.17).[11] The *default swap* basis is the difference between default swap spreads and bonds' asset swap spreads (spreads relative to the Libor).[12] There are several fundamental reasons why the default swap basis is normally positive. The most compelling is the traditional principle of "absence of arbitrage opportunity." Were the basis to become negative, it would offer a risk-free gain to anyone investing in a country's bond while buying protection for

the same maturity.[13] It is not clear whether the CDS price or the cash price of the underlying bonds is the leading price. This will vary depending on the market context and the difference among the participants in the markets. When spreads follow the long-term spread-narrowing trend, traditional investors in emerging bonds will set the price. If new information emerges that justifies a reappraisal by the market, CDS premiums may be adjusted much more rapidly than the bond spread, resulting in a sudden, if temporary, widening of the basis. The explanation offered here is that hedge funds will react—and perhaps overreact—more promptly to news than will traditional cash investors. With the broadening of the market and the increasing presence of hedge funds and banks' proprietary trading desks, the bias is toward active trading, which should improve price discovery in the CDS market.

The growing EMCDS market, while immature, has the potential to benefit emerging economies. EMCDSs are very liquid and more available than emerging market cash bonds, most of which are held until maturity. Many participants with strong views on emerging names, including hedge funds and banks' proprietary desks, have joined the EMCDS market so as to engage in active value trading in credit-risk premiums. Market data show that CDS spreads react more promptly to market developments than do corresponding cash market spreads (and may even overreact to adverse news). On balance, that alertness means greater efficiency in credit pricing and stronger market discipline—in other words, a reduction in the asymmetry of information between lender and borrower, something from which emerging market finance can benefit.

EMCDS markets are highly liquid and have shown strong resilience to idiosyncratic shocks, such as Argentina's default. However, despite considerable improvement in transparency under the auspices of ISDA, transparency in CDSs still lags behind emerging bond markets where, similarly trading takes place only in the private, over-the-counter market. The market has expanded to include new names, such as Peru, the Philippines, Slovakia. It is reasonable to expect corporate names to join as well, as private entities in emerging market economies tap increasingly global debt markets. The great concentration of the market in

Figure 2.17 Five-year CDS and ASW spreads for selected countries, 2002–5

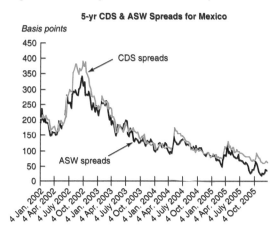

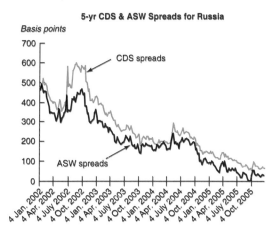

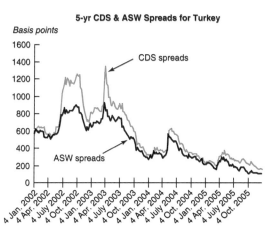

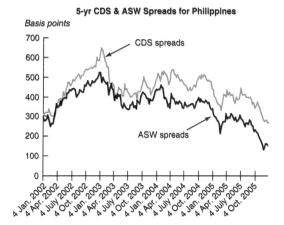

Sources: Bloomberg and World Bank staff calculations.
Note: ASW = asset swap; CDS = credit default swap.

the hands of a small number of dealers poses a risk, however, that an adverse credit event in a major financial center would have potentially serious repercussions on CDS market liquidity.

Local-currency bond markets provide important new sources of capital

The rapid development of local-currency bond markets in emerging market economies signifies governments' successful responses to the string of financial crises of the 1990s. Local-currency bond markets, now the fastest growing segment of emerging market debt, are in many cases helping to correct mismatches of currencies and maturities in the countries affected, thereby contributing to greater financial stability. From a global perspective, the local-currency bond markets in emerging

economies are still relatively small, accounting for just 7.9 percent of global domestic debt market as of September 30, 2005. Local currency bond markets are concentrated in eight countries (Brazil, China, India, the Republic of Korea, Malaysia, Mexico, Turkey, and South Africa) that together make up three-quarters of the entire market.

Robust domestic bond markets enable monetary authorities to conduct monetary policy through open-market operations. It is widely understood that well-developed capital markets enhance financial stability by diversifying both the avenues for investing savings and the sources of funding for investment activities beyond the banking sector. A vibrant bond market, supported by well-functioning and well-regulated derivative markets, enables market participants to better manage their financial risks through swaps and futures and attract foreign investors. Furthermore, domestic debt instruments with long duration are also ideally suited for infrastructure projects, especially those conducted by subsovereign borrowers earning revenues in local currencies.

Driven largely by domestic institutional and individual investors, local-currency debt markets have grown rapidly, moving from an aggregate outstanding level of $1.3 trillion at the end of 1997 to $3.5 trillion in September 2005 (figure 2.18). The countries of East Asia have led the way—the region accounts for 51.7 percent of total

Figure 2.18 **Trends in domestic debt securities in emerging markets, by region, 1997–2005**

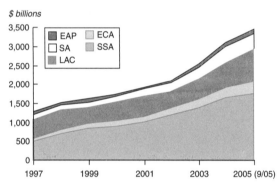

Sources: Bank for International Settlements data and World Bank staff calculations.

Figure 2.19 **The size of the domestic bond market in selected countries**

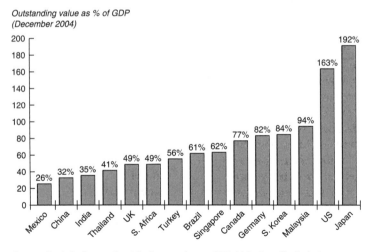

Sources: Bank for International Settlements data and World Bank staff calculations.

local-currency debt in emerging markets, followed by Latin America (24.3 percent), Eastern Europe (12.2 percent), South Asia (9.1 percent), and Africa (2.8 percent).

Local currency bond markets in developing countries are diverse in their size, issuers, liquidity, supporting infrastructure, and degree of openness to foreign investors. Ten of the fifteen largest local-currency bond markets in the world (measured as a percentage of GDP) in 2004 were in emerging markets (figure 2.19). The three largest markets (China, India, and Mexico), while small relative to GDP (below 35 percent), have substantial growth potential in light of recent reforms undertaken by these countries.

Governments are the largest issuers in emerging local-currency bond markets, accounting for 65 percent of local-currency bond markets in September 2005. Governments are followed by financial institutions (25 percent) and corporations (10 percent). Relative to the United States—the world's most diversified local bond market—bond markets in emerging economies are still highly concentrated in government bonds (figure 2.20). The challenge for emerging market countries is to further diversify their markets by building up other segments.

The bond markets in East Asia grew rapidly from $400 billion in 1997 to $1.6 trillion by September 30, 2005. Since 1997, governments in East Asia have issued large amounts of local-currency bonds to restructure the banking system and revive the corporate sector. This has helped establish risk-free interest rate benchmarks that enabled the corporate sector, seeking to restructure its balance sheets, to issue bonds in the local market. Bond-market development in East Asia gained further momentum in December 2002 with the launching of the Asian Bond Market Initiatives (ABMI) by the ASEAN+3 group.

Corporate bond markets have been more difficult to establish than government bond markets in emerging markets because of the small issue size, lack of a yield curve, difficulties with proper disclosure of accounting information, and general weakness in corporate governance. However, several countries, including Chile, the Republic of Korea, and Malaysia have been able to build relatively large corporate bond markets over the past decade. In the Republic of Korea, the stimulus for developing a functioning corporate bond market

Figure 2.20 Bond market profile in selected countries, September 2005

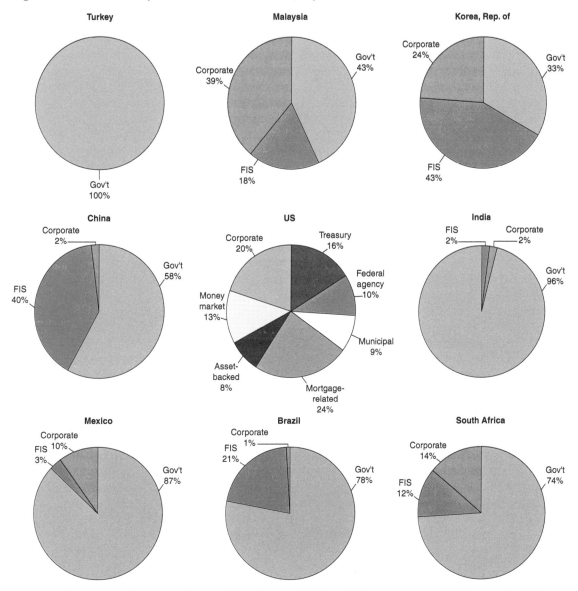

Sources: Bank for International Settlements Quarterly Review, December 2005, Bond Market Association, and World Bank staff calculations.
Note: FIS = financial institutions.

came in the aftermath of the 1997–8 crisis. Before 1997, all corporate bonds in Korea had been guaranteed by commercial banks, which masked the differential credit risk of corporate bonds.

The development of *municipal bond* markets is likely to become more important, given the growing role of subnational bodies in financing infrastructure projects, which have revenues and expenses in local currencies.

The investor base widens for local-currency bonds

Foreign investors. Until recently, the domestic bond markets of major emerging markets were largely closed to foreign investors. The obstacles to investment took many forms—administrative, regulatory, fiscal, infrastructural, and informational. Since the East Asian crisis of 1997, however, these markets have become much more open,

Box 2.6   The role of multilateral development banks in developing local-currency bond markets

Multilateral development banks (MDBs) meet part of their general funding requirements by issuing bonds denominated in the currencies of emerging markets. Such issues by MDBs can be standard setters in local-currency bond markets. Although they are likely to be small relative to the size of the domestic bond market, they can play a catalytic role by removing the policy and regulatory impediments to foreign investment and accelerating the development of necessary market infrastructure. They can also help create a long-term benchmark, which in turn may facilitate issuance of local-currency bonds by corporations.

During 2000–5, the total raised by MDBs in 24 markets through 534 bond issues was $21.4 billion (see figure and table). MDB issuance gained momentum in 2005, with 121 issues totalling $5.2 billion. The largest issuer was the European Investment Bank, which accounted for $10 billion, or 47 percent of total issuance, followed by the World Bank ($2.7 billion). The Inter-American Development Bank (IDB) and European Bank for Reconstruction and Development (EBRD) were also

active issuers. The Asian Development Bank (ADB), which recently became active, has issued bonds denominated in Indian rupees, Malaysian ringgits, Chinese yuan, Philippines pesos, and Thai baht. Overall, most of the local-currency borrowing by the MDBs occurred in Hong Kong dollars, Taiwanese dollars, South African rand, Turkish lira, and Polish zlotys.

Successful bond issuance by MDBs requires several supporting policies as well as market infrastructure. These include: (i) the existence of a clearly defined and sound regulatory framework; (ii) a disclosure-based regulatory system; (iii) an efficient clearing and settlement system; and (iv) the existence of an investor base, particularly institutional investors such as pension funds and insurance companies. Success in local markets also requires a nondiscriminatory tax structure and exemption from exchange controls. The experience of Malaysia, and Mexico in facilitating issuance of bonds by MDBs should be of interest to other emerging economies.

Source: Dealogic Bondware.

Local-currency bond issuance by multilateral development banks, 2000–5

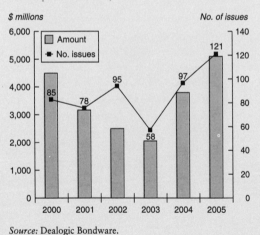

Source: Dealogic Bondware.

Bond issuance in non-G-10 currencies by supranationals, January 2000–October 2005

Issuers	No. of Issues	Amount ($ millions)	Percent
European Investment Bank—EIB	256	10,054	47.0
World Bank	91	2,722	12.7
Inter-American Development Bank—IDB	49	2,257	10.5
European Bank for Reconstruction & Development—EBRD	50	1,628	7.6
International Finance Corp.—IFC	19	1,550	7.2
Nordic Investment Bank	38	1,490	7.0
Asian Development Bank	9	808	3.8
Council of Europe Development Bank	4	348	1.6
African Development Bank—AfDB	4	221	1.0
Central American Bank for Economic Integration—CABEI	9	164	0.8
Eurofima	5	152	0.7
Total	534	21,395	100

Source: World Bank staff estimates based on Dealogic Bondware.

especially in East Asia, where many impediments to foreign investment have been removed (Takeuchi 2005). The only major markets in Asia that still limit access are China and India, where fixed-income investments are allowed only by qualified foreign institutional investors up to a

ceiling of $10 billion. Several multilateral development banks played key roles in removing obstacles to foreign investment in developing markets by issuing bonds in the currencies of China, Thailand, Malaysia, Mexico, and the Philippines (box 2.6).

Gradual but steady liberalization of capital accounts in several developing countries has led to a general increase in investment interest by foreign investors (see chapter five). In the past, institutional investors in developed countries, especially the United States and United Kingdom, did not view emerging market equity or bonds, regardless of their denomination, as a separate asset class. Instead, they were considered as a small component of broad indexes such as Morgan Stanley's All Country World Index. Most institutions would allocate a small amount of their investments to emerging market equity. In the case of emerging market debt, the allocation was usually made as a part of the Lehman Aggregate Plus Index or the High Yield Index. However, returns from U.S.-dollar-denominated emerging market debt were attractive, and some investors have been willing to assume the associated risks to obtain attractive risk adjusted returns.

Local-currency bonds were rarely considered by institutional investors, since they involved high currency convertibility risk, on top of the interest rate and credit risks associated with fixed-income investments. However, efforts by several countries to build their domestic bond markets have begun to bear fruit. Their recent performance, as well as the potential for currency appreciation in several markets, is drawing the attention of growing numbers of fund managers. Investments by foreign institutional investors in local-currency bond markets have been facilitated by the introduction of several local-currency bond indexes such as JPMorgan Chase's Emerging Market Local Currency Index (ELMI) and the Lehman Global Aggregate Index, which includes a small percentage of emerging market bonds. During 2000–5, the JPMorgan Chase ELMI+ (Local Currency) index generated an annual average return of 9.9 percent, well above the average return of 1.91 percent on the U.S. Treasury's one-year, constant maturity bills (figure 2.21).

Investment in U.S. dollar–denominated debt, as measured by the EMBI Global index, outperformed the ELMI+ (Local Currency), with an average annual return of 15.31 percent from 2000 to 2005. However, the volatility of the local-currency bond was less than that of the EMBI Global during the same period (figure 2.22).

Although data are limited, it appears from the IMF's 2003 consolidated portfolio survey that foreign flows to local-currency bond markets have

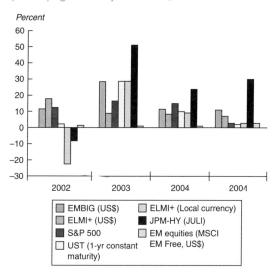

Figure 2.21 Performance of local-currency bonds (ELMI+) against major indexes, 2002–5

Sources: JPMorgan Chase, Datastream, Bloomberg.

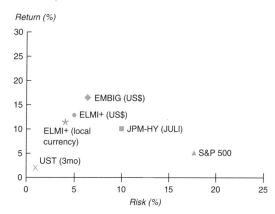

Figure 2.22 Returns vs. volatility of selected bond indexes, 2000–5

Sources: JPMorgan Chase, Datastream, Bloomberg.

been relatively modest in comparison with the size of these markets. Flows are reported to be higher in 2005, but no segregated information is available.

In contrast to the East Asian approach of opening domestic bond markets to foreign investors, the major countries of Latin America and the Russian Federation have taken a different approach, issuing bonds denominated in local currency in the international markets (Tovar 2005). In November 2004, the Colombian government raised the equivalent of $375 million by issuing a six-year bond. This was followed in January 2005 by a second issue for $124 million. In September 2005, Brazil issued global bonds totaling 3.4 billion reals ($1.5 billion) with a maturity of 10 years and a 12.5 percent coupon. By issuing local-currency bonds in international markets, these Latin American countries have tried to tap international investors while changing the currency mix of their debt portfolio.

The barriers facing foreign investors seeking to enter the domestic bond markets of countries (such as Brazil and Colombia) that have opted to issue local-currency bonds in international markets include registration requirements and withholding taxes. In February 2006, Brazil took several steps to increase the attractiveness of its domestic bond markets to foreign investors. These included exempting investors from transaction taxes and withholding tax on interest income, and permitting tax-free migration between equities and fixed-income instruments.

Domestic investors. Domestic investors, both institutional and individual, thus far have been the major investors in local-currency bond markets, especially government bonds. Bond investments have become an acceptable and preferred asset class in the portfolios of institutional investors (pension funds, insurance, and mutual funds) in emerging markets because of the high volatility experienced in emerging equity markets after 1997. Pension funds and insurance companies have long-term liabilities, best funded by high-quality debt instruments such as long term government bonds. Retail investors, too, look for relatively safe instruments that will nevertheless bring them higher yields than bank deposits.

The funds managed by institutional investors in emerging markets have grown in recent years because of several factors—among which are the excess of national savings over national investment, particularly in several East Asian countries; pension reforms (in Chile, Mexico, and Thailand, for example); rapid growth of the insurance industry in many countries, especially China and Thailand; and growth of collective investment schemes (mutual funds and other similar arrangements) in most emerging markets covered in this chapter.

At the end of June 2005, the East Asian central banks, through the Executives' Meeting of East-Asia and Pacific Central Banks (EMEAP), had in-

vested $3 billion in the Asian bond markets through two funds. Although they represent a relatively small share of official reserves, these investments are expected to play a catalytic role in the development of domestic bond markets. The larger of the funds, the Asian Bond Fund (ABF2), was launched in December 2004 to invest $2 billion in local currency bonds. ABF2 has two components: a Pan-Asian Bond Index Fund (PAIF) and a Fund of Bond Funds (FoBF). The PAIF is a single bond fund investing in sovereign and quasi-sovereign local-currency-denominated bonds issued in the eight EMEAP markets. The FoBF is a two-layered structure with a parent fund investing in eight subfunds, each of which will invest in sovereign and quasi-sovereign local-currency-denominated bonds issued in the EMEAP economies. The ABF2 has started to invest in domestic bond markets, helping in the process to create eight local-currency bond market indices.

Local-currency bond markets present new opportunities and new challenges
Bringing local currency bond markets in emerging economies up to the standards of markets in developed countries will require concerted efforts in several areas. Countries at an *early stage* of bond-market development should focus on the infrastructure of the primary market (issuance) and related markets. The pertinent areas include: (1) risk-free interest rate benchmarks; (2) a well-functioning primary dealer system (a network of financial intermediaries); (3) credible credit ratings; (4) efficient trading platforms; (5) sound and safe clearing and settlement systems; and (vi) a diversified investor base.

Countries at an *advanced stage* of market development will need to undertake additional reforms to improve the efficiency of their bond markets. These reforms include: (1) strengthening primary dealer systems by offering them liquidity supports through repurchase agreements, in return for market making; (2) creation of a securities borrowing and lending facility to enable primary dealers to borrow securities from institutional investors for trading purposes; (3) establishment of a central information system to disseminate bond-market information similar to those functioning in the Republic of Korea, which enable implementation of market-to-market valuation of fixed-income instruments; (4) diversification of local-currency bond markets through promotion of corporate and municipal bonds; (5) expansion of an investor base for bond markets; (6) development of derivatives markets to facilitate risk management; (7) increased participation of foreign investors through removal of impediments such as withholding tax and capital controls.

The efforts made by the East Asian countries in developing their domestic bond markets have met with some early success and could provide a case worth watching by other emerging economies.

Foreign institutional investors provide benefits to local bond markets in several ways. First, they can increase liquidity. Second, given their large capital base and experience in fixed-income markets, they can play the role of primary dealers and market makers, the absence of which is a major gap in most emerging markets. Third, they can improve the efficiency of the market by deploying state-of-the-art technology and services available in the international capital markets. Finally, they can introduce new investors to the domestic market, help broaden the investor base, and play a key role in developing capacity in domestic capital markets.

However, growing local-currency debt markets present new challenges to decision makers. Government debt denominated in the local currency will need to be managed with as much care as debt denominated in international currencies and on an integrated basis. The establishment of an independent debt-management office should be considered to manage both domestic and international debt within the country's overall macroeconomic framework. In this regard, the experiences of Sweden and New Zealand could be of interest to developing countries. Capacity building in risk management (currency, interest rate, and duration) will also be needed to ensure that public debt is properly managed.

Prospects for private capital flows

Private capital flows to developing countries increased sharply in 2005, but the outlook through 2007 is mixed. Debt flows are likely to remain subdued because of accumulated foreign exchange reserves, substantial repayments, and pre-

funding of future requirements by developing countries during 2005. In February 2006, Brazil, Colombia, and República Bolivariana de Venezuela announced debt-buyback programs that together could lower their foreign currency–denominated external debt by about $16 billion (see the annex to this chapter for a discussion of buybacks). Meanwhile, Mexico announced another buyback in March, repurchasing $2.9 billion of its less-traded global bonds. These buybacks are in line with the liability-management and deleveraging practices that many developing countries have pursued over the past few years to improve the terms and risk profile of their external debt. Buybacks could be especially significant for Brady debt—only about $9 billion of Brady bonds (about 6 percent of the original issue) will remain outstanding after Brazil and República Bolivariana de Venezuela conclude their buybacks. The supply of foreign currency bonds is likely to be limited, except from a few countries (Bulgaria, Hungary, Turkey) with large external financing requirements. Turkey alone is expected to account for one-third of the external financing demands of emerging markets. In 2005, several countries were successful in altering their debt profile by refinancing foreign debt through domestic bond markets. In coming years, some developing countries—among them Brazil, Colombia, Malaysia, Mexico and Thailand—are likely to raise most of their funds in domestic bond markets. Therefore, sovereign issues in the international bond market are likely to become more scarce. Banking flows are also likely to taper off from their record level in 2005, as mergers and acquisitions in the oil industry are completed.

However, the supply of bonds from corporate issuers is likely to increase with the revival of private investment in Asia and Latin America. Demand from international investors is likely to be buoyant, because yields on corporate bonds are higher than those on sovereign issues. Foreign flows into some local-currency bond markets are likely to increase because of the limited supply of external debt denominated in foreign currency, and because of the potential for currency appreciation.

FDI flows are expected to grow, although at a slower rate than the last year. High commodity prices are likely to boost investment in extractive industries, while ongoing liberalization in China,

India, and other countries should increase FDI in the services sector. Given fundamental macroeconomic improvements in several developing countries and projected annual growth of around 5 percent, the prospects for equity mar-kets in developing countries are better than for those of the developed countries. This bodes well for future equity flows into emerging markets in 2006–7. However, the pace will be more mea-sured than in 2005.

Annex: Commercial Debt Restructuring

Developments in 2005 and the first quarter of 2006[14]

The period under review saw major debt-management activities in developing countries, some of which were resolutions of previously defaulted debts, such as the conclusion of Argentina's debt-restructuring program and Iraq's restructuring of debt incurred under Saddam Hussein's reign. Some of these debt-management activities involved stressed-debt restructuring, such as the Dominican Republic's $1.1 billion debt-exchange operation. Others involved another wave of Brady buyback operations and announcements, which will retire most of the remaining Brady bonds outstanding. Brady retirements are in line with the liability-management practice and deleveraging that many developing countries have pursued over the past few years to improve their external debt terms and risk structure.

Brady bond restructuring

Brazil. Two buyback operations in 2005 retired $5.6 billion of Brazil's Brady bonds. In July 2005, Brazil used the proceeds from a new 12-year global bond (A-bond) to buy back $4.5 billion of its outstanding C-bonds (or capitalization bonds). The global A-bond issue was priced at a premium and carried a coupon of 8 percent. In October 2005, Brazil completed its second buyback operation, retiring the remainder of its C-bonds (worth about $1.1 billion). In February 2006, Brazil announced that it will buy back all of its remaining Brady bonds by exercising the embedded call options, effectively marking the end of the country's restructured debt era.

Bulgaria. Two buyback operations in 2005 retired all of Bulgaria's remaining Brady debt outstanding (about $1.5 billion). In January 2006, Bulgaria exercised embedded call options to fully retire just under $938 billion of interest arrears bonds (IABs) that were to expire in 2011. In July 2005, Bulgaria also bought back all of its front-loaded interest reduction bonds (FLIRBs), worth about $608 million, in an operation generating a $648 billion reduction in outstanding debt and about $120 million in debt-service expenses over the next 7 years. By retiring the entire outstanding FLIRBs and IABS, Bulgaria fully redeemed its Brady bonds, issued in 1994 to restructure its debt to the London Club of commercial creditors.

República Bolivariana de Venezuela. In February 2006, República Bolivariana de Venezuela announced plans to buy back $3.9 billion worth of outstanding Brady bonds, leaving only $487 million outstanding in the market, in an operation to be financed by the country's large oil revenues and international reserves. According to the government, the deal will reduce external debt to 21 percent of GDP by end-2006, down from 23.4 percent at end-2005. This operation will also enable the government to realize $670 million in interest payment savings in 2006, and a further $600 million per year in interest and principal savings through 2020. The country had previously bought back $3.8 billion of Brady bonds in 2003 and an additional $2.2 billion in 2004.

Other bond market restructurings

Argentina. In June 2005, Argentina finally completed a debt-restructuring operation involving more than $100 billion in defaulted bonds and interest arrears. Argentina swapped about $62.3 billion in defaulted bonds and $680 million in interest payments for $35.3 billion in 11 new bond issues denominated in yen, euros, dollars, and pesos. This operation resulted in a 75 percent net present value reduction in principal for bondholders, with about 76 percent of bondholders accepting the deal. According to government estimates, the transaction is expected to result in debt-payment savings of more than $67 billion.

Colombia. Two buyback operations in 2005–6 retired about $1.1 billion of Colombia's external debt. In September 2005, Colombia used the proceeds from a reopening of its 20-year global bond to buy back $497 million of dollar-denominated bonds maturing in 2007, 2010, 2011, 2016, 2027, and 2033, and 136 million in bonds maturing in 2008 and 2011. This operation yielded savings of $135 million in interest payments and improved the country's dollar yield curve. In March 2006, the Colombian government bought back about $601 million of dollar- and euro-denominated bonds maturing between 2006 and 2011, using $365 million of cash on hand and $306 million of the proceeds from the reopening of a 2015 peso bond.

Dominican Republic. In May 2005, the Dominican Republic restructured about $1.1 billion of its external debt through two exchange offers, which converted $500 million of 2006 bonds into new 5-year amortizing bonds, and $600 million of 2013 bonds into new 11-year amortizing bonds. The new 5-year and 11-year bonds carry coupons of 9.5 percent and 9.04 percent, respectively. The exchange deal extended the maturities of the country's outstanding bonds by 5 years and resulted in about $100 million of interest savings in 2005 and 2006. Approximately 94 percent of eligible bondholders participated in the exchanges. In July 2005, the Dominican Republic reopened the exchange offer, which boosted participation to about 97 percent.

Iraq. In October 2005, Iraq concluded a two-phase commercial debt restructuring with small creditors holding $35 million or less of debt incurred under Saddam Hussein's reign. Of about $1.6 billion in eligible claims, it is estimated that 71 percent of creditors accepted the deal and only 8 percent of creditors elected to reject. In January 2006, the government of Iraq completed a debt-exchange operation with commercial creditors holding more than $35 million of debt incurred under Saddam Hussein's reign, swapping about $14 billion in defaulted debt for a new eurobond issue worth bout $2.7 billion. In accordance with a December 2005 agreement, the holder of each $100 of tendered claims received a new bond with a $20 face value, carrying a coupon of 5.8 percent and amortizing between 2020 and 2028. Some creditors received a floating rate note paying 50 basis points over Libor in lieu of the new bond. Further notes up to an additional $800 million may be issued for other eligible outstanding claims on the same terms.

Mexico. In October 2005, the Mexican government carried out a debt-management operation to retire about $1.4 billion of global bonds with 10 different maturities between 2007 and 2033 through open-market repurchase. In November 2005, Mexico became the first developing country to issue warrants that allow investors to exchange dollar-denominated bonds for peso-denominated debt at specific strike dates in 2006. The exchange operation involved three series of warrants, which can be exercised up to a maximum of $2.5 billion in bonds potentially exchanged for domestic peso bonds. The transaction was part of the government's continuing effort to shift its financing to local-currency debt markets. In March 2006, Mexico retired $2.9 billion worth of global bonds due to mature between 2007 and 2031, and issued $3 billion of new global bonds due in 2017. The new global issue carried a coupon of 5.63 percent, and was priced to yield 5.74 percent, or 105 basis points above comparable U.S. Treasuries.

Panama. In November 2005, Panama exchanged $820 million of short-dated dollar bonds for a new $980 million global bond due in 2026. The new issue was priced at a discount with a coupon of 7.13 percent, yielding 7.42 percent, or 263 basis points over the U.S. Treasury rate. In a transaction intended to improve the long end of the government's yield curve, in January 2006 Panama exchanged about $1.1 billion of global bonds due in 2020, 2023, and 2034 for a new $1.4 billion global bond due in 2036. This exchange operation retired $117 million of 2020s, $617 million of 2023s, and $327 million of 2034s. The new issue was priced at 98.4 percent of face value to yield 6.94 percent, or 230 basis points over the U.S. Treasury rate.

Notes

1. The concentration pattern was similar to bank lending except for the Philippines, which attracted very little bank lending.

2. International Financial Services, London, 2005.

3. InterSec reports that U.S. fund managers' allocations to international stocks rose from 13 percent in 2004 to 15 percent in 2005.

4. The growth in FDI was led by the United Kingdom, where FDI inflows almost tripled to a record high after almost $100 billion worth of asset restructuring of a large oil company. Because of the restructuring of the Shell Transport and Trading Company and Royal Dutch Petroleum Company into Royal Dutch Shell, Royal Dutch Shell was classified as a foreign company for UK balance-of-payments purposes. That resulted in a sharp increase in FDI into the United Kingdom. FDI flows to Canada, Germany, and United States also increased in 2005 after significant reductions since 2000. In 2004, after a continuing decline, FDI flows to Germany slumped into negative numbers as changes in corporate tax laws led to large repayments of intercompany loans (OECD 2005).

5. The Foreign Investment Advisory Service (FIAS), part of the International Finance Corporation, advises governments on how to attract and retain FDI by providing investment climate diagnostics and developing customized long-term FDI promotion strategies that fit each client country's needs, objectives, and capacity.

6. In 2005, SAB-Miller bought a brewery company for $7.8 billion bringing approximately US$1 billion worth of FDI into Columbia. In addition, Philip Morris bought a local tobacco producer for $350 million.

7. Itaú BBA has opened its first office in China. Brazil's second-leading commercial bank is targeting Chinese and Brazilian companies doing business in both markets.

8. French Vodafone increased its share in Vodacom from 35 percent to 50 percent. The deal represents the second-largest inflow of foreign direct investment into South Africa after the Barclays-ABSA deal.

9. In a perfect international market, covered interest arbitrage implies that spreads on bonds issued by the same issuer in different currencies are just a function of respective interest rates and net exchange rates. Thus $S_e = \left(\dfrac{1+r_e}{1+r_d}\right)S_d$

where S_e and S_d are spreads on the euro and the dollar, respectively and r_e and r_d are corresponding interest rates in euros and dollars. See Kercheval, Goldberg, and Berger (2003) and Berger and Stovel (2005) for more detail.

10. See "Deutsche Bank Ousts Citigroup: Demand for euro-denominated issues puts sales on a record pace for 2005," *Bloomberg Markets,* November 2005.

11. Some studies have provided empirical evidence of the comovement of the two asset prices for investment-grade bonds (Blanco, Brennan, and Marsh 2005).

12. In theory, under the absence-of-arbitrage-opportunity hypothesis, a par floating rate note and a CDS on the same issuer should have the same spread. If the spread of the latter was strictly larger, a risk-free gain would be possible by entering into the following trade: (i) purchase of a par floating rate note paying a coupon of Libor plus a spread; (ii) fund the purchase in the repo market, paying the general-collateral repo rate, which is typically close to Libor; and (iii) buy protection on the issuer's name in the CDS market, paying the premium.

13. However, in practice, the arbitrage cannot be implemented at all times and under all market conditions.

14. As of April 7, 2006.

References

A.T. Kearney. 2005. "2005 Foreign Direct Investment Confidence Index." www.atkearney.com.

BIS (Bank for International Settlements). Various issues. *BIS Quarterly Review.* Basel. www.bis.org.

Blanco, Roberto, Simon Brennan, and Ian W. Marsh. 2005. "An Empirical Analysis of the Dynamic Relation between Investment-Grade Bonds and Credit Default Swaps." *Journal of Finance* 60 (5): 2255–81.

Bloomberg Markets. 2005. "Deutsche Bank Ousts Citigroup: Demand for Euro-Denominated Issues Puts Sales on a Record Pace for 2005." November. http://www.bloomberg.com/media/markets/index.html

Breger, Ludovic, and Darren Stovel. 2005. "Global Integration of Developed Credit Markets." *Journal of Portfolio Management* (Spring).

Business China. 2005. "Bankable Prospects." October 10.

Duffie, Darrell. 1999. "Credit Swap Valuation." *Financial Analysts Journal* (January–February).

Emerging Market Traders Association. 2003. "2003 Annual Debt Trading Volume Survey." New York. www.emta.org.

Fitch Ratings. 2004. "Global Credit Derivatives Survey 2004." http://www.fitchratings.com

IMF (International Monetary Fund). 2003. "Coordinated Portfolio Investment Survey 2003." Statistics Department, Washington, DC.

———. 2005. *Global Investor Survey 2005.* Washington, DC.

International Financial Services. 2005. "Fund Management." London. August.

Jarrow, Robert A., and Stuart M. Turnbull. 1995. "Pricing Derivatives on Financial Securities Subject to Credit Risk." *Journal of Finance* 50 (1).

Kalotay, Kalman. 2006. "The Impact of EU Enlargement on FDI Flows." *International Finance Review* 6: 473–99.

Kercheval, Alec, Lisa Goldberg, and Ludovic Breger. 2003. "Modeling Credit Risk: Currency Dependence in Global Credit Markets." *Journal of Portfolio Management* (Spring): 90–100.

OECD (Organisation for Economic Co-operation and Development). 2005. "Recent Trends in Foreign Direct Investment in OECD Countries." Investment Division, Paris. http://www.oecd.org/investment

Takeuchi, Atsushi. 2005. "Study of Impediments to Cross-border Bond Investment and Issuance in Asian Countries." Paper prepared for discussion at the working group of the ASEAN+3 Asian Bond Market Initiatives. December.

Tovar, Camilo E. 2005. "International Government Debt Denominated in Local Currency: Recent Developments in Latin America." *BIS Quarterly Bulletin* (December): 109–18. http://www.bis.org/publ/qtrpdf/r_qt0512.pdf

UNCTAD. (United Nations Conference on Trade and Development). 2004. *World Investment Report 2004.* New York: UNCTAD.

———. 2005. *World Investment Report 2005.* New York: UNCTAD.

USA Today. 2005. "Only the Bravest of Bankers Boldly Go to China." January 19, 2005.

World Bank. 2005. *World Development Report 2005: A Better Investment Climate for Everyone.* Washington, DC: World Bank.

World Bank. Various years. *Global Development Finance.* Washington, DC: World Bank.

3

Supporting Development through Aid and Debt Relief

Development finance moved to center stage at a series of major international forums in 2005. The High-Level Forum on Aid Effectiveness held in Paris in March set out to change how aid is delivered and managed. The Commission for Africa issued a report in March urging donors to scale up aid for Africa significantly. Expectations for a big push in development assistance with a strong focus on Africa escalated over the course of the year, leading up to the G-8 Summit in Gleneagles, Scotland, in July, where "Africa and Development" was one of two main themes. The United Nations World Summit followed in New York in September to assess progress toward the Millennium Development Goals (MDGs) and reinforce commitments on the part of donor and recipient countries. Multilateral trade liberalization also played a central role in the development agenda in 2005. Although the World Trade Organization (WTO) Ministerial Meeting in Hong Kong (China) in December did not complete the Doha Development Round as planned, "aid for trade" surfaced as a major policy initiative, with new commitments by advanced countries to enrich development assistance.

Broad agreement surfaced at the international forums about the need to provide more aid resources, particularly to poor countries in Africa, and to further reduce the debt burdens of heavily indebted poor countries (HIPCs) in order to free up financial resources for meeting the MDGs. There was also strong emphasis on the importance of debt sustainability in underpinning growth, and thereby alleviating poverty over time. This chapter addresses these broad objectives—namely, enhancing the aid effort, particularly in the context of Africa; provid-

ing further debt relief to HIPCs; and helping to ensure that developing countries can maintain sustainable debt levels over time. It highlights recent trends in each of these areas and reflects on how the policy initiatives announced over the course of 2005 are likely to influence development finance over the balance of the decade. The main messages are:

- Official development assistance (ODA) increased sharply in 2005, reaching 0.33 percent of gross national income (GNI) in donor countries, up from a low of 0.22 percent in 2001, just below the 0.34 percent level attained in the early 1990s. Although most of the record $27 billion increase in 2005 is accounted for by debt relief grants provided to just two countries (Iraq and Nigeria), the underlying trend indicates that donors have continued to enhance their aid effort. Based on existing commitments, ODA is expected to decline in 2006–7, as debt relief falls to more normal levels, but then to rise gradually through the end of the decade to reach 0.36 percent of GNI in 2010.
- Donors have taken steps to improve: (1) the *allocation* of aid, by providing more aid resources to the poorest countries, particularly those in Sub-Saharan Africa, where the amount of aid may double by the end of the decade; (2) the *composition* of aid, by providing more grants in place of concessional loans in an effort to reduce countries' debt service burden and improve debt sustainability; and (3) the *effectiveness* of aid, by developing a framework that includes tangible indicators and targets designed to gauge development progress over time.

- Debt relief provided under the HIPC Initiative and the Multilateral Debt Reduction Initiative (MDRI) will significantly reduce the debt burdens of poor countries that qualify. The debt of 17 countries that have already reached the completion point under the HIPC Initiative will fall from 55 percent of GDP (before HIPC debt relief) to 13 percent (after MDRI debt relief). Other poor countries have made considerable progress in reducing their debt burdens from very high levels, but much more needs to be done, particularly in Sub-Saharan Africa.
- Debt sustainability in many of the HIPCs has been enhanced by other factors, including stronger economic growth, foreign reserve accumulation, improved external balances, and higher inflows of foreign direct investment (FDI) and remittances. Going forward, low-income countries, HIPCs and non-HIPCs alike, face the challenge of financing their development plans without compromising debt sustainability over the long term. Countries can enhance debt sustainability by pursuing macroeconomic policies that maintain economic and financial stability and by making progress on structural reforms to improve their policy and institutional frameworks.

Recent trends and prospects for foreign aid

ODA continues to rise

At the United Nations World Summit in September in New York countries reaffirmed the Monter-

rey Consensus, recognizing that a substantial increase in foreign aid was required to achieve internationally agreed goals, including the MDGs. Donors continue to deliver on their promise. According to the Development Assistance Committee (DAC) of the Organisation for Economic Co-operation and Development (OECD), net ODA disbursements by DAC member countries increased by a record $27 billion in 2005, reaching $106.5 billion (table 3.1).

Relative to gross national income (GNI) in DAC member countries, ODA increased to 0.33 percent in 2005, up from a low of 0.22 percent in 2001, but still remains slightly below the 0.34 percent level reached in the early 1990s (figure 3.1).

The rise reflects debt relief and other special-purpose grants

However, much of the increase in ODA was due to debt relief grants, which totaled $23 billion in 2005, up from $4 billion in 2004 (table 3.2). This largely reflected nearly $14 billion in debt relief provided to Iraq and a little over $5 billion to Nigeria by their Paris Club creditors. Excluding debt relief, ODA increased by 8.7 percent in real terms, up from average annual rate of 5.6 percent in 2002–4.

At the UN Conference on Financing for Development in Monterrey in 2002, donors pledged that debt relief would not displace other components of ODA. It is difficult to assess whether donors have honored their pledge in the absence of an explicit counterfactual demonstration of the amount of ODA that would have been provided in the absence of debt relief. The share of debt relief

Table 3.1 Net ODA disbursements, 1990–2005

$ billions

	1990	1995	2000	2001	2002	2003	2004	2005[a]
DAC donors	54.3	58.8	53.7	52.4	58.3	69.1	79.6	106.5
G7 countries	42.4	44.7	40.2	38.2	42.6	50.0	57.6	80.1
United States	11.4	7.4	10.0	11.4	13.3	16.3	19.7	27.5
Japan	9.1	14.5	13.5	9.8	9.3	8.9	8.9	13.1
United Kingdom	2.6	3.2	4.5	4.6	4.9	6.3	7.9	10.8
France	7.2	8.4	4.1	4.2	5.5	7.3	8.5	10.1
Germany	6.3	7.5	5.0	5.0	5.3	6.8	7.5	9.9
Canada	2.5	2.1	1.7	1.5	2.0	2.0	2.6	3.7
Italy	3.4	1.6	1.4	1.6	2.3	2.4	2.5	5.1
Memo item:								
EU countries	28.3	31.2	25.3	26.4	30.0	37.1	42.9	55.7

Source: OECD Development Assistance Committee (DAC).
a. Preliminary.

Figure 3.1 Net ODA to developing countries, 1990–2005

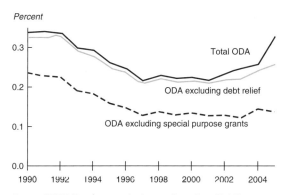

Source: OECD Development Assistance Committee (DAC).

Table 3.2 ODA and debt relief grants in 2005
$ billions

	ODA	Debt relief grants	ODA excluding debt relief grants	Percent change in ODA excluding debt relief grants in real terms[a]
DAC donors	106.5	23.0	83.5	8.7
G7 countries	80.1	20.2	59.9	8.9
United States	27.5	4.1	23.4	16.2
Japan	13.1	3.6	9.5	12.1
United Kingdom	10.8	3.7	7.1	–1.7
France	10.1	3.2	6.9	0.0
Germany	9.9	3.6	6.3	–9.8
Canada	3.7	0.5	3.2	17.8
Italy	5.1	1.7	3.4	40.0
Memo item:				
EU countries	55.7	27.9	27.8	3.8

Source: OECD Development Assistance Committee (DAC).
a. Takes into account inflation and exchange-rate movements.

in ODA has risen from an average of 3.7 percent in the 1990s to 6.6 percent in 2002–4, followed by a sharp increase to 22 percent in 2005. ODA, net of debt relief, has risen relative to GNI in donor countries, but at a more modest pace than overall ODA (figure 3.1). Thus, some, but not all, of the scaling-up in aid can be attributed to debt relief.

Debt relief together with other special-purpose grants—for technical cooperation, emergency and disaster relief, and administrative costs—accounted for three-quarters of the bilateral portion of ODA in 2005, well above the 53 percent average of the 1990s (table 3.3). Excluding the $19 billion in debt relief provided to Iraq and Nigeria, special-purpose grants still accounted for two-thirds of bilateral ODA in 2005. Emergency and distress relief grants increased by $5 billion in 2005, $2.2 billion of which was provided in response to the December 2004 tsunami. However, part of remaining $2.8 billion increase reflects a modification in the definition to include reconstruction grants.[1]

ODA net of special-purpose grants totaled $45 billion in 2005, unchanged from 2004, but up significantly from a low of $30 billion in 2001. However, relative to GNI in DAC member countries, ODA net of special-purpose grants has shown little increase over the past 10 years (1996–2005), averaging 0.14 percent, remaining well below the 0.23 level attained in the early 1990s (figure 3.1). Thus, the increase in the ODA as a percent of GNI over the past few years reflects higher special purpose grants.

The shift from concessional loans to grants continues

Bilateral donors have continued to shift their resources from concessional loans to grants, with the goal of limiting the rise in the debt burdens of aid recipients and thereby prevent a recurrence of

Table 3.3 Main components of bilateral ODA, 1990–2005
$ billions

	1990	1995	2000	2001	2002	2003	2004	2005[a]
Total ODA	54.3	58.8	53.7	52.4	58.3	69.1	79.6	106.5
Bilateral ODA	38.5	40.5	36.1	35.1	40.8	49.8	54.4	82.0
Debt relief	1.5	2.7	1.6	2.0	3.7	6.8	4.2	23.0
Technical co-operation	11.4	14.3	12.8	13.6	15.5	18.4	18.8	21.6
Emergency/distress relief	1.1	3.1	3.6	3.3	3.9	6.2	7.3	12.7
Administrative costs	2.0	2.9	3.1	3.0	3.0	3.5	4.0	4.0
Special purpose grants:	15.9	23.0	21.0	21.8	26.1	34.8	34.3	61.3
Multilateral ODA	15.8	18.3	17.7	17.3	17.5	19.3	25.1	24.5
Total ODA less debt relief	52.7	56.1	52.2	50.5	54.6	62.3	75.4	83.5
Total ODA less special purpose grants	38.4	35.8	32.7	30.6	32.2	34.2	45.2	45.2

Source: OECD Development Assistance Committee (DAC).
Note: a. Preliminary.

Figure 3.2 Bilateral ODA loans and grants, 1990–2005

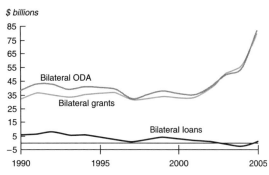

Source: OECD Development Assistance Committee (DAC).

lending/debt forgiveness cycles that have occurred over the past few decades. Net concessional lending from bilateral donors has averaged close to zero over the past five years (2001–5), implying that disbursements of new concessional loans equaled repayments (interest and principle) on existing loans on average, whereas in the early 1990s new lending exceeded repayments by about $6 billion on average (figure 3.2).

Donors are providing more assistance to the least developed countries and those affected by conflict

Donors have been reallocating development assistance to the poorest countries. The amount of ODA allocated to the least developed countries (LDCs) has increased substantially since the late 1990s, while that allocated to other low-income countries has been relatively constant in nominal terms. The share of total ODA allocated to the LDCs grew from a low of 30 percent in 1999 to a high of 45 percent in 2003, while the share allocated to other low-income countries declined from 29.5 percent to 19 percent in 2004 (figure 3.3).[2]

From a regional perspective, donors have been reallocating development assistance to countries in Sub-Saharan Africa and the Middle East. The share of total ODA allocated to Sub-Saharan Africa increased from a low of 25 percent in 1999 to 40 percent in 2004,[3] while that allocated to Asia declined from 44 percent to 35 percent. Donors are committed to continued increases in Africa's share of ODA over the balance of the decade.

A portion of the rise in ODA over the past two years reflects increased assistance for countries affected by conflict. The share of total ODA

allocated to the Middle East rose from 4.5 percent in 2002 to 11.6 percent in 2004, with most of the increase going to Iraq, Afghanistan, and Jordan (table 3.4). Aid to Iraq rose from an average of only $90 million in 2000–2 to $3.2 billion in 2003–4, making it the largest recipient of ODA. Aid to Iraq is likely to rise further, as its agreement with Paris Club creditors in November 2004 included $30 billion in debt relief that that will result in a major increase on Iraq's share of ODA beginning in 2005. Similarly, aid to Afghanistan increased from $0.5 billion to $1.4 billion over the same period. Increases in aid to Iraq, Afghanistan, and the Democratic Republic of the Congo account for over two-thirds of the increase in total ODA in 2003–4.

More "aid for trade" is on the way

Donors also are focusing more aid resources to bolster the capacity of the poorest countries to participate in trade and manage the adjustment costs of liberalization. This entails providing assistance for trade policy and regulations (technical assistance for product standards, integration of trade with development plans, trade facilitation), trade development (trade promotion, market development activities) and building infrastructure (transport, energy, and telecommunications). The amount of aid devoted to trade-related assistance has risen over the past few years, increasing from 3.6 percent of total aid commitments in 2002 to 4.4 percent in 2003, with infrastructure accounting for a further 25 percent.[4]

The G-8 Summit in Gleneagles gave important high-level endorsement for "aid for trade" initiatives that aim to build the physical, human, and

Figure 3.3 Share of total ODA allocated to LDCs and other low-income countries, 1990–2004

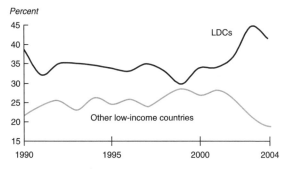

Source: OECD Development Assistance Committee (DAC).

Table 3.4 Net ODA disbursements to the ten largest recipient countries
$ billions, average over period

1990–9		2000–2		2003–4	
Egypt	2.23	Indonesia	1.35	Iraq	3.24
China	1.82	China	1.18	Dem. Rep. of Congo	3.09
Indonesia	1.47	Egypt	1.12	Afghanistan	1.45
Poland	1.33	Serbia & Montenegro	1.05	China	1.36
India	1.07	Mozambique	1.00	Vietnam	1.07
Philippines	0.90	Vietnam	0.94	Ethiopia	1.03
Bangladesh	0.75	Tanzania	0.88	Tanzania	1.00
Mozambique	0.72	India	0.78	Egypt	0.98
Thailand	0.70	Pakistan	0.76	Indonesia	0.85
Tanzania	0.68	Bangladesh	0.57	Jordan	0.76
Memo items:					
Iraq	0.16	Iraq	0.09		
Afghanistan	0.11	Afghanistan	0.47		
Dem. Rep. of Congo	0.18	Dem. Rep. of Congo	0.20		
Net offical assistance disbursements by largest recipients[a]					
Russian Fed.	1.22	Russian Fed.	1.12	Russian Fed.	1.03
Israel	1.33	Israel	0.57	Israel	0.46

Source: OECD Development Assistance Committee (DAC).
a. Included in official aid (OA), but not official development assistance (ODA).

institutional capacity of poor countries so that they can play a more prominent role in the negotiation of multilateral trade agreements and benefit more fully from the outcomes. The G-8 asked multilateral institutions to provide additional assistance to poor countries to develop their trade capacity and ease the adjustment costs arising from trade liberalization. In response, the World Bank and the International Monetary Fund (IMF) proposed to enhance the Integrated Framework for Trade-related Technical Assistance for the LDCs (box 3.1), a move endorsed at the annual meetings of the IMF and the World Bank in September and at the WTO Hong Kong Ministerial in December.

Although the Doha Development Round was not completed as planned at the WTO Ministerial Meeting in Hong Kong in December 2005, modest progress was made. In particular, participants agreed to phase out agricultural subsidies by 2013, and developed countries agreed to provide market access (free from quotas and duties) to the LDCs on 97 percent of their tariff lines.

Donors have enhanced their commitments to scale up aid

At the G-8 Summit in Gleneagles, Scotland, donors announced their commitment to increase ODA by $50 billion by 2010 (in real terms) from 2004 levels. Many donor countries have made explicit commitments to scale up aid significantly over the medium term. Five of the 22 DAC member countries have already increased ODA to levels that exceed the UN target (Norway, 0.87 percent of GNI; Denmark, 0.85 percent; Luxembourg, 0.83 percent; Sweden, 0.73 percent; the Netherlands, 0.73 percent). The European Union has pledged to increase ODA provided by its member countries from 0.35 percent of GNI in 2004 to 0.7 percent by 2015, with an interim target of 0.56 percent by 2010.[5] Moreover, six EU member countries announced commitments to attain the 0.7 percent UN target prior to 2015 (Belgium and Finland by 2010; France, Ireland, and Spain by 2012; and the United Kingdom by 2013).

Other donors have made commitments that are not linked to the UN target. For example, ODA provided by the United States is projected to decline from $27.5 billion in 2005 ($23.4 billion excluding debt relief grants) to $24 billion in 2006 (in real terms) and remain at that level to 2010, based on commitments announced on the margins of the G-8 Summit.[6] At the G-8 Summit, Japan announced its intention to increase ODA by $10 billion over the next five years. Projections based on these commitments imply that the share of total ODA provided by the United States will decline from 26 percent in 2005 to 19 percent in 2010, while that provided by the EU member countries as a group will increase from 54 percent to 63 percent (table 3.5).

Box 3.1 The Integrated Framework for Trade–Related Technical Assistance

The Integrated Framework for Trade-Related Technical Assistance (IF) brings together the International Monetary Fund, International Trade Centre, United Nations Conference on Trade and Development, United Nations Development Programme, World Trade Organization, the World Bank, and bilateral donors to: (i) integrate trade into the national development plans of LDCs; and (ii) assist in the coordinated delivery of trade-related technical assistance. The IF is built on the principles of country ownership and partnership. It consists of diagnostic studies, technical assistance projects, and capacity-building projects valued at up to $1 million per country.

By the end of 2005, diagnostics had been completed in 20 countries, with a further 17 countries in the process

or applying to join. As of September 2005, 30 capacity-building projects had been approved in 12 countries, amounting to $10 million, and 17 donors, including the World Bank, had pledged a total of $34 million to the IF Trust Fund.

To date, the IF has completed several capacity-building projects; made solid progress in the difficult task of coordinating donors and international agencies; contributed to increased understanding of the constraints facing poor countries; and brought IF governments to the table on trade. Of the eight IF countries that had completed diagnostics at the time of their poverty reduction strategy, three incorporated the recommendations, and two were working to do so for their next poverty reduction strategy.

Table 3.5 Donors' shares of ODA in 2005, projected 2010

Percent

	2005	2005 (excluding debt relief)	2010
United States	25.8	28.0	18.7
Japan	12.3	11.4	9.3
United Kingdom	10.1	8.5	11.4
France	9.4	8.2	11.0
Germany	9.3	7.6	12.1
Netherlands	4.8	5.7	4.0
Italy	4.7	4.0	7.2
Sum:	76.5	73.4	73.7
Memo item:			
EU Members	53.9	49.2	63.4

Source: Projections by the OECD DAC Secretariat.

ODA is expected to decline as a percentage of GNI in the short run and then increase gradually over the balance of the decade

ODA is expected to decline in 2006 as the debt relief component falls to more normal levels (figure 3.4). ODA will continue to be affected by further debt relief to be provided to Iraq and Nigeria by its Paris Club creditors over the coming few years, but in smaller amounts than in 2005. This explains the transitory nature of the ODA surge in 2005. Based on current commitments of DAC donors, the OECD DAC Secretariat is projecting that ODA will decline from 0.33 percent of GNI in 2005 to

about 0.29 percent in 2006–7 and then rise gradually over the balance of the decade as a percent of their GNI, reaching 0.36 percent in 2010, just slightly above levels attained in the early 1990s.

The projections imply that ODA as a ratio to GNI in donor countries will increase by about 0.017 of a percentage point per year on average over the period 2005–10. Extrapolating this rate of increase would mean that the UN target of 0.7 percent would not be attained until 2030, 15 years after the 2015 deadline set for attaining the MDGs. The UN Millennium Project (2005) estimates that financing the MDGs requires an increase in ODA (excluding debt relief) to 0.46 percent of GNI by 2010, suggesting that current commitments fall short. There is, however, a high degree of uncertainty surrounding such estimates.[7] Moreover, the *quality* of aid, is as, or perhaps even more, important than the *quantity* of aid for supporting developing countries progress on the MDGs. For example, enriching special purpose grants rather than direct budgetary support could have quite different implications for the ability of developing countries to fund programs that are deemed to be critical for accelerating progress of the MDGs.

Commitments to increase ODA have been made despite the very high level of general government deficits in many donor countries. Fiscal deficits are expected to exceed or be close to 3 per-

Figure 3.4 Net ODA as a percentage of GNI in DAC donor countries, 1990–2005 and projected 2006–10

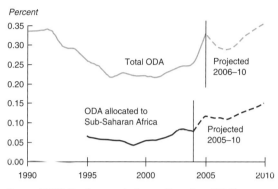

Source: OECD Development Assistance Committee (DAC); projections by the OECD DAC Secretariat.

Table 3.6 General government financial balances in 2004, projected 2005–7
Percent of GDP

	2004	2005c	2006c	2007c
United States[a]	–4.7	–3.7	–4.2	–3.9
Japan[a]	–6.5	–6.5	–6.0	–6.0
United Kingdom	–3.2	–3.1	–3.0	–3.2
France	–3.6	–3.2	–3.2	–3.0
Germany	–3.7	–3.9	–3.6	–2.6
Netherlands	–2.1	–1.6	–1.8	–1.5
Italy	–3.3	–4.3	–4.2	–4.8
Weighted average:[b]	–4.3	–3.9	–4.0	–3.8

Source: OECD Economic Outlook No. 78 Annex Table 27.
a. Including social security.
b. Weighted using shares of ODA in 2005 listed in Table 3.5.
c. Projected.

Table 3.7 ODA as a percentage of fiscal expenditures and revenues in 2004, projected 2006
Percent

	Expenditures[a]		Revenues[b]	
	2004	2006c	2004	2006c
United States	0.46	0.49	0.53	0.55
Japan	0.51	0.55	0.51	0.55
United Kingdom	0.84	0.90	0.90	0.97
France	0.79	0.87	0.85	0.93
Germany	0.59	0.72	0.64	0.78
Netherlands	1.56	1.65	1.64	1.71
Italy	0.30	0.64	0.32	0.70

Source: OECD Economic Outlook No. 78 Annex tables 2 and 26.
a. General government total outlays.
b. General government total tax and nontax receipts.
c. Projected.

cent of GDP in 2005/6 in six of the seven largest DAC donor countries, which together accounted for three-quarters of total ODA in 2004 (table 3.6). However, ODA makes up less than 1 percent of fiscal revenues and expenditures in six of the seven major donor countries (the Netherlands being the exception) (table 3.7). Donors have examined several innovative financing mechanisms that could augment aid flows, including the International Finance Facility for Immunization, advance market commitments for vaccines, and airline departure taxes.[8]

Donors have agreed to provide significant increases in aid for Africa

With 10 years remaining for developing countries to meet the MDGs, Africa is the only continent not on track to meet any of the goals. The past year was to be the year of Africa. It began with a report issued by the Commission for Africa in March. British Prime Minister Tony Blair had launched the commission in February 2004 to take a fresh look at Africa's past and present, as well as the international community's role in its development path. The report called for a doubling of aid by 2010, while recognizing the need for African countries to improve governance and accelerate policy reforms so that higher amounts of aid could be absorbed effectively. Countries at the African Union Summit in June reaffirmed their commitment to promoting economic growth and reducing poverty. In turn, at the G-8 Summit in July, "Africa and Development" was adopted as one of two main themes. The G-8 leaders supported the

recommendations of the Africa Commission (including the doubling of aid to Sub-Saharan Africa by 2010), while underlining the importance of good governance, democracy, and transparency on the continent. Building on this momentum, the World Bank presented its Africa Action Plan in September, setting out a program of concrete, results-oriented actions for the Bank and development partners to assist all African countries to meet as many MDGs as possible.

Current commitments by donors imply a significant scaling-up in aid to low-income countries in Sub-Saharan Africa. Donors have committed to increase total ODA by about $50 billion by 2010 (in real terms), at least half of which is slated for Sub-Saharan Africa. This would double the amount of aid to the region by 2010 and raise its share of total ODA from 40 percent in 2004 to almost 50 percent in 2010.

The new commitments have raised concerns about absorptive capacity

The commitment by donors to double the amount of aid to Sub-Saharan Africa by 2010 raises the question of absorptive capacity. There is a concern that a substantial increase in aid flows to some countries could have unfavorable macroeconomic repercussions. Specially, there is a risk that a surge in aid flows could lead to an appreciation of the real exchange rate (either through inflation or the nominal exchange rate), which could in turn undermine competitiveness and thereby curtail exports. This so-called Dutch disease could undermine growth, particularly in countries where the export sector provides a key source of productivity growth (because of dynamic externalities such as learning by doing).

Assessing the overall consequences of a surge in aid flows requires considering the potential benefits, along with the costs. For example, investments in public infrastructure could boost productivity and thereby improve competitiveness, offsetting the impact of a real exchange rate appreciation. Moreover, higher spending on programs needed to accelerate progress on the MDGs could also enhance growth over the longer term (education and health being prime examples). The empirical evidence on the macroeconomic consequences of aid surges is inconclusive.[9] Recent aid surges in a number of African countries have coincided with a *depreciation* of the real exchange rate, contrary to theory.[10] It is unclear, however, whether that outcome reflected productivity-enhancing benefits of higher aid, or whether the higher aid was not spent or "absorbed" by recipient countries.[11] Donors and recipient countries need to pay careful attention to the macroeconomic consequences of higher aid flows for inflation, domestic interest rates, and fiscal balances, taking into account the high degree of uncertainty surrounding the effects on competitiveness and productivity.

Moreover, Bourguignon and Sundberg (2006a and 2006b) stress that absorptive capacity is a dynamic concept that depends on the composition and sequencing of aid, as well as characteristics of the local economy (labor markets, institutions, demand side constraints, etc.). And as such, a country's absorptive capacity can be enhanced by strategic planning that aims to identify key constraints to growth and expand its productive capacity through targeted and carefully sequenced investments (developing public infrastructure and labor market training initiatives being prime examples) and through improvements in governance. Current proposals under study involve scaling up aid significantly with predictable flows of grant-financed aid to selected countries that have relatively strong institutions and governance. The historical record provides few examples along these lines and, hence, it is difficult to estimate the response of key macro variables—the real exchange rate, interest rates, inflation, and output growth—under such circumstances. Researchers have developed modeling frameworks that can provide insights into the complex linkages between the sequencing and components of aid and the growth process, taking into account some of the constraints that can hinder development. As an example, model simulations reported by Sundberg and Lofgren (2006) indicate that a cost-minimizing strategy for achieving the MDGs in the case of Ethiopia entails a front-loaded expansion in infrastructure spending with constantly growing social spending.

Improving aid effectiveness plays a critical role in the development agenda

In addition to their commitments to scale up the volume of aid, donors promised to improve the effectiveness of aid. Ministers of developed and developing countries responsible for promoting development, along with heads of multilateral and bilateral development institutions, together representing 90 countries and 26 multilateral organizations, participated in the OECD High-Level Forum in March. Participants at the Forum recognized that while the volumes of aid and other development resources must increase to achieve the MDGs, aid effectiveness must increase commensurately to support partner-country efforts to strengthen governance and improve development performance. To this end, the "Paris Declaration on Aid Effectiveness" committed donor countries, partner countries, and multilateral institutions to:

- Strengthen partner countries' national development strategies and associated operational frameworks
- Increase alignment of aid with partner countries' priorities, systems, and procedures, and help to strengthen their capacities

- Enhance donors' and partner countries' respective accountability to their citizens and parliaments for their development policies, strategies, and performance
- Eliminate duplication of efforts and rationalize donor activities to make them as cost-effective as possible
- Reform and simplify donor policies and procedures to encourage collaborative behavior and progressive alignment with partner countries' priorities, systems, and procedures
- Define measures and standards of performance and accountability of partner-country systems in public financial management, procurement, fiduciary safeguards, and environmental assessments, in line with broadly accepted good practices and their quick and widespread application.

Tangible indicators and targets were established so that progress toward the commitments could be tracked. To this end, donor and partner countries are working together to develop an international monitoring system that will enable them to measure progress toward the targets identified in the Paris Declaration.

Debt relief: improving and maintaining debt sustainability

Progress continues on reducing the debt burdens of the poorest countries, particularly those in Africa. Debt relief is provided under the HIPC Initiative, through the Paris Club, and on a bilateral basis. According to the data reported by OECD DAC donors, grants provided for debt relief from all three sources have increased significantly over

the past few years, reaching $23 billion in 2005, largely due to $19 billion in debt relief provided by the Paris Club to Iraq and Nigeria. In the three years prior to 2005, debt relief grants averaged $6.7 billion, well above the $3.4 billion average in 1990–2002, with most of the additional resources going to the poorest countries, particularly those in Sub-Saharan Africa (table 3.8). Of the total $20 billion in debt-relief grants provided by DAC donors over the period 2002–4, more than half was allocated to the LDCs, up from an average share of 29 percent over the period 1990–2001. Countries in Sub-Saharan Africa received almost three-quarters of debt relief provided in 2002–4, up from just over a third during the period 1990–2001.

The HIPC Initiative is significantly reducing the debt service burdens of some poor countries
The HIPC Initiative has substantially eased the debt-service burden of a small group of poor countries, most of which are in Africa (box 3.2).[12] The 28 countries that reached the "decision point" for debt relief under the initiative prior to 2006 received $2.3 billion per year in debt relief from 2001 to 2005, equal to 2.2 percent of their GDP and 9.2 percent of their exports.[13] The HIPC Initiative has provided debt relief equal to about half of the debt service due from the group. Debt-service payments for the 28 countries equaled 1.8 percent of their collective GDP in 2005 (down from 3.2 percent in 2000); were it not for debt relief under HIPC, they would have been an estimated 3.8 percent of GDP in 2005 (figure 3.5).

The amount of debt relief provided has varied considerably across countries. In 4 of the 28 countries that reached the decision point prior to 2006, HIPC debt-service reduction exceeded 5 percent of GDP on average over the period 1998–2006, but

Table 3.8 Debt-relief grants provided by DAC donor countries, by income and region of beneficiary, 1990–2005
$ billions

	1990	1995	2000	2001	2002	2003	2004	2005
Debt relief grants	4.3	3.7	2.0	2.5	4.5	8.3	7.1	23.0
Allocation across income classifications								
Least-developed countries	0.9	0.9	1.2	1.1	2.2	5.6	3.4	—
Other low-income countries	1.1	0.6	0.3	0.8	1.1	2.2	2.7	—
Allocation across regions								
Sub-Saharan Africa	2.2	1.2	1.2	1.3	3.0	6.5	5.0	—
Other regions	2.2	2.6	0.8	1.2	1.6	1.9	2.1	—

Source: OECD Development Assistance Committee (DAC).

Box 3.2   The HIPC Initiative

The HIPC Initiative was launched by the World Bank and the International Monetary Fund (IMF) in 1996, amid growing concerns that excessive debt was crippling efforts to reduce poverty in some of the poorest countries. It was based on agreement by multilateral organizations and governments to offer a fresh start to countries that were making efforts to reduce poverty by reducing their external debt burdens to sustainable levels. The HIPC Initiative was enhanced in 1999 to provide deeper and faster debt relief to a larger group of countries and to increase the links with poverty reduction efforts in those countries.

There are currently 40 countries eligible for the HIPC Initiative, 33 of which are in Sub-Saharan Africa. So far 29 countries have reached the "decision point" at which donors make a commitment to provide the debt relief necessary to meet a specified debt ratio. The Republic of Congo reached the decision point in March 2006. Of these, 19 have reached the "completion point," at which they receive irrevocable debt relief. Honduras, Rwanda,

and Zambia reached the completion point in 2005, followed by Cameroon in May 2006. The debt relief accorded the remaining 10 decision-point countries will not become irrevocable until they pass the completion point. All 10 decision-point countries are expected to reach the completion point by the end of 2007. The 11 remaining countries that are already eligible for the HIPC Initiative are referred to as the "pre-decision" countries. All 11 countries are expected to reach the completion point by the end of 2010.*

The HIPC initiative is estimated to cost about $41 billion in debt relief to the 29 countries that have reached the decision point, measured in net present value terms at the end of 2004. Most of the debt relief will be provided by multilateral creditors (50 percent) and official bilateral creditors (47 percent). Commercial creditors (3 percent) have played a relatively minor role.

*See World Bank 2006b (p. 20 Annex 2.3) for a list of estimates for completion-point dates.

Estimated costs of the HIPC Initiative
$ billions, net present value at end-2004

	Completion point (18 countries)	Decision point (11 countries)	Total (29 countries)
Multilateral creditors	14.5	5.8	20.3
of which:			
World Bank	7.0	2.3	9.3
IMF	2.2	0.8	3.0
AfDF/AfDB	1.9	1.5	3.4
IDB	1.3	0.0	1.3
Other	2.1	0.9	3.0
Official bilateral creditors	12.3	7.0	19.3
of which:			
Paris Club	8.9	5.8	14.7
Other	3.3	0.3	3.7
Commercial creditors	0.7	0.8	1.5
Total	27.5	13.6	41.1

Sources: World Bank and IMF 2005 (table 2) and World Bank Staff estimates.

less than 1 percent in 4 other countries (figure 3.6).[14] There are also large differences between countries' debt-service burdens. In 2005, debt-service payments exceeded 5 percent of GDP in 4 countries, but was less than 1 percent in 4 other countries (figure 3.7). This reflects the fact that some countries had higher debt-service burdens prior to HIPC debt relief and that some countries received more HIPC debt relief than others.

Debt relief provided under the HIPC Initiative will free up additional resources in recipient coun-

tries only if it does not displace other components of foreign aid. As with the more general case of debt relief mentioned above, it is difficult to assess whether HIPC debt relief has been additional in the absence of an explicit counterfactual showing. The share of ODA allocated to the 29 decision-point HIPCs has increased substantially over the past few years, rising from 19 percent in 1999 to 28.5 percent in 2004. This suggests that HIPC debt relief has not displaced other components of ODA. However, the share of ODA allocated to countries in Sub-Saharan Africa and to the LDCs increased by even more during this period.

The Paris Club plays an important role in the HIPC Initiative

The Paris Club has made an important contribution to the debt relief provided to HIPCs. Initially, the Paris Club provided cash-flow relief to distressed debtors (debt restructuring), but no debt relief in the sense of reducing the net present value of the debt (box 3.3). However, in the mid-1980s it became apparent that debt burdens in many low-income countries were unsustainable and that debt relief was needed. Beginning in 1988, the Paris Club began providing concessional debt relief to poor countries, first under *Toronto Terms*,

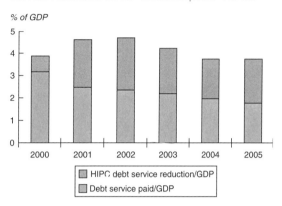

Figure 3.5 Debt-service payments and HIPC debt service reduction for 28 "decision point" HIPCs

Sources: World Bank and IMF 2005 (table 1A) and staff estimates.

Figure 3.6 Debt-service reduction provided by the HIPC Initiative to 25 decision-point countries

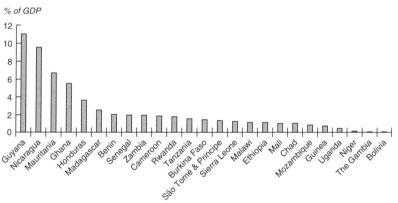

Source: World Bank staff estimates.

Figure 3.7 Debt service paid by 25 decision-point HIPCs, 2000 versus 2005

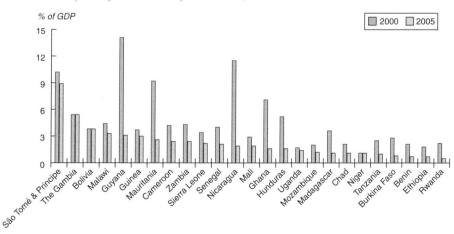

Source: World Bank staff estimates.

Box 3.3 The Paris Club

The year 2006 will mark the fiftieth anniversary of the establishment of the Paris Club of Creditors. Historically this informal body has met in Paris to: (i) review the external debt-servicing performance of debtor countries; (ii) develop rules and mechanisms that may be used to resolve debt-payment difficulties; and (iii) negotiate debt rescheduling or reduction agreements with debtor countries. Since 1956, the club's 19 creditor members (along with about a dozen invited creditor countries) have reached more than 400 agreements with debtor countries. Initially, the Paris Club provided only cash-flow relief to countries experiencing temporary balance-of-payments difficulties, while maintaining the present value of creditors' claims. In the past 15 years, however, the club has engaged increasingly in debt-reduction operations covering not only debt flows but also debt stocks.

The Paris Club took on greater importance with the onset of the 1980s debt crisis. The number of agreements concluded by the club since the early 1980s has been almost three times the number reached during the first 25 years of its existence. Since 1983, the total amount of debt covered in agreements concluded by the Paris Club or ad hoc groups of Paris Club creditors has been $504 billion.

The activities of the Paris Club have been governed by five basic principles:

1. *Creditor solidarity.* The members of the Paris Club act as a group in their dealings with a particular debtor country. For debtors this implies that any country seeking a debt rescheduling from the club must agree to treat all its members in the same way; for creditors it implies that club members will refuse to consider a request from a debtor to reschedule debt on a purely "bilateral" basis, that is, outside of the Paris Club framework.
2. *Commitment to economic reform.* Debt rescheduling requires an economic policy plan aimed at correcting deficiencies that have brought about the need for debt treatment. As a general rule, such a plan takes the form of an economic adjustment program officially supported by the International Monetary Fund (IMF) although in a few cases the Paris Club did not require an IMF program.
3. *Comparable treatment.* The debtor country must secure from all other creditors debt relief terms that involve treatment comparable to those agreed with the Paris Club. Formerly private creditors were not affected by the comparability-of-treatment clause. However, beginning in 1998 (for Pakistan) the Paris Club has asked some debtors to obtain comparable debt relief from bondholders.
4. *Agreement by consensus.* This principle requires that the Paris Club act only with the concurrence of all of its participants.
5. *Case-by-case approach.* Paris Club members reserve the right to apply the principles in a flexible manner so as to meet the particular requirements of a specific debtor.

In October 2003, the Paris Club adopted a new approach to treating debt in countries that were not eligible for the HIPC Initiative. The *Evian Approach* was designed to ensure that debt restructuring was granted only in cases of imminent default and that the debt treatment provided reflected countries' financial needs and the objective of ensuring debt sustainability. Debt sustainability therefore plays a central role in determining whether and to what extent countries receive debt relief. The adoption of the *Evian Approach* was followed by two major agreements that provided record amounts of debt relief. In November 2004, the Paris Club agreement with Iraq considered $37 billion in debt, canceling $30 billion (80 percent) and rescheduling the rest. In October 2005, the Paris Club reached an agreement with Nigeria concerning $30 billion in debt, $18 billion (60 percent) of which was canceled.

which provided for a 33 percent reduction in the net present value of the debt. It soon became evident that even more relief was required to reduce debt burdens to sustainable levels. The terms offered by the Paris Club were made more generous in a series of steps. In 1991 *London Terms* allowed for a 50-percent reduction in net present value; in 1994, *Naples Terms* allowed for debt relief of as much as 67 percent.

Since 1997, debt relief provided by the Paris Club has been an integral part of the HIPC Initiative. To be eligible for the HIPC Initiative, a country's debt must exceed certain threshold levels. Either external debt must be at least 150 percent of exports, or public debt must be at least 250 percent of revenues (in net present value terms), after receiving debt relief from the Paris Club under *Naples Terms*.[15] Under the HIPC Initiative, countries benefit from debt reduction from all creditors (which include the Paris Club and other bilateral official creditors, multilateral creditors, and commercial creditors) in an amount that reduces their debt burden to the threshold levels. In principle, the burden of debt relief is to be shared equally among all creditors. However, participation is voluntary. In practice, most commercial creditors have not participated,[16] while the Paris Club creditors have provided much more than their share of the debt relief. In most cases, Paris Club creditors have cancelled all of the debt owed to them by countries that have reached the completion point.[17] In contrast, other official bilateral creditors have committed so far to less than half of their share of debt relief.[18]

HIPC debt relief could lead to more litigation by commercial creditors

Sharing the burden of debt relief equally across all creditors is complicated by the "collective action" problem. Some commercial creditors have an incentive to "hold out" of an agreement, preferring to pursue their claims through litigation in hopes of obtaining more favorable terms. In corporate bankruptcies, the legal system prevents creditors from engaging in such "free-riding" and imposes rules for collective action. But in the case of sovereign debt restructuring, there is no overriding legal system that has such jurisdiction over all creditors. Hence, collective action cannot be imposed through legal means. Some commercial creditors have prevailed in litigation against HIPCs. There are currently 24 litigation cases on record against HIPCs, 4 of which were new in 2005; court awards to creditors total $586 million, of which countries have paid only about $35 million.[19] Al-

though the amounts paid are small relative to the total amount of debt relief committed by the HIPC Initiative ($38 billion in net present value terms), judgments in favor of creditors set a precedent that could lead to more litigation. Debt relief frees up financial resources, leading creditors to reassess their chances of obtaining a significant judgment in their favor. Thus further debt relief could make the litigation strategy even more alluring.

Further debt relief is envisioned under the HIPC Initiative and the Multilateral Debt Relief Initiative

The HIPC initiative will continue to reduce debt-service burdens. In 2006/7, some $2.6 billion in relief will be provided annually to the 29 decision-point countries, up from an average of $2.3 billion provided during 2001–5. Debt service by these countries is projected to remain unchanged in 2006/7 relative to their GDP and exports, but the total amount of debt relief provided under the HIPC Initiative will increase over time as additional countries reach the decision point and completion point.

Following on the HIPC initiative, the Multilateral Debt Relief Initiative (MDRI) will achieve further, significant reductions in the debt burden of poor countries (box 3.4). The MRDI calls for complete cancellation of debt owed to the International Development Association (IDA), the IMF,

Box 3.4   The MDRI

The Multilateral Debt Relief Initiative (MDRI) was proposed in June 2005 by the G-8 Finance Ministers as a way to free up additional resources to help poor countries with high debt levels make progress toward the Millennium Development Goals. Under the MDRI, three multilateral institutions—the International Development Association (IDA), the International Monetary Fund (IMF), and the African Development Fund (AfDF)—will cancel all claims on countries that reach the completion point under the HIPC initiative. The IMF and IDA have approved debt relief under the MDRI for 17 of the 18 HIPCs that have already reached the completion point. The exception, Mauritania, will qualify for debt relief under the MDRI after implementing key public expenditure management reforms. (Approval by the AfDF is expected to come in April 2006.)

Although the MDRI is a common initiative, the approach to coverage and implementation varies somewhat across the three institutions.* The IMF Executive Board modified the proposal to reflect the Fund's requirement that the use of IMF resources be consistent with uniformity of treatment. Thus, it was agreed that all countries with per capita income of $380 a year or less (HIPCs and non-HIPCs) would receive MDRI debt relief financed by the IMF's own resources. Two non-HIPCs—Cambodia and Tajikistan—were certified as eligible for MDRI debt relief from the IMF on this basis. HIPCs with per capita income above that threshold would receive MDRI relief from bilateral contributions administered by the IMF.

*See World Bank (2006a) for a more detailed discussion of the implementation of the MDRI.

and the African Development Fund (AfDF) by countries that reach the HIPC completion point. The process of reaching the HIPC completion point includes conditions relating to governance, accountability, and transparency.

The MDRI can be interpreted as an extension and a deepening of the HIPC Initiative. Eligibility will require meeting the HIPC completion-point criteria, which include (i) satisfactory macroeconomic performance under an IMF poverty reduction and growth facility program (PRGF) or equivalent; (ii) satisfactory performance in implementing a poverty reduction strategy; and (iii) the existence of a public expenditure management system that meets minimum standards for governance and transparency in the use of public resources.

The objective of the MDRI is to provide additional support to HIPCs to reach the MDGs, while ensuring that the financing capacity of the international financial institutions is preserved. Debt stocks in the 18 countries that reached the HIPC completion point prior to 2006 will be reduced by an estimated $17 billion (in net-present-value terms, valued at end-2004), with most of the reduction coming from cancellation of IDA credit repayments of $12 billion (table 3.9).[20] If all 11 decision-point countries were to reach the completion point by the end of 2007, the total amount of debt relief would be almost $22.4 billion, an amount equal to 56 percent of the debt relief provided under the HIPC initiative to the same set of countries ($40 billion).

For the 18 HIPCs that reached the completion point prior to 2006, the MDRI will reduce debt service payments by $0.9 billion on average in 2007–17 and then rise to a peak of $1.5 billion on average in 2022–4 (figure 3.8). The total amount of debt relief provided by the MDRI will rise over time as additional countries reach the completion point.[21] The modest increase in 2006 reflects the fact that the MDRI will not be implemented by IDA until July 2006 (the beginning of its fiscal year).

Figure 3.8 Debt-service reduction to be provided by the MDRI, 2006–45

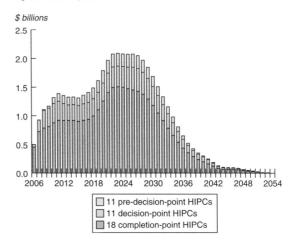

$ billions

Source: World Bank staff estimates.

The two-humped shape of the debt-service-reduction profile is due to the fact that the bulk of outstanding IMF loans to these countries are scheduled to mature within three to six years (figure 3.9). Outstanding IDA and AfDB loans have a much longer duration (extending out to 40 years), so the debt-service-reduction profile is much more gradual once the IMF loans have disappeared from the picture.

The MDRI will affect flows of assistance from IDA and the AfDF to recipient countries in two ways. First, annual gross assistance from IDA and the AfDF to a given country will be reduced by the amount of debt relief provided that year. Second,

Table 3.9 Debt-service reductions to be provided by the MDRI
$ billions, net present value at end-2004

	Completion-point countries (18)	Decision-point countries (11)	Total for 29 countries	Pre-decision point countries (9)	Total for 38 countries
IDA	12.1	2.8	14.9	1.2	16.1
IMF	2.8	1.4	4.2	0.3	4.5
AfDF	2.3	1.1	3.4	0.3	3.6
Total	17.2	5.3	22.4	1.8	24.2

Source: World Bank staff estimates.

Figure 3.9 Debt-service reduction to be provided to 18 completion-point HIPCs under the MDRI, 2006–45

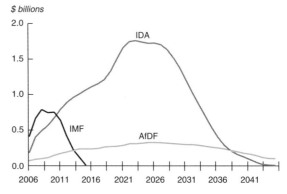

$ billions

Source: World Bank staff estimates.

donors will make additional contributions to compensate IDA and the AfDF for the total reduction in gross assistance flows in each year. Donors have specified that the additional contributions are to be calculated relative to a baseline that maintains current contribution levels in real terms (adjusted for inflation). Under the current replenishment of IDA (IDA14) donors have agreed to make contributions of almost $15 billion between July 2006 and June 2008, or about $5 billion per year. Debt relief on IDA loans under the MDRI will be financed by donors over and above the $5 billion level, measured in real terms to compensate for the effect of inflation.[22] If the annual inflation rate were constant at 2 percent, the baseline contribution level would rise to $5.4 billion in 2010 and $8.0 billion in 2030 in nominal terms (figure 3.10 and table 3.10). Donors' commitment to compensate IDA for the total reduction in gross assistance flows is equal to the debt service reduction provided to the recipient countries (figure 3.8). Donors' total financing commitment comprised of compensation for the effect of inflation and for the reduction in gross assistance flows rises to $7.0 billion in 2010 and $9.7 billion by 2030. Donors' commitment to preserve financing of the AfDF is specified in a similar manner.

The additional resources provided to refinance IDA and the AfDF will be reallocated to recipients using each institution's existing performance-based allocation mechanism, thereby alleviating the risk of "moral hazard" associated

Table 3.10 Donors' commitment to refinance IDA for debt relief provided under the MDRI, selected years
$ billions

	2006	2007	2010	2020	2030
Baseline for IDA replenishments	5.0	5.1	5.4	6.6	8.0
Compensation for reduction in gross assistance flows (equal to debt service reduction)	0.8	1.2	1.6	1.7	1.6
Total financing commitments	5.8	6.3	7.0	8.3	9.7

Source: World Bank staff estimates.

with providing debt relief to countries with the highest debt burdens. In other words, debt relief provided under the MDRI will result in an increase in aid (above countries' initial allocation), only to the extent that the country shares in the performance-based allocation. Countries that do not qualify for debt relief under the MDRI may qualify for the reallocated resources and thereby benefit from the initiative.

Although the amount of debt relief provided under the HIPC Initiative has been small relative to the total amount of foreign aid received by all developing countries, it is substantial for many of the individual countries that qualify. In 2004, HIPC debt-service reductions provided to the 27 countries that reached the completion point prior to 2005 totaled $2.3 billion, an amount equal to just 3 percent of total ODA ($79.6 billion), but 12 percent of ODA received by the 27 countries ($18.6 billion). Moreover, HIPC debt-service reductions exceeded 20 percent of ODA received by 8 of the 27 countries. Additional debt service reductions provided by the MDRI are expected to keep pace with the scaling up of aid to the HIPCs. In 2007, debt-service reductions provided by the HIPC Initiative and MDRI combined are projected to remain at about 12 percent of the amount of ODA received by countries that reach the completion point.

A gap is opening between countries that qualify for debt relief and those that do not

Taken together, debt relief provided by the HIPC Initiative and the MDRI will substantially reduce the debt burdens of qualifying countries. For the 18 countries that reached the completion point prior to 2006, the HIPC Initiative reduces their total debt stock from 55 percent of their GDP to 30 percent; the MDRI then reduces it further to 13 percent (in net present value terms). In 4 of the 18

Figure 3.10 Donors' commitment to refinance IDA for debt relief provided under the MDRI, 2006–45

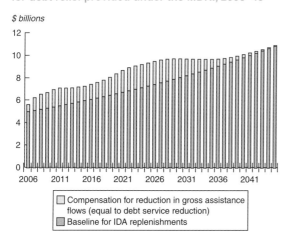

$ billions

Legend: Compensation for reduction in gross assistance flows (equal to debt service reduction); Baseline for IDA replenishments

Source: World Bank staff estimates.

countries the debt-to-GDP ratio will decline by more than 90 percentage points. Debt stocks will fall below 30 percent of GDP in all countries except one (Guyana), and in 10 of the 18 countries, debt will fall below 10 percent of GDP, well below the average for developing countries ([32] percent in 2005) (figure 3.11).[23] Similar reductions would result for other countries that reached the HIPC completion point.

For the 11 HIPCs that have reached the decision point, but not the completion point, the median debt burden was 41.2 percent of GDP in 2004 (in present value terms), which is below that for middle-income countries (44.8 percent) (table 3.11). Similar results hold for the low-income countries that are not currently eligible for the HIPC Initiative (the "other low-income countries" reported in table 3.11). Relative to exports, however, the debt burden in the 11 decision-point HIPCs is significantly higher than in other low-income countries (183.7 percent

compared to 99.5 percent). All 11 countries are expected to reach the completion point by the end of 2007, which will reduce their debt burdens significantly (to less than 15 percent of GDP and 50 percent of exports in most cases). For the 11 countries that are currently eligible for the HIPC Initiative but have not yet reached the decision point, the median debt burden was 67.1 percent of GDP and 150.4 percent of exports in 2004. These countries therefore have a very strong incentive to reach the decision and completion points, in order to qualify for debt relief under the HIPC Initiative and the MDRI.

Debt relief raises concerns about excessive borrowing in the future

The low debt burdens in countries receive MDRI debt relief will improve their creditworthiness significantly, raising concerns that they might borrow excessively from nonconcessional sources. This could offset the efforts made to improve debt sustainability, leading to yet another lending-forgiveness cycle. But why would countries borrow "excessively"? And why would private creditors be willing to lend "excessively"?

Determining whether countries are borrowing excessively is not straightforward. Loans used to finance investment projects that generate revenues will not erode debt sustainability if the rates of return cover the cost of financing. From this perspective, debt sustainability is determined by the quality of the investments made, not by the quantity borrowed.

Accessing external private capital entails significant risks, but it also provides potential benefits. Financial crises have led to major setbacks in many emerging market economies over the past few decades. On the other hand, external private capital can play a valuable role in the development process, particularly for countries in which domestic savings are inadequate to finance productive investment projects with high private and social rates of return. Countries therefore face the challenge of balancing the potential risks and benefits.

Part of the concern about excessive nonconcessional borrowing stems from the incentive problems associated with providing publicly funded debt-relief initiatives. The public funding introduces an element of moral hazard into borrowing and lending decisions. If borrowers and lenders perceive publicly funded debt relief as an

Figure 3.11 Debt burdens in 18 completion-point HIPCs, before and after the HIPC and MDRI debt relief

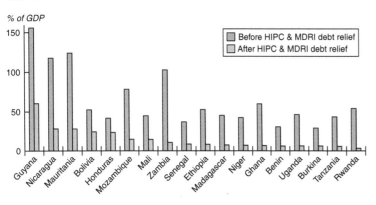

Source: World Bank staff estimates.

Table 3.11 Net present value of external debt relative to GNI and exports, 2004

Percent

	Number of countries	Median of present value of debt/exports	Median of present value of debt/GNI
Completion-point HIPCs	18		
after HIPC debt relief, prior to MDRI		102.2	27.6
after HIPC debt relief and MDRI		41.1	8.6
Decision point HIPCs	11	183.7	41.2
Pre-decision-point HIPCs	9	150.4	67.1
Other low-income countries	18	99.5	46.3
Middle-income countries	76	98.0	44.8

Sources: World Bank Debtor Reporting System and staff estimates.

ongoing feature of the development agenda, countries have an incentive to increase borrowing beyond prudent levels, under the expectation that debt relief will be provided by donors if they encounter difficulties in meeting their debt-service obligations. Similarly, some investors might believe that their exposure to poor countries is reduced by an implicit guarantee of publicly funded debt relief, which would limit their downside risk, making them willing to lend at a lower rate.

Another factor underlying the concern about excessive nonconcessional borrowing stems from the inherent trade-off in scaling up the financial resources required to accelerate progress on MDGs while maintaining debt sustainability. Grants provide countries with financial resources without sacrificing debt sustainability. But the availability of grants is limited. Loans provide additional financial resources, but raise the risk of debt distress, particularly when loans are made on nonconcessional terms. Countries may be more willing to accept a higher risk of debt distress in order to gain additional resources. Official creditors may prefer a more prudent approach to borrowing; one

that puts more weight on debt sustainability, with the aim of preventing a recurrence of lending-forgiveness cycles.

The Debt Sustainability Framework (DSF) for low-income countries developed jointly by the IMF and the World Bank provides a framework for managing the risks associated with additional borrowing (box 3.5). The DSF captures the distinction between concessional and nonconcessional borrowing by measuring debt in net present value terms. Nonconcessional borrowing raises the debt burden by more (in net present value terms) for the same amount of financial resources. In other words, borrowing on concessional terms improves the trade-off between debt sustainability and resource flows. More generally, it is the overall degree of concessionality in a country's loan portfolio that determines how many more resources can be provided without sacrificing debt sustainability.

The DSF can be used to assess the risks associated with additional borrowing. Assessing the risks are complicated by the high degree of uncertainty surrounding economic projections over long time horizons (measured in decades), especially when the

Box 3.5 The DSF for low-income countries

The International Monetary Fund (IMF) and World Bank jointly assess debt sustainability in countries that receive credits and grants from the International Development Association (IDA) and that are eligible for resources under the IMF's Poverty Reduction and Growth Facility (PRGF). The DSF is used by IDA and the African Development Fund (AfDF) to allocate credits (not loans) to countries. It is also used by the Paris Club to help determine whether a country's debt is sustainable and, if it is not, how much debt relief would be required to attain debt sustainability over the long term.

The objective is to monitor the evolution of countries' debt-burden indicators and to guide future financing decisions. The DSF traces the evolution of external and public debt and debt-service indicators over the long term with reference to a baseline projection based on realistic assumptions. Stress tests are conducted to illustrate the implications of adverse shocks to key macroeconomic variables (typically lower growth, higher interest rates, and an exchange rate depreciation), along with other selected scenarios of specific interest to the country under study (for example, an increase in a contingent liability of the public sector).

The external debt burden of each country is assessed over the projection horizon with reference to threshold levels that depend on the quality of a country's policies and institutions. The World Bank's Country Policy and Institutional Assessment (CPIA) is used to classify countries into three performance categories (strong, medium, and poor). Debt thresholds for strong policy performers are highest. The risk of external debt distress is then assessed with reference to four risk classifications: low, medium, high, and "in debt distress." Empirical studies indicate that low-income countries with better policies and institutions have a lower risk of debt distress (see IMF and World Bank 2004 and the references therein).

The risk classifications do not fully capture the complexity of the assessment. For example, in cases where the various indicators give different signals, there is still a need for careful interpretation and judgment. Furthermore, vulnerabilities related to domestic public debt should also be taken into account. The past record in meeting debt-service obligations may also be a factor in determining the classification, especially for countries at high or moderate risk of debt distress.

additional borrowing is used to fund projects and programs that have the potential to enhance economic growth significantly over the long term. Managing the risks by setting limits on additional borrowing would require agreement among all creditors on the assessment of debt sustainability and the degree of risk to be tolerated. In the case of the main multilateral creditors, there is typically some scope for agreement on the major issues, and moral suasion can be used to enforce limits on additional borrowing. However, reaching agreement among all prospective creditors is generally be problematic, and, under such conditions, moral suasion is likely to be ineffective in enforcing borrowing limits. For countries with IMF programs, the collective-action problem is addressed by setting limits on additional borrowing, which help ensure that additional resource flows do not endanger debt sustainability. However, for countries without an IMF program, it will be difficult to monitor and set limits on nonconcessional borrowing.

What has been the experience so far for countries that have already received HIPC debt relief? Has their borrowing increased significantly?

Net official lending to decision-point HIPCs has been stable

Net concessional lending from the official sector to the 27 HIPCs that reached the decision point prior to 2005 declined significantly in the mid-1990s (figure 3.12).[24] The transitory increase in 2002 was partly due to a resumption in concessionary lending to the Democratic Republic of the Congo (DRC) in 2002.[25] Non-concessional lending from the official sector to the 27 countries has

been declining for several years, resulting in lower debt service costs. Since 1990, repayments on outstanding loans have exceeded disbursements of new loans by 0.4 percent of GDP on average.

Net private debt inflows to 27 HIPCs that reached the decision point before 2005 *contracted* by $0.75 billion (0.7 percent of GDP) on average over the period 2000–3, before rebounding to $0.5 billion in 2004 (0.4 percent of GDP).[26] The rebound in 2004 was lower than in other low-income countries, where net private debt inflows increased from an average level of $0.4 billion (0.05 percent of GDP) in 2000–3 to $7.2 billion (0.7 percent of GDP) in 2004. The rebound in 2004 was mainly concentrated in 4 of the 29 decision-point HIPCs: Tanzania ($168 million, 1.5 percent of GDP), Honduras ($151 million, 2.0 percent of GDP), Cameroon ($133 million, 0.9 percent of GDP), and the Democratic Republic of the Congo ($88 million, 1.3 percent of GDP). The private debt burden of the 27 countries as a group has declined significantly, falling from more than 20 percent in the early 1990s to less than 9 percent in 2004, comparable to the level in other low-income countries but well below that for middle-income countries (25 percent in 2004). Private debt exceeded 20 percent of GDP in only 2 of the 27 countries in 2004 (Nicaragua at 25 percent and Mozambique at 23.4 percent), while 13 countries recorded ratios of private debt to GDP of under 5 percent.

International credit-rating agencies have recently begun issuing sovereign debt ratings for some low-income countries. Credit ratings enhance transparency and help private investors assess the risk of holding sovereign debt. Thirteen of the 29 decision-point HIPCs are currently rated by international agencies (table 3.12). Benin, Ghana, and Senegal are rated B+ by Standard and Poor's; Ghana and Mozambique are rated B+ by Fitch. These ratings, the highest among low-income countries, are three notches below investment grade, making it difficult for countries to expand their access to international bond markets. Bank loans and short-term debt account for most of the outstanding private debt (90 percent in 2004) issued by the 29 countries. Medium- and long-term bonds account for a negligible portion, less than 0.1 percent in 2004, down from almost 4 percent in 1993. In 2004, net inflows of medium- and long-term bonds to the 29 countries totaled only $345 million (0.3 percent of GDP), and were con-

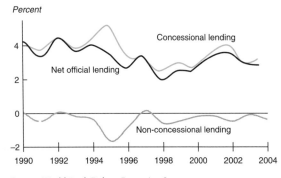

Figure 3.12 Net official lending to 27 decision-point HIPCs as a percent of GDP, 1990–2004

Percent

Source: World Bank Debtor Reporting System.

Table 3.12 Credit ratings for decision-point HIPCs
Rating of foreign currency long-term debt[a]

	Moody's	Standard & Poor's	Fitch
Benin		B+	B
Bolivia	B3	B	B–
Burkina Faso		B	
Cameroon		CCC	B–
Ghana		B+	B+
Honduras	B2		
Madagascar		B	
Malawi			CCC
Mali		B	B–
Mozambique		B	B+
Nicaragua	Caa1		
Senegal		B+	
Uganda			B

Sources: Moody's, Standard & Poor's, and Fitch.
a. As of March 8, 2006.

centrated in just three countries: Honduras ($162 million, 2.2 percent of GDP), Senegal ($92 million, 1.2 percent of GDP), and Ethiopia ($71 million, 0.9 percent of GDP). The creditworthiness of HIPCs that reach the completion point will be enhanced by further debt relief under the MDRI. However, other factors such as the quality of policy and institutional frameworks, and political risk, will continue to have an important influence on credit ratings by international agencies.

The decline in debt service burdens is supported by stronger economic growth

Growth has picked up over the past few years in most HIPCs, helping reduce their debt service burden, measured relative to GDP (table 3.13). Real GDP growth in the 27 HIPCs that reached the decision point before 2005 averaged 4.6 percent over the period 2000–5, up considerably from an average rate of 2.6 percent in the 1990s and just 1.8 percent in the 1980s. The pickup in growth has been broadly based across countries—real GDP growth exceeded 4 percent in 16 of 27 decision-point HIPCs in 2000–5.

It is important to recognize, however, that the range of outcomes was broad—annual per capita real GDP growth *declined* in 9 of the 27 countries. Moreover, the average increase in real GDP growth in 27 decision-point HIPCs over the sub-periods 1990–9 versus 2000–5 (1.9 percentage points) was the same as in "other low-income countries" (countries that currently are not eligible for the HIPC Initiative) and in middle-income countries. Furthermore, the increase in growth also reflects

the fact that HIPCs are required to establish a track record of macroeconomic stability in order to reach the decision point. Real GDP growth increased by only half of a percentage point during this period in the 11 countries that are eligible for the HIPC Initiative but had not yet reached the decision point by the end of 2004 (these are the "pre-decision-point HIPCs" in table 3.13). Clearly, growth has been influenced by many factors beside debt relief.

According to the "debt overhang" hypothesis, excessive debt can seriously impede countries' growth potential.[27] Much of the theoretical literature has focused on the adverse incentive effects of excessive debt. Excessive debt raises concerns that the government may resort to inflationary finance or large tax increases to meet its debt-service obligations or that it may default on its obligations at some point in the future. These concerns deter private investment, which curtails growth. Moreover, in countries that are unable to meet their debt-service obligations, governments can be discouraged from carrying out structural reforms if most of the benefits were used to augment debt-service payments.

The theoretical literature suggests that external borrowing may foster growth up to some threshold level, beyond which adverse incentives begin to dominate. But empirical research on this issue has been inconclusive, on the whole. There is a high degree of uncertainty surrounding estimates of threshold levels and the effect of debt relief on growth. Recent empirical studies by Clements and others (2003) and Pattillo and others (2004) suggest that the amount of debt relief provided by the

Table 3.13 Average annual real GDP growth, 1990–2005
Percent

	No. of countries	Average real GDP growth[a]		
		1980–9	1990–9	2000–5
Decision-point HIPCs[b]	27	1.8	2.6	4.6
Pre-decision-point HIPCs[c]	11	2.6	1.7	2.2
Other low-income countries	19	4.7	2.7	4.6
Middle-income countries	77	3.5	2.8	4.8

Source: World Bank Debtor Reporting System and staff estimates.
a. Real GDP growth rates are first averaged over indicated sub-periods for each country and then unweighted averages are calculated across countries.
b. Burundi and Congo reached the decision point prior to 2005 and are therefore classifed as pre-decision-point HIPCs for the purpose of these calculations.
c. Real GDP data is unavailable for 2 of the 11 pre-decision-point HIPCs (Myanmar and Somalia).

HIPC Initiative should raise countries' annual per capita real GDP growth rates by about 1 percentage point.[28] That estimate is broadly consistent with recent trends—annual per capita real GDP growth increased by about 2 percentage points on average for the HIPCs over the periods just before and just after reaching their respective decision points.[29]

The "debt overhang" literature stresses that debt relief can strengthen incentives to promote domestic investment and structural reforms. Providing more aid in the form of grants in place of concessionary loans can provide the same incentive effects (because it reduces the net present value of debt), but this may not be the case for greater aid in the form of grants allocated to reduce debt-service payments. In the absence of a credible multiyear commitment, recipient countries face uncertainty about their ability to use grants to service debt. The irrevocable nature of HIPC debt relief upon reaching the completion point provides such a commitment.

Debt burdens are not the only indicator of sustainability; other factors are important, as well. Episodes of debt distress often have occurred in emerging market economies with moderate, or even low, debt.[30] Moreover, adverse shocks to economic growth and the terms of trade have had a greater influence on debt burdens in low-income countries than has the amount of borrowing undertaken (IMF 2003). Various indicators of countries' external positions can provide additional insights into debt sustainability.

Debt sustainability in some countries has been enhanced by reserve accumulation, higher exports, and higher inflows of FDI, remittances, and aid

Foreign reserves enable countries to meet their debt-service obligations in the event of adverse financial or economic developments, thereby reducing of the risk of a liquidity crisis. Reserves in the 29 decision-point HIPCs as a group have increased substantially since the early 1990s, rising from 2.6 percent of GDP in 1990 to a high of 13.3 percent in 2004, before declining to 11.9 percent in 2005 (table 3.14). In 2004, reserves provided cover for more than six months of imports in one-third of the countries, whereas in 1990 none of the countries had enough reserves to cover six months of imports.

The external position of the 29 decision-point HIPCs has also been strengthened by an expansion of trade. More open economies are better able to adjust to external shocks. Exports by the 29 countries as a group have increased from 20 percent of GDP in the early 1990s to almost 30 percent in 2005, but the figure remains well below the level in middle-income countries (estimated at 40 percent in 2005).

Non-debt-creating resource flows, notably from FDI, workers' remittances, and foreign aid, can help countries meet their external financing needs by generating a relatively stable stream of foreign exchange earnings. FDI and remittance inflows to the 29 decision-point HIPCs as a group have risen considerably since the early 1990s (table 3.14). FDI and remittance inflows provide important sources of external finance to most countries, with FDI inflows exceeding 3 percent of GDP in one-half of the countries, and remittances exceeding 3 percent of GDP in about one-third. ODA has risen from a low of 12 percent of GDP in 29 decision-point HIPCs as a group to 20.5 percent in 2003–4, which is comparable to the level received in the early 1990s.

Sizable external and fiscal imbalances remain

The current-account deficit for the decision-point HIPCs as a group narrowed from 8.9 percent of GDP in 1999 to 5.1 percent in 2005. But large imbalances remain in some countries: deficits exceed 10 percent of GDP in one-third of the 29 countries. Those countries still rely heavily on external financing, making them vulnerable to external shocks. In 2005, current-account deficits widened by more than 3 percent of GDP in 6 of the 29 countries, mainly due to higher oil-import bills. The value of oil imports increased from 3.5 percent of GDP in decision-point countries in 2002 to 7.6 percent in 2005.

The analysis to this point has focused mainly on external debt burdens. However, there is growing concern about fiscal imbalances and rising domestic debt burdens in some countries. Data limitations make this issue difficult to analyze. Nonetheless, the available data indicate cause for concern in some HIPCs. General government budget balances have improved over the past few years for the decision-point HIPCs as a group, reaching –3.2 percent of GDP in 2005, up from –4.3 percent in 2003. However, fiscal deficits exceed 5 percent of GDP in 8 of the 26 countries for which data are available. Gross domestic debt issued by the public sector increased by more than 5 percent of GDP over the period 1998 to 2004 in 4 of the 11 HIPCs where data are available.[31] In 2004 gross domestic debt exceeded 20 percent of GDP in 5 of the 11 HIPCs. For countries where the public debt burden is high and rising, the gains in debt sustainability provided by HIPC debt relief have been eroded by financing public debt in the domestic market.

The challenge ahead: accessing external capital, while maintaining debt sustainability

Low-income countries, HIPCs and non-HIPCs alike, face the challenge of balancing the potential risks of external borrowing against the benefits. The debt burden is an important factor in assessing those risks, but it is not the only factor. Much of the buildup in the debt burden in the HIPCs from the mid-1980s to the mid-1990s can be explained by their weak policy and institutional frameworks, low capacity for debt management, lack of export diversification, and limited fiscal revenue capacity (Sun 2004). To the extent that these factors have not improved significantly in countries that reach the HIPC completion point, debt sustainability will be an ongoing concern, despite the substantial amount of debt relief pro-

Table 3.14 Indicators of external position of the 29 decision-point HIPCs, 1990–2005

Percent

	1990	1995	2000	2001	2002	2003	2004	2005
Foreign reserves/GDP	2.6	6.8	8.2	8.9	11.5	12.8	13.3	11.9
Exports/GDP	21.1	23.9	28.3	25.3	24.9	25.6	28.4	29.5
Current account/GDP	−4.8	−6.0	−7.1	−7.0	−7.9	−5.9	−5.4	−5.1
FDI/GDP	0.5	1.8	3.6	3.7	4.0	3.3	3.1	—
Remittances/GDP	1.2	1.4	2.0	2.3	2.5	2.7	2.8	—
ODA/GDP	21.2	18.1	15.3	17.2	16.0	20.3	20.7	—

Sources: World Bank Debtor Reporting System and staff estimates.

vided to the countries. Countries can enhance debt sustainability by building up foreign reserves to levels that provide adequate insurance against external shocks, and by pursuing macroeconomic policies that aim to maintain a low and stable inflation environment, along with a sound fiscal framework. Debt sustainability can also be enhanced by implementing structural reforms designed to improve institutional frameworks. This includes initiatives aimed to promote trade, FDI, and remittance inflows; advance export diversification; augment capacity for debt management; raise fiscal revenue capacity; and improve the investment climate through better governance and sound institutions. In addition to helping to maintain debt sustainability over the long term, improving policies and institutional frameworks along these lines will play a critical role in improving aid effectiveness and more generally, in helping countries attain their development objectives.

Annex: Debt Restructuring with Official Creditors

This appendix lists official debt restructuring agreements concluded in 2005. Restructuring of intergovernmental loans and officially guaranteed private export credits take place under the aegis of the Paris Club. These agreements are concluded between the debtor government and representatives of creditor countries. The terms of Paris Club debt treatments are recorded in an agreed-upon minute. To make the terms effective, debtor countries must sign a bilateral implementing agreement with each creditor (see box 3.3).

Burundi On July 29, 2005, Burundi reached its decision point under the enhanced Initiative for Heavily Indebted Poor Countries (enhanced HIPC Initiative). In accordance with the agreement reached in March 2004,[32] Paris Club creditors increased debt reduction to 90 percent of the net present value of eligible external debt (Cologne terms), from 67 percent (Naples terms, or "traditional relief"), for maturities falling due between July 29, 2005, and December 31, 2006.

Dominican Republic In October 2005, the Paris Club creditors reached agreement with the Dominican Republic to consolidate around $137 million of debt service payments falling due in 2005, of which $50 million related to ODA loans. The rescheduling was conducted according to "classic terms," whereby claims are to be repaid progressively over 12 years, including a 5-year grace period, with 14 semi-annual repayments increasing from 5.5 percent of the amount rescheduled to 9.08 percent. ODA loans were to be rescheduled at interest rates at least as favorable as the original concessional rates and no higher than the appropriate market rate, and non-ODA loans

were to be rescheduled at the appropriated market rate. Paris Club creditors also agreed to review the external financing needs of the Dominican Republic in December 2005 in connection with satisfying the conditions for the third review under the IMF Stand-by Arrangement, with a view to providing additional relief in 2006, if needed.

Honduras In May 2005, the Paris Club creditors reached agreement on debt reduction for Honduras, which had reached its completion point under the enhanced HIPC Initiative on April 5, 2005. Of the $1.474 billion due to the Paris Club creditors as of March 31, 2005, $1.171 billion was treated on Cologne terms (debt reduction to 90 percent of the net present value [NPV] of eligible external debt), of which $206 million was cancelled as the Paris Club share of the effort in the enhanced HIPC Initiative, $110 million was rescheduled, and $855 million was cancelled on a bilateral basis. As a result of the agreement and additional bilateral assistance, Honduras' debt to Paris Club creditors was reduced from $1,474 million to $413 million.

Kyrgyz Republic In March 2005, Paris Club creditors agreed with the government of the Kyrgyz Republic to a reduction of its public external debt. The comprehensive debt treatment under the Evian Approach covered $555 million of debt due to the Paris Club creditors as of March 1, 2005, of which $124 million was cancelled and $431 million rescheduled. According to the agreed rescheduling terms, non-ODA commercial credits were cancelled by 50 percent ($124 million) and the remaining 50 percent will be repaid over 23 years, with a 7-year grace period at the appropriate market rate. ODA credits ($306 million) will be repaid over 40 years with a 13-year grace period at interest rates at least as favorable as the concessional rates applying to these loans. Moratorium interest due under the agreement will be capitalized at 85 percent in 2005, 75 percent in 2006, 70 percent in 2007 and 65 percent in 2008. The capitalized interest amounts will be repaid over 23 years including a 7-year grace period.

Nigeria The October 2005 debt deal with Nigeria was the single largest debt relief granted to any African country, effectively providing debt cancellation estimated at $18 billion (including moratorium interest), which represents about 60 percent of its debt owed to Paris Club creditors (an overall reduction in its debt stock by an estimated $30 billion). This Paris Club agreement was made possible following the achievement by Nigeria of (1) progress in pursuing an ambitious economic reform program, which aims to accelerate growth and reduce poverty; (2) the World Bank's reclassification of the country from "blend" to "IDA only," paving the way for Paris Club creditors to grant debt relief along the Naples terms; and (3) negotiation of an agreement with the IMF for a non-lending Policy Support Instrument (PSI), which formalizes continuing IMF surveillance.

The debt relief agreement was to be implemented in two phases in consonance with the implementation of the IMF PSI approved on October 17, 2005. In the first phase, Paris Club creditors grant a 33 percent cancellation of eligible debts after payment of arrears estimated at $6.3 billion by Nigeria. In the second phase, after approval of the first review under the PSI by the IMF and repayment of post-cutoff-date debt, Paris Club creditors would grant an additional tranche of cancellation of 34 percent on eligible debts and Nigeria will buy back the remaining eligible debt. Paris Club creditors are to be paid $12.4 billion in total, with $6.3 billion to clear arrears and $6.1 billion for the buyback. Full implementation of the Paris Club deal, scheduled to be completed in April 2006 and following the IMF first review of the PSI, would reduce Nigeria's total outstanding external debt from $35 billion to $5 billion.

Peru In June 2005, the Paris Club creditors agreed on Peru's offer to prepay up to $2 billion of its non-ODA debt falling due between August 2005 and December 2009. Under the agreement, prepayment would be made at par and offered to all creditors. Participation by Paris Club members was voluntary, although a majority of the group's creditors agreed to accept the prepayment offer.

Poland In January 2005, Poland announced its intention to prepay portions of its €12.3 billion debt falling due to the Paris Club between 2005 and 2009. Although Poland had prepaid around €4.5 billion of its Paris Club debt by end-May 2005, because the prepayment was financed by sovereign bond issues, it did not contribute to any appreciable reduction of external debt. However, the deal lengthened the average maturity terms of Poland's external debt, removing the bulge in the country's debt repayments in 2005–9 and reducing refinancing risk.

Russian Federation In May 2005, the Paris Club creditors agreed on the Russian Federation's offer to prepay $15 billion of its debt at par. Participation by Paris Club members was voluntary, although an overwhelming majority of the group's creditors agreed to participate. This prepayment offer translates into major interest savings for Russia and is the largest such offer by a debtor country to the Paris Club creditors.

Rwanda The Paris Club creditors agreed on 100 percent cancellation of Rwanda's debt in May 2005, following a month after Rwanda reached its completion point under the enhanced HIPC Initiative. Around $90 million in debt due to Paris Club creditors as of March 31, 2005, was treated on Cologne terms (debt reduction to 90 percent of the NPV of eligible external debt), of which $82.7 million ($61.7 million in ODA loans and $21 million in non-ODA commercial credits) was cancelled as the Paris Club share of the effort in the enhanced HIPC Initiative. A further $7.7 million in ODA loans was to be cancelled as a result of additional debt relief granted by creditors on a bilateral basis.

São Tomé and Principe In September 2005, the Paris Club creditors reached agreement on the retroactive rescheduling of São Tomé and Principe's debt service payments falling due between May 01, 2001, and December 31, 2007. The treatment was on Cologne terms (cancellation of 90 percent of the NPV of eligible external debt), with ODA credits to be repaid over 40 years with a 16 year-grace period.

Zambia In May 2005, the Paris Club creditors agreed to reduce Zambia's debt stock under the Enhanced HIPC Initiative, a month after Zambia had reached its completion point. Of the total $1.92 billion due to the Paris Club creditors as of March 31, 2005, $1.763 billion was treated on Cologne terms (90 percent cancellation rate). Of this latter amount, $1.403 billion in pre-cut-off date debt ($461 million in ODA loans and $942 million in non-ODA commercial credits) was cancelled as the Paris Club share of the effort in the enhanced HIPC Initiative. A further $360 million ($298 million in pre- and post-cutoff-date ODA loans and $62 million in post-cutoff-date non-ODA commercial credits) was to be cancelled on a bilateral basis. As a result of the agreement and additional bilateral assistance, Zambia's debt to Paris Club creditors was reduced from $1.92 billion to $124 million. Paris Club creditors also agreed to reschedule 50 percent of the debt service payments due in 2005, 2006, and 2007 on the debt remaining due after additional bilateral cancellation.

Debt treatment for countries affected by the tsunami

Following meetings in January and March 2005, Paris Club creditors reviewed the debt treatment of the tsunami-affected countries and agreed not to expect any debt payments on eligible sovereign claims from these countries until December 31, 2005. Two countries, Indonesia and Sri Lanka, took up the offer. According to the terms of treatment set in May 2005, these two countries were to repay the deferred debt over 5 years with 2-year grace periods. Under treatment were 100 percent of the amounts of principal and interest due between January 1, 2005 and December 1, 2005 on loans from Paris Club creditors having an original maturity of more than one year. For Indonesia, the total amount treated was $2.704 billion, including $2.056 billion of principal and interest on ODA loans and $648 million of non-ODA credits. For Sri Lanka, the total amount treated was around $227 million, including $213 million of principal and interest on ODA loans and 15 million of non-ODA credits.

Notes

1. The definition of emergency and distress relief grants was modified in 2005 to included reconstruction grants. The modification was not applied to previous years. The amount of reconstruction grants reported by donors in 2005 will not be known until the OECD DAC reports the components of ODA in December 2006.

2. OECD DAC data on the allocation of ODA across income classifications and regions in 2005 will not be available until December 2006. The calculations refer to the portion of ODA that is allocated across income classifications and regions. In 2000–4, 26 percent of ODA was not allocated across income classifications and 17 percent was not allocated across regions, on average.

3. The United Nations' LDC income classification overlaps the World Bank's Sub-Saharan Africa region, but not completely—32 of the 49 LDCs are in the Sub-Saharan Africa region; 32 of the 43 low-income countries in the Sub-Saharan Africa region are LDCs.

4. As measured by the WTO/OECD-DAC Trade Capacity Building Database.

5. The *collective* interim target of 0.56 percent in 2010 entails individual targets of 0.51 percent for the 15 "original" EU countries, along with 0.17 percent targets for the 10 countries that joined the European Union in 2004.

6. Projections of ODA based on donor commitments are reported by OECD (2006, table 1.1).

7. See World Bank (2004, chapter 11) for a discussion of the difficulties entailed in estimating the amount of aid required to finance the MDGs.

8. See World Bank (2006, pp. 77–8) for a detailed discussion of innovative financing mechanisms.

9. See IMF (2005a, annex 2, and 2005b) and Isard and others (2006) for a survey of recent studies.

10. Documented in IMF (2005b).

11. See IMF (2005b) for an analysis of whether recent large aid surges in five African countries were "spent" or "absorbed."

12. All but 4 of the 29 HIPCs that have reached the decision point are in Sub-Saharan Africa.

13. The Republic of the Congo only reached the decision point in March 2006 and hence did not receive any debt service reduction from the HIPC initiative over the period 2000–5.

14. The Democratic Republic of the Congo and Gineau-Bissau are both excluded from the calculations underlying figures 3.6 and 3.7 because they did not service their debt payments in 2000–3.

15. To qualify for "traditional debt relief" provided by the Paris Club, countries must generally have a Poverty Reduction and Grant Facility (PRGF) program with the IMF.

16. Commercial creditors account for only 2 percent of debt relief due under the HIPC Initiative.

17. See IMF and World Bank (2005, section III).

18. See IEG (2006: 8–9) for a more detailed discussion of creditors' commitments to HIPC debt relief.

19. World Bank and IMF (2005: 18–20).

20. Mauritania has reached the completion point under the HIPC Initiative but has not yet qualified for debt relief under the MDRI, pending implementation of key public expenditure management reforms. The calculations reported in the text assume that Mauritania will qualify by the end of 2006.

21. The calculations underlying figure 3.8 assume that countries will reach their respective completion points on the dates listed in World Bank 2006b (annex 2.3).

22. The baseline for refinancing IDA is specified in SDRs with an inflation adjustment factor based on a three-

year moving average, so the U.S. dollar equivalent will vary over time.

23. The higher debt burdens in Guyana, Nicaragua, Bolivia, and Honduras largely represent debt owed to the Inter-American Development Bank, which is not forgiven under the MDRI.

24. Burundi and the Republic of Congo are excluded from these calculations because they reached the decision point after 2004. Net official lending in figure 3.12 includes *concessional* and *non-concessional* loans from official creditors, whereas all bilateral loans discussed in the context of ODA (figure 3.2) are *concessional* (by definition).

25. Prior to 2002, the DRC was in arrears with multilateral institutions and hence did not receive any concessional loans from official sources. In 2002 the DRC received $607 million in net concessional lending from official sources, an amount equal to 11 percent of GDP.

26. Net private debt inflows are comprised of net changes in public and publicly guaranteed debt, private nonguaranteed debt, commercial bank loans and other private credit.

27. See Clements and others (2003) and Pattillo and others (2004) for recent reviews of the theoretical and empirical literature on "debt overhang."

28. The empirical results reported by Clements and others (2003) also imply that the impact on growth could be stronger if some of the debt-service reduction were allocated to public investment. For instance, annual per capita GDP growth would be augmented by an additional 0.5 percentage point if half of HIPC debt relief were allocated to public investment.

29. This result is strongly influenced by large increases in just a few countries, notably Chad, where real GDP per capita increased from an average rate of –0.9 percent over the period 1991–2000 to 13.6 percent in 2001–04. The *median* increase is only 1.5 percentage points.

30. This is documented by Reinhart, Rogoff, and Savastano (2003), who coined the term "debt intolerance." They examined 33 debt-distress episodes in emerging market economies over the period 1970–2001. Of these, four involved countries with ratios of external debt to GDP of less than 40 percent; another seven involved ratios of less than 50 percent.

31. Calculations are based on World Bank staff estimates of gross general government debt.

32. The March 2004 agreement treated $85 million in arrears in principal and interest as of December 31, 2003 and of maturities in principal and interest falling due from January 1, 2004 to December 31, 2006. The rescheduling was on Naples terms (67 percent NPV debt reduction of eligible external debt), with non-ODA credits cancelled by 67 percent (around $4.4 billion) and the remainder rescheduled over 23 years with a 6-year grace period, at market interest rates, and ODA credits rescheduled over 40 years with a 16-year grace period.

References

Bourguignon, François, and Mark Sundberg. 2006a. "Constraints to Achieving the MDGs with Scaled-Up Aid"

DESA Working Paper ST/ESA/2006/DWP/15, United Nations Department of Economic and Social Affairs, New York. March. http://www.un.org/esa/desa/papers/2006/wp15_2006.pdf

Bourguignon, François, and Mark Sundberg. 2006b. "Absorptive Capacity and Achieving the MDGs." Unpublished paper, World Bank, Washington, DC. March.

Clements, Benedict, Rina Bhattacharya and Toan Quoc Nguyen. 2003. "External Debt, Public Investment, and Growth in Low-Income Countries" IMF Working Paper 03/249, International Monetary Fund, Washington, DC.

IEG (Independent Evaluation Group). 2006. "Debt Relief for the Poorest: An Evaluation Update of the HIPC Initiative." World Bank, Washington, DC.

IMF (International Monetary Fund). 2003. "Fund Assistance for Countries Facing Exogenous Shocks." Policy Development and Review Department, Washington, DC. August. http://www.imf.org/external/np/pdr/sustain/2003/080803.htm.

———. 2005a. *The Macroeconomic Challenges of Scaling Up Aid to Africa—A Checklist for Practitioners.* SM/05/179. Washington, DC: IMF. www.imf.org/external/pubs/ft/afr/aid/2006/eng/index.htm.

———. 2005b. "The Macroeconomics of Managing Increased Aid Flows—Experiences of Low-Income Countries and Policy Implications." SM/05/306, Policy Development and Review Department, Washington, DC. August. http://www.imf.org/external/np/pp/eng/2005/080805a.pdf

IMF (International Monetary Fund) and World Bank. 2004. "Debt Sustainability in Low-Income Countries: Further Considerations on an Operational Framework and Policy Implications." September. http://www.imf.org/external/np/pdr/sustain/2004/091004.htm.

———. 2005. "Heavily Indebted Poor Countries (HIPC) Initiative—Status of Implementation." August. http://siteresources.worldbank.org/INTDEBTDEPT/Resources/081905.pdf

Isard, Peter, Leslie Lipschitz, Alexandros Mourouras, and Boriana Yontcheva, eds. 2006. *The Macroeconomic Management of Foreign Aid: Opportunities and Pitfalls.* Washington, DC: IMF.

OECD. 2006. *2005 Development Cooperation Report.* Paris: OECD.

Pattillo, Catherine, Hélène Poirson, and Luca Ricci. 2004. "What Are the Channels through Which External Debt Affects Growth?" Working Paper 04/14, International Monetary Fund, Washington, DC.

Reinhart, Carmen, Kenneth Rogoff, and Miguel Savastano. 2003. "Debt Intolerance." Brookings Papers of Economic Activity 1: 1–74.

Sun, Yan. 2004. "External Debt Sustainability in HIPC Completion Point Countries." Working Paper 04/160, International Monetary Fund, Washington, DC.

Sundberg, Mark, and Hans Lofgren. 2006. "Absorptive Capacity and Achieving the MDGs: The Case of Ethiopia." In *The Macroeconomic Management of Foreign Aid: Opportunities and Pitfalls,* ed. Peter Isard, Leslie Lipschitz, Alexandros Mourouras, and Boriana Yontcheva. Washington, DC: International Monetary Fund.

UN Millennium Project. 2005. Investing in Development: A Practical Plan to Achieve the Millennium Development Goals. Overview. http://www.unmillenniumproject .org/reports/index.htm.

World Bank. 2005. Global Economic Prospects 2006. Washington, DC: World Bank.

World Bank. 2004. Global Monitoring Report 2004. Washington, DC: World Bank.

World Bank. 2006a. Global Monitoring Report 2006. Washington, DC: World Bank.

World Bank. 2006b. "IDA's Implementation of the Multilateral Debt Relief Initiative." Resource Mobilization Department, Washington, DC. March.

4

Financial Integration among Developing Countries

Developing countries have become important sources of lending and investment to other developing countries. In years past, most of the capital exported from developing countries found its way to industrial countries, usually to help wealthy individuals safeguard their assets. During the past decade, however, developing countries have become a significant source of foreign direct investment (FDI), bank lending, and even official development assistance (ODA) for other developing countries. This expansion in South–South capital flows reflects developing countries' increasing integration into global financial markets. As developing countries' incomes rise and their banks and firms become increasingly sophisticated, it is natural that they should become more important sources of foreign lending and investment and that a portion of these flows should go to other developing countries. At the same time, South–South capital flows may have implications for developing-country recipients that differ from the implications of capital flows coming from rich countries. The purpose of this chapter is to present data on this growing trend and to evaluate its implications for development. The principal issues are (i) the forces that have propelled South–South financial integration, and (ii) the differences between South–South interactions and financial integration between developing and high-income countries.

The main messages are:

- Capital flows among developing countries increased rapidly over the past 10 years, driven by the technological innovations that support globalization generally, rising incomes in developing countries, and increasingly open policies toward trade and financial markets. South–South financial integration has progressed more rapidly than North–South integration, as South–South trade has expanded more rapidly than North-South trade (capital flows often follow trade) and developing countries have eased constraints on outward investment.

- Developing-country multinationals enjoy some advantages over industrial-country firms when investing in developing countries because of their greater familiarity with technology and business practices suitable for developing-country markets. However, developing-country multinationals also face greater impediments in their home countries than do industrial-country multinationals. Impediments may take the form of bureaucratic constraints on outward investment, other financial constraints, and a paucity of institutional support and business services.

- South–South capital has helped to sustain FDI flows in developing countries even as FDI from industrial countries has declined. It has made more capital available to low-income countries, because developing-country investors are often more willing to handle the special risks encountered in poor countries. In some cases, South–South investment may also confer benefits because firms in receiving countries may find it easier to absorb technology from a developing-country investor than from an industrial-country investor, as developing-country investors are likely to rely on technology appropriate for a developing-country setting.

- Most South–South capital flows occur within the same geographic region, both because they follow trade (and a large share of trade is regional) and because proximity, common language, and cultural and ethnic ties reduce the risks of lending and investment.

• Developing-country banks are more likely than industrial-country banks to invest in small developing countries with weak institutions. Especially in low-income countries, the performance of foreign banks from developing countries (both in terms of asset quality and efficiency) does not differ from that of foreign banks from rich countries, suggesting that developing-country banks do not pose an additional risk to vulnerable low-income countries because of poor management or weak finances.

• Initiatives to promote the integration of developing countries' stock exchanges have made little progress, and many developing-country capital markets remain more integrated with major international financial markets than with other developing-country markets. Nevertheless, there are recent signs of change, with fewer new issues on U.S. exchanges, in particular, and increased local issuance. Many exchanges may benefit from closer South–South cooperation, including by encouraging cross-border listings and investment, and information/technology sharing.

The growth of South–South capital flows

Financial transactions among developing countries increased substantially in the past decade (see annex 1).[1] South–South FDI, for example, increased from $14 billion in 1995 to $47 billion in 2003. The share of South–South flows in total FDI to developing countries rose from 16 percent in 1995 to 36 percent in 2003, a higher share than that of South–South exports in developing countries' total trade and of South–South remittances in their total remittance receipts (figure 4.1).[2] Syndicated loans grew from $0.7 billion in 1985 to $6.2 billion in 2005. The share of South–South flows in total cross-border syndicated lending was 3 percent in 1985, during the Latin American debt crisis, when syndicated loans to Latin America and other major debtors plummeted. That share fell to 1 percent in 1995, with the recovery from the debt crisis, and then rose to 3.4 percent in 2005. By contrast with FDI and bank lending, developing-

country stock markets have shown little integration in the form of cross-border listings or establishment of regional stock exchanges.[3]

The growing financial integration of developing countries is driven by the same forces that are increasing integration between developing and high-income countries. Technological advances have reduced the costs of transport and communications, facilitating greater cross-border integration and encouraging the growth of cross-border production networks that involve expanded trade and financial transactions. Income growth has been accompanied by increased sophistication in financial systems, facilitating outward investment. Income growth also is associated with more diverse consumption choices, stimulating international trade. In turn, the rise in international trade has provoked greater cross-border financial transactions. The very large differences in wage levels and capital intensity of production within the developing world also have stimulated South–South flows.

The rise in capital flows among developing countries also reflects the increased importance of developing countries in the global economy. The developing world's share of global GDP rose modestly from about 18 percent in 1990 to 20 percent in 2004, but its share in international trade grew more quickly—from 15 percent in 1991 to 26 percent in 2004. The growing importance of some of the larger developing countries is reflected in their increasingly prominent role in global economic negotiations, particularly within

Figure 4.1 South–South capital flows by type, 2005

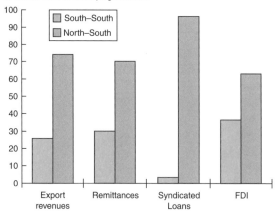

% of total flows to developing countries

Sources: UN Comtrade database; World Bank staff estimates.
Note: Data are for 2005, except for FDI (2003).

the World Trade Organization (WTO). WTO's Ministerial Meeting in Cancun in 2003 showed that coalitions of developing countries (notably the G-20, but also the G-90 group of the poorest countries[4]), if they maintained solidarity, could play a major role in determining the outcome of

negotiations on issues of concern to them (Narlikar and Tussie 2004). The emergence of the G-20 has been characterized as moving the WTO from a group dominated by the Quad (Canada, the European Union, Japan, and the United States) to a multipolar environment (Amorim

Box 4.1   Developing countries as aid donors

The Millennium Development Goals call for a global partnership for development. Historically, that partnership has been understood as a matter of North–South cooperation, but that interpretation fails to acknowledge the growing role of developing countries as sources of official development assistance (ODA). In recent years, however, recognition of the importance of South–South cooperation has come from several quarters—among them the Development Assistance Committee (DAC) of the Organisation for Economic Co-operation and Development (OECD), the European Union, and the United Nations Development Programme (UNDP).

Brazil, Chile, China, India, South Africa, and Thailand are among the developing countries that now provide aid to others in the developing world. There is evidence that the resources involved in South–South aid initiatives may be increasing. China recently announced an increase in its assistance to developing countries over the next three years, including $10 billion dollars in concessional loans and preferential export credits. In February 2006, Turkey became a member of the OECD Development Centre, demonstrating its commitment to providing development assistance to developing countries.

Developing countries often provide aid through partnerships with traditional donors and international institutions (so-called triangular cooperation). For example, in cooperation with Britain's Department for International Development (DFID) and the U.N. Aids Program, the government of Brazil launched the International Centre for Horizontal Technical Cooperation to fight HIV/AIDS in Latin American countries. The center has allowed Brazil, which already has the region's best record in fighting HIV/AIDS, to strengthen its capacity to provide AIDS-related technical assistance to other Latin American countries.

Data on the magnitude of South-South development assistance are scarce, although initiatives to improve collection are underway.[a] DAC, the South-South Unit of the UNDP, and the World Bank have formed a partnership to collect information about South-South aid and provide a platform for developing countries to share their experiences.

Data from the World Bank Debtor Reporting System indicate that concessional loans from developing countries have shown no clear trend over the past decade, but tend to

be dominated by disbursements from just a few countries and show large variability from year to year because of substantial, one-time loans. China accounted for 58 percent of concessional lending from developing countries from 1994 to 2004, and Turkey (due to one disbursement in 1996), the Russian Federation, and Mauritius (due to one disbursement in 2004) for another 30 percent. Fifteen (mostly low-income) countries received some 70 percent of South–South concessional loans during 1994–2004. Sub-Saharan Africa received the greatest amount of South-South concessional loans (47.5 percent), followed by Latin America and the Caribbean (26.5 percent) and Europe and Central Asia (19.1 percent). In 2004 South–South concessional loans made up just 2 percent of all concessional lending to developing countries. Data on grants are not available.

Like other South–South flows, South–South concessional loans are, once we exclude disbursements by China, mostly intraregional (78 percent). Case studies confirm the strong intraregional pattern of South–South development assistance. For example, 90 percent of Thailand's ODA supports infrastructure projects in Cambodia, Laos, Myanmar, and the Maldives (Ministry of Foreign Affairs of Thailand), and 73 percent of India's non-plan grants and loans from 1997–2004 went to neighboring countries (Ministry of Finance of India).

Most emerging donors appear to have a special interest in providing development assistance to African countries. Long a donor in Africa, China, since 2000, has formalized its relationship with the continent through the Forum for China-African Cooperation. Brazilian cooperation with Africa encompasses many areas, including agriculture, infrastructure, trade, and public administration. The country has written off more than $1 billion in debts of African countries. The Russian Federation, too, has written off a substantial amount of African debt, partly under the HIPC initiative. It is studying the possibility of a full HIPC debt write-off for loans not falling under ODA.

a. DAC provides data on official development assistance for its members and for some non-DAC donors. These include high-income donors, such as Saudi Arabia, where development assistance has accounted for more than 1.3 percent of GDP over the past five years, and some developing-country donors, mostly in Eastern Europe. Since the most prominent emerging donors are not included in the DAC database, however, the numbers do not provide an accurate picture of South–South aid.

2005). More than any previous round of trade negotiations, the Doha Round has been shaped by the actions and positions of developing countries (Zedillo, Messerlin, and Neilson 2005). Another indication of their increasing importance is that a few developing countries have become sources of official development assistance (box 4.1).

South–South financial integration has been given a boost by the rapid opening of developing economies. About half of 77 developing countries rated on a leading index of openness to trade showed some improvement from 1995 to 2005, whereas only 5 showed deterioration (figure 4.2). The rest were unchanged.[5] By contrast, nearly all high-income countries showed no major change in their trade policies over this period, because they already were relatively open economies: the average trade index of high-income economies was more than two points better (on a 1-to-5 scale) than that of developing countries.[6] Moreover, South–South trade expanded more quickly than North–South (box 4.2). Because capital flows often follow trade, this has meant more rapid South–South financial integration as well.

Similarly, a majority of 76 rated developing countries became more open to foreign investment over the past 10 years, while only 8 instituted more restrictive policies. In part this reflects an easing of constraints on outward investment, leading to increased South–South capital flows. The difference between high-income and developing countries is less stark for foreign investment than for trade, as high-income countries in 1995 were only slightly more open than developing countries, and 9 of the 21 rated high-income countries adopted more open regimes over the past 10 years. However, the major sources of outward investment and lending from high-income countries, such as the United States and Germany, already had relatively open regimes in the early 1990s, so their outward capital flows did not receive any further impetus from policies becoming more open.

Another spur to South–South capital flows has been the rise of regional trade agreements (RTAs) among developing countries. RTAs have mushroomed: since 1990, their number rose from 50 to nearly 230.[7] Activity has been particularly intense in Latin America, Africa, and Asia.

- In Latin America, Mexico and Chile have concluded a series of agreements since the launch of the North American Free Trade Agreement (NAFTA) in 1994.
- In Africa, the countries of eastern and southern Africa established a common market in 1993; the East African Community was formed in the mid-1990s; and the Southern Africa Development Community (SADC) signed a trade cooperation protocol in 1996.
- In Asia since 2000, India has made agreements with the Southern Cone Common Market (MERCOSUR) and Thailand; China has concluded bilateral trade accords with the countries of the Association of Southeast Asian Nations (ASEAN); and the countries of South Asia reached a free trade agreement in 2004.

It is unclear whether such agreements have made a major contribution to South–South trade and capital flows—or simply reflect their increase.

Figure 4.2 Growing openness of developing countries to trade and capital flows, 1995–2005

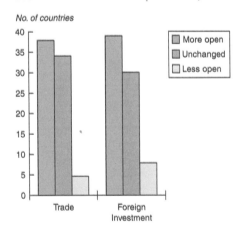

No. of countries

Legend:
- More open
- Unchanged
- Less open

Source: Heritage Foundation.
Note: Number of countries rated more open, unchanged, or less open on Heritage Foundation index of openness for period 1995–2005.

Foreign direct investment in the developing world
South–South FDI is increasing

FDI flows from developing countries to other developing countries increased from an estimated $14 billion in 1995 to $47 billion in 2003 (table 4.1). Increased South–South flows have provided

Box 4.2 South–South FDI and trade

Trade and FDI flows are closely linked (Aizenman and Noy 2005; Albuquerque, Loayza, and Serven 2005; Swenson 2004). At times FDI is a substitute for trade, as when the investment is designed to serve the host market while reducing transport costs or circumventing tariff barriers. However, as trade barriers have come down and the importance of global production networks has risen, FDI and trade have become increasingly complementary (World Bank 2005a). Trade flows also can facilitate FDI by increasing investors' access to information (Portes and Rey 2005).

South–South trade grew rapidly over the past decade, reaching $562 billion in 2004 compared to $222 billion in 1995. From 2000 to 2004, South–South trade grew at an annual rate of 17.6 percent, faster than South–North and North–South exports (12.6 percent and 9.7 percent, respectively). South–South trade made up 26 percent of developing countries' exports in 2004.

Most South–South trade occurs within the same region, although cross-regional trade has also been growing rapidly. In 2004, for example, China was the fourth-largest export destination for Argentina and Brazil. The rapid growth in South–South trade is linked to high growth rates in developing countries, substantial reductions in tariff barriers, and falling transport costs.

The impact of increased investment on South–South trade is hard to measure. However, the surge in trade in raw materials (126 percent from 1995 to 2003) was in line with increasing South–South FDI flows in extractive sectors (see figure). Also, the growth in trade in intermediate goods (91 percent) and capital goods (213 percent) reflects the increased integration of production networks among developing countries, which is stimulated both by North–South and South–South investments.

Composition of South–South exports, 1995 and 2003

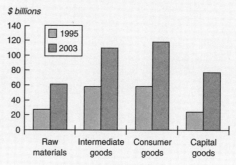

Source: UN Comtrade database.

partial compensation for the decline in FDI flows from high-income countries—from $130 billion in 1999 to $82 billion in 2003.

More than 50 developing countries have reported FDI outflows over the past decade, although the data are notoriously understated (World Bank 2004). It is clear that most developing-country FDI comes from the same middle-income countries that account for the lion's share of developing-country economic activity. The 10 countries that accounted for 73 percent of FDI inflows from 2000 to 2004 also were the source of 87 percent of the total outflows (both to developed and developing countries) during the same period.

The expansion of FDI outflows has been driven by developing countries' increasing openness to capital and trade, and by their increasing participation in international production networks. Because of increased globalization of economic activities, developing-country companies face growing competition in sales and in access to resources and

Table 4.1 South–South FDI as a share of global FDI, 1999–2003
$ billions

	1995	1999	2000	2001	2002	2003e
Total inflows (1)	90.3	163.5	154.7	159.3	135.3	129.6
from high-income OECD (2)	48.1	95.4	93.7	84.8	55.1	59.4
from high-income non-OECD (3)	28.2	35.0	22.7	24.8	27.2	22.8
South–South FDI (1)-(2)-(3)	14.0	33.1	38.3	49.7	53.0	47.4
South–South FDI (percent)	*15.5*	*20.2*	*24.8*	*31.2*	*39.2*	*36.6*

Source: World Bank staff estimates.
Note: The South–South estimates are based on 35 countries that account for 85 percent of total FDI flows to developing countries. The estimates are based on the World Bank's classification of developing countries.
e = estimate.

strategic assets. As many developing-country governments have eased their policies toward capital outflows, their companies, like industrial-country multinationals, have expanded their operations abroad. South–South FDI flows have also increased in response to the significant rise in South–South trade.

Most South–South FDI goes to countries in the same region

Many expanding developing-country firms tend to invest regionally before taking on the rest of the world because of familiarity gained through trade or ethnic and cultural ties. The regional agreements that began to proliferate in the mid-1990s (World Bank 2005b) also have encouraged intraregional trade and investments. For example, 75 percent of the outward investments of Hungarian firms were within Europe (Elteto and Katalin 2003 and table 4.2); almost 40 percent of Russian firms' investments abroad have been in Europe and Central Asia (Vahtra and Liuhto 2004); and the Russian Federation accounts for one-third of Turkey's recent FDI outflows. Encouraged by cooperation arrangements, ASEAN countries have been the top destination for Thai companies (Mathews 2005). South African investments in other developing countries are largely in the southern part of Africa (Goldstein 2003). Following trade liberalization in Latin America, multinationals from Argentina, Brazil, and Chile expanded their regional operations (Chudnovsky and Lopez 2000).

Nevertheless, some developing-country multinationals are venturing beyond their region. For example, in 2004 about half of China's outward FDI went to natural resources projects in Latin America; Malaysia has emerged as a significant new source of FDI in South Africa (Padayachee and Valodia 1999); and Brazil has considerable investments in Angola and Nigeria (Goldstein 2003).

South–South FDI is concentrated in services and extractive industries

While data on the sectoral composition of South–South FDI are not available, a substantial amount of South-South FDI is known to be in services (in-

Table 4.2 Regional FDI by multinationals from selected countries

Share of total investment occurring within region

	Regional (South–South)
China	20.7
India	25.4
Hungary	75.1
Thailand	58.8
Turkey	32.0
Russian Fed.	37.0

Source: Goldstein (forthcoming).

frastructure, in particular) and the extractive industries, as shown by data on mergers and acquisitions (M&A) and privatization transactions (annex 2).

South–South FDI in services increased over the last decade, in tandem with the global surge in services sector FDI and the liberalization of the services sector in many developing countries.[8] Developing economies attracted substantial FDI flows from both high-income and other developing countries through the privatization of state-owned assets. Developing-country firms enjoy some advantages in services sector FDI, because services often require proximity between producers and consumers, and often favor cultural and ethnic familiarity.[9] Moreover, developing-country firms can take advantage of their experience in managing the regulatory process (De Sol 2005; Lisitsyn and others 2005) and create regional networks. Nevertheless, FDI from high-income countries is also highly concentrated in the services sector.

The significant rise of South–South FDI in the infrastructure sector, which began in the late 1990s, often was achieved through partnerships between developing- and industrial-country firms. This expansion by northern investors slowed following stock market declines in the industrial countries and in response to problems of corporate governance in some companies and poor regulation in many developing countries. But developing-country firms continued their expansion through buyouts of the assets of their northern partners, privatization and acquisitions deals, and licenses (annex 2).[10] Between 1998 and 2003, developing countries received almost $160 billion in foreign investment in infrastructure, while developing-country firms invested more than $30 billion in developing-country infrastructure projects. These data represent commitments for selected projects, and thus the totals cannot be compared to the net-flows data usually shown for FDI (see World Bank 2005a for details). Nevertheless, the commitments data do show that a very significant proportion of FDI flows to developing countries (from both the North and the South) is devoted to infrastructure. South–South flows were greatest in telecommunications and, geographically, in Africa (figure 4.3).

Almost 30 percent of FDI in developing countries' telecommunications during 1998–2003 came from southern telecommunications companies, more than 85 percent of it intraregional. Financial and equity investors from the South—such as investment banks, private equity funds, and mutual funds—also have become direct investors in the sector, in addition to participating through South–South cross-border lending and syndicated loans, as discussed in detail later in the chapter (World Bank 2006).

Developing-country multinationals also invest in noninfrastructure services, taking advantage of brand-name recognition, physical proximity, regional distribution networks, taste similarities, and advantages offered by bilateral arrangements. Considerable South–South investment has occurred in banking, as we shall see later in this chapter. Other examples include the growing number of supermarket chains, food companies, pharmaceutical firms, hospitals, and airline carriers from developing countries.[11] In some cases, northern investors undertake investments in developing countries through their subsidiaries in another developing country—for example, Wal-Mex, Wal-Mart's joint venture with a Mexican company.

Developing-country firms (mainly in Asia) have made a small but increasing number of investments in research and development (R&D) in other developing countries (UNCTAD 2005a). China and India are among the largest recipients of R&D-related investments from developing countries, with investment from one another and from Malaysia and Thailand.[12]

The extractive sector (particularly oil and gas) also attracts increasingly large amounts of South–South FDI, mostly through state-owned companies (table 4.3). In recent years, high-

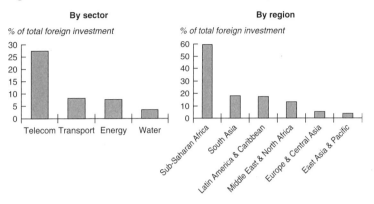

Figure 4.3 South–South FDI in infrastructure and by region, 1998–2003

Source: World Bank (2005c).

growth economies, such as China and India, have acquired oil-and-gas assets or licenses in other developing countries (annex 2). Developing-country companies also are investing in exploration projects. For example, Petronas (Malaysia), which has strong technical competencies in deep-water exploration, has invested in exploration and production projects in more than 20 developing countries (Goldstein forthcoming). Countries that are large oil-and-gas producers, such as República Bolivariana de Venezuela, invest in other developing countries as they integrate their downstream operations such as refining, distribution, and retailing.

South–South FDI in the nonoil mining sector is also increasing. The resource-rich African region has attracted the interest of companies from China, India, South Africa, and other developing countries.[13] Chinese investments in nonoil mining

Table 4.3 Selected southern multinationals in the oil-and-gas sector, 2004

Corporation (home country)	Ownership	Total assets in 2004 ($ billions)	Areas of activity
CNPC (China)	State	110.6	Canada, Ecuador, Kazakhstan, Mauritania, Myanmar, Sudan, R. B. de Venezuela
Indian Oil Corp.	State	10.9	Islamic Rep. of Iran, Libya
Lukoil (Russian Federation)	Private	29.8	Iraq, Romania, Ukraine, Bulgaria, Canada, Uzbekistan
PDVSA (R. B. de Venezuela)	State	13.4	Argentina, Belgium, Brazil, Chile, Germany, Paraguay, United States (Citgo)
PEMEX (Mexico)	State	84.1	Argentina
Petrobras (Brazil)	State	19.4	Libya, Mexico, Nigeria, Tanzania
Petro China (China)	State	58.8	Nigeria, Sudan, R. B. de Venezuela
Petronas (Malaysia)	State	53.5	Cambodia, Chad, Islamic Rep. of Iran, Myanmar, Sudan, Turkmenistan
Saudi Aramco (Saudi Arabia)	State		Canada, China, United States

Sources: UNCTAD, ECLAC, and Oil & Gas Journal Special Report 2001, company annual reports, company Web sites.

projects have been growing in Latin America, and several Russian companies have investments in Central Asia and the Middle East (Vahtra and Liuhto 2004).[14]

Recent bilateral and regional initiatives among developing countries are centered on cooperation in resource-seeking projects, including a proposal to create a regional state-owned energy company in Latin America; joint-venture projects involving India, Bangladesh, Myanmar, and Thailand; China's agreements with Argentina and Brazil to cooperate in mining, oil, and infrastructure projects (UNCTAD 2005b); and partnerships between China and India for the acquisition of energy assets.

Manufacturing also receives considerable South–South FDI flows, although projects tend to be smaller than the large privatization and M&A deals in services and the extractive industries. Developing-country multinationals have invested in efficiency-seeking activities abroad following erosion in their competitiveness, at home and in export markets, because of currency appreciation, increased labor costs, or other causes (Mirza 2000). In many middle-income countries, higher living standards are reflected in increased labor costs.[15] Developing-country manufacturing firms also invest abroad to sell into the target markets or to access other markets, sometimes through special arrangements. Examples include the investments in India and Thailand of Chinese white goods producer Haier, and the plants in China, Egypt, India, and Ethiopia of Russian automobile manufacturer UralAZ plants (Vahtra and Liuhto 2004). Special arrangements play an important role in attracting South–South FDI to low-income countries. Chinese, Indian, Malaysian, and Sri Lankan textile companies have investments in Africa to export garments to U.S. and European markets through free trade agreements. Some developing-country firms are investing in the manufacture of generic drugs in Africa because WTO provides that patents may be broken in cases of national emergency. A few Indian and Chinese companies are introducing anti-malarial and AIDS drugs under such arrangements (Goldstein and others 2006).[16]

In some cases, FDI from high-income countries has facilitated South–South flows in the manufacturing sector. For example, Mexican Bimbo, a food producer, has invested abroad since becoming McDonalds' exclusive supplier in Latin America and more recently in Europe.

State-owned and small and medium enterprises are investing abroad

State-owned enterprises (SOE) in extractive industries and infrastructure are a considerable source of South–South FDI flows.[17] The role of SOEs in overseas investments is significant in China, where 43 percent of outward FDI stock in 2003 was held by SOEs (Giroud 2005). This indicates that a considerable portion of South–South FDI may be driven not only by economic but also by political and strategic factors.[18] SOEs usually have an advantage over privately owned firms, since they enjoy better financing terms when funded by state-owned banks. In some cases, governments negotiate packages of investment deals that may give additional bargaining power to SOEs.[19]

Small and medium enterprises (SMEs) also provide a significant amount of investment in other developing countries.[20] In India, for example, SMEs accounted for 26 percent of overseas projects (6.7 percent of the value) in manufacturing and 41.1 percent (47.1 percent of the value) in the software industry (Pradhan 2005). Almost three-fourths of companies investing abroad in Poland and Estonia, and about one-third in the Czech Republic and in Hungary, are SMEs (Sevtlicic and Rojec 2003).

Southern multinationals are supported by government incentives

In addition to easing restrictions on capital outflows, some developing-country governments have provided fiscal and other incentives for outward investment, particularly South–South FDI. China's Export-Import Bank, for example, provides loans for investments in resource development and infrastructure, as well as for projects that facilitate trade. If the investment is in an aid-receiving country, firms can receive preferential loans under Chinese aid programs or projects (UNCTAD 2005b). Malaysia supports special deals for FDI outflows to countries such as India, the Philippines, Tanzania, and Vietnam (Mirza 2000). The Thai government promotes Thai firms' involvement in infrastructure projects in selected developing countries in the region (UNCTAD 2005b).

Some regional arrangements, such as SADC, ASEAN, MERCOSUR, and the Andean Community offer various incentives for outward investment within the region, including lower tax and tariff rates and easier profit repatriation. Some members of the regions maintain bilateral investment agreements and double-taxation treaties.

Whether these incentives encourage or direct FDI outflows, and at what fiscal cost, is unclear. UNCTAD (1998) found that incentives had a positive, but minimal, effect. On the other hand, Hallward-Dreimeier (2003), using only OECD countries, and Tobin and Rose-Ackerman (2005), using a larger sample of countries, found that incentives can further increase FDI flows in countries only where the environment for FDI is already strong. Banga (2003) shows that India's fiscal incentives and lower tariff rates attracted investors from developing countries only; the removal of restrictions was necessary to attract investments from developed countries. Interviews with Malaysian investors suggest that tax and fiscal incentives were not important (UNCTAD 2005a). In some cases, incentives simply generate so-called round-tripping (capital outflows to finance investment back in the home country). For example, India's advantageous tax treaty with Mauritius encourages many Indian investors to incorporate in Mauritius in order to benefit from this tax treatment (Shah and Patnaik 2005).

Developing-country multinationals may enjoy some advantages over industrial-country firms when investing in developing countries

Compared to their northern counterparts, developing-country multinationals may enjoy some advantages when investing in developing countries. Companies with a significant regional presence often benefit from well-established distribution networks. Because of their experience in their home markets, they are often in a position to use locally available inputs more efficiently. And some developing-country firms are more familiar than northern firms with lower-cost production processes that are appropriate for developing-country markets. For example, India's Tata Group produces a car that is significantly less expensive than those of the major automobile companies.[21] While the car lacks some of the qualities desired by industrial-country consumers, it has found a ready market in India and several other developing countries. Finally, developing-country firms may also use technologies that are better suited to conditions in developing countries. For example, in Vietnam, TVs made by China's TCL are the most popular brand, as their powerful color TV receivers provide clear reception even in remote areas (Yi 2004).

Geographical proximity and cultural similarities can make coordination of foreign operations more effective (IMF–World Bank 2005; UNCTAD 2005b). Developing-country firms may have a comparative advantage over companies from developed countries in doing business in challenging economic and political conditions because of their experience in their home economies (Claessens and Van Horen 2006). This sort of advantage brought higher rates of return for northern investors that partnered with Chilean companies to invest in Latin America than for those that invested alone (De Sol 2005). The relative success in Uganda of MTN (the South African telecommunications company), compared with its competitors from developed countries, was traceable to its in-house expertise in managing pertinent economic and political risks (Goldstein 2003).

Developing-country firms may also be more willing to assume the risks of postconflict and other politically difficult situations (Sull and Escobari 2004). For example, Chinese companies (not all of them SOEs) are the only foreigners that have invested in Sierra Leone since the end of the civil war. Egypt's Orascam is the only foreign telecom company operating in Iraq (EIU 2005).

Institutional, financial, and operational impediments constrain FDI from developing countries

Despite these advantages, developing-country firms face institutional procedures, financial restrictions, and operational problems in their home countries that can make it difficult for them to invest abroad.

Institutional procedures. Many developing countries still have various levels of capital controls, and firms may be subject to regulatory burdens to obtain access to foreign exchange. For example, in addition to several capital-control procedures, China's regulations require its multinationals (state-owned or private) to submit a certificate of establishment of the firm in China, contracts and agreements relating to the overseas project, various elements of a project feasibility study, assessments of the project made by the Chinese embassy in the host country, and audited financial reports and bank statements—all before proceeding with an overseas investment (FIAS 2005). Such requirements have increased costs and in some cases prevented SMEs from investing abroad, while some larger firms have used off-shore platforms for their foreign investments. For example, many Chinese companies use their Hong Kong affiliates as a base from which to expand overseas (UNCTAD 2003).

Developing countries often lack the institutional infrastructure needed to provide foreign investors with the support services that their counterparts in developed countries take for granted. Access to knowledgeable consulting firms, business associations, banks, and other sources of information about overseas markets and practices is more difficult to obtain in most parts of the developing world. Unlike in developed economies, services that promote outward investment are nonexistent or in their infancy in most developing countries. These handicaps have affected the development and operations of overseas projects, particularly for companies relatively new to outward FDI.

Financial restrictions. Developing-country firms, particularly SMEs, face more severe financial constraints than do their industrial-country counterparts, because local financial markets are less developed. And access to international financial markets is limited and costly for many of these firms, since they carry the sovereign risk of the home country in addition to their company risks (IMF–World Bank 2005). These challenges sometimes lead large and successful developing-country multinationals to migrate to industrial countries. For example, South African Brewery moved its headquarters to Britain in 2001 to improve its risk rating and position itself for global expansion. India's Ispat Corporation moved to the Netherlands for similar reasons.

Operational challenges. Developing-country firms that invest abroad face operational issues that vary with the firm's level of experience as a foreign investor and to some extent with the business environment in the firm's home country. For example, with limited experience in FDI, some Chinese investors find it difficult to formulate projects that fit in with the culture, market characteristics, and regulatory environment of foreign countries (FIAS 2005). Some developing-country multinationals may have overbid for large assets due to lack of experience (IMF–World Bank 2005; *Financial Times* 2004). This is not an unusual phenomenon: Japanese firms experienced similar challenges when they started to venture abroad in the late 1980s (Goldstein forthcoming). The World Bank Group has made efforts to assist developing-country multinationals in overcoming the institutional, financial, and operational challenges they face (box 4.3).

South–South FDI may generate important benefits for developing countries

The emergence of the South as a substantial source of FDI for developing countries may have significant implications for economic development. First, South–South FDI represents an opportunity for low-income countries. Except in the extractive sector, most northern multinationals are unlikely to invest in small markets, as market size is a major determinant of North–South FDI (Levy-Yeyati, Ugo, and Stein 2002; Stein and Daude 2001). In contrast, southern multinationals tend to invest in neighboring developing countries with a similar or lower level of development than their home country (World Bank 2005a). South–South FDI flows, however small, are significant for many poor countries, particularly those that are close to major investors. For example, India (in hotels and

---

Box 4.3 The World Bank Group and South–South flows

The World Bank Group, particularly the International Finance Corporation, has several programs to help developing-country multinationals. IFC's Foreign Investment Advisory Service (FIAS) is surveying firms and assessing the need for technical assistance to governments to enhance the investment climate as it affects outward FDI. The Multilateral Investment Guarantee Agency (MIGA) supports the efforts of local export-credit agencies to serve emerging South-South investors through coinsurance and reinsurance arrangements. In addition, MIGA's recently launched Small Investment Program—which offers a streamlined insurance package and underwriting process—is designed to increase South-South investment.

manufacturing) and China (in manufacturing) account for more than half of FDI in Nepal. Most FDI in Mongolia comes from China and the Russian Federation. An Indian company is securing approval for a $2.5 billion investment project in Bangladesh, which will be the largest foreign investment in the country. Moreover, low-income countries receive almost one-third of their banking sector FDI from other developing countries (see the section on banking in this chapter).

Second, in some cases, developing countries may see greater positive spillovers from FDI originating in developing countries than from investments originating in industrial countries.[22] To the extent that developing-country firms provide technologies that are more suitable for other developing countries (compared with more sophisticated technologies used by industrial-country firms), developing countries may be in a better position to absorb them. Baldwin and Winters (2004) find that a country's absorption capacity is greater with a smaller technological gap between the foreign firm and domestic firms. Kabelwa (2004) finds that narrower technological gaps between developing-country multinationals and host economies, compared with their industrial-country counterparts, foster positive spillovers. Schiff and others (2002) found that the extent of spillovers from participation in trade (as opposed to FDI) depends on the sector: companies in low R&D-intensive industries benefit more from trading with other developing-country firms than with firms from industrial countries, while companies in high R&D industries benefit more from trading with firms from industrial countries. However, the importance of this advantage, which is most significant in manufacturing, is unclear, as South-South FDI is heavily concentrated in extractive industries and infrastructure, where such spillovers are limited.

South–South FDI is not always more beneficial than North–South FDI. Over the years, many northern multinationals have participated in initiatives to improve the transparency of their foreign operations, as well as the environmental and labor standards observed in those operations.[23] Such initiatives are less likely to have been implemented by southern companies, which also may have low environmental and labor standards (Goldstein forthcoming; IMF–World Bank 2005). That said, compliance with corporate governance standards by

developing countries is increasing, although significant regional and sectoral variations in compliance remain (OECD 2005b). Ultimately, of course, it is the host country's responsibility to improve its business environment and regulatory system to realize the development potential of FDI.

Outward investment (including to high-income countries) may also generate benefits to the investing economy through increased competitiveness and exports. Surveys report that direct presence in foreign markets has enabled many Southern firms to increase their competitiveness and to respond better to consumer demand.[24] Geographic risk diversification and market access can be crucial for some southern firms that are faced with volatile home markets.

South–South banking

Traditionally, banks have followed their clients overseas. Thus the growing importance of developing-country firms in overseas trade and investment has led to an expansion of cross-border activities by developing-country banks, both through lending and through investment carried out by branches and subsidiaries. As is the case with other financial flows to developing countries, foreign bank lending is dominated by industrial-country banks. However, developing-country banks are playing a growing and already important role, especially in low-income countries. Because they are willing to penetrate markets where banks from industrial countries are reluctant to go, these banks may provide an important new source of external finance for low-income countries.

The rise in South–South cross-border banking is driven by several factors
The recent increase in banks' cross-border activities has come in response to global economic trends, liberalization of the financial sector in many developing countries, and advances in technology.

Economic trends. The general expansion of syndicated lending to developing countries and the growing importance of developing-country lenders in such lending reflect a favorable external financing environment characterized by ample global liquidity, as well as improved economic conditions and greater openness to trade and capital flows in many developing countries. As South–South trade and FDI have expanded, many banks have followed their clients. FDI in banking is correlated with bilateral trade and FDI between source and host countries (Grosse and Goldberg 1991; Brealey and Kaplanis 1996; Williams 1998; Yamori 1998). Preferential trade agreements, which have burgeoned in number and scope since the 1990s (WTO 2003), are opening new opportunities for banks to provide trade finance. For example, Banco de Chile, the country's second-largest bank in terms of assets, recently opened a branch in Beijing—reportedly to position itself to benefit from a new free-trade accord between the two countries (*Latin Finance* 2005). A number of Central American banks (e.g., Panama's Banistmo, El Salvador's Banco Cuscatlan) are seeking growth opportunities in other Central American retail financial markets to capitalize on regional trade integration and the recently concluded Central American Free Trade Agreement (CAFTA). Standard Bank of South Africa has established a sizable presence in southern and eastern Africa, reflecting South Africa's increased investment in and trade with the region.

Migration. Banks have expanded cross-border activities to serve growing numbers of expatriates. For example, Pakistan's Habib Bank has targeted a well-established customer base of expatriates through its branch network in South Asia.

Financial sector liberalization. The liberalization of developing countries' banking sectors and the sale of state-owned banks have increased opportunities for cross-border lending and investment by developing-country banks. Rules governing cross-border lending and the establishment of branches and subsidiaries by foreign banks have been eased—in many cases under the impetus of WTO commitments, notably in the Asia-Pacific region (Capital Intelligence and EIU, various issues).

Technology. Advances in telecommunications and information technology are enabling banks and other financial institutions—including those based in developing countries—to better manage cross-border activities. Banks based in Asia-Pacific, the Middle East, and elsewhere have been investing heavily in electronic delivery systems and other technologies to enhance their ability to offer a wider array of financial services at a distance from headquarters.[25] Sri Lanka's Commercial Bank of Ceylon and Hungary's OTP Bank, among others, have boosted their investment in technol-

ogy to support a strategy of greater focus on serving SMEs and retail credit clients.

The several motives behind the expansion of South–South banking can be illustrated by the experience of the State Bank of India (SBI) and ICICI Bank, India's largest privately owned bank. Both are undertaking overseas expansions in Asia, Africa, and the Middle East to tap retail credit clients, to facilitate increasing trade and investment flows between India and other countries, to provide foreign currency–denominated loans to the overseas affiliates of Indian companies, and to provide remittance and retail credit services for Indian expatriates (Capital Intelligence, various issues; State Bank of India 2005; and ICICI Bank 2005).

South–South bank lending has grown
There are two sources of data on developing countries' foreign bank lending (see annex 1 for data sources and definitions). The Bank for International Settlements (BIS) in Basel publishes data on the foreign lending of banks from a few developing countries. Dealogic Loanware reports data on syndicated loan transactions, which are loans arranged by a group of banks (referred to as a syndicate).

Syndicated lending. Most syndicated loans to developing countries are made by groups of banks in high-income countries. In the past 20 years, however, the volume of syndicated lending from developing countries and the number of banks participating in syndicates have grown sharply. South–South syndicated flows are estimated to have increased from $0.7 billion in 1985 to $6.2 billion in 2005, although the data have shown substantial variability across years and countries.[26] The number of developing countries receiving such flows also has grown, from 19 in 1985 to 41 in 2005.[27]

The rise in South–South syndicated lending partly reflects the overall rise in syndicated lending to developing countries from all sources, which increased by almost the same amount from 1985 to 2005. Indeed, the share of South–South lending in total developing-country borrowing from the syndicated loan market equaled 3 percent in 1985 during the debt crisis. However, once lending from industrial countries picked up, the share of South–South lending fell to 1 percent in 1995, but then rose to 3.4 percent in 2005 (table 4.4). Borrowers in Europe and Central Asia and the Middle East and North Africa sourced the largest portion

Table 4.4 South–South cross-border syndicated lending, 1985–2005
$ millions

Borrower's region of domicile	1985	1995	2004	2005
Eastern Europe & Central Asia	234.4	31.2	1,420.0	2,719.7
Middle East & North Africa	326.8	109.1	694.2	1,120.9
Sub-Saharan Africa	8.7	130.0	986.8	364.0
South Asia	15.0	12.9	349.7	463.8
East Asia & Pacific	56.4	431.6	470.5	872.0
Latin America & Caribbean	54.2	165.1	301.7	686.1
Total	695.5	879.9	4,222.9	6,226.5
Total syndicated lending to developing-country borrowers	22,895.6	91,943.2	112,238.2	184,034.7
South–South share in syndicated lending to developing countries	3.0	1.0	3.8	3.4

Source: World Bank staff estimates based on loan syndicate transactions reported in Dealogic Loanware dataset.

of their syndicated loans from nonlocal developing-country banks (4.2 percent overall for both regions), while borrowers in Latin America continued to source the smallest portion (about 1.8 percent overall).

The growing participation of developing-country banks in syndicated lending also reflects the increasing size and sophistication of those banks. As syndicates typically are unwilling to include banks that are relatively unknown or unreliable, the growing role of developing-country banks in syndicates is one indication of their arrival as major players in global finance. For many banks, participation in recent South–South syndicated loans has been one element in a strategy of expansion into other developing countries through loans, acquisitions, and greenfield investments.[28]

Despite the growth of South–South lending, some aspects of developing countries' participation have changed little over the years. Participation by local banks in syndicated loan transactions remains strong.[29] Also, banks domiciled in developing countries tend not to be the lead arrangers or major participants in a syndicate, given their relative capital constraints compared with major industrial-country banks. Nevertheless, nonlocal developing-country banks participated in a mandated lead arranger role in nearly one-quarter of all South–South cross-border syndicated loan transactions in 2005 (49 of 206 transactions).[30] South Africa's Standard Bank was particularly active, as a mandated lead arranger for 28 transactions in 2005.

The regional distribution of South–South syndicated lending flows as compared with syndicated lending flows to developing countries from all sources was broadly similar last year. Borrowers in

Eastern Europe and Central Asia attracted the highest share from both source groupings (35 percent and 44 percent, respectively), while borrowers in Sub-Saharan Africa attracted the lowest share (6 percent) from both source groupings. Notably, East Asia and Pacific attracted a much smaller share in 2005 from both source groupings (14 percent and 17 percent, respectively) compared with a decade earlier, just a few years ahead of the financial crisis. In 1995, East Asia and Pacific received nearly half of syndicated lending flows destined for developing countries—sourced both on a cross-border South–South basis and from all lending sources worldwide The share of Eastern Europe and Central Asia, in particular, was significantly smaller (at just 4 percent and 7 percent, respectively).

Cross-border lending reported to the Bank for International Settlements (BIS). Cross-border lending by banks located in developing countries that report to the BIS (that is, countries with significant cross-border lending) has increased significantly, reaching $94 billion in 2005 (figure 4.4).[31] While in 1999 no developing country reported to the BIS, by 2005 six developing countries (Brazil, Chile, India, Mexico, Panama, and Turkey) were reporting data; more are expected to follow soon. About 85 percent of the cross-border lending was to the banking sector (the average across all countries was 65 percent), indicating that a substantial share of this lending represents international transactions between affiliates of the same bank.

The above data indicate the growing importance of certain developing countries as banking centers from which domestic and foreign banks operate, but they capture external positions in all countries (including high-income countries). Data

Figure 4.4 Cross-border lending to all countries by banks in developing countries, 2000–5

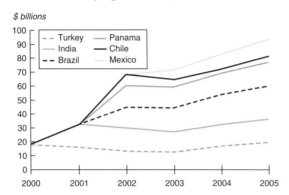

Source: Bank for International Settlements.
Note: Yearly data are averages based on quarterly data.

from countries that report the destination of their foreign claims (so far only Brazil, Chile, Mexico, and Panama) indicate that the South–South component is growing.[32] For example, foreign claims on developing countries reported by Brazilian banks rose from $1 billion in the fourth quarter of 2002 to $2 billion in the third quarter of 2003, while Chilean banks' foreign claims on developing countries rose from $176 million to $891 million in the same period. The increase in South–South foreign claims by banks from Panama rose only by 10 percent, and foreign claims on developing countries by Mexican banks decreased in the last two years. However, on average the increase of South–South foreign claims reported by these four countries has been more significant than the 58 percent rise in total North–South foreign claims (from all high-income to all developing countries).

South–South bank ownership is significant

Banks from 40 developing countries (most of them middle-income) hold 5 percent of the $944 billion dollars in foreign bank assets in developing countries (based on Bankscope data; see annex 1).[33] Excluding Panama (an important offshore center), the biggest investors are banks in South Africa, Malaysia, and Hungary. The pattern of ownership differs significantly by region. In South Asia, 20 percent of foreign bank assets are held by banks in other developing countries.[34] In Europe and Central Asia the same share is just 2 percent (table 4.5).[35] While these data indicate that participation by developing-country banks is significant, banks from high-income countries still account for 95 percent of total foreign bank assets in developing countries. Moreover, all foreign banks account for only 16 percent of total banking sector assets in developing countries. South–South bank ownership thus accounts for less than 1 percent of total bank assets in developing countries. Northern foreign banks in developing countries—with median assets of $361 million—tend to be larger than southern foreign banks—with median assets of $92 million. Southern bank participation is more important in terms of the number of banks.

South–South banking increases opportunities for low-income countries

Banks from industrialized countries and developing countries alike tend to invest in countries with which they have strong trade linkages, that share a common language and legal system, and that are nearby. But because developing-country banks have more experience doing business in a challeng-

Table 4.5 Source of foreign bank assets, by region
% of foreign bank assets in host region owned by banks in other regions

Host region	Source region							
	East Asia & Pacific	Europe & Central Asia	Latin America & Caribbean	Middle East & North Africa	South Asia	Sub-Saharan Africa	High-income countries	Total
East Asia & Pacific	6.39	..	..	..	..	..	93.57	100
Europe & Central Asia	..	1.84	..	0.01	..	0.03	98.11	100
Latin America & Caribbean	..	..	4.78	..	..	..	95.26	100
Middle East & North Africa	..	..	..	8.91	..	..	91.19	100
South Asia	..	..	..	..	0.74	19.51	79.83	100
Sub-Saharan Africa	0.07	0.03	0.02	0.29	1.99	14.12	83.54	100

Source: World Bank Staff estimates based on Bankscope.
Note: Foreign assets are averages over the 2000–4 period. A foreign bank is defined to have at least 50 percent foreign ownership as of December 2005.
.. = Negligible.

ing economic environment, they have a comparative advantage over industrialized-country banks when entering low-income countries (box 4.4). As a result, low-income countries, which have problems attracting bank lending from industrial country banks, are benefiting disproportionately from the increased supply of banking services from other developing countries.

Cross-border investment by developing-country banks is more significant in low-income countries (27 percent of foreign bank assets and 47 percent of the number of foreign banks) than in middle-income countries (4 percent of foreign assets and 22 percent of foreign banks) (figure 4.5). The correlation between income level and the share of banks from developing countries in foreign bank assets is −0.37, which is statistically significant. In addition, low-income countries are also important in South–South syndicated lending; their share increased from 3 percent ($24 million) in 1985 to 17 percent ($1 billion) in 2005, although the vast majority of this latter amount was concentrated in a few countries in East and South Asia (notably, India).

South–South banking takes place largely within the region

Foreign investment and lending by developing-country banks is regionally concentrated. In East Asia and the Pacific, Europe and Central Asia, and the Middle East and North Africa, practically all developing-country foreign banks are from the same region (table 4.5). In Sub-Saharan Africa, banks from other regions account for only 14 percent of developing-country foreign banks. By contrast, almost all developing-country foreign banks in South Asia are from Sub-Saharan Africa. However, these data reflect ownership by branches and holding companies of banks from OECD countries based in Mauritius (an offshore banking center) that own Indian banks.

Intraregional transactions are becoming less dominant in South–South cross-border syndicated lending. In 2005, 52 percent of this lending was to borrowers in the same region as the lenders, down from 66 percent in 1985.[36] Intraregional lending remained particularly important in East Asia (where 97 percent of South–South cross-border loans are intraregional) and Latin America (83 percent) in 2005. Cross-regional South–South lending

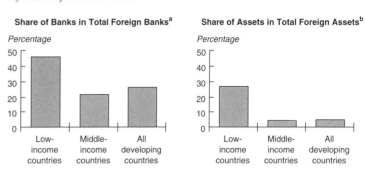

Figure 4.5 South–South foreign bank entry in developing countries, by country income level

Share of Banks in Total Foreign Banks[a]

Percentage

Share of Assets in Total Foreign Assets[b]

Percentage

Source: World Bank Staff estimates based on Bankscope.
Note: "Southern foreign banks" are those banks headquartered in a developing country. A foreign bank is one that had at least 50 percent foreign ownership as of December 2005.
a. Number of southern foreign banks as a percentage of all foreign banks (left panel).
b. Bank assets held by southern foreign banks as a percentage of total foreign assets, averaged over 2000–4 (right panel).

was particularly important in India (where 76 percent of South–South lending was cross-regional), Kazakhstan (83 percent), and the Russian Federation (77 percent). Important motivations for cross-regional South–South bank lending include trade financing (which accounted for the vast majority of cross-regional loans in 2005) and the desire to serve expatriates. In addition to these purposes, major uses of intraregional loans were the financing of acquisitions and other expansion plans (particularly in East Asia) and infrastructural development projects in power, telecommunications, and transport (in both East Asia and Latin America).

The dominance of intraregional cross-border banking in part reflects the importance of intraregional trade and FDI flows (discussed earlier) and the priority being given to regional cooperation and integration in policy agendas. In addition, geographic proximity often implies a common cultural heritage, language, or ethnic ties, making it easier for banks to assume more risk.

Just as local banks have an advantage over foreign banks due to their greater knowledge of local conditions and their ability to screen and monitor local borrowers (Nini 2004), foreign banks from within the same geographic region may have an advantage over other nonlocal lenders. This greater familiarity means that banks from the same region can lend more than nonregional banks and are more likely to expand beyond the traditional focus on corporate banking

Box 4.4 Determinants of South–South foreign bank entry

The economic literature on the determinants of foreign bank entry has not distinguished between foreign ownership by banks from industrial countries and developing countries. (see, for example, Buch and DeLong 2004; Focarelli and Pozzolo 2000; and Galindo, Micco, and Serra 2003). However, country studies and anecdotal evidence suggest that industrial-country banks invest in developing countries for different reasons than do developing-country banks. To address this issue, we estimated a model of decisions by foreign banks to enter developing-country markets. We measure foreign bank penetration, the dependent variable, in terms of the level of total assets owned by foreigners. The model is explained in detail in annex 3.

The results (see table) reveal some important similarities and differences between the determinants of foreign bank investment in developing countries by industrial-country and developing-country banks:

- FDI by both industrial-country and developing-country banks is strongly related to bilateral trade flows, one indicator of integration between source and host countries. Essentially, banks tend to follow their customers.
- Colonial ties are an important explanation of foreign bank penetration by industrial-country banks, but less so for developing-country banks.
- A common language, which reduces the cost of foreign banking, is a significant determinant of foreign bank entry for both industrial- and developing-country banks.
- Distance is negatively related to foreign bank entry, but the effect appears to be smaller for banks from developing countries than for banks from industrial countries.
- After controlling for distance, a common border is not a significant determinant of foreign bank entry.
- Banks from industrial countries tend to go to large developing countries, while banks from developing countries tend to enter the smaller developing countries. In addition, the depth of the financial sector is negatively correlated with foreign ownership by industrial-country banks, but positively with ownership by developing-country banks
- Banks from industrial and developing countries are equally likely to be deterred from entering a developing country with a different legal system.

Determinants of foreign bank entry: northern versus southern foreign banks

	Northern bank	Southern bank
Colonial linkages	0.757*	0.699*
Border	0.297	0.297
Common language	0.338*	0.338*
Distance	−0.153*	−0.123*
Trade	0.014*	0.014*
GDP	0.040*	−0.009*
Financial sector depth	−0.048*	0.008*
Different legal system	−0.045*	−0.045*
Quality institutions	0.006	−0.060*
Observations	5,532	

Source: World Bank staff calculations.
Note: Mean of dependent variable = 0.59
* = significant at level of at least 10 percent.

- After controlling for all of the above determinants of FDI, the quality of institutions does not appear to influence the decision by an industrial-country bank to enter a developing country. However, banks from developing countries are more likely to enter developing countries with weak institutions. This result seems to indicate that banks from developing countries, being more familiar with working in domestic environments where institutional development is low, are more suited to investing in such markets.

The coefficients in the table express the marginal effects of the impact of the respective variable on foreign ownership by northern and southern banks. The marginal effects capture the combined effect of the impact of the explanatory variable on the probability of entering the host country and on the amount of FDI.

Overall, the model provides support for the conclusions in the literature that FDI in foreign banking is strongly related to economic integration, common language, and proximity; this holds true for both industrial and developing-country banks. More interestingly, it appears that developing-country banks are more likely to invest in small developing countries with weak institutions, where industrial country banks are reluctant to go. These results indicate that FDI decisions are not so much influenced by the absolute amount of risk faced by firms, but rather by a given firm's ability to bear that risk better than other investors.

For a more detailed discussion, see Van Horen (2006).

to sectors that require new and different sources of information. For example, in some developing countries, foreign banks from the same region have given more emphasis to providing retail financial services (mortgages, consumer loans, debt and credit card services, and remittance services for expatriates) and loans to SMEs.[37]

Developing-country banks are not a significantly greater source of poor asset quality or management

Investments in the banking sector of developing countries by banks from other developing countries could create instability if those banks were poorly managed or if their asset quality were low. As with industrial-country banks, however, the record of entry into developing-country financial systems by banks from other developing countries is mixed. For example, Ecobank, a successful private sector banking group based in 13 countries in West and Central Africa, has strengthened the banks it has taken over. Standbic, a South African bank, greatly improved the soundness and efficiency of the United Commercial Bank of Uganda.[38] By contrast, several branches of the Meridian Bank of Zambia were liquidated after a major run on its deposits (Rakner, van de Walle,

and Mulaisho 1999). The directors of the bank were prosecuted for criminal charges for allegedly having received deposits while knowing that the bank was insolvent.[39]

The available data, however, do not indicate that, on average, developing-country banks investing in low-income developing countries are significantly weaker than industrial-country banks that do the same. The asset quality of developing-country banks in these countries is lower than that of banks from high-income countries, but the differences are not statistically significant (table 4.6). Similarly, indicators of efficiency and operational performance in low-income countries are slightly better for northern banks, but not by enough to be statistically significant. In middle-income countries there is some indication that banks from high-income countries seem to outperform developing-country banks, both in asset quality and in efficiency and operational performance. However, since penetration of the banking sector by developing-country banks is especially prevalent in low-income countries, the risks posed by southern foreign banks to their host countries because of possible poor capitalization or management are not significantly greater than similar risks posed by northern banks.

Table 4.6 Performance indicators for northern and southern foreign banks, selected aggregates, 2000–4
Ratios in percentages

		Asset quality		Efficiency and operational performance				Memo
		Loan loss reserves/ gross loans	Loan loss provision/net interest revenue	Net interest margin	Return on average assets	Cost-to-income ratio	Net income/ total assets	No. of countries (banks)
Low-income countries	North foreign	7.05	15.54	9.47	1.88	65.80	1.77	30 (74)
	South foreign	6.92	26.11	8.94	0.84	90.90	0.77	30 (63)
Middle-income countries	North foreign	**6.42**	27.03	6.38	**1.14**	73.73	0.81	53 (439)
	South foreign	**11.38**	49.12	7.82	**−0.35**	76.04	0.17	53 (87)
All countries	North foreign	**6.50**	25.43	6.86	**1.25**	72.64	0.94	83 (513)
	South foreign	**9.46**	39.54	8.30	**0.16**	82.26	0.42	83 (150)

Source: World Bank staff estimates based on Bankscope.
Note: Ratios are calculated for each bank in each country and then averaged for North and South foreign banks separately within an income level. Host and source countries that are offshore banking centers are excluded from the sample.
Pairs of entries that are significantly different from each other at the 10% level of significance are shown in bold.
The ratio of loan-loss reserves to gross loans indicates how much of the total portfolio has been provided for but not charged off. Given a similar charge-off policy, the higher the ratio, the poorer the quality of the loan portfolio. Loan-loss provision over net interest revenue is the relationship between provisions in the profit-and-loss account and interest income over the same period. This ratio should be as low as possible. Net interest margin is the ratio of net interest income to earning assets. The higher this figure, the cheaper the funding or the higher the margin the bank is commanding. Higher margins are desirable as long as asset quality is maintained. Return on average assets looks at the returns generated from the assets financed by the bank. The cost-to-income ratio measures the overheads and costs of running the bank as percentage of income generated before provisions. It is a measure of efficiency, although if the lending margins in a particular country are very high then the ratio will improve as a result. Net income to total assets shows the profitability of the bank.

South–South banking can strengthen domestic financial services but may entail some risks

Even if foreign bank entry does not generate a capital inflow (because subsidiaries may generate their funds locally), it can improve the quality and availability of domestic financial services. Increased competitive pressure can lead to stronger credit growth, more aggressive provisioning behavior, and higher loss-absorption capacity—all of which can help stabilize domestic banking systems (Crystal, Dages, and Goldberg 2001). Managerial and technology spillovers may benefit domestic banks, as well. Foreign banks also can help stimulate the development of the underlying supervisory and legal system by pressuring host-country governments to improve institutions, thereby enhancing the country's access to the international capital market (see, for example, Levine 1996). Claessens, Demirguc-Kunt, and Huizinga (2001) find that greater presence of foreign banks (from high-income countries) is associated with reductions in profitability, lower noninterest income, and lower overall expenses of domestic banks. South–South foreign banking is too recent a phenomenon to permit a judgment about whether entry by banks from developing countries produces the same effects. It is possible that developing-country banks are less sophisticated in technology and banking practices, so that they would not generate the same degree of competition and hence not lead to the same efficiency gains. Alternatively, as argued elsewhere in this chapter, host countries may find it easier to adapt technology from other developing countries, thus increasing spillovers. In the absence of empirical work, one can only speculate on which effect may be more important.

South–South banking has the potential to direct capital away from the source country, thus reducing the supply of credit available to market participants that are already credit deprived. This can happen when total lending by participating banks is constrained by their available capital or the availability of skilled staff (as opposed to being constrained by the lack of investment opportunities in the domestic market). As capital is scarce in most developing countries, it is widely presumed that domestic lending is constrained by capital availability, at least in countries where the investment climate is adequate to support increased economic activity. The fact is, however, that in some countries the poor investment climate severely reduces the availability of profitable investment opportunities; in such cases banks' cross-border lending may not reduce the effective supply of domestic credit.

Entry by developing-country foreign banks may increase credit volatility. In general, foreign banks increase credit volatility if they quickly decrease their exposure to the country when domestic conditions deteriorate (Caballero 2002) or reduce their lending when deteriorating economic conditions in their home country reduce their capital. On the other hand, foreign banks may reduce credit volatility because they are less reliant on erratic local deposits—their reputation for soundness may attract local deposits during a credit crisis, thus reducing outflows from the domestic financial system.

Overall, developing-country banks may make a greater contribution to instability than industrial-country banks. Developing-country banks are more likely to be subject to financial crises in their home country than are industrial-country banks, and thus are more likely to reduce credit due to sharp changes in their capital. For example, banks from Latin America are more likely to react with a reduction in credit when they experience a reduction in real deposits than are banks from developed countries (IDB 2002). Furthermore, the less secure reputations of developing-country banks indicate that they may play a less important role in attracting local deposits during a domestic credit crisis.

Developing-country stock exchanges
Emerging trends in regional versus international integration

A feature common to many nations' efforts to develop their financial sectors over the past several decades has been the establishment of a national stock exchange—or the expansion of an existing one. It has been argued that such a development can be an important step toward a modern, well-functioning financial sector—as a means of increasing and improving the allocation of savings and investments.[40] Many international organizations, including the World Bank, have supported these efforts (IFC 1991). As a result, there are currently some 85 stock exchanges operating in some

75 developing countries.[41] Many of the exchanges have very low ratios of market capitalization to GDP and are characterized by lack of depth (low turnover), inadequate transparency, operational inefficiency, and poor regulation, calling into question the notion that they contribute to efficient resource mobilization and allocation.[42] Consequently, in the past several years, there has been growing interest in the possible advantages of consolidating national stock exchanges in developing countries and so addressing the impediments of small size, illiquidity, and inadequate market infrastructure (table 4.7).

Limited progress toward regional integration, but some positive signs

Stock exchanges across developing regions have introduced various initiatives over the past decade to forge closer regional links both intraregionally and, in some cases, extraregionally. Thus far, however, actual progress toward merging or integrating stock exchanges among developing countries has been limited.

Many developing-country capital markets remain more integrated with the major international financial markets than with other developing countries. In part, this is due to a lack of intraregional harmonization of tax, accounting, disclosure, and other stock-market listing and trading regulations and procedures. In Asia, for example, stock markets remain fragmented and poorly integrated, and cross-border listings between developing-country exchanges remain uncommon.[43] Overseas listings by companies domiciled in Asian developing economies are still more likely to take place via depositary receipt and other issues on developed-country exchanges, particularly in Hong Kong (China), Singapore, Japan, New York, London, and, increasingly for South Asian firms in recent years, Luxembourg.[44] Cross-border listings by firms in southern Africa on the Johannesburg and other national exchanges in the subregion are not uncommon.[45] However, many of the largest South African companies moved their primary listings from Johannesburg to the London Stock Exchange (particularly during the 1990s), citing a need for access to a much larger capital market.

Neither Asia nor Latin America has taken a strong intraregional approach—at least in practice—toward developing national equity markets. In Asia,

Table 4.7 Stock exchanges in selected developing countries, December 2005

Market	Company listings	Market capitalization ($ millions)	Market capitalization as % of GDP	Annual turnover ratio (%)
Botswana	18	2,438	25	2.1
Ecuador	32	3,215	98	4.2
Ghana	30	1,661	21	3.2
Latvia	45	2,527	16	7.9
Oman	96	15,269	45	31.5
Philippines	235	40,153	44	14.0
Sri Lanka	239	5,720	26	18.3
Trinidad & Tobago	37	16,971	120	3.8
Tunisia	46	2,876	10	8.9
Ukraine	221	24,976	35	2.5

Sources: Standard & Poor's, *Emerging Stock Markets Review* (January 2006); Standard & Poor's *Global Stock Markets Factbook,* 2005; World Bank database (for GDP data).
Note: Annual turnover ratios are calculated by dividing the total value traded in 2004 by average market capitalization for 2003 and 2004.

the focus of intraregional initiatives in recent years has been bond markets—via the ASEAN+3 initiatives to develop an intraregional bond market. But, so far, although issues of foreign currency–denominated bonds by Asian sovereigns and private firms have increased, most tend to be denominated in U.S. dollars, and most of the investment in these issues is sourced from Europe or the United States—albeit with a significant amount coming from Asian investors residing there.[46]

In Latin America, by contrast, recent efforts to develop capital markets have focused on the equity markets and have included some plans that take an intraregional approach. The region's two largest exchanges, in Mexico and Brazil, signed an agreement in 2005 that will soon allow cross-border investments in shares on their exchanges. Since the 1990s, the MERCOSUR countries have taken steps to encourage more cross-border trading in the markets of Argentina, Brazil, Paraguay, and Uruguay. Nevertheless, the actual volume of cross-border listings and investment in intraregional securities between developing countries in Latin America remains small.[47]

Steps to increase intraregional cooperation—rather than outright integration—as a means of developing national capital markets are increasingly evident, particularly in the form of an increase in agreements between developing-country stock exchanges to encourage more cross-border listings and investment, information and technology sharing, training, and staff exchanges. Some

Figure 4.6 Developing-country firms shift away from ADRs

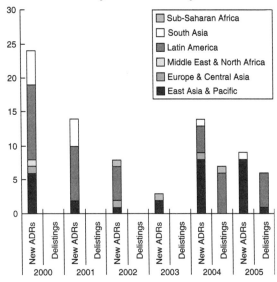

No. of new ADRs/delistings on U.S. stock exchanges

Source: Bank of New York Depositary Receipts Division.

of these agreements also promote joint efforts to develop new financial products and develop the stock-brokerage profession. A growing number of such cooperation agreements has been signed with exchanges outside the region—in developed as well as other developing countries.

Signs of a move away from American Depositary Receipts (ADRs) and toward more local listings

Developing-country firms may be less likely in the future to list on major international financial centers' markets than on domestic markets. In part, this is due to the recovery of trading activity and share prices in developing-country stock markets—reversing the downturns of the late 1990s (see box 2.2). That recovery has been driven by rapid economic growth and greater corporate earnings, as well as by local stock-market regulatory reforms to increase local trading activity, attract more investors and issuers to local and regional markets, and improve efficiency and competitiveness. There also is an ongoing effort—apparent across all developing-country regions—to bring financial reporting and disclosure standards more in line with international standards.

At the same time, increased regulatory and disclosure requirements in industrial-country markets, and their associated costs, are giving some impetus to local initiatives to develop capital markets, including those taking an intraregional approach. More costly and complicated documentation requirements, and significantly increased human resource and other capacity requirements for compliance with the more stringent reporting standards of Section 404 of the U.S. Sarbanes-Oxley Act of 2003, have coincided with an apparent decline in the attraction of an overseas listing on a U.S. exchange in recent years—particularly for companies based in Latin America, and also for many companies based in Asia (see figure 4.6).[48] New issues of depositary receipts by Latin American firms on U.S. exchanges declined from 11 in 2000 to none in 2005.[49] Moreover, there were six delistings of ADRs in 2005, five of which involved Latin American firms. At the same time, more companies in middle-income countries in Latin America and elsewhere have made initial public offerings (IPOs) or other forms of share issues in recent years (see also figure 2.9).

More must be done to improve financial intermediation at the national level

Regional cooperation and, possibly at a later stage, integration could improve the liquidity, efficiency, and competitiveness of securities exchanges in developing countries. But for many emerging markets, further progress in developing well-functioning national securities markets (and financial markets generally) is needed ahead of moves to integrate those markets. Hasty integration of several small, illiquid national stock markets would likely create nothing more than a large, illiquid regional market. Short of full integration, underdeveloped national exchanges could meanwhile benefit from the steps they have been taking to encourage closer cooperation, including through cross-border listings and investment, and through information and technology sharing.[50] More intraregional trading activity could also facilitate the privatization of large corporations, by providing a market for large share issues that could not be absorbed on a national basis.

Beyond general progress in strengthening national financial markets, several steps are important at the national level to facilitate eventual cross-border integration. Countries participating in cross-border trades must have convertible currencies and would have to liberalize those remaining controls and other restrictions on capital flows that impede cross-border trading, payments, and settlements. Harmonizing regulatory and policy frameworks would facilitate cross-border listing and investment and would be a prerequisite to actual integration.[51]

Conclusion

Available data indicate that more developing countries are lending to and investing in other developing countries. The expansion of South–South capital flows reflects both the general growth of cross-border financial transactions in the wake of globalization and the increasing size and sophistication of developing-country banks and multinationals. Greater South–South flows promise greater resources for low-income countries, a more efficient allocation of capital by lenders and investors familiar with developing-country conditions, and potentially greater transmission of technology and know-how from FDI.

The potential benefits of greater South–South integration are supported by anecdotes, a few empirical studies, and deduction and inference from the history of North–South capital flows, rather than by a large body systematic research. The fact is that the data on South–South capital flows are limited, and assem-bling those data from available sources is an arduous task (see annex 1). Moreover, very little research has been done on South–South financial integration. In part this reflects the relative novelty of developing countries as a significant source of capital, in part the absence of data, and in part the desire of development economists to focus their energies on the principal source of capital flows to developing countries (the high-income countries).

We hope that this foray into South–South capital flows will draw greater attention to developing countries as a source of capital. Greater efforts to collect data are essential to progress. Further empirical research could focus on (1) the extent of spillovers from South–South FDI and how these differ from spillovers from North–South FDI; (2) the impact of government impediments to, and incentives for, outward investment in developing countries; (3) the impact of developing-country banks on macroeconomic instability in their foreign markets, including the extent to which developing-country banks transmit crises from source to host country and whether the quality of management and financial soundness of internationally active developing-country banks differs greatly from high-income country banks; (4) the circumstances under which efforts to increase the integration of regional capital markets are likely to improve their efficiency; and (5) circumstances under which regional trade agreements and other forms of regional integration have a positive impact on economic growth and development.

Chapter 4 Annexes

Annex 1: Data on South–South capital flows

Most countries do not routinely publish data on capital flows by source country. Thus it is not possible to rely on official sources to calculate the portion of capital flows to developing countries that come from other developing countries. In constructing a database on South–South capital flows, we have relied on a variety of sources, including the Bank for International Settlements (BIS), Loanware, Bankscope, the United Nations Conference on Trade and Development (UNCTAD), the Organisation for Economic Co-operation and Development (OECD), the International Monetary Fund (IMF), and the World Bank.

Measuring South–South loans

BIS recently has begun publishing data on lending by banks domiciled in some developing countries. However, data are available only since 2000, and only for five countries (Brazil, Chile, India, Mexico, and Turkey). Moreover, data are available for all of these countries only since 2003. While the BIS data do provide some indication of the role of banks in developing countries as lenders, they cannot provide a very complete picture of South–South lending.

Most of our analysis of South–South lending, therefore, is based on data on syndicated loans obtained from Loanware, although considerable work was required to calculate the share of South–South transactions. While many transaction entries detail the allocation of loans among all participating banks, others do not, depending on the disclosure practices of particular syndicates. Where participation by all banks is disclosed, nonlocal developing-country bank partici-

pation in a loan is taken directly from Loanware. Where loan-allocation details for a particular loan transaction are not disclosed, an estimate of the cross-border South–South lending component for that transaction is derived by multiplying the total transaction amount by the average share of non-local South–South lending in syndicated loan transactions with some portion of developing-country bank participation arranged for borrowers in the region that year.[52]

Measuring South–South foreign bank ownership

Data on foreign banks in developing countries, as well as related financial variables, are based on Bankscope and include all active commercial banks, saving banks, cooperative banks, bank holding companies, and middle and long credit banks that were available in Bankscope as of December 2005. When ownership information is not available in Bankscope, information is gathered from banks' Web sites or other Internet sources.[53] We determine whether each bank is foreign-owned, that is, whether at least 50 percent of the bank's shares are owned by foreigners. In addition, the percentage of shares are summed by country of residence of the shareholder, and the country with the highest percentage of shares is appointed as the source country. Ownership is based on the direct ownership structure; indirect ownership is not taken into account.

Countries with fewer than five active banks in Bankscope were excluded from the sample. In addition, Guatemala was excluded, as ownership information was available for only a small portion of the country's banks. We were left with a sample of 103 developing countries. In total, the database provides us with information on ownership and related financial variables for 2,297 banks, of which 35 percent are foreign owned.

Measuring South–South foreign direct investment

Developing countries do not report the source of FDI inflows. Therefore, data on South–South FDI flows are calculated by comparing total FDI inflows to developing countries with FDI outflows from high-income to developing countries; the difference is South–South FDI flows. First, FDI outflows from high-income countries to developing countries are calculated. For high-income OECD countries, the OECD provides data on FDI outflows to 35 developing countries that account for 85 percent of all FDI inflows to developing countries. For high-income countries that are not part of the OECD, including several offshore centers, data on FDI outflows are taken from the IMF and UNCTAD. Since detailed destination data are not available, we assume that all of the FDI outflows from high-income non-OECD countries went to developing countries. (This assumption leads to an underestimation of South–South FDI flows.) Second, data on FDI inflows (to the 35 developing countries covered by the OECD database) are taken from the World Bank. South–South FDI

flows (to the 35 developing countries) are then approximated by FDI inflows in developing countries that are not from developed countries (Aykut and Ratha 2004).

The estimation technique suffers from the several weaknesses, some of which will lead to an underestimation, some an overestimation, of South–South FDI. First, FDI outflows to developing countries may be underreported by the high-income countries. It is likely that a portion of the FDI outflows that are not identified by country go to developing countries, which would imply an overestimation of South–South FDI. Second, FDI inflows are likely to be underreported by some developing countries, which would imply that our data are underestimates of South–South FDI. Third, round-tripping of flows (the export of capital to a foreign country for the purpose of investment back in the home country, often to benefit from tax incentives) will lead to overestimation of South–South FDI flows. Fourth, transactions channeled through offshore financial centers may be misclassified as FDI. Fifth, FDI from the North may be channeled through a developing country to another high-income country (indirect FDI flows), causing an overestimation of South–South flows. And finally, relying on a sample of 35 developing countries may lead to an underestimation of the level of South–South flows.

Annex 2: Selected South–South M&A deals by southern multinationals in service sector, 2000–5

In services sector

Year	Acquiring company	Country	Acquired company	Country	Sector	Value ($ millions)
2005	America Movil	Mexico	TIM Peru	Peru	Telecommunications	500
2004	Anglogold Ltd	South Africa	Ashanti Goldfields	Ghana	Gold ores	1500
2004	Sinergy	Brazil	Avianca	Colombia	Air transportation	400
2004	CEZA.S.	Czech Republic	Capital Electricity Colombia	Bulgaria	Electric services	400
2004	Teléfonos de Mexico	Mexico	Telecomunicaciones	Colombia	Telecommunications	400
2004	Teléfonos de Mexico	Mexico	Embratel	Brazil	Telecommunications	400
2004	Vempelcom	Russia	Kar-tel	Kazakhstan	Telecommunications	400
2004	YTL Power	Malaysia	Jawa Power	Indonesia	Electric services	200
2004	Teléfonos de Mexico	Mexico	Chilesat	Chile	Telecommunications	130
2004	Teléfonos de Mexico	Mexico	Techtel	Argentina	Telecommunications	100
2002	Vodacom	South Africa	Vodacom Mozambique	Mozambique	Telecommunications	260
2002	Ressano Garcia Railways company	South Africa	Caminhos de Ferro Mozambique	Mozambique	Cyclical services	78
2001	MTN	South Africa	MTN	Nigeria	Telecommunications	285
2001	Teléfonos de Mexico	Mexico	Comcel	Columbia	Telecommunications	257
2001	Industrial Development Corporation	South Africa	Mozal II	Mozambique	Basic industries	160
2001	Vodacom	South Africa	Vodacom Congo	Republic of Congo	Telecommunications	142
2000	Orascom	Egypt	Telecel	12 African countries	Telecommunications	413
2000	Teléfonos de Mexico	Mexico	ATL	Brazil	Telecommunications	345
2000	Teléfonos de Mexico	Mexico	Conecel	Ecuador	Telecommunications	153
1998	Teléfonos de Mexico	Mexico	TelGua	Guatemala	Telecommunications	700

In extractive sector

Year	Acquiring company	Country	Acquired company	Country	Location of the acquired asset	Value ($ millions)
2005	Andes Petroleum	China	EnCana	Canada	Ecuador	1420
2005	CNPC	China	Petro Kazakh	Canada	Mainly in Kazakhstan	4180
2005	CNOOC	China	MEG Energy	Canada	Canada	120
2005	Sinopec Group (50%) and ONGC (20%)	China-India	National Iranian Oil Company	Iran	Yadavaran Oil Fields in Iran	$70–100 billion over 30 years
2004	CNPC	China	Plus Petrol Norte	Peru		200
2004	Gazprom	Russia	Lietuvos	Lithuania	Lithuania	50
2004	Metorex	South Africa	Ruashi Mining	D. R. Congo	D. R. Congo	86
2004	Rangold Resources	South Africa	Loulo Concessions	Mali	Mali	80
2004	Rangold Resources	South Africa	Licences and assets	Angola	Angola	15
2003	CNOOC	China	Tangguh LNG project	Indonesia		275
2003	CNPC	China	Oil field	Kazakhstan	N Buzachi	200
2003	Investor Group	China	Amerada Hess	Indonesia		164
2003	Sinochem	China	Ecuador Block 16	Ecuador		100
2003	Lukoil	Russia	Beopetro	Serbia	Serbia	130
2003	AngloGold	South Africa	Ashanti	Ghana	Ghana	274
2003	Impala Platinum	South Africa	Zimbabwe Plat. Mes	Zimbabwe	Zimbabwe	85
2003	Impala Platinum	South Africa	Hartley Platinum Mines	Zimbabwe	Zimbabwe	80
2003	Impala Platinum	South Africa	Platinum mines	Zimbabwe	Zimbabwe	19
2003	Sasol	South Africa	Escravos gas to liquid plant	Nigeria	Nigeria	undisclosed
2002	CNOOC	China	Repsol YPF SA	Spain	Indonesia	591.9
2002	PetroChina Corp	China	Devon Energy	—	Indonesia	262
2002	Escom Holding	South Africa	Grand Inga Falls	D. R. Congo	D. R. Congo	1200
2001	Saso Oil	South Africa	Pande Teemanegasfields	Mozambique	Mozambique	581
2000	AngloGold	South Africa	Ashanti Goldfields	Tanzania	Tanzania	83
1998	China National Petroleum Corp	China	Oil Field	R. B. de Venezuela		240.7
1997	China National Petroleum Corp	China	Aktyubinskmunaygaz	Kazakhstan		325

Source: UNCTAD and news sources.
Note: — denotes not available.

Annex 3: Model of determinants of bank ownership

The following is an explanation of the model used in box 4.4. To test the differences between determinants of foreign bank entry in developing countries by banks from developing countries and from high-income countries, we estimate the following model using Tobit:

$$
\begin{aligned}
FC_{ij} = {} & \alpha_1 Collinks_{ij} + \alpha_2 Collinks_{ij} * D^S \\
& + \beta_1 Border_{ij} + \beta_2 Border_{ij} * D^S \\
& + \gamma_1 Comlang_{ij} + \gamma_2 Comlang_{ij} * D^S \\
& + \delta_1 Dist_{ij} + \delta_2 Dist_{ij} * D^S + \kappa_1 Trade_{ij} \\
& + \kappa_2 Trade_{ij} * D^S + \lambda_1 GDP + \lambda_2 GDP \\
& * D^S + \mu_1 Findepth + \mu_2 Findepth \\
& * D^S + \varphi_1 Legaldif + \varphi_2 Legaldif * D^S \\
& + \theta_1 Inst + \theta_2 Inst * D^S + \rho_1 Entryres \\
& + \rho_2 GDPsource + \rho_3 GDPcapsource \\
& + \rho_4 Dregion + \tau_1 constant + \varepsilon_{ij}
\end{aligned}
$$

The dependent variable is defined as the ratio of the sum of assets of banks in host country i of which a source country j owns 50 percent or more equity, divided by the total amount of banking assets in host country i. *Collinks* is a dummy with a value of 1 if the host and source countries have had colonial links either between colonizer and colony or between those countries colonized by the same colonizer. D^s is a dummy with a value of 1 if both host and source country are a developing country. *Border* is a dummy with a value of 1 if the countries share a border. *Comlang* is a dummy with a value of 1 if the countries share the same language. *Dist* refers to the log of the distance between the host and source countries. *Trade* is the log of exports plus imports in 2000 between the two countries. *GDP* is the log of the host country's GDP in 2000. *Findepth* is the log of M2 as a percentage of GDP in the host country in 2000. *Legaldif* is a dummy with a value of 1 if the origin of the legal system of the host and source countries differs. *Inst* is the simple average of six indicators of quality of institutions in the host country in 2000 as measured by Kaufmann, Kraay, and Mastruzzi (2005). *Entryres* is a dummy with a value of 1 if foreign bank entry is restricted. *GDPsource* and *GDPcapsource* are the logs, respectively, of GDP and GDP per capita in the source country in 2000. *Dregion* are dummies for each region.

Notes

1. See annex 1 for the methods used to compile data on South-South transactions.

2. Data on bilateral remittance flows are not available. The estimate in figure 4.1 assumes that bilateral remittances are a function of the stock of migrants in the sending country. This estimate is consistent with the fact that nearly half of the migrant stock from the South migrate to another country in the South.

3. It is difficult to obtain data on foreigners' purchases of stock issues. But see figure 2.14 on initial public offerings in emerging markets.

4. The G-20 and G-90 groups were formed at the time of the WTO ministerial in Cancun in September 2003. The G-20 includes some of the larger developing countries, while the G-90 is made up of countries from the African, Caribbean, and Pacific (ACP) group, the African Union, and the least developed countries.

5. According to the index published by the Heritage Foundation. See http://www.heritage.org/research/features/index/downloads.cfm.

6. These are unweighted averages. The average for high-income countries includes non-OECD countries.

7. The discussion of RTAs is taken from World Bank (2005b).

8. World FDI in services quadrupled between 1990 and 2002 (UNCTAD 2004). By 2002, the services sector accounted for 70 percent and 47 percent of FDI stock in developed and developing countries, respectively (World Bank 2004).

9. The services sector includes electricity, gas, water, transport, communication, construction, wholesale and retail trade and repairs, hotels and restaurants, transport, storage and communications, finance and insurance, real estate, renting, and business services, public administration, defense, education, health, social services, social and personal service activities, and recreational, cultural, and sporting activities. Not all services are nontradable or require physical proximity.

10. For example, America Movil (Mexico) bought out the shares of its partners (SBC and Bell Canada) in Brazil and of its partner (Bell Canada) in Colombia in 2002.

11. See Goldstein (forthcoming) and Pradhan (2005).

12. Examples include the Indian R&D center of Chinese white goods producer Haier, and Russian design and R&D centers for the shipping industry and drilling platforms (Vahtra and Liuhto 2004).

13. The extractive industries also attract a large share of developed-country FDI in Africa. In 2002, 53 percent of FDI from four major developed-country investors in Africa (France, the Netherlands, the United Kingdom, and the United States) was in the extractive sector (World Bank 2004, figure 3.6).

14. China has partnerships or investments in oil and gas exploration projects in Cuba, Peru, and República Bolivariana de Venezuela.

15. For example, a Turkish soap and detergent producer (Evyap) opened factories in Egypt and Ukraine and is planning to open one in Russia to escape uncompetitive

labor costs at home and growing competitive pressures in these markets (IMF–World Bank 2005). Mauritius has received significant FDI in the textile and clothing sector but moved part of its production to lower-cost neighboring Madagascar and Mozambique in response to cost pressures from Asia (Goldstein 2003).

16. In June 2005, India's Ranbaxy won approval to make lamivudine tablets for Africa under the U.S. President's Emergency Plan for AIDS Relief.

17. Examples of SOEs in other sectors include Telekom Malaysia, Eskom, and Transet of South Africa.

18. For example, South African SOEs have invested in Africa in part to promote the New Partnership for African Development (UNCTAD 2005a).

19. In July 2005, China's CNPC was awarded four oil blocks in Nigeria in exchange for investing in the construction of a hydropower plant ("China Goes Shopping," *Financial Times,* March 8-16, 2005).

20. SMEs have 1,000 or fewer employees (OECD 2005a).

21. Since 1998, the Tata Group has been selling a family sedan for $4,000 to $6,000. It announced plans to introduce a $2,000 car by 2008 ("Getting the Best to the Masses," *Business Week,* October 11, 2004).

22. Positive spillovers are benefits that the domestic economy enjoys but does not pay for, due to the presence of foreign firms. Such benefits may include the availability of information and technology or the increased supply of trained workers (where, because of job mobility, the foreign firm does not capture the full return to training).

23. Some of these initiatives are the OECD Guidelines for Multinational Enterprises, the OECD Convention Against Bribery of Foreign Public Officials in International Transactions, and various initiatives that promote transparency in the extractive industries.

24. A survey of 200 outward investors from Eastern Europe and Central Asia (Sevtlicic and Rojec 2003) showed that most companies that have invested abroad—mainly in other developing countries—increased exports and improved their financial performance. In India, outward investment enhanced the export performance of SMEs in manufacturing, compared with those that did not invest abroad (Prahdan 2005).

25. See *The Banker* (2005), *Global Finance* (2004 and 2005), Capital Intelligence (2004 and 2005), *EIU Country Finance* (2004 and 2005), *Latin Finance* (2005), and information posted on various bank Web sites.

26. Data reflect participation by nonlocal developing-country banks in cross-border syndicated lending to borrowers based in developing countries (see annex 1).

27. This increase is due in part to the rise in the number of countries following the breakup of the Soviet Union. Seven of the former Soviet republics received syndicated lending in 2005.

28. Examples include the State Bank of India and Oman's Bank Muscat.

29. In a sample of 1,143 cross-border syndicated loan transactions, local banks in eastern Europe accounted for 13 percent of the total loan amount, and local banks in Latin America for 16 percent (Nini 2004).

30. A mandated lead arranger is a bank (or banks) responsible for originating, structuring, and syndicating a loan transaction.

31. This includes international transactions of the banks with any of their own affiliates and with Panama, an offshore center. Excluding Panama, cross-border lending originating from developing countries amounted to $77 billion in 2005

32. Foreign claims include cross-border loans by the bank's head offices or its affiliates, and local loans by affiliates located in another country

33. Total assets are averaged over 2000-4. These numbers include offshore centers. Excluding FDI in and from offshore centers, developing-country banks hold 3 percent of foreign bank assets in developing countries.

34. The data for South Asia reflect banks domiciled in Mauritius (an offshore banking center), most of which owned by banks from high-income countries that have set up subsidiaries in India.

35. Excluding FDI to and from offshore centers, Sub-Saharan Africa shows the highest percentage of developing countries' banks in total foreign bank entry (13.3 percent), followed by East Asia and the Pacific (10 percent), and the Middle East and North Africa (6.6 percent). In the other regions South-South activity accounts for less than 2 percent of FDI in the banking sector.

36. Some banks, such as India's Bank of Baroda and the State Bank of India, Jordan's Arab Bank, and the Bank of China have been active participants in cross-border syndicated transactions for borrowers outside their regions since at least 1985.

37. Examples include plans by a number of Kazakh banks to offer financial leasing services (a growing financial product geared to SMEs) in Eastern Europe and Central Asia. Evidence on the kinds of financial services provided by developing-country banks can be found in *Capital Intelligence* (various country reports through the end of 2005), *The Banker* (various issues in 2005), and information provided on the banks' Web sites.

38. This discussion is based on conversations with World Bank staff.

39. The prosecution was reported in Zambia News Online. http://www.africa.upenn.edu/Newsletters/zno24.html

40. Engberg (1975) saw a role for capital markets in raising domestic savings and contributing to their more efficient allocation, even in less developed economies. Engberg also argued that the broader range of financial assets associated with capital market development could raise personal savings rates. Levine (1990) showed that a stock market can positively impact growth by providing a means of trading the ownership of firms (shares) without disrupting the operating and productive processes within those firms and by providing a way for investors to diversify their portfolios. See also Demirgüc-Kunt and Maksimovic (1996); Boyd and Smith (1998); Levine and Zervos (1998); Arestis, Demetriades, and Luintel (2001).

41. The number of countries with a stock exchange is actually greater than 75, but several exchanges are inactive or have negligible trading activity.

42. Forty-six of the 80 stock markets categorized as "emerging markets" in Standard & Poor's *Global Stock Markets Factbook 2005* had a market capitalization of $10 billion or less in October 2004. In contrast, just 3 of the 29 developed-economy stock exchanges had a market capitalization of $10 billion or less. Stock markets in many developing economies rival those in developed economies when viewed in terms of the ratio of market capitalization to gross national income, however. Market capitalization is only one factor in determining the relative level of development of a stock exchange (Standard & Poor's 2005).

43. According to the IMF's *Asia-Pacific Outlook,* September 2005, at least 95 percent of the listings on Asian national stock exchanges are local listings.

44. Indian firms issuing global depositary receipts (GDRs) on the Luxembourg Stock Exchange (citing cost, time, and marketing advantages) accounted for the majority (23) of the 42 total depositary receipts newly issued on the main depositary receipt listing markets in 2005 (the United States, the United Kingdom, and Luxembourg). The issuance of GDRs by developing-country firms may improve efficiency in the home market due to increased competitive pressures on standards, procedures, and operations, but it may also impose costs due to diversion of order flow abroad. The net impact on market liquidity and capitalization from cross-border listings may depend on the proportion of trading volume that shifts overseas, relative sizes of the home and overseas markets, and changes, following the cross-border listing, in the extent of home-market segmentation due to investment barriers and intermarket information transparency (Hargis and Ramanlal 1996; Hargis 1997; and Domowitz, Glen, and Madhavan, 1998). More recent research (Karolyi 2004) found that an increase in issues of American Depositary Receipts (ADRs) by firms in an emerging market economy may be a result, rather than a cause, of deteriorating local market conditions.

45. More than 70 percent of the equities listed on the Namibia Stock Exchange (NSX) are dual listed on the Johannesburg Stock Exchange, and the vast majority of NSX trading takes place in these dual listed stocks (Johannesburg Securities Exchange 2005). For a region-specific assessment of whether cooperation and integration of stock exchanges in southern and eastern Africa could offer a way of overcoming impediments to the development of these exchanges, see Irving (2005).

46. Bank for International Settlements, 2005.

47. Despite a significant amount of foreign investment in securities traded on the region's two largest exchanges, in Brazil and Mexico, the vast majority of it comes from developed economies.

48. In October 2005 China Construction Bank, which had reportedly been considering a listing on the NYSE, opted instead to list on the Hong Kong, China exchange, with an IPO of $8 billion—China's largest to date and the largest worldwide since 2001. In the past few years, the international financial press has contained numerous additional reports of firms domiciled in developing countries that have abandoned plans to list on the major U.S. exchanges and, to some extent, on the London Stock Exchange, because of more onerous listing requirements and associated higher costs. The European Union also has been taking steps to increase the stringency of its reporting and disclosure requirements for companies that list on EU stock exchanges, including through a transparency directive slated to take effect in 2006.

49. Although a Chilean firm issued new ADRs in 2005, this transaction was an exchange of existing depositary receipts due to a company merger.

50. The impact of South–South cross-border listings on developing countries' stock exchanges is an important area for research, given the increasing number of agreements between developing countries' stock exchanges that encourage cross-border listings and investment.

51. This would involve harmonizing not only stock-market regulations, listing requirements, and procedures for trading, clearing, and settlement, but also transaction fees, accounting and disclosure standards, corporate governance standards, common standards for stockbrokers, and national rules for capital gains and withholding taxes. Such efforts, as well as the development of common infrastructure and systems, may have to address limitations in national markets, such as poor institutional capacity for enforcing regulations, rudimentary stock-market infrastructure, poor and unreliable access to information and communications technology, and exchanges at significantly different stages of development. A regional securities regulatory body would be essential if integration were to proceed to the point of forming a regional exchange.

52. For example, the South–South cross-border lending component of a qualifying syndicated loan ("loan A") for a borrower in East Asia in 2005 that does not reveal loan-allocation details is estimated by multiplying the average share (15 percent) of nonlocal South–South lending in all qualifying transactions for East Asia that reveal loan-allocation details by the total "loan A" transaction amount. A qualifying transaction is defined for this purpose as a syndicated loan disbursed to a borrower in a developing country, whereby one or more banks domiciled in other (nonlocal) developing countries participate in the syndicate. In cases where loan-allocation details are unavailable for all qualifying syndicated transactions in a particular region, as in Latin America in 1985 and 1995 and in the case of all regions in 1985 (with the exception of two transactions), the estimate is derived from an average of all transactions that provide loan-allocation data for the region in the time series.

53. Currently our sample does not include Costa Rica, the Dominican Republic, or Panama.

References

Aizenman, Joshua, and Ilan Noy. 2005. "FDI and Trade—Two Way Linkages?" NBER Working Paper 11403, National Bureau of Economic Research, Cambridge, MA.

Albuquerque, R., N. Loayza, and L. Servén, L. 2005. "World Market Integration through the Lens of Foreign Direct Investment." *Journal of International Economics* 66 (2): 267–95.

Amorim, Celso. 2005. "Brazil Redraws the Trade Map." *Global Agenda.* http://www.globalagendamagazine.com/2005/celsoamorim.asp.

Arestis, Philip, Panicos Demetriades, and Kul Luintel. 2001. "Financial Development and Economic Growth: The Role of Stock Markets." *Journal of Money, Credit, and Banking* 33: 16–41.

Aykut, Dilek, and Dilip Ratha. 2004. "South–South FDI Flows: How Big Are They?" *Transnational Corporations* 13 (1).

Baldwin, Robert, and L. Alan Winters, eds. 2004. *Challenges to Globalization: Analyzing the Economics*. Chicago: University of Chicago Press.

Banga, Rashmi. 2003. "Impact of Government Policies and Investment Agreements on FDI Flows." Working Paper 116, Indian Council for Research on International Economic Relations, New Delhi.

Bank for International Settlements. 2005. *BIS Quarterly Review* (June).

Boyd, J., and B. D. Smith. 1998. "The Evolution of Debt and Equity Markets in Economic Development." *Economic Theory* 12: 519–60.

Brealey, R., and E. C. Kaplanis. 1996. "The Determination of Foreign Banking Location." *Journal of International Money and Finance* 15: 577–97.

Buch, Claudia M., and Gayle Delong. 2004. "Cross-Border Bank Mergers: What Lures the Rare Animal?" *Journal of Banking and Finance* 28: 2077–102.

Capital Intelligence. Various years. "Country Banking Reports." http://www.ciratings.com/.

Caballero, R. 2002. "Coping with Chile's External Vulnerability: A Financial Problem." Unpublished paper, Massachusetts Institute of Technology, Cambridge, MA.

Chudnovsky, Daniel, and Andres Lopez. 2000. "A Third Wave from Developing Countries: Latin American TNCs in the 1990s." *Transnational Corporations* 9 (2).

Claessens, Stijn, Asli Demirgüc-Kunt, and Harry Huizinga. 2001. "How Does Foreign Entry Affect Domestic Banking Markets?" *Journal of Banking and Finance* 25: 891–911.

Claessens, Stijn, and Neeltje Van Horen. 2006. "Location decisions of foreign banks and competitive advantage." Unpublished paper. World Bank, Washington, DC.

Crystal, J., G. Dages, and L. Goldberg. 2001. "Does Foreign Ownership Contribute to Sounder Banks in Emerging Markets? The Latin American Experience." Federal Reserve Bank of New York Staff Reports 137, New York.

Demirgüc-Kunt, A., and V. Maksimovic. 1996. "Stock Market Development and Firm Financing Choices." *World Bank Economic Review* 10: 341–70.

De Sol, Patricio. 2005. "Why Join a Chilean Firm to Invest Elsewhere in Latin America?" Unpublished paper, Pontificia Universidad Católica de Chile. http://www.ingenieriaindustrial.cl/documentos/182.pdf

Domowitz, Ian, Jack Glen, and Ananth Madhavan. 1998. "International Cross-Listing and Order Flow Migration: Evidence from an Emerging Market." *Journal of Finance* 53 (December): 2001–27.

EIU (Economist Intelligence Unit). Various dates. "Country Finance Reports." http://www.eiu.com.

———. 2005. "Country Report for Iraq." September.

Elteto, Andrea, and Antaloczy Katalin. 2003. "Outward Foreign Direct Investments from Poland." In *Facilitating Transition by Internalization: Outward Direct Investment from Central European Countries in Transition*, ed. M. Svetlicic and M. Rojec. Aldershot, Hampshire, UK: Ashgate.

Engberg, H. L. 1975. "The Nairobi Stock Exchange: An Organized Capital Market in a Developing Country." *Journal of Management Studies* 8.

Erdilek, Asim. 2005. "Case Study on Outward FDI by Enterprises from Turkey." Background paper for UNCTAD conference on "Enhancing the Productive Capacity of Developing Country Firms through Internationalization," Geneva, December 5–7.

FIAS (Foreign Investment Advisory Service). 2005. "Survey of Chinese MNCs." International Finance Corporation, Foreign Investment Advisory Service, Washington, DC.

Financial Times. 2004. "Chinese Companies Acquire a Taste of Western Targets." October 19, 2004

Focarelli, D., and A. Pozzolo. 2000. "The Determinants of Cross-Border Bank Shareholdings: An Analysis with Bank-Level Data from OECD Countries." *Proceedings* (Federal Reserve Bank of Chicago, May): 199–232.

Galindo, Arturo, Alejandro Micco, and Cesar Serra. 2003. "Better the Devil That You Know: Evidence on Entry Costs Faced by Foreign Banks." IADB Working Paper 477, Inter-American Development Bank, Washington, DC.

Giroud, Axele. 2005. "Chinese Outward FDI." Background paper for UNCTAD conference on "Enhancing the Productive Capacity of Developing Country Firms through Internationalization," Geneva, December 5–7.

Global Finance. Various issues. http://www.gfmag.com.

Goldstein Andrea. 2004. Regional Integration, FDI, and Competitiveness in Southern Africa. Paris: Organisation for Economic Co-operation and Development.

———. Forthcoming. *Emerging Multinationals in the Global Economy: Data Trends, Policy Issues, and Research Questions*. London: Palgrave Macmillan.

Goldstein, Andrea, Nicolas Pinaud, Helmut Reisen, and Michael-Xiaobao Chen. 2006. "The Rise of China and India: What Is in It for Africa?" Development Center Paper, Organisation for Economic Co-operation and Development, Paris.

Grosse, R., and L. G. Goldberg. 1991. "Foreign Bank Activity in the United States: An Analysis by Country of Origin." *Journal of Banking and Finance* 15: 1092–1112.

Hallward-Driemeier, Mary. 2003. "Do Bilateral Investment Treaties Attract Foreign Direct Investment? Only a Bit—and They Could Bite." Policy Research Working Paper 3121, World Bank, Washington, DC.

Hargis, K. 1997. "ADRs in Emerging Equity Markets: Market Integration or Fragmentation?" Working Paper D97-17, Center for International Business Education and Research, University of South Carolina, Columbia.

Hargis, K., and P. Ramanlal, 1998. "When Does Internationalization Enhance the Development of Domestic Stock Markets?" *Journal of Financial Intermediation* 7 (3): 263–92.

ICICI Bank. 2005. http://www.icicibank.com.

IDB (Inter-American Development Bank). 2002. *Beyond Borders: The New Regionalism in Latin-America*. Washington, DC: Johns Hopkins University Press.

IFC (International Finance Corporation). 1991. "Financing Corporate Growth in the Developing World." IFC Discussion Paper 12, International Finance Corporation, Washington, DC.

IMF (International Monetary Fund). 2005. "Asia-Pacific Outlook." Washington, DC. September.

IMF–World Bank. 2005. "FDI Monitoring Working Project—interviews with major investors both from developing and developed countries."

Irving, Jacqueline. 2005. "Regional Integration of Stock Exchanges in Eastern and Southern Africa: Progress and Prospects." IMF Working Paper 122, International Monetary Fund, Washington, DC.

Johannesburg Securities Exchange. "Dual Listed Company Information." http://www.jse.co.za.

Kabelwa, George. 2004. "Technology Transfer and South African Investment in Tanzania." Globalisation and East Africa Working Paper 10, Economic and Social Research Foundation, Dar es Salaam.

Karolyi, A. 2004. "The Role of American Depositary Receipts in the Development of Emerging Equity Markets." Review of Economics and Statistics 86: 670–90.

Latin Finance. 2005. "Daily Briefs." http://www.latinfinance.com.

Levine, Ross. 1990. "Stock Markets, Growth, and Policy." Working Paper 484, World Bank, Washington, DC.

———. 1996. "Foreign Banks, Financial Development, and Economic Growth." In International Financial Markets, ed. E. B. Claude. Washington, DC: AEI Press.

Levine, Ross, and Sara Zervos, 1998. "Stock Markets, Banks, and Economic Growth." American Economic Review 88: 537–58.

Levy-Yeyati, Eduardo, Panizza Ugo, and Ernesto Stein. 2002. "The Cyclical Nature of North–South FDI Flows." Business School Working Paper 15, Universidad Torcuato Di Tella, Buenos Aires.

Lisitsyn, Nikita, Sergi F. Sutyrin, Olga Y. Trofimenko, and Irina V. Vorobieva. 2005. "Outward Internationalisation of Russian Leading Telecom Companies." Electronic Publications of Pan-European Institute 1/2005, Turku School of Economics and Business Administration, Turku, Finland. http://www.tukkk.fi/pei

Mathews, John. 2005. "Enhancing Productive Capacity of Developing Country Firms through Internationalization." Discussion paper for UNCTAD conference on "Enhancing the Productive Capacity of Developing Country Firms through Internationalization," Geneva, December 5–7.

Mirza, Hafiz. 2000. "The Globalization Business and East Asian Developing Country Multinationals." In The Globalalization of Multinational Enterprise Activity and Economic Development, ed. Neil Hood and Stephen Young. New York: St. Martin's Press.

Narlikar, Amrita, and Diana Tussie. 2004. "The G-20 at the Cancun Ministerial: Developing Countries and Their Evolving Coalitions in the WTO." World Economy 27 (7): 947–1148.

Nini, Greg. 2004. "The Value of Financial Intermediaries: Empirical Evidence from Syndicated Loans to Emerging Market Borrowers." U.S. Federal Reserve International Finance Discussion Paper 820, Washington, DC.

OECD 2005a. "Centre for Entrepreneurship, SMEs, and Local Development." http://www.oecd.org/department/0,2688,en_2649_33956792_1_1_1_1_1,00.html.

———. 2005b. "Corporate Responsibility Practices of Emerging Market Companies—A Fact-Finding Study." OECD, Paris.

Oil & Gas Journal Special Report. 2001. http://www.ogj.com

Padayachee, Vishnu, and Imraan Valodia. 1999. "Malaysian Investment in South Africa." Journal of Contemporary African Studies 17.

Portes, R., and H. Rey. 2005. "The Determinants of Cross-Border Equity Flows." Journal of International Economics 65 (2): 269–96.

Pradhan, Java Prakash. 2005. "Outward Foreign Direct Investments from India: Recent Trends and Patterns." Unpublished paper, Centre for the Study of Regional Development, Jawaharlal Nehru University, New Delhi.

Rakner, L., N. van de Walle, and D. Mulaisho. 1999. Zambia. Washington, DC: World Bank.

Schiff, Maurice, Yanling Wang, and Marcelo Olarreaga. 2002. "North–South and South–South Trade-Related Technology Diffusion: An Industry-Level Analysis." Policy Research Working Paper 2861, Development Research Group, World Bank, Washington, DC.

Svetlicic, Marjan, and Matija Rojec. 2003. Facilitating Transition by Internalization: Outward Direct Investment from Central European Countries in Transition. Aldershot, Hampshire, UK: Ashgate.

Shah, Ajay, and Ila Patnaik. 2005 "India's Experience with Capital Flows: The Elusive Quest for a Sustainable Current Account Deficit." NBER Working Paper 11387, National Bureau of Economic Research, Cambridge, MA.

Standard & Poor's. 2005. Global Stock Markets Factbook. New York: Standard & Poor's.

———. Various dates. Emerging Stock Markets Review.

State Bank of India. 2005. "In the News." http://www.statebankofindia.com.

Stein, E., and C. Daude. 2001. "Institutions, Integration, and the Location of Foreign Direct Investment." Unpublished paper, Inter-American Development Bank, Research Department, Washington, DC.

Sull, Donlad, and Martin Escobari. 2004. "Creating Value in an Unpredictable World." Business Strategy Review 15 (3): 14–20.

Swenson, D. L. 2004. "Foreign Investment and the Mediation of Trade Flows." Review of International Economics 12 (4): 609–29.

The Banker. Various issues in 2005. http://www.thebanker.com/.

Tobin, Jennifer, and Susan Rose-Ackerman. 2005. "Foreign Direct Investment and the Business Environment in Developing Countries: The Impact of Bilateral Investment Treaties." Research Paper 293, Yale Law Centre for Law, Economics and Public Policy, New Haven, CT.

UNCTAD. 1998. World Investment Report 1998. Geneva: UNCTAD.

———. 2003. "China: An Emerging FDI Outward Investor." Geneva: UNCTAD.

———. 2004. World Investment Report—2004." Geneva: UNCTAD.

———. 2005a. World Investment Report—2005." Geneva: UNCTAD.

———. 2005b. Country Case Studies presented at UNC-TAD Expert Meeting on "Enhancing the Productive Capacity of Developing Country Firms through Internalization," Geneva, December 5–7.

Vahtra, Peeter, and Kari Liuhto. 2004. "Expansion or Exodus? Foreign Operations of Russia's Largest Corporations." Electronic Publications of the Pan-European Institute 8/2004, Turku School of Economics and Business Administration. http://www.tukkk.fi/pei

Van Horen, Neeltje. 2006. "Foreign Bank Entry in Developing Countries: Origin Matters." Unpublished paper, World Bank, Washington, DC.

Williams, B. 1998. "Factors Affecting the Performance of Foreign-Owned Banks in Australia: A Cross-Sectional Study." *Journal of Banking and Finance* 22: 197–219.

World Bank. 2002. *Global Economic Prospects 2003.* Washington, DC: World Bank.

———. 2004. *Global Development Finance 2004.* Washington, DC: World Bank.

———. 2005a. *Global Development Finance 2005.* Washington, DC: World Bank.

———. 2005b. *Global Economic Prospects 2006.* Washington, DC: World Bank.

———. 2005c. "Developing Country Investors and Operators in Infrastructure, Phase 1 Report." Public Private Infrastructure Advisory Facility, World Bank, Washington, DC.

———. 2006. *Information and Communications for Development.* World Bank, Washington, DC

WTO (World Trade Organization). 2003. *World Trade Report.* Geneva: World Trade Organization.

Yamori, N. 1998. "A Note on the Location Choice of Multinational Banks: The Case of Japanese Financial Institutions." *Journal of Banking and Finance* 22: 109–20.

Yi, Ren. 2004. "Motivations for Chinese Investment in Vietnam." University of Melbourne Working Paper.

Zedillo, Ernesto, Patrick Messerlin, and Julia Nielson. 2005. *Trade for Development: Achieving the Millennium Development Goals.* UN Millennium Project Task Force on Trade. London: Earthscan.

5

Challenges in Managing Capital Flows

The surging flows of international private capital and favorable global economic environment present a significant opportunity for developing countries, particularly for the middle-income countries that are the major recipients of capital flows. These and other countries that have embraced sound macroeconomic fundamentals, open international trade, and financial integration must now find ways to leverage their gains, while building an institutional and policy environment that will maintain the confidence of investors and insulate the economy from external shocks. Few policy decisions would appear as important to future growth and financial stability as those capable of preventing a recurrence of the market and policy failures of the 1990s. Although initial conditions point to better management of capital flows this time around, significant downside risks remain.

At an annual average growth rate of 5.4 percent over the past four years (2002–5), economic activity in developing economies has expanded more than twice as fast as in high-income countries. And as authorities have increasingly adopted price stability—often in the context of inflation targeting—as an integral part of their macroeconomic management, inflation has fallen dramatically in virtually all developing countries, from an annual median of 11.5 percent during 1993–6 to 4.5 percent during 2002–5. At the same time, greater autonomy in monetary policy, afforded by the widespread transition to flexible exchange rates, has allowed authorities to lower local interest rates, which, in many developing countries, are now converging to international levels. With lower local interest rates and greater exchange rate flexibility, the incentive to resort to short-term external borrowing has been reduced, thereby addressing a major policy failure that accompanied the capital surge of the mid-1990s.

These positive developments do not come without risk. Progress in macroeconomic stabilization and reform since the Asian financial crisis has not been fully matched by improvements in corporate governance; in many countries, adherence to global standards and norms is still a work in progress. Many countries still lack adequate capacity to manage risks associated with managed-float exchange rate regimes and partially liberalized capital markets. The large buildup of official foreign exchange reserves by many countries, particularly in Asia, has resulted in a high concentration of currency and interest rate risks on central banks' balance sheets, with potentially adverse fiscal consequences. On the international front, growing uncertainty about the sustainability of the current pattern of global capital flows, in which developing countries export capital to the rest of the world, particularly the United States, constitutes a major vulnerability in international capital markets. The current episode of strong capital flows to developing economies coincided initially with a considerable easing of monetary policy in industrial countries; that period came to an end in the United States in mid-2004 and in the Euro Area more recently. Rising interest rates in the industrialized world may keep some investors closer to home.

This chapter highlights the implications of recent changes in the macroeconomic and financial environment for policy makers in developing countries. It also maps out broad strategies for managing the influx of capital to serve long-term growth and development objectives. Given the differences among developing countries in their stage of economic development, and the considerable variation in the amount and impact of different kinds of private flows, policy makers will necessarily be guided by country-specific considerations in determining the course of policy. But overall, the three core dimensions of *managing capital flows* at the current juncture are likely to be (i) ensuring macroeconomic stability and sustaining the confidence of investors so that access to international capital markets is sustained and enhanced; (ii) implementing appropriate policies and risk-management strategies to encourage allocation of capital to long-term investment and growth; and (iii) designing appropriate safeguards to enhance resilience through self-insurance and adherence to global norms and standards.

The key messages emerging from the analysis presented in this chapter are:

- Policy responses in the current period of increased capital inflows have differed in important respects from those that prevailed during the previous boom in the mid-1990s. Governments have generally managed to avoid excessive expansion of aggregate demand and large current-account deficits. Their policies have supported modest allocations of foreign capital resources to domestic investment, although the major chunk has been used to build up foreign exchange reserves. So far, fewer countries have seen their real exchange rate appreciate than during the 1990s boom. In many countries, investment rates have not yet risen to the peaks they reached before the East Asian crisis. In Indonesia, Malaysia, and Thailand, for example, investment rates remain lower than precrisis levels by 10 to 20 percentage points of GDP. At the same time, the surge in portfolio inflows has been associated with a dramatic escalation of stock market prices and valuations in many developing countries, particularly in Asia, raising the risk of asset price bubbles—and of reversals of capital flows should those bubbles burst. For oil-importing countries, higher oil prices and the consequent adjustment in the current-account balance have partly offset the impact of strong capital inflows.

- That many developing countries have accumulated foreign exchange reserves far in excess of the level required for intervention and liquidity purposes reflects in part a clear proclivity to self-insure against global financial shocks. As the volume of reserves increases, however, so does the importance of balancing their use for intervention and insurance purposes against their domestic resource costs. Allowing local institutional investors to diversify their investment portfolio globally, while ensuring more effective regulation, could provide a viable channel of capital outflow, as well as an opportunity to further diversify risk. Further, permitting such investments would have the effect of transferring foreign exchange rate risks, currently concentrated on the books of central banks, to domestic institutional investors that have a long investment horizon and can benefit from a more diversified international portfolio. Moreover, opening up a channel for capital outflows would also help to avoid the excessive exchange rate appreciations that can result from surges in capital flows.

- As developing countries become more open to international financial markets, designing and building a sound regime of external financial policy making and regulation presents an urgent challenge. A consensus has formed around the three core components of such a new regime—membership in a credible currency union, such as the European Union, or an exchange rate that reflects market forces; gradual opening of the capital account; and a monetary policy framework that favors price stability. These elements are present to varying degrees in many developing countries involved in private capital markets. Roughly one-half of developing countries are now operating under a floating exchange rate regime (free or managed), while the 11 new and aspiring members of the European Union are taking steps to peg their currencies to the euro. Priority now must be given to two points. First, the complex web of capital controls and exchange rate restrictions that persists in many countries should be simplified and, as macroeconomic policies improve and local capital markets develop, eased gradually over time. During the transition, curbs on short-term debt inflows may need to be maintained, or even strengthened, while restrictions on outflows are eased. Second, authorities must build a system of risk management robust enough to respond to the needs of a more flexible exchange rate and open capital account.

- The development and partial application of a set of international norms and standards on transparency, corporate governance, and regulation and supervision of national financial systems has helped increase the confidence of foreign investors in emerging market economies. To promote stability and maintain a financial environment conducive to a balanced expansion and deployment of capital flows in developing countries, the international community must be assiduous in promoting the further application of those norms and standards.

- The world economy is moving toward a multipolar international monetary system in which policy interactions among the major industrial countries of the G-3—*and with key emerging market economies*—will be essential in securing an orderly adjustment of the prevailing global imbalances in external payments. One effect of inclusive interactions would be to lessen market anxiety over the course of global interest rates and capital flows. Emerging market economies, which would suffer disproportionately from the instability induced by a disorderly adjustment, share with the industrial countries the desire for a multilateral approach that will include corrective actions in deficit and surplus countries alike. In addition, policy makers in emerging market economies should take advantage of the opportunity presented by the current benign global financial market environment to build institutions and mechanisms that will enable them to navigate their economies in a world of increasingly open capital accounts and market-based exchange rates.

Two booms in capital flows—what has changed?

The present surge in capital flows to developing countries differs substantially from the previous episode in the mid-1990s. Greater global economic and financial integration, improved domestic macroeconomic conditions, and sounder domestic policies and institutions have enhanced the capacity of policy makers to deal with infusions of private capital. Compared with the situa-

tion in the 1990s, many developing countries today have significantly lower external debt burdens, fewer currency mismatches in their debt structures, higher reserves of foreign exchange, a more flexible exchange rate regime, and more open capital accounts. But the benign external environment in which these improvements were made may become less so in the next few years, as the major industrial countries tighten their monetary policy and as markets come to reassess their views and expectations regarding the evolution of global interest rates and capital flows.

Since the early 1990s, developing countries have experienced two episodes of heavy influx of private capital. The first, occurring in the middle of the past decade (1992–7), resulted in an increase in capital inflows from 3.2 percent of developing countries' aggregate GDP in 1992 to 5.1 percent in 1997. The second began in 2002 and continues to date. So far, it has brought a cumulative total of $1,316 billion in capital to the developing world (approximately $350 billion annually averaged over 2002–5). This last episode has led to an increase in private capital flows from 2.8 percent of developing countries' aggregate GDP in 2002 to 5.1 percent in 2005.

The macroeconomic consequences and policy responses associated with the previous surge have been explored in a large body of academic literature (Johnson and others 2000; Radelet and Sachs 1998; Corsetti, Pesenti, and Roubini 1998). The data from that period reveal several interesting patterns for developing countries that had access to international capital markets: a considerable acceleration in economic growth, a rise of two percentage points in the ratio of investment to GDP, and a considerable and widespread appreciation of national currencies in real terms (19 percent). Moreover, about one-third of the inflowing capital was allocated to the accumulation of official reserves of foreign exchange, which rose, in aggregate, from $216 billion at the end of 1992 to $572 billion at the end of 1997. These facts provide a good point of comparison for the current influx in private capital to developing countries.

Looking at the cross-country distribution of capital inflows during current episode (see figure 5.1), 67 percent of developing countries received private flows within the range of 2 to 10 percent of their GDP, and a further 16 percent received capital flows of more than 10 percent of their

Figure 5.1 Distribution of private capital flows across developing countries, 2002–4

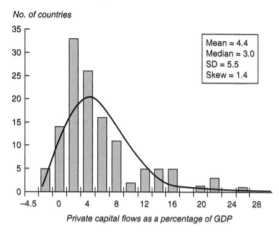

No. of countries

Mean = 4.4
Median = 3.0
SD = 5.5
Skew = 1.4

Private capital flows as a percentage of GDP

Source: World Bank Debtor Reporting System and staff estimates.
Note: 134 developing countries for which we had data were used. Private capital flows to GDP were averaged over the 3 years.

GDP. The correlation between capital inflows and per capita income is positive but relatively low (0.18), reflecting the fact that many low–income countries also have attracted private capital flows, including The Gambia, Mozambique, Tanzania, and Vietnam.

The Asian financial crises of the mid-1990s provide a cautionary example of the potential macroeconomic effect on recipient countries of large capital inflows. At that time, inflows generated a sequence of currency misalignment, asset price escalation, excessive expansion of aggregate demand, inflationary pressures, current-account imbalances, capital losses on central banks' balance sheets, and financial instability—a calamitous chain of events that affected individual countries in very different ways. A large body of theoretical and empirical research over the past decade has attempted to identify confluences of global financial-market conditions and specific developing-country characteristics that could lead to a recurrence of that sequence (World Bank 1997; Calvo and others 1996; Edwards 2001; Chinn and Ito 2002; Kletzer and Spiegel 2004). That literature, combined with recent experience, points to five important trends, domestic and global, distinguishing the present cresting of capital flows from the previous episode:

- The *pattern* of private capital flows to developing countries has changed in two important respects: first, the share of short-term debt in

total debt flows has declined for virtually all major debtors, particularly in crisis-affected countries; second, the composition of flows has rotated toward equity, particularly foreign direct investment (FDI).

- The shift toward more flexible exchange rate regimes has helped overcome a major policy failure underlying the financial crises of the 1990s. That shift, in conjunction with improved macroeconomic conditions, has facilitated a continued process of relaxation or removal of formal controls on many capital-account transactions in many developing countries, despite the severity and global nature of the 1997 financial crisis.

- The current account in many developing countries, particularly major oil exporters and emerging Asia, has moved from deficit to sizable surplus, contributing to the accumulation of foreign exchange reserves. The initial impetus came from countries' strenuous external adjustments to the crises of the 1990s, but high commodity prices, robust global growth over the past few years and intervention to maintain undervalued exchange rates for the purposes of export competitiveness have sustained and, in some cases, amplified the effect. These developments have combined to improve the external debt burdens of developing countries, as debt/export ratios and debt/GDP ratios have declined since their peaks in 1997–8.

- The accelerated development of local bond markets in many countries after the crises of the 1990s has been helpful to the development of a more balanced financial structure, reducing dependence on the banking sector and short-term foreign capital as sources of financing. The presence of a well-functioning government bond market facilitates the conduct of monetary policy through open market operations and helps improve debt management. (This development is discussed in chapter 2.)

- External changes that are likely to affect the climate for capital flows include the euro's growing role as a major international reserve currency, which widens policy makers' choices. Higher international interest rates and likely volatility in exchange rates, by contrast, will constrain policy making. The long and aggressive phase of monetary easing that started in the United States in 2001 came to an end in June 2004, with the Euro Area following suit a few months later. (See Chapter 1.)

The first three of those trends are discussed below.

The composition of capital flows is changing

The composition of private foreign capital flowing to developing countries during the current surge has shifted decisively toward equity, predominantly FDI. The shift reflects government policies that encourage equity and aim to reduce dependence on external borrowing. Thus, on average, FDI accounts for 57 percent of private capital flows to developing countries (figure 5.2), much higher than portfolio equity (9 percent) and higher even than short- and long-term bank debt combined (33 percent). In the mid-1990s, by contrast, the same figures were 47 percent for FDI, 11 percent for portfolio equity, and 42 percent for debt. The trend toward equity in the composition of private capital flows has been particularly pronounced in the two regions (Latin America and the Caribbean and East Asia and the Pacific) that were most directly affected by the string of financial crises in the 1990s.

Greater reliance on equity financing also improves countries' external liability profile, because equity flows are more focused on long-term economic prospects and offer better risk-sharing characteristics than debt flows. Moreover, FDI tends to be more stable than debt, in the sense that current FDI is strongly correlated to its past levels; the coefficient of persistence of FDI, using a simple autoregressive estimation for a sample of developing countries, is found to be on average 0.62, while it is 0.52 on debt (both short and long term).[1]

An indication of the improvement brought about by the changing composition of capital flows is the significant reduction in the ratio of external debt to gross national income (GNI) for developing countries as a whole—from a peak of 44 percent in 1999 to about 34 percent in 2004—and particularly for countries in East Asia and Latin America. In Europe and Central Asia, however, the ratios remain relatively high compared with those seen in the early 1990s.

A further sign of improved external liability positions in the developing world can be found in the ratio of foreign exchange reserves to short-

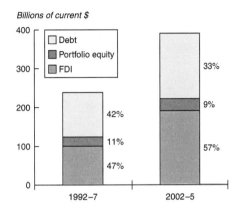

Figure 5.2 Composition of financial flows to developing countries, 1992–7 and 2002–5

Billions of current $

Source: World Bank Debtor Reporting System and staff estimates.

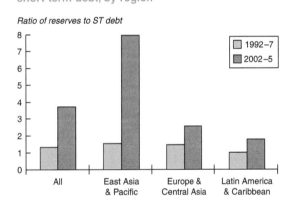

Figure 5.3 Ratio of foreign exchange reserves to short-term debt, by region

Ratio of reserves to ST debt

Source: World Bank Debtor Reporting System and staff estimates.

term debt. Developing countries as a group are now much better equipped than previously to deal with the potential volatility of private capital flows. Looking at reserve holdings on a regional basis, each of the regions holds in the form of reserves at least 1.5 times their short-term debt (figure 5.3). The ratio is particularly high in East Asia (8.3), largely because of China, whose accumulated reserves are 38 times greater than its short-term debt. The rising ratio of reserves to short-term debt reflects not only the spike in reserve holdings, but also the decline in short-term debt as a percentage of total debt in most developing countries since the mid-1990s (table 5.1).

The rotation towards equity and reduced reliance on short-term debt flows have significant policy implications for the management of capital flows to developing countries, as they enhance the scope for monetary policy autonomy. Equity flows, in contrast to debt flows, tend to move countercyclically with local interest rates, increasing during periods of low domestic interest rates due to the positive impact of low interest rates on domestic growth and corporate profitability and valuation. The classical Mundell-Fleming model (Mundell 1963, Fleming 1962) of the open economy and the implied impossible trinity—that countries can pursue only two of the three objectives of fixed exchange rates, free capital mobility, and independent monetary policy—is predicated on the assumption that capital inflows are composed predominately of short-term debt. In an equity dominated pattern of capital flows, authorities have more autonomy in pursuing interest rate policies geared toward domestic goals.

Countries now have more flexible exchange rates and more open capital accounts

Policies on exchange rates and capital controls are particularly important for developing countries, because external developments have a greater effect on domestic inflation, monetary transmission, and financial stability in developing countries than in industrial countries. Most developing countries are already more open to international trade in goods and services than are developed countries: from 2002 to 2004, developing countries' trade averaged 54.5 percent of GDP, compared to 39 percent in developed countries. But developing countries as a group also face a potentially higher degree of volatility in capital flows, and changes in the exchange rate may translate more quickly into domestic inflation than in developed countries.[2] Even with their recent progress in launching local-currency debt issues on global markets (see Chapter 2), developing countries still have much larger shares of their external debt denominated in foreign currencies than do industrial countries (Eichengreen and Hausmann 1999; Hawkins and Turner 2000). Such conditions predispose an economy to greater vulnerability to external financial shocks.

Virtually all capital flow–related financial crises of the 1990s involved a fixed peg or crawling band exchange rate regime and considerable currency mismatch on the balance sheets of both public and private borrowers (Fischer 2001; Goldstein 2002). When countries maintain such exchange rate regimes (fixed pegs or crawling

Table 5.1 Ratio of short-term debt to total debt in major borrowing countries, 1996–2004
Percent

Country	Short-term debt/total debt		
	1996	2004	Change
China	19.7	47.2	27.5
Poland	6.1	17.0	10.9
Czech Rep.	28.5	37.5	9.0
Russian Fed.	9.5	17.8	8.4
Hungary	12.3	19.5	7.2
Venezuela, R. B. de	7.9	12.2	4.3
Egypt	7.4	9.7	2.3
Algeria	1.0	2.0	1.0
India	7.2	6.1	−1.1
Turkey	21.7	19.7	−2.0
Argentina	21.2	16.2	−4.9
Nigeria	18.1	12.8	−5.3
Pakistan	9.4	3.5	−6.0
Malaysia	27.9	21.9	−6.0
Colombia	20.4	14.2	−6.2
Indonesia	25.0	17.4	−7.6
Chile	25.7	17.5	−8.2
Brazil	19.8	11.4	−8.4
Philippines	18.1	8.3	−9.8
Mexico	19.1	6.6	−12.5
South Africa	41.6	27.8	−13.8
Peru	22.2	8.0	−14.2
Thailand	42.3	22.4	−19.9
Average[a]	**18.8**	**16.4**	**−2.4**

Sources: IMF, International Financial Statistics and World Bank staff estimates.
Note: Major borrowing countries, based on the average volume of total debt stock over the period of 1996–2004 (in descending order).
a. Excluding South Africa.

bands), investors and borrowers may believe there is less need to hedge currency movements, and the risk of borrowing in foreign currency appears to be reduced, encouraging excessive exposure. However, if a crisis does hit, and the central bank cannot maintain the peg or band, the costs to the banking system and corporate sector can be substantial and damaging.

Partly due to this experience, several developing countries have adopted greater exchange rate flexibility, moving to a variety of managed-float regimes, with central banks retaining the ability to intervene in the market to influence the exchange rate and limit volatility. Since the early 1990s, nearly 50 developing countries have abandoned fixed or crawling pegs in favor of managed floats or fully flexible exchange rates (figure 5.4). Notable examples are Mexico (1994), Indonesia (1997), Colombia (1999), Brazil (1999), Chile (1999), and the Russian Federation (2002). In July 2005, the Bank Negara Malaysia adopted a man-

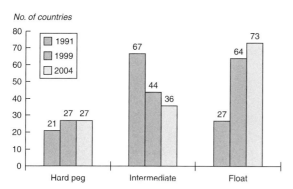

Figure 5.4 Changes in exchange rate flexibility, 1991–2004

No. of countries

Sources: IMF Annual Report on Exchange Arrangements and Exchange Restrictions and World Bank staff estimates.

aged float for the ringgit with reference to a currency basket and the People's Bank of China revalued the renminbi and announced that it would be determined with reference to a currency basket.

Evidence also suggests that many developing countries pursuing a managed float are tolerating a greater degree of short-term fluctuation in their currencies.[3] Figure 5.5 displays the frequency distribution of daily percentage changes in the bilateral exchange rates of currencies in several crisis-affected countries against the U.S. dollar during the current and previous surges in capital flows. The left panel shows movements during the 1990s surge; the right panel shows current movements. The bell-shaped daily fluctuations in exchange rates in the current episode indicate two-way movements in bilateral exchange rates.

Successful management and operation of a flexible exchange rate regime requires proper policy frameworks, market microstructure, and institutions to ensure smooth functioning of foreign exchange markets. Policy decisions must be made about whether to rely on interest rates and intervention to stabilize exchange rates at times of high volatility or uncertainty. Such decisions require an assessment of the underlying sources of exchange rate volatility, which in the context of many developing countries often implies gauging the sustainability of capital flows. For example, policy makers might ask whether a surge in capital flows was composed primarily of volatile portfolio capital or speculative debt, on the one hand, or more stable and predictable FDI flows, on the other. When

pressure on the exchange rate stems from temporary shocks or volatile capital flows, intervention and interest rates, singly or in combination, should be considered as tools to limit short-run exchange rate fluctuations.

There are institutional and microstructure requirements associated with managing a flexible exchange rate regime. The key steps involve the development of local money, capital, and cross-border derivatives markets to provide the necessary depth, sophistication, and hedging possibilities for managing currency risk, thereby providing stability for private agents and the economy as a whole.

Real exchange rate appreciation has been mild

A significant, sustained, and rapid appreciation in a country's real exchange rate is one of the precursors of a currency crisis.[4] Figure 5.6 shows the movements in real effective exchange rates in two of the regions that experienced some of the largest exchange rate corrections during the crises of the 1990s. The appreciation in real exchange rates in the last few years has been much milder than during that period. Latin America shows stronger appreciation over 2004–5 than does East Asia.

Looking at some individual countries, the real exchange rate appreciated in 60 percent of developing countries over the period 1993–6, while only about one-third experienced an appreciation in 2002–4. Moreover, the range of appreciations during the second surge has been significantly smaller (figure 5.7).[5]

Easing of capital controls

Since the 1990s, the shift to floating exchange rates, the convergence of the currencies of Eastern Europe toward the euro, and the deepening of local capital markets have enabled many developing countries to ease capital controls and foreign exchange restrictions. Progress in formulating and implementing such liberalization measures across developing countries has been uneven, however, as countries have moved at different paces and with different degrees of rigor (see box 5.1). The clearest trend is in the liberalization of exchange rate restrictions. The number of countries that declared their currencies convertible on the current account, which often precedes capital-account convertibility, rose from approximately 62 in 1990 (or 40 percent of the IMF's membership) to 164 in 2004 (or almost 90 percent of the IMF's membership).

Figure 5.5 Frequency distribution of daily percentage changes in exchange rates for selected developing countries, 1993–6 vs. 2003–5

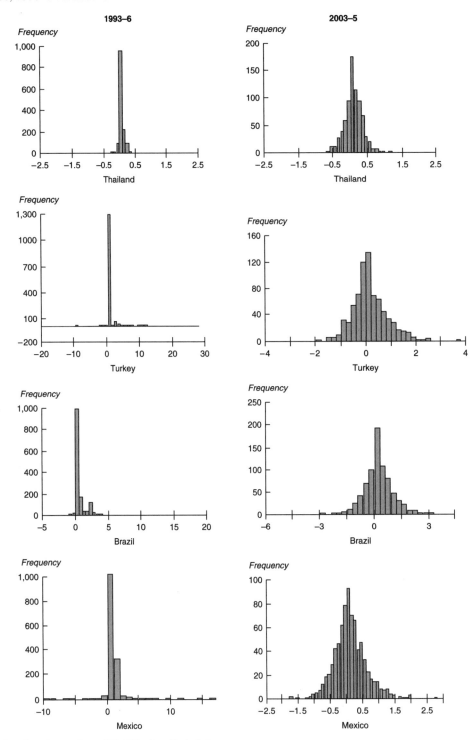

Sources: Bloomberg data service and World Bank staff calculations.
Note: The figures show the frequency distribution of daily percentage changes in the exchange rate between local currency and U.S. dollars. Increases in the exchange rate represent depreciations against the U.S. dollar, and decreases represent appreciation.

Figure 5.6 Movements in real effective exchange rates in East Asia and Latin America, 1993–2005

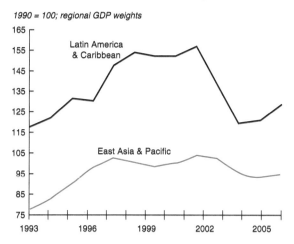

1990 = 100; regional GDP weights

Sources: IMF, International Financial Statistics and World Bank staff calculations.

Figure 5.7 Real exchange rates for selected countries that receive higher-than-average private capital inflows as a ratio to GDP, 1994–7 and 2002–5

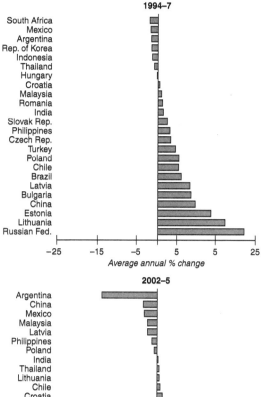

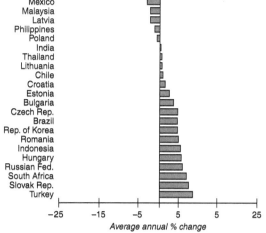

Sources: Bank for International Settlements and World Bank staff estimates.

Three trends stand out in the liberalization of capital-account transactions:

- The easing or removal of quantitative restrictions on residents' issuance of securities, including debt, and outward FDI by private resident entities
- The relaxation of limits on nonresidents' access to local money and securities markets
- The reduction or elimination of taxes on capital-account transactions.

In Chile, for example, the limit on outbound foreign investment by private pension funds was increased in 2003–4 from 16 to 30 percent, enabling local investors to hold diversified portfolios despite the small size of local capital markets. In Malaysia and Thailand, approved domestic institutional investors may now invest up to 10 percent of their assets abroad. In the Republic of Korea, residents are encouraged to invest in overseas mutual funds to mitigate the impact of foreign inflows. And in India, new measures have relaxed overseas investment restrictions on banks and mutual funds, allowing banks to invest in money market and debt instruments abroad and raising from $500 million to $1 billion the limit on mutual funds' investments in companies listed abroad. In Brazil this year, foreign investors were exempted from a 15 percent withholding tax on local government debt investments.

Many countries with open capital accounts have floating exchange rates

The growing group of developing countries that are considered relatively open to capital movements appears in table 5.2. A variety of indices of financial openness were used to compile the list (Chinn and 2002; Miniane 2004; Edwards 2005; Quinn 1997; and Brune and others 2001). The countries in the table all have achieved currency

Box 5.1   Preconditions for capital-account liberalization

By the early 1990s, under the Code of Liberalization of Capital Movements of the Organization for Economic Co-operation and Development (OECD), developed countries had moved to open their capital accounts fully to cross-border financial transactions, including capital-market securities, money-market operations, and derivatives instruments. Developing countries, by contrast, have continued to maintain, though in varying degrees, a wide range of administrative capital controls and foreign exchange restrictions. Capital-account regulation ranges from quantitative limitations on certain transactions (or on associated transfers of funds) to indirect measures intended to influence the economic incentives of engaging in certain transactions (IMF various years; Dailami 2000; and Eichengreen 2001). Although country circumstances vary, controls generally have three goals: to discourage short-term external debt flows in favor of longer-term investments, such as FDI (a motivation that gained momentum after the East Asian crises); to enhance monetary autonomy and exchange rate stability; and to allow time for the establishment of an institutional and policy framework within which capital-account liberalization will be successful (Rodrik 1999; Stiglitz 2002).

The liberalization of capital accounts must be accompanied by sound economic policies and institutions, so that governments are prepared to deal with the volatility inherent in capital markets. The preconditions for a safe transition to a more open capital account in most developing countries include a track record of fiscal prudence and stability (specifically, low inflation and a low fiscal deficit), a deep and well-regulated financial system, and adequate levels of reserves to provide the necessary buffer against adverse external shocks. Against such a backdrop, a deliberate and sequenced opening will signal to financial markets the government's commitment to sound finance, thereby contributing to more stable capital flows. Once capital-account liberalization has progressed, it is very costly to reverse, and the reinstitution of capital controls should be considered a last resort, appropriate only when alternative policy options have been exhausted. Even then, authorities would have to consider the reputational costs of invoking controls and carefully assess the likelihood that the controls would meet their declared objectives in today's large and rapidly changing global financial environment (Goldfajn and Minella 2005; Edwards 2005; Carvalho and Garcia 2005).

convertibility on the current account of the balance of payments—but they maintain some controls on capital-account transactions. The table also reports on three other aspects of these countries' external financial profile: exchange rate regime, monetary policy framework, and the number of years that currency convertibility on current accounts (signifying acceptance of IMF Article VIII) has been in effect. It also indicates whether there exists an offshore nondeliverable foreign exchange forward market (NDF)[6] for each currency. Most countries that are largely open to capital-account transactions maintain a flexible exchange rate arrangement. This affords policy makers a degree of autonomy in setting interest rates to achieve price stability, something particularly desirable for countries such as Brazil, Chile, Mexico, the Philippines, South Africa, and Thailand, which have adopted inflation targeting as an anchor for monetary policy.

Along with the shift to greater exchange rate flexibility, a number of developing countries have moved to inflation targeting regimes. Twelve of the 32 developing countries considered to be rela-

tively open to capital movements had adopted inflation targeting regimes by the end of 2005—several in the course of the year (table 5.2). Recent research (IMF 2006) indicates that a number of developing countries that have pledged to use inflation targeting as their monetary policy framework have had better macroeconomic performance and in particular have outperformed countries with other frameworks.[7]

Six of the same 32 countries allow offshore trading in their currencies through NDFs, which are similar to ordinary forward foreign exchange contracts, with the exception that at maturity they do not require physical delivery of currencies and are typically settled in U.S. dollars. NDFs are largely short-term instruments—one month to one year—and are increasingly relied upon by foreign investors to hedge their exposures against currencies that are not traded internationally and that are not convertible on capital-account transactions. Once a country permits convertibility and develops onshore foreign exchange markets, NDF markets tend to diminish. Although NDFs are helpful instruments for managing cross-border

Table 5.2 Profile of external financial policy for developing countries considered relatively open to capital movements

As of 2005

Largely open countries	Exchange rate regime	Monetary policy	Years since article VIII assumed	Offshore currency derivatives market
Bolivia	Intermediate	Exchange rate anchor	38	
Botswana	Intermediate	Exchange rate anchor	10	
Costa Rica	Intermediate	Exchange rate anchor	40	
Croatia	Floating	IMF program	10	
Czech Rep.	Floating	Inflation target	10	
Dominican Rep.	Floating	—	52	
Ecuador	Hard peg	Exchange rate anchor	35	
Egypt, Arab Rep. of	Floating	M aggregate	1	
El Salvador	Hard peg	Exchange rate anchor	59	
Estonia	Hard peg	—	11	
The Gambia	Floating	—	12	
Guatemala	Floating	Inflation target	58	
Hungary	Intermediate	Inflation target	9	
Indonesia	Floating	Inflation target	17	Yes
Jamaica	Floating	M aggregate	42	
Jordan	Hard peg	Exchange rate anchor	10	
Kenya	Floating	IMF program	11	
Latvia	Intermediate	Exchange rate anchor	11	
Lebanon	Intermediate	Exchange rate anchor	12	
Mexico	Floating	Inflation target	59	Yes
Nicaragua	Intermediate	Exchange rate anchor	41	
Panama	Hard peg	Exchange rate anchor	59	
Peru	Floating	Inflation target	44	Yes
Philippines	Floating	Inflation target	10	Yes
Poland	Floating	Inflation target	10	
Romania	Floating	Inflation target	7	
Slovak Rep.	Floating	Inflation target	10	Yes
Thailand	Floating	Inflation target	15	Yes
Trinidad & Tobago	Hard peg	—	12	
Turkey	Floating	Inflation target	15	
Uruguay	Floating	M aggregate	25	
Zambia	Floating	M aggregate	3	

Sources: World Bank staff calculations based on Ito and Menzies 2002; Miniane 2004; Edwards 2005; Quinn 1997; Brune and others 2001 and Annual Report on Exchange Arrangements and Exchange Restrictions, IMF, various years.
Note: Monetary policy: Inflation target = Public announcement of medium-term numerical targets for inflation with an institutional commitment by the monetary authority to achieve those targets. M aggregate = Monetary authority uses its instruments to achieve a target growth rate for a monetary aggregate that becomes the nominal anchor or intermediate target of monetary policy. Exchange rate anchor = Monetary authority stands ready to buy and sell foreign exchange at quoted rates to maintain the exchange rate at its predetermined level or range. IMF program = Implementation of monetary and exchange rate policy within the confines of a framework that establishes floors for international reserves and ceilings for net domestic assets of the central bank.

currency risk, regulatory agencies in developing countries need to keep a close eye on them, given the illiquidity of the currencies that underlie NDF transactions and the potential for speculative behavior.

Many countries now show surpluses on both their current and capital accounts

Developing countries as a group have undergone a significant turnaround in the past several years in their external payment positions, moving from an aggregate current-account deficit of $89 billion (1.6 percent of GDP) in 1998 to a sizable surplus of $248 billion (2.6 percent of GDP) in 2005 (fig-

ure 5.8). This stands in marked contrast to the pattern observed in the first capital boom of 1992–7, when developing countries as a whole ran an aggregate current-account deficit of 2 percent of GDP per year (or an aggregate deficit of $547.7 billion from 1992–7).

Much of the current-account surplus accumulated during the present surge is attributable to oil exporters and emerging Asia, which are benefiting from high oil prices and strong export growth, respectively. The net oil-exporting countries as a group have seen large gains in their current-account surpluses, posting an aggregate surplus of close to $219 billion in 2005, up from $50 billion

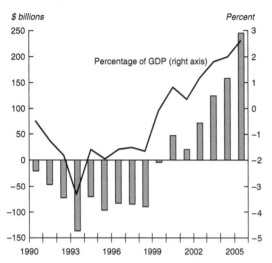

Figure 5.8 Current-account balance, developing countries, 1990–2005

Sources: IMF, International Financial Statistics and World Bank staff calculations.

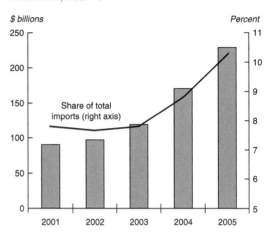

Figure 5.9 Value of oil imports, oil-importing countries, 2001–5

Sources: World Bank Debtor Reporting System and staff estimates.

Table 5.3 Current account aggregated by region, 1997–2005
$ billions

	1997	1998	1999	2000	2001	2002	2003	2004	2005e
All developing countries	−84.7	−89.4	−4.1	47.1	18.8	69.8	122.3	153.1	248.4
East Asia and Pacific	17.2	59.8	60.3	53.7	39.8	61.2	74.9	93.6	143.4
Europe and Central Asia	−27.7	−24.5	−1.3	16.3	17.6	5.6	−2.0	4.2	23.2
Latin America and Caribbean	−65.3	−89.4	−55.4	−46.8	−51.9	−14.9	8.4	19.0	33.9
Middle East and North Africa	4.5	−9.7	6.2	25.3	15.4	12.0	28.3	41.0	76.0
Others	−13.3	−25.4	−13.2	−0.7	−0.2	8.1	14.3	−2.3	−23.5
Memo item									
Oil exporting countries	−32.5	−47.5	26.9	87.4	41.4	49.3	91.3	131.2	219.0
Oil importing countries	−52.2	−42.0	−30.9	−40.3	−22.6	20.6	31.0	21.9	29.5
excl. China	−89.2	−73.4	−52.0	−60.8	−40.0	−14.9	−14.9	−46.6	−97.2

Sources: IMF, International Financial Statistics and World Bank data reporting system.
e = estimate.

in 2002. By contrast, the current-account position of oil-importing developing countries has increased from a surplus of $21 billion in 2002 to a surplus of $30 billion in 2005. The rise in their oil import bills from an aggregate value of $91.2 billion in 2001 to $229.8 billion in 2005 (now equal to approximately 10 percent of their total imports of goods and services—figure 5.9) is substantially greater than the change in their current account, as the boom in non-oil commodity prices has cushioned somewhat the impact of rising oil prices.

Meanwhile, the Eastern Europe and Central Asia regions have recorded a large surplus, largely because of strong oil exports from the Russian Federation that mask deficits elsewhere in the re-

gion. And in Latin America, thanks to favorable prices for many non-oil commodity exports and relatively strong global economic growth, the region's surplus increased in 2005 to $33.9 billion (table 5.3)—the largest current-account surplus recorded for that region in 25 years.

The overall surpluses appearing on the current and capital accounts of the balance of payments of many countries reflect an increase in holdings of foreign currency due to net inflows from trade, workers' remittances, and financial transactions (table 5.4).

For developing countries as a whole, these inflows have increased steadily since 2000. In 2005, the combined current accounts and recorded capi-

Table 5.4 Sources of reserve accumulation, 1997–2005
$ billions

	1997	1998	1999	2000	2001	2002	2003	2004	2005e
Change in reserves	52	16	33	45	82	172	292	405	392
Current account balance	–85	–89	–4	48	21	72	124	158	246
Balance on goods & services	–53	–44	33	76	48	86	107	128	146
Net workers' remittances	71	73	77	84	96	113	141	160	167
Capital account	332	260	241	211	210	209	303	418	464
Net private capital flows	293	199	198	188	154	172	272	397	483
Net official capital flows	38	61	42	23	55	38	31	22	–19
Residents' foreign asset accumulation and errors & omissions	195	155	204	213	148	109	136	172	318

Sources: IMF, International Financial Statistics and World Bank data reporting system.
e = estimate.

tal accounts of the developing world amounted to $710 billion (7 percent of their aggregate GDP), of which $392 billion was channeled into reserves by the official sector and the rest invested abroad by residents in the form of FDI, portfolio holdings, and other vehicles. (The cited figures include errors and omissions in the balance-of-payments accounts.) The opening of capital accounts by many developing countries in recent years has increased opportunities for capital outflows by firms and other private investors seeking to improve their returns through international diversification.

Policy responses to such influx of liquidity must take into account the difference in the dynamics and cyclical characteristics of current-account positions and private capital flows. Private capital flows to developing countries tend to move pro-cyclically, in line with global economic activity as expressed in GDP, trade, and commodity prices. They increase during upswings in commodity prices, for example, and decrease during downturns, which tends to amplify balance-of-payment swings from oil and other commodities. Current-account positions, by contrast, are less volatile than capital flows; they move in a countercyclical fashion with respect to the business cycle (Lane 2003). Box 5.2 provides an estimate of the sensitivity of private capital flows to international commodity price movements from 1980 to 2005. For developing countries as a whole, private capital flows were twice as large during upturns as they were during downturns, averaging $237 billion (in constant U.S. dollars) during upswings in commodity prices, and $109 billion during downswings.

While capital flows tend to rise during upswings of economic cycles and decline in bad times, remittances tend to be countercyclical rela-

tive to recipient countries' economies. Remittances (which are the largest source of external financing in many developing countries) may rise when the recipient economy suffers a downturn in activity, or because of macroeconomic shocks due to financial crisis, natural disaster, or political conflict (Clarke and Wallsten 2004, Kapur 2003, Yang 2004 and 2005), as migrants may send more funds during hard times to help their families and friends.[8] According to official statistics, in 2005 remittance flows are estimated to have exceeded $233 billion worldwide, of which developing countries received $167 billion.

Current-account surpluses have fed foreign exchange reserves

Although the pace of foreign exchange reserve accumulation slowed somewhat in 2005 in several developing countries, including India, Thailand, and Malaysia, the conversion of current-account surpluses into official reserves has continued. For developing countries as a group, the stock of official foreign exchange reserves reached $2 trillion by the end of 2005, compared to $1.6 trillion in 2004 and $1.2 trillion in 2002. In 2005, 92 of 127 developing countries increased their reserves, with the largest accumulations occurring in China and oil-exporting countries (figure 5.10). In relation to the size of their international trade, developing countries' reserve holdings are now twice as large as those in developed countries (figure 5.11). Demand for official foreign currency reserves in major industrial countries has been more subdued, given their free-floating exchange rates, well-developed capital markets, and less vulnerable economies. At the end of 2005, the Euro Area reported $167 billion in reserves (European Central

Box 5.2   Capital flows are procyclical with respect to non-oil commodity markets

Capital flows to developing countries tend to move procyclically with world commodity prices, increasing when commodity prices are high and decreasing when they are low. Two factors account for this. First, commodity prices typically are negatively correlated with fixed income and equity markets in advanced countries. Capital is pushed to the developing world when returns in mature capital markets are low (typically during upturns), and vice-versa. Second, commodities still account for a large share of developing-country exports and production, affecting their terms of trade and real exchange rates, and potentially influencing business-cycle fluctuations, particularly in countries characterized as having "commodity currencies" (Chen and Rogoff 2002; Mendoza 1995; Cashin and others 2003). Thus the rise in aggregate demand increases domestic borrowing. Equally, as developing countries tend to face quantitative constraints on their borrowing, the rise in creditworthiness that comes with higher earnings on commodity exports increases foreign lenders' willingness to supply funds. The relationship between capital flows and commodity prices is displayed in the figure below, which shows the behavior of net private capital flows (deflated by the U.S. GDP deflator) to developing countries, and the world price (in real terms) of their non-energy commodity exports from 1980 to 2005.

This co-movement poses a problem for the management of capital flows in developing countries because, when commodity prices are falling (signaling a downturn in economic activity), capital flows also tend to fall, potentially exacerbating the effects of an economic downturn for the developing country.

Over the period 1980–2005, downswings in world commodity prices (for those commodities that form a sig-

nificant portion of developing-country exports) averaged 16 years, while upswings averaged 8.5 years. For developing countries as a whole, private capital flows were twice as large during upturns as they were during downturns, averaging $237 billion (in constant U.S. dollars) during upswings in prices, and $109 billion during downswings. This tendency is also confirmed by detailed regional analyses using region-specific commodity price indices (excluding energy) and capital flow data. The correlation between private capital flows and commodity prices is particularly pronounced in East Asia, Europe and Central Asia, and Latin America. During the upturns in commodity prices, private capital flows in East Asia, for example, were 3.1 times larger than they were during downturns. Similarly, in Europe and Central Asia, private capital flows were 3.2 times larger during upturns than downturns. In the other three regions, private capital flows in total are more modest, although they also tend to move procyclically.

The recent surge in private capital flows is a good illustration of this experience. Net private capital flows rose from $154 billion in 2001 to an estimated $483 billion in 2005, while non-oil commodity prices increased by 55 percent, and oil prices by 119 percent, in dollar terms. This raises an important issue for oil importers: because the non-oil commodity-price cycle may have reached a peak, while oil prices are likely to remain high (see chapter 1), oil importers face the prospect of further declines in their terms of trade, coupled with a fall in private capital flows. It remains to be seen whether the improved macroeconomic environment achieved in recent years will be sufficient to cope with a substantial fall in both export revenues and external finance.

Private capital flows in line with non-oil commodity prices

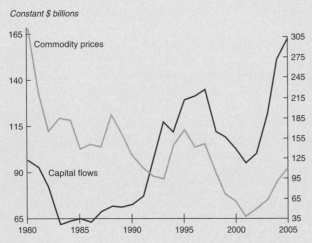

Sources: World Bank Debtor Reporting System and staff estimates.

Volume of private capital flows during cycles, 1980–2005

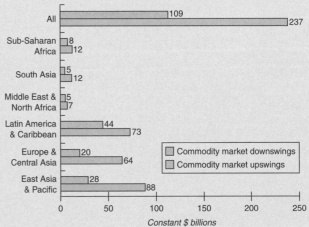

Sources: World Bank Debtor Reporting System and staff estimates.

Figure 5.10 Foreign exchange reserves, by region, 1995–2005

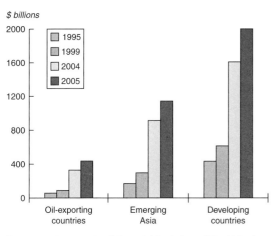

Sources: IMF, International Financial Statistics and World Bank staff calculations.

Figure 5.11 Foreign exchange reserves as a share of trade, 1970–2003

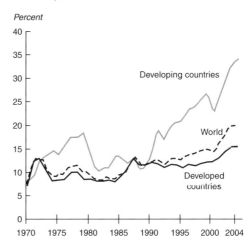

Source: World Bank staff calculations.

Bank and Euro-System); the United States, $37.8 billion (combined reserves of the Federal Reserve's Open Market Account and the Treasury Department's Exchange Stabilization Fund); the United Kingdom, $40.9 billion; and Japan, $828.8 billion, the largest amount among the developed countries.

The large-scale reserve buildups in developing countries reflect central banks' policies of intervening in foreign exchange markets. In practice, the central banks purchase from private and public entities part or all of their inward flow of foreign exchange, paying for them with a mix of local currency and debt instruments. Massive foreign exchange intervention, therefore, is very likely to have expansionary domestic monetary implications in many developing countries. The authorities in

many high-reserve countries have so far managed to contain expansionary outcomes through large-scale and routine sterilizations using open-market operations and other means. In almost all countries included in table 5.5, the change in net foreign assets on the central bank's balance sheets between 2001 and 2005 has been largely offset by a decrease in net domestic assets, leaving reserve money largely unchanged as a percentage of GDP.

The accumulation of reserves has concentrated risks on central bank balance sheets

The effect of the sterilization of capital flows is to transfer much of the currency risk associated with the intermediation of capital flows to the public sector, particularly to the central bank. When the

Table 5.5 Changes in central bank balance sheets, 2001–5
% change relative to GDP

	Net foreign assets			Net domestic assets			Reserve money		
	2001	2005	Change	2001	2005	Change	2001	2005	Change
Brazil	5.0	5.2	0.2	10.8	4.8	–6.0	6.6	11.1	4.5
China	19.6	34.4	14.8	22.0	6.7	–15.3	42.3	35.3	–7.0
Czech Rep.	22.5	25.0	2.5	–2.2	–5.0	–2.8	22.3	10.7	–11.5
India	10.2	20.2	10.0	8.0	0.2	–7.8	13.8	16.3	2.5
Malaysia	35.0	57.4	22.4	–6.8	–6.5	0.3	12.0	11.0	–1.0
Mexico	7.2	9.6	2.5	–1.7	–0.6	1.0	5.7	8.0	2.3
Poland	13.3	14.3	0.9	2.2	–1.5	–3.7	8.2	7.9	–0.3
Russian Fed.	9.9	24.3	14.3	5.0	–8.5	–13.5	10.8	13.7	2.9
Thailand	20.2	30.0	9.8	9.1	10.1	1.0	14.2	20.9	6.7
Turkey	–3.1	6.2	9.3	22.9	4.9	–18.1	10.1	8.4	–1.8
Venezuela, R. B. de	10.5	24.9	14.5	0.0	–2.3	–2.3	7.3	9.2	1.9

Sources: World Bank Data Reporting System and World Bank staff estimates.

central bank carries out an open-market sterilized intervention, it finances its purchase of foreign exchange reserves by issuing an equivalent amount of domestic public debt in the form of government (or central bank) securities. Reserves are typically invested in certain classes of foreign assets deemed to be of "reserve quality" or are used to pay down existing external public debt. At the end of 2005, foreign exchange reserves accounted for about three-fourths of the average assets of central banks of the countries with the largest reserve holdings, ranging from 27 percent in Brazil to 93 percent in Malaysia (table 5.6). Since the interest rates on reserve-grade assets are seldom as high as those on domestic securities, the mismatch often represents a significant loss of revenue, so that more debt has to be issued to cover the shortfall.

The chief domestic implication of high reserves is a large accumulation of public debt. As domestic securities are the counterpart liabilities to foreign assets on the central bank's balance sheet, the bank must be concerned about the effects of a rise in local interest rates. Whether they are issued in the form of the central bank's own obligations or drawn from its existing inventory of government securities, the securities issued to balance out foreign currency reserves must compete for the available supply of domestic savings with securities issued by the private sector. In some countries, such as China, the supply of domestic securities issued by the central bank has grown very rapidly in recent years, from 2.2 percent of GDP in 2003 to 11 percent of GDP in 2005 (box 5.3).

Table 5.6 Foreign currency reserves and foreign assets as shares of total central bank assets in countries with high reserve accumulations, 2005
Percent

Country	Foreign reserves/ Total assets	Net foreign assets/ Total assets
Brazil	27.9	20.9
China	84.8	79.4
India	79.2	88.7
Malaysia	93.1	90.8
Mexico	86.4	86.3
Poland	91.8	93.1
Russian Fed.	84.8	89.7
Thailand	63.8	67.1
Turkey	62.9	27.3
Venezuela, R. B. de	73.9	95.1
Average	**74.9**	**73.8**

Sources: IMF, International Financial Statistics, and World Bank staff calculations.

The upward pressure on local interest rates induced by reserve accumulation could have the perverse effect of reinforcing the need for more reserves, as higher interest rates could attract larger volumes of private inflows. Higher local rates may well conflict with the government's policy of stimulating investment and growth. And they almost always cause an increase in the government's public debt; such public finance issues arise even if these assets are held by agencies other than central banks. The fact that governments tend to entrust the responsibility for accumulation and management of official reserves to their central banks adds to the complexity of the problem at hand by bringing to the fore the unique institutional character of central banks, their role in monetary and exchange rate management, and their particular accounting and reporting norms and standards. Central banks have a monopoly position in issuing domestic currency and the rules and agreements governing the distribution of their profits and dividends to the treasury vary considerably and are often determined by negotiation (Courtis and Mander 2003).[9]

Countries are adjusting the currency composition of their reserves

The range of foreign assets of reserve quality encompasses virtually all government securities issued by large industrial countries that are denominated in major currencies and traded in deep liquid markets. The two key qualifying conditions for reserve assets are that they need to be readily available to and controlled by national monetary authorities (IMF 2001). Official holders of reserves may need to access them quickly and under difficult market conditions, when the ability to turn reserve assets into cash for intervention purposes at the prevailing market price is of the first importance.[10]

Almost 93 percent of developing countries' reported official reserve holdings as of the end of 2005 were invested in three major currencies: the U.S. dollar, the euro, and the Japanese yen.[11] The euro's share increased from 20 percent of reserves held at end-2000 to 29 percent in 2005, while the share of U.S. dollar reserves declined from 68 percent to 60 percent during the same period (figure 5.12).

The dominant role of the U.S. dollar is likely to have persisted into 2006, as much of the reserve

Box 5.3 Central bank debt in China

In the face of large capital inflows, the People's Bank of China (PBC) has had to act to stabilize monetary growth, a challenge complicated by the fact that, until July 2005, the PBC pegged the Chinese currency to the U.S. dollar. A close examination of the PBC balance sheet reveals a significant level of sterilization in the form of PBC securities issued to offset the domestic monetary consequences of PBC's purchases of foreign exchange. In 2004 and 2005, the PBC issued bonds worth 805 billion and 922 billion yuan, respectively, in local markets, raising the outstanding stock of such bonds from 303 billion yuan in 2003 to 2,033 billion yuan in 2005 (figure at left). In addition, the authorities have relied on administrative mea-

sures, including reserve requirement ratios on domestic banks and credit ceilings on overheated sectors, such as real estate and infrastructure, in order to tighten monetary conditions and contain the inflationary consequences of large reserve accumulation. Such measures, coupled with the closed nature of China's capital markets, have enabled the PBC to follow a prudent course of monetary policy. The pace of growth in the money supply (M2) remained within PBC's target of 15 percent for much of 2004–5, but the rate of growth seems to have accelerated since the third quarter of 2005, possibly because of PBC's move to ease its efforts on sterilization so as to buffer the impact of a currency revaluation (figure at right).

Domestic bond issuance by China's central bank, 2001–5

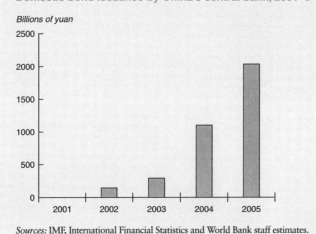

Sources: IMF, International Financial Statistics and World Bank staff estimates.

China's money supply and reserve money, 2000–5

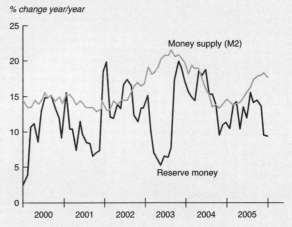

Sources: IMF, International Financial Statistics and World Bank staff estimates.

accumulation during the year was done by Asian and oil-exporting countries, whose main exports are priced in dollars and whose currencies are in many cases either linked to the dollar or to a basket of currencies in which the dollar is heavily weighted. Although models of optimal portfolio investment allocation call for more euros in developing countries' reserve holdings (box 5.4), further shifts into euro reserves are likely to be hampered by several factors:

- *Inertia.* Holdings of reserve currency reflect the currency's importance in other areas, such as trade, which evolve slowly. A prime example is the time it took for the U.S. dollar to overtake

the pound sterling as the world's major currency, despite the fact that the U.S. economy had overtaken Britain's long before (Cohen 2000).

- *First-mover risks.* Choosing an alternative currency is risky for any individual holder, since it depends for its success on others also deciding to use that currency. In other words, there are network externalities, and such externalities may justify historical dependence on the use of that currency as a medium of exchange.

- *Effects on exchange rates.* Switching out of the incumbent reserve currency may induce adverse movements in dollar/euro exchange rates, so large holders may be reluctant to switch from the existing reserve holdings.

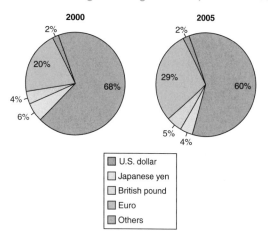

Figure 5.12 Currency composition of developing countries' foreign exchange reserves, 2000 and 2005

Sources: IMF, International Financial Statistics and World Bank staff calculations.

Such a consideration may be important in the current context for official holders of U.S. dollars in Asia and for oil exporters, and any diversification is likely to be incremental through purchase of non-dollar assets in the future, depending on the pace of their reserve accumulation.

- *Depth.* No market in euro-denominated government bonds, or indeed in the world, is as deep and liquid as that for U.S. Treasury securities. Although the aggregate issuance of Euro Area government debt is of the same order of magnitude as that of U.S. Treasury issues, Euro Area debt is the debt of 12 sovereign entities, rather than one. So far, there has been only limited coordination of the schedule and structure of issues (Bernanke 2004). There is also a lack of debt instruments with short maturities, since Euro Area governments issue relatively few short-term bills.[12]

The effect of the recent influx of capital flows on domestic investment and asset prices

Improved macroeconomic fundamentals, increased exchange rate flexibility, and greater financial openness have enhanced the ability of national policy makers to deal effectively with the ongoing surge in capital flows. Two domestic

changes associated with that surge have already become clear. They are an increase in domestic investment in most recipient countries and a sharp escalation in asset prices in local equity markets. These effects must be considered to be the initial manifestations of the current surge—longer term consequences are still in the making.

Our analysis of monetary aggregates, based on a sample of 72 developing countries with access to international capital markets, provided no clear signal of excess money supply growth associated with the surge in private flows.[13] Simple correlation and cross-country regression analyses revealed no statistically significant relationship between private capital flows and indicators of domestic money and credit supply. One plausible explanation is the possibility of a shift in demand for real money balances, brought about as many countries have lowered their inflation while simultaneously experiencing robust economic growth. Higher demand for money has absorbed some liquidity reducing the pressure on domestic inflation. Such findings are also consistent with the conclusion that, to date, countries have elected to respond to the surge by accumulating (and sterilizing) large quantities of reserves. This policy response is understandable: authorities in recipient countries see the surge as temporary and seek to avoid adjustments in the current accounts of their balance of payments. Sustained access to capital flows over time, however, is necessary for capital inflows to have a tangible impact on economic growth—to the extent that they increase domestic investment or lead to increased domestic financial intermediation (Bailliu 2000) or to enhanced domestic firm productivity. Reserve accumulation and sterilization cannot be a long-term solution to capital inflows, particularly if developing countries remain attractive for foreign investment in the coming years.

Capital flows are sometimes associated with increased domestic investment

Private capital flows can contribute meaningfully to domestic investment, particularly if they are sustained. The influx of private capital flows is associated with increased domestic investment, on average, as well as for most of the 72 developing countries in our sample. Table 5.7 compares the investment performance (aggregate domestic investment as a percentage of GDP) of a large

Box 5.4   Optimizing allocations in reserve portfolios

The currency composition of reserves can be viewed in terms of a mean-variance, or capital-asset-pricing, model. Such models typically quantify the attractiveness of reserve assets in optimal portfolios over the long run, in the absence of other factors. In the real world, the choice of reserve currency is subject to considerable inertia, that is, it evolves slowly.

Thus portfolios based on an optimal reserve-portfolio model, when compared to actual reserve holdings, provide an indication of long-run trends in the composition of reserves (after inertia has worked itself out), rather than predictions of near-term reserves changes. The table below provides the optimal reserve allocation across four currencies (U.S. dollar, euro, Japanese yen, and the pound ster-

ling) for a representative country consuming a basket of goods with the same proportions as the SDR weights, on the basis of historical returns on government bonds since the euro's introduction.

A comparison of real SDR returns on the major reserve currencies since 1999 (table below) shows that the pound sterling had the highest ex post return. While the euro's mean return was higher than the dollar's, its standard deviation was considerably larger. As a result, the representative country would hold a proportion of its reserves in euros lower than its SDR weight, while the dollar's proportion would be slightly higher.

Source: IMF Annual Report 2005.

Real returns expressed in SDRs, January 1999–September 2005
% per annum

	Mean	Standard deviation	Correlations			
			Dollar	Pound	Yen	Euro
U.S. dollar	1.98	15.88	1.00	−0.33	−0.09	−0.82
British pound	4.82	17.16	−0.33	1.00	−0.24	0.19
Japanese yen	1.55	26.53	−0.09	−0.24	1.00	−0.32
Euro	3.66	21.86	−0.82	0.19	−0.39	1.00

	Optimal share	SDR weight
U.S. dollar	1.98	15.88
British pound	4.82	17.16
Japanese yen	1.55	26.53
Euro	3.66	21.86

sample of recipient countries during the first three years of the current surge (2002–4) with the preceding three years (1999–1). On average, across countries, investment rates stand approximately at the pre–Asian crisis level, although many countries have not yet reached that level. In Indonesia, Malaysia, and Thailand, investment rates remain lower than pre-crisis levels by 10 to 20 percentage points of GDP, suggesting that the over-exuberance in investor behavior during the previous capital flow surge has not yet materialized, although a few countries, such as China, exhibit potential signs of overheating.

Simple cross-country regression of domestic investment on private capital flows or the components of those flows reveals that the FDI component of capital flows has the strongest correlation

with domestic investment during 2002–4.[14] This result may reflect the higher share of FDI in capital flows in 2002–4, as compared with 1992–7, since inbound FDI adds directly to domestic investment (see box 5.5). In addition, FDI has the potential to generate positive spillovers in the form of technology transfers, knowledge diffusion, and forward and backward linkages, potentially adding stimulus to overall domestic investment spending (Razin 2003; Alfaro, Chanda, and others 2004).

The capital flows surge has not (yet) resulted in excessive demand expansion

One of the questions that arises during the current surge in capital flows, particularly in the quickly growing economies of China and India as well as in some of the oil exporting Eastern European

Table 5.7 Investment performance during the surge in capital flows, 2002–4

Investment as a % of GDP (averages)

Selected Countries	Average over 1994–6	1999–2001	2002–4	Change (2002/4–1999/2001)
Azerbaijan	22.7	22.6	45.6	23.0
Bangladesh	19.2	23.3	23.3	0.0
Botswana	25.4	23.7	27.6	4.0
Brazil	21.8	21.1	18.8	–2.3
Chile	25.6	21.5	23.2	1.7
China	40.5	37.4	43.2	5.8
Colombia	24.5	13.9	14.9	1.0
Croatia	19.0	22.4	28.8	6.4
Ecuador	21.0	20.2	25.9	5.8
Egypt, Arab Rep. of	16.8	18.6	17.0	–1.6
El Salvador	18.4	16.7	16.4	–0.3
Hungary	23.4	28.8	24.9	–3.9
India	23.9	22.9	22.8	0.0
Indonesia	31.2	18.3	20.4	2.1
Jordan	32.2	22.0	22.1	0.2
Kazakhstan	22.7	20.9	26.1	5.2
Malaysia	42.1	24.5	21.9	–2.6
Mexico	21.7	22.8	21.0	–1.7
Morocco	20.6	23.2	23.5	0.2
Nigeria	16.7	21.3	23.3	2.0
Pakistan	19.0	16.7	17.1	0.4
Peru	23.3	20.2	18.7	–1.4
Philippines	23.5	19.6	17.1	–2.5
Poland	18.9	23.4	19.1	–4.3
Russian Fed.	24.9	18.5	20.7	2.2
South Africa	17.4	15.9	17.0	1.1
Sri Lanka	25.7	25.8	22.7	–3.0
Thailand	41.4	22.5	25.3	2.9
Tunisia	24.8	27.1	25.0	–2.2
Turkey	23.8	21.5	23.3	1.7
Venezuela, R. B. de	16.3	26.1	19.3	–6.8
Vietnam	26.9	29.5	34.2	4.7
Zambia	12.3	18.8	24.6	5.8
Total	23.8	21.9	23.3	1.3

Sources: IMF, International Financial Statistics and World Bank staff calculations.
Note: A selection of countries is presented; the overall average represents results for a sample of 72 developing countries with access to international capital markets. The countries in the sample account for more than 95 percent of private capital flows to developing countries.

countries, is whether private capital flows are contributing to overheating. Several traditional markers of overheating (acceleration in inflation, rapid increases in domestic investment, and consumer goods imports) have not been evident so far during this current surge. Inflation has decreased in many developing countries (table 5.8) and remained relatively low, and currencies have not experienced significant appreciation in terms of their real effective exchange rate (as noted earlier). Moreover, there is no sign so far of a run-up in consumption and imports, and thus of current-account deficits or of sharp rises in domestic investment. It does not yet appear that the current surge in private capital flows has resulted in the kind of overheating of domestic economies seen just before the East Asian crisis. It is still early, however. Should the surge continue, it could result in higher inflation, currency appreciation, and declines in current-account balances over the next few years.

Capital flows are associated with escalation in asset prices

Although inflation as a whole has remained subdued in most developing countries, one indicator of potential demand pressures is the sharp rise in stock prices. The stock market capitalization of countries included in the Standard and Poor's/IFCI index[15] rose from $1.7 trillion at the end of 2002 to $4.4 trillion at the end of 2005 (figure 5.13). In particular, market capitalization of Asian stock markets tripled during the same period, and stock prices in other major emerging markets saw large increases (more than 100 percent in some cases) in both local currency and U.S. dollar terms (table 5.9). For many countries, stock markets have now recovered to the levels they attained before the East Asian crisis.

The sharp response of these markets to inflows of portfolio capital can be explained by their small size, limited liquidity, and high concentration in a few large issues. As shown in figure 5.14, turnover ratios, as a percentage of market capitalization, for most emerging stock markets in 2004 were less than 40 percent while for the NYSE and NASDAQ they were 90 percent and 249 percent, respectively. India and Thailand were the exceptions with turnover ratios over 100 percent. Trading in most emerging markets is also highly concentrated; for example, in Mexico, trading in eight stocks accounted for 62.7 percent of total trades on the exchange. Therefore, relatively small foreign portfolio inflows can have a major impact on the stock prices in these exchanges.

One benefit of the rise in stock market valuation has been its contribution to corporate restructuring in several developing countries, especially in East Asia. The high market valuations combined with low local interest rates, have made it possible for many firms to pay off debt, thus reducing leverage. The two most highly leveraged corporate sectors—those of the Republic of Korea and Thailand—reduced their debt-to-equity ratios below 75 percent by 2004, down sharply from nearly 400 percent in 1997 (figure 5.15).

Box 5.5 Investment and private capital flows

In order to more carefully examine the relationship between private capital flows and investment, a more rigorous analysis is required. In principle, both capital flows and domestic investment are endogenous variables affected by third factors (such as the investment climate, productivity, international interest rates, and economic growth). Because factors that stimulate domestic investment also tend to attract private capital flows (and vice versa), the high correlation of capital flows with investment is not surprising. The influence of third variables also suggests that the relationship between capital inflows and domestic investment is nonlinear, so that capital inflows have a positive and significant effect on investment only once a threshold level of financial and economic development has occurred (Rioja and Valev 2004; Bailliu 2000; Alfaro and others 2004).

Econometric analysis offers a more rigorous explanation of the dynamics of capital flows and domestic investment in recipient countries. The underlying methodology and estimation are summarized in the annex. Some key findings are presented below:

- There is strong statistical evidence that suggests private capital flows contribute to increased domestic investment across developing countries with access to international capital markets.

- Taking into account financial development and trade openness, while controlling for other determinants of domestic investment, econometric analysis indicates that for countries reaching a minimum threshold of financial development and capital-account openness, private capital inflows can have a positive and significant impact on investment.

- Financial development affects the ability of developing countries to attract private capital flows and use them for domestic investment. For example, our estimates indicate that in Ghana, where the ratio of M2 to GDP is 17 percent, a one-percentage-point increase in private capital flows (as a share of GDP) would result in an increase in investment of 0.40 percent of GDP, but only if Ghana's domestic financial size (ratio of M2 to GDP) was developed to reach 74 percent, a level comparable to Malaysia's.

- Similarly, a country like Brazil could experience an increase in investment of up to 1 percent of GDP as a result of a one-percentage-point (of GDP) increase in private capital flows—if it became as open to financial flows as Mexico (provided those resources were channeled into domestic investment and not reserve accumulation).

Moreover, since the Asian financial crises, developing countries have made some progress in establishing the institutional and regulatory foundations they need to manage capital flows. At the same time, they have considerably improved corporate financial soundness, as firms in virtually all crisis-affected countries have reduced leverage, enhanced profitability, and undertaken financial restructuring. That progress needs to be set against still evolving reforms in the areas of corporate governance, risk management, and transparency. Weak governance results in poor financial reporting and disclosure, as well as insufficient management accountability, allowing resources to be used for personal or unrelated uses. It can also provide incentives for short-term gain rather than long-term stability.

The links between financial soundness and good corporate governance are clear. Recent research has provided evidence that the quality of corporate governance is positively related to growth opportunities and the need for external financing (Pinkowitz and others 2003). Poor corporate governance limits the ability of firms to raise capital and grow, as capital markets place a lower value on poorly governed firms. Recent research has also highlighted the importance of the country-level dimension of corporate governance, including the relationship between the quality of a country's institutions and the legal protection given to investors' rights, on the one hand, and the effect on investors' potential returns and overall decisions to invest in a particular country, on the other (Doidge and others 2004).

Lessons and policy agenda

In the last few years, many developing countries have deepened their integration into global capital markets through greater exchange rate flexibility, development of local capital markets, reduced dependence on short-term external debt, and gradual liberalization of cross-border trade in financial

Table 5.8 Indicators of overheating in selected developing countries, 2002–4

Change from immediately preceding 3 years: annual period averages in %

Selected countries	Current account balance			GDP growth			Inflation		
	1999–2001	2002–4	Change	1999–2001	2002–4	Change	1999–2001	2002–4	Change
Azerbaijan	−5.7	−23.7	−17.9	9.5	11.0	1.5	−1.7	3.0	4.7
Bangladesh							3.3	4.0	0.7
Botswana	11.3	6.3	−5.0	6.1	4.8	−1.3	8.0	8.0	0.0
Brazil	−4.5	0.4	4.8	2.2	2.5	0.4	6.3	10.0	3.7
Chile	−0.9	−0.3	0.6	2.0	3.9	1.8	3.7	2.0	−1.7
China	1.8	3.4	1.6	7.5	9.0	1.5	−0.3	0.0	0.3
Colombia	0.1	−1.3	−1.4	0.1	3.3	3.2	9.3	6.3	−3.0
Croatia	−4.4	−7.1	−2.7	2.1	4.4	2.2	4.3	2.0	−2.3
Ecuador	2.7	−2.7	−5.3	0.5	4.2	3.7	62.0	7.7	−54.3
Egypt, Arab Rep. of							2.7	6.3	3.7
El Salvador	−2.1	−3.9	−1.8	2.4	1.9	−0.5	2.3	2.7	0.3
Hungary	−7.5	−8.3	−0.7	4.4	3.5	−0.9	9.7	5.7	−4.0
India	−0.5	0.9	1.4	5.4	6.5	1.1	4.3	4.0	−0.3
Indonesia	4.4	2.9	−1.5	3.2	4.8	1.6	12.0	8.3	−3.7
Jordan							1.3	2.3	1.0
Kazakhstan	−1.8	−1.2	0.5	8.7	9.5	0.8	9.7	6.3	−3.3
Malaysia	11.2	11.0	−0.2	5.1	5.5	0.4	2.0	1.3	−0.7
Mexico	−3.0	−1.5	1.5	3.4	2.2	−1.2	10.7	5.0	−5.7
Morocco	0.9	3.2	2.2	2.4	4.0	1.6	1.3	2.0	0.7
Nigeria	8.1	11.9	3.8	2.8	5.3	2.5	11.0	14.0	3.0
Pakistan	0.3	3.0	2.6	3.3	4.9	1.6	3.7	4.3	0.7
Peru	−2.6	−1.1	1.5	1.3	4.6	3.2	3.0	2.0	−1.0
Philippines	6.5	3.3	−3.2	4.1	4.7	0.5	5.7	4.0	−1.7
Poland	−5.5	−3.0	2.5	3.0	3.5	0.5	7.7	2.3	−5.3
Russian Fed.	13.9	8.9	−5.0	7.2	6.4	−0.8	42.7	13.7	−29.0
South Africa	−0.2	−1.4	−1.3	3.1	3.4	0.3	5.3	5.7	0.3
Sri Lanka	−3.8	−1.9	2.0	2.9	5.3	2.4	8.3	8.0	−0.3
Thailand	7.7	5.1	−2.7	3.8	6.1	2.3	1.3	2.0	0.7
Tunisia	−3.5	−2.8	0.7	5.2	4.3	−0.9	2.7	3.3	0.7
Turkey	0.4	0.1	−0.3	−1.6	7.6	9.2	58.0	26.3	−31.7
Venezuela, R. B. de.	4.6	11.5	6.9	0.4	0.3	−0.1	17.7	25.0	7.3
Vietnam	3.2	−2.9	−6.2	6.2	7.3	1.1	0.7	5.0	4.3
Zambia	−14.4	−6.3	8.1	3.6	4.4	0.8	24.7	22.0	−2.7
Total	**0.4**	**1.7**	**1.3**	**3.4**	**4.9**	**1.5**	**15.9**	**10.4**	**−5.6**

Sources: IMF, International Financial Statistics and World Bank staff calculations.

Figure 5.13 Market capitalization

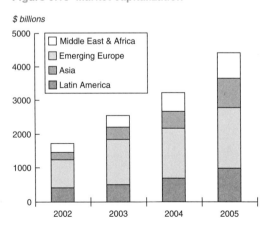

Sources: World Federation of Exchanges and World Bank staff calculations.

Figure 5.14 Turnover on world stock exchanges, 2004

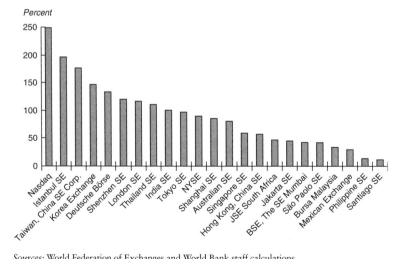

Sources: World Federation of Exchanges and World Bank staff calculations.

Table 5.9 Stock market performance in emerging markets, 2002–5
% increase in stock market valuation

Region/Country	Local currency		U.S. dollar	
	% change, 2002–5	Average annual change, 2002–5	% change, 2002–5	Average annual change, 2002–5
Latin America				
Argentina	277.1	92.4	319.2	106.4
Brazil	167.4	55.8	305.3	101.8
Chile	107.3	35.8	143.4	47.8
Mexico	181.9	60.6	177.3	59.1
Peru	136.5	45.5	142.4	47.5
Asia				
China	92.2	30.7	97.1	32.4
India	165.8	55.3	183.1	61.0
Indonesia	183.6	61.2	158.0	52.7
Malaysia	36.6	12.2	37.4	12.5
Philippines	113.0	37.7	114.5	38.2
Thailand	128.3	42.8	140.0	46.7
Europe				
Czech Rep.	442.9	147.6	290.9	97.0
Hungary	175.2	58.4	189.1	63.0
Poland	111.6	37.2	149.1	49.7
Russian Fed.	181.9	60.6	213.4	71.1
Turkey	244.8	81.6	323.5	107.8
Middle East & Africa				
Egypt, Arab Rep. of	887.0	295.7	947.6	315.9
Morocco	68.6	22.9	84.6	28.2
South Africa	90.5	30.2	157.7	52.6

Sources: Standard & Poor's IFCI index and World Bank staff calculations.

Figure 5.15 Ratios of debt to equity in selected countries, 1996–2004

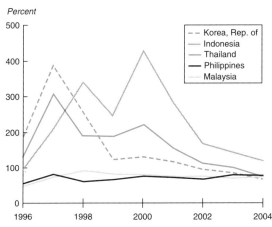

Sources: Thomson Financial and World Bank staff calculations.

assets. Those developments, coupled with the shift from potentially volatile short-term debt to more stable FDI, have improved the context for capital flows, raising the likelihood that the economic outcomes of the present surge in capital flows will be better than those observed in the 1990s. The associ-

ated policy agenda for developing countries is broad and complex. However, several key themes are clear.

Policy responses to the latest surge in private flows have included the buildup of large foreign exchange reserves.

Governments have attempted to minimize the macroeconomic problems associated with large inflows of foreign capital by recycling those resources into official reserves. Central banks have purchased foreign exchange from local banks and other authorized financial intermediaries and invested the proceeds in liquid assets in major industrial countries, particularly in U.S. Treasuries. Recognizing that this process cannot continue indefinitely, policy makers in developing countries are exploring alternative policies, including improving the return on reserve holdings by asset diversification, transferring part of the currency risk to the private sector (notably by allowing institutional investors to invest some portion of their foreign-currency earnings overseas, rather than selling them to the central bank), relying more on the stabilizing role of exchange rate changes, and encouraging expansion in aggregate demand (both consumption and investment). In East Asia, efforts are being made to increase the size and depth of regional financial markets to recycle reserves into productive investments within the region. Such policy responses need to be orchestrated carefully, taking into account the potential threats of macroeconomic imbalances, overheating, and asset-price escalation, as well as the need to improve risk management practices.

For countries with large holdings of foreign exchange reserves, allowing local institutional investors to diversify their investment portfolio globally could provide a viable channel of capital outflow, as well as an opportunity for greater risk diversification. Allowing such investments would have the salutary effect of transferring foreign exchange risks, currently concentrated on central banks' books, to domestic institutional investors, which have a longer investment horizon and can benefit from a more diversified international portfolio. Other vehicles for reducing the pressure on the central banks' balance sheets might include the creation of specialized investment vehicles similar to the Government Investment Corporation of Singapore, the Korea Investment Corporation, and Kazanah in Malaysia to manage a portion of foreign exchange reserves for long-term investment.

The assets of institutional investors in several developing countries, especially in East Asia and Latin America, have been growing at a fast clip due to rapid growth of pension funds and insurance companies. The establishment of corporate pension funds in countries such as the Republic of Korea and Thailand has contributed to that growth. Until recently, institutional investors in most developing countries have followed very conservative investment policies, with government securities accounting for the lion's share of their assets. Institutional investors in most developing countries are generally prohibited from investing in foreign securities. Exceptions include Chile, Malaysia, the Republic of Korea, and Thailand. At the end of 2004, Chile's institutional investors held 27.3 percent of their assets in foreign securities, compared with just 2.8 percent for Thailand and Korea, which only recently have gained the right to make limited overseas investments.

Oil exporters face a different set of policy challenges, including the need to design appropriate stabilization funds and to rely on market instruments to hedge against volatility in the oil market.

Oil exporters, most of which are heavily dependent on a single commodity for foreign ex-

change, face opportunities and challenges distinct from those of other developing countries.[16] Oil is a commodity with an active spot market, as well as a growing liquid futures market that offers up to 5-year contracts, affording oil-exporting countries a broad range of options and market instruments, such as oil derivatives, to manage the future stream of foreign exchange revenues. But, in practice, governments have been reluctant to enter futures and derivatives markets for several reasons, including their limited capacity for large-scale hedging, insufficient expertise to trade successfully, and limited access for countries with poor credit.

A high concentration in a single export commodity translates into a high degree of volatility in export earnings. In 2005, 14 of 31 oil-exporting countries depended on oil exports for more than 50 percent of their foreign exchange—among them Libya (94 percent), Saudi Arabia and Kuwait (85 percent), and Iran (73 percent). Several countries have put aside a fraction of their oil revenues in so-called stabilization funds or funds for the future. Experience with such funds has been mixed. To make the best of them, robust governance and legal frameworks are required to insulate the funds from political interference. The government must set clear investment objectives, adopt sound investment policies, and appoint professional managers to invest money with proper safeguards and transparency.

The development of international norms and standards on transparency, corporate governance, and regulation of national financial systems has raised the confidence of foreign investors in emerging market economies.

A hallmark of efforts to improve the international financial architecture in the late 1990s was the development, by the international financial community, of a set of international norms and standards on transparency, corporate governance, and regulation and supervision of financial systems. The new standards were designed specifically to guide the countries affected by the Asian crises of the late 1990s to return to international financial markets, and more generally to pave the way for the gradual and sequential liberalization of international capital movements. International scholars have argued that the adoption of open-door financial policies and practices tends to cluster in time and space (Simmons and Elkins 2004) and that governments comply with international norms and legal commitments if their peers do so and if the reputational cost of reneging is perceived to be high (Simmons 2000). Those arguments have provided a strong intellectual basis for a standards-centered approach to bolster market confidence.

Building on the success of earlier norms embodied in the IMF's safeguards assessments and the Special Data Dissemination Standards (adopted in 1996), international norms on transparency, financial infrastructure, and corporate governance were formulated on the basis of voluntary compliance, with monitoring responsibility assigned to multinational financial institutions. At the request of a member country, the IMF and the World Bank assess compliance with the international standards by preparing and publishing reports on the observance of standards and codes (ROSCs). International norms—standards of appropriate and broadly accepted behavior—enhance stability as investors are able to form accurate expectations of governments' behavior.

The world is moving toward a multipolar international monetary system in which the monetary and financial policies of the major industrial countries of the G-3—and of key emerging market economies that are important players in global trade and finance—are of predominant importance.

One aspect of the new multipolar world is that the U.S. dollar is no longer without a serious competitor as an international currency. The emergence of a large and deep market for euro-denominated securities widens the opportunities for diversification available to developing countries as well as to other countries. Accumulating euro-denominated financial assets in proportion to the Euro Area's share of global production and trade allows governments to hedge against real-side fluctuations. The euro also provides a potential anchor currency for economies closely linked to the existing Euro Area that wish to peg to a major and widely circulated currency.

The emergence of the euro alongside the dollar may introduce some instability, however, as the lack of synchronization between the United States and the Euro Area may occasionally produce large movements in exchange rates that could have serious consequences for developing countries. Policy coordination may not be necessary in normal times, when floating exchange rates and monetary policies oriented primarily to domestic targets for inflation and economic activity facilitate adjustment to the shocks hitting the two regions. But at times of financial market instability, policy coordination may be needed to limit large swings in exchange rates.[17]

A second aspect of the multipolar world is that a wider set of countries now matter in the resolution of policy imbalances. Developing countries, which would suffer disproportionately from the instability induced by a hard landing, have a shared interest in seeing multilateral cooperation in international monetary relations. The scope of cooperation should cover global liquidity, the optimal mode of adjustment, and the role of key currencies. The large size of the U.S. current account deficit has as its counterpart large surpluses in Asia and among oil exporters. The anticipated need for a real effective depreciation of the dollar to help correct that deficit will have to occur against a wider set of currencies than those of the industrial countries (the Plaza Agreement involved the G-5 countries), which may well make policy coordination more difficult. However, it is clear that countries with large reserve holdings have a shared interest in a smooth adjustment of dollar's exchange rate.

Managing capital flows effectively will remain critical to ensuring economic progress in developing countries

Private capital flows to developing countries hit an historic high in 2005, but there remains considerable room for growth, given developing countries' demographic profiles, per capita investment levels ($400 in 2004, compared with $6,000 in developed countries), and economic prospects. Investors in developed countries invest less than 3 percent of their portfolios of common stocks in developing countries; and only 5 percent of global bonds issued in recent years originated in developing countries. As developing countries' financial markets become increasingly integrated with global financial markets, those percentages are likely to rise (as are developing countries' holdings of foreign assets). To take advantage of those opportunities and protect market access, it will be essential for developing countries to vigorously maintain macroeconomic stability. They also will need to strengthen domestic financial markets and institutions to cope more effectively with the risks associated with growing capital flows and to maximize the efficiency of capital allocation. Sustaining the economic policies and institutions that can effectively deal with capital flow surges is likely to remain a key issue for developing countries for many years to come.

Annex: Capital Flows and Domestic Investment

Because private capital flows may have a larger impact on investment where the financial sector is well developed and restrictions on capital movements are few (Bailliu 2000), we studied interactions between private capital flows, financial development, and capital controls. We tested the relationship between private capital flows and investment in a simultaneous equation system, where we were interested in both the direct effect of private capital flows on investment and the indirect effect, which was determined through the interaction of private capital flows with financial development and capital account restrictions, respectively.

The dependent variables in our analysis are investment and private capital flows, each as a percentage of GDP. The explanatory variables include trade openness, financial development, capital controls, and a set of control variables. Trade openness (TO) is defined as exports plus imports divided by GDP. Financial development (FD) is measured using M2. Restrictions on movements of private capital (CC) are measured by the Chinn-Ito index (2002). The index is larger when there are fewer capital controls. Private capital flows (CF/GDP) include both debt and equity flows. The control variables are: government size (measured by government expenditure) and institutional development (measured by the Freedom House index of political freedom). Several other control variables were tried (such as average years of schooling, inflation rates, and the extent of paved roads), but they proved insignificant in the analysis.

The motivation for including these control variables comes from several theoretical relationships. Government size is a control for policy at the country level. Political freedom is a proxy for institutional quality. The data set consists of a panel of observations for a sample of 72 developing countries with access to international capital markets. The sample was drawn from all regions and includes countries in a broad range of developmental stages. China was excluded because of the size of its money supply in relation to GDP, which is far greater than any other developing country and might have biased the results. The data were averaged over five-year intervals over 1980–2004 to produce a set of five observations per country. The simultaneous equation model we used in our analysis takes into account the endogeneity of investment and private capital flows and is written as follows:

$$\left(\frac{1}{GDP}\right)_{it} = \alpha_i + \beta_1\left(\frac{CF}{GDP}\right)_{it} + \beta_2\left(\frac{FD}{GDP}\right)_{it} + \beta_3\left(\frac{CC}{GDP}\right)_{it} + \beta_4\left(\frac{CF}{GDP}\right)_{it} * \left(\frac{FD}{GDP}\right)_{it} + \beta_5\left(\frac{CF}{GDP}\right)_{it} * \left(\frac{CC}{GDP}\right)_{it} + \gamma_i X_{it} + \varepsilon_{it} \quad (5.1)$$

is the equation for investment and

$$\left(\frac{CF}{GDP}\right)_{it} = \phi_i + \delta_1(growth)_{it} + \delta_2\left(\frac{FD}{GDP}\right)_{it} + \delta_3\left(\frac{CC}{GDP}\right)_{it} + \theta_i X_{it} + \varepsilon_{it} \quad (5.2)$$

is the equation for private capital flows.

Table 5A.1 Domestic investment and private capital flows

Iterated 3SLS regressions

Dependent variable is private capital flows			Dependent variable is investment		
Variables	Regression 1	Regression 2	Variables	Regression 1	Regression 2
GDP per capita	0.000005*	0.000005*	Private capital flows	1.37*	1.58*
GDP growth	0.62*	0.62*	GDP per capita	−0.000008*	−0.000008*
Trade openness	0.12*	0.12*	Trade openness	−0.04	−0.15
M2	−0.05*	−0.05*	M2	0.10*	0.14*
Capital controls	−0.002	−0.002	Capital controls	0.001	−0.002
Gov't spending	0.021	0.021	PCF × M2		−1.2
Political freedom	0.001	0.001	PCF × capital controls		0.11
			Gov't spending	0.12*	0.11*
			Political freedom	−0.002*	−0.002*
Constant	−0.03*	−0.02*	Constant	0.17*	0.15*

Note: Regression 1 is without interaction effects; regression 2 is with interaction effects. Iterated 3SLS iterates over the estimated disturbance covariance matrix and parameter estimates until they converge. The technique does not require the assumption that errors are normally distributed. PCF = private capital flows.

* = significance at the 5-percent level or better.

In each equation, X represents a vector of country specific characteristics: openness to trade, GDP per capita, government spending, and political freedom. We used an iterated three-stage least squares (3SLS) technique (Zellner and Theil 1962) to estimate the simultaneous equation system to take into account the nonlinearity of the investment equation and the endogeneity of the regressors. First, estimation of private capital flows (column 1) showed that GDP per capita, GDP growth, and trade openness had positive and significant effects on private capital flows, while financial development measured by M2 had a small negative effect. For the baseline regression (shown in the first column of the right-hand panel) of investment, we found that private capital flows, government spending, and financial development (measured by M2) had a positive and significant effect on domestic investment. Political freedom also had a significant effect—the coefficient is negative because higher values of political freedom in this index imply less freedom. Capital controls and trade openness were insignificant at the 10-percent level. (The coefficient estimates from the 3SLS are presented.)

Next we performed a 3SLS regression that included, in the equation for investment, the interaction effects reported in column (2) in the table, which shows first that when interaction effects are included, private capital flows and M2 have positive, significant, and direct effects on domes-

tic investment, whereas GDP per capita and political freedom (the absence of freedom) have small negative effects. Turning to the interaction terms, private capital flows have both a direct and indirect effect on domestic investment. The indirect effect comes through the extent of financial development and capital controls, which is determined by the coefficient estimates on the interaction terms (PCF × M2 and PCF × capital controls).

We then considered the marginal effects (obtained by differentiating investment with respect to capital flows using the coefficient estimates from our estimations) of capital flows on growth and investment. We calculated the net effect (both direct and indirect) of private capital flows on investment as:

$$\beta_1 + \beta_4 \left(\frac{FD}{GDP} \right)$$

for the interaction with financial development and as

$$\beta_1 + \beta_5 \left(\frac{CC}{GDP} \right)$$

for the interaction with capital controls. From this, we determined the effect that deepening the financial sector or loosening capital controls might have on investment through their interactions with private capital. (An example is discussed in the text.)

Notes

1. The coefficient of persistence referred to here is measured as the coefficient on the lagged term in the regression of the annual ratios of FDI to GDP and debt to GDP, respectively, against a constant and their one-year lag values for each of the 72 developing countries with access to international capital markets over the period 1980–2004.

2. The conventional wisdom was that pass-through of exchange rate changes into import prices is relatively rapid and more complete in developing than developed countries (Ho and McCauley 2003). Rapid pass-through was cited as a rational for exchange rate management, as changes in exchange rates could translate into significant inflationary pressure. However recent research has shown that pass-through underwent a transformation during the 1990s for many developing countries and now is much slower and less complete (Frankel, Parsley and Wei 2005), although still faster and more pervasive than for developed countries.

3. Even when countries announce greater exchange rate flexibility as a policy, their day-to-day practice may be quite different. See Calvo and Reinhart (2002) for a discussion.

4. See for example, Schneider and Tornell (2004) and Fischer (2001). The increased vulnerability from real exchange rate appreciation comes through loss of trade competitiveness and possible worsening of current account balances.

5. During 2002–4, about half of the variation in the real effective exchange rate appears to have come from the nominal exchange rate, rather than from movements in relative prices. A simple variance decomposition of the real effective exchange rate into its components (nominal exchange rate and differences between relative prices) shows that the nominal rate accounts for about 53 percent of the variation in the real rate during this period.

6. The offshore nondeliverable forward market for selected currencies is typically used to hedge currency risks in markets where capital controls prevent effective onshore currency risk hedging.

7. The move to inflation targeting may be a consequence of the shift in many developing countries to policies that promote macroeconomic stability. If that is so, it cannot be credited directly with improving macroeconomic performance. As discussed in IMF (2006), the available evidence is only suggestive; the time series is too short and the number of countries with such targets are too few to make a definitive statement.

8. Yang (2005) found that the increase in remittances makes up for 13 percent of income losses in the current year and 28 percent within four years of a hurricane. In contrast, increases in ODA and FDI make up for roughly 26 and 21 percent within four years.

9. Also, despite considerable progress in recent years in achieving convergence of financial accounting standards between the United States and European Union, and in implementing the IMF's safeguards assessment policy, there is yet no accepted international accounting standards that are suited to the nuances of central banks' particular role and mandate. Important questions remain on the proper treatment of unrealized gains or losses, asset valuation, and reporting and disclosure of derivatives contracts that the central bank may be counterparty to either for risk management or foreign exchange intervention purposes (see, for example, Hawkins 2003).

10. In this regard, reserves need to be distinguished from other assets held by the official sector primarily for investment purposes, rather than for intervention in the foreign exchange market.

11. Swiss francs and several other currencies are used as foreign exchange reserves, but their shares are too small to be meaningful in this analysis.

12. It is possible to imagine innovative solutions that would increase the liquidity of European markets, for instance the creation of a single issuer of government short-term paper, as proposed by Alexandre Lamfalussy (Speech at the European Central Bank, April 29–30, 2002). However, the prospect for such an institution, which presumably would buy up all the Euro Area governments' issues, seems distant.

13. The 72 countries in our sample account for more than 95 percent of all private capital flows to developing countries. The countries in the sample range from large emerging markets (such as China, Malaysia, and Thailand) to small commodity-based economies. They were drawn from all regions and from both mid- and low-income categories.

14. The implication is that capital inflows and investment are correlated—at least some of the capital inflows are going to domestic investment. As the regression excludes other determinants of investment, the degree of this relationship may be overstated.

15. Excluding Bahrain, Israel, Republic of Korea, Saudi Arabia, and Taiwan (China).

16. In the last two years, oil-exporting countries have benefited from the sharp increase in oil prices. In 2005, total oil exports from developing countries increased to an estimated $522.7 billion, up 37.6 percent from 2004. Oil exports from the Middle East were estimated at $242.7 billion, 46.4 percent of the total. In addition to the Middle Eastern countries, the Russian Federation was one of the major beneficiaries of the hike in the price of oil.

17. In the mid-1980s, when the U.S. dollar was widely perceived to be overvalued, the Plaza Agreement of September 1985 helped bring it to a "soft landing". In the current environment a coordinated policy of intervention in foreign currency markets is neither desirable nor feasible, given the changes in global finance market conditions and actors over the past two decades.

References

Alfaro, Laura, Areendam Chanda, Sebnem Kalemli-Ozcan, and Selin Sayek. 2004. "FDI and Economic Growth: The Role of Local Financial Markets." *Journal of International Economics* 64 (1): 89–112.

Bailliu, Jeannine. 2000. "Private Capital Flows, Financial Development, and Economic Growth in Developing Countries." Bank of Canada Working Paper 2000-15.

Bernanke, Ben. 2004. "What Have We Learned from the Euro at Five?" Remarks made at the conference on "The Euro at Five: Ready for a Global Role." Institute for International Economics, Washington, DC, February 26.

Brune, Nancy, Geoffrey Garrett, Alexandra Guisinger, and Jason Sorens. 2001. "The Political Economy of Capital Account Liberalization." Paper prepared for presentation at the 2001 Annual Meetings of the American Political Science Association, San Francisco, August 31.

Calvo, Guillermo A., Morris Goldstein, and Eduard Hochreiter. 1996. *Private Capital Flows to Emerging Markets after the Mexican Crisis*. Washington, DC: Institute for International Economics.

Calvo, Guillermo A., and Carmen M. Reinhart. 2002. "Fear of Floating." *Quarterly Journal of Economics* 117 (2): 379–408.

Carvalho, Bernardo S. de M., and Márcio G. P. Garcia. 2005. "Ineffective Controls on Capital Inflows under Sophisticated Financial Markets: Brazil in the Nineties." Paper presented at the Inter-American Seminar on Economics entitled "Strengthening Global Financial Markets," December 1–3. http://www.nber.org/books/IASE05/.

Cashin, Paul, Luis Cespedes, and Ratna Sahay. 2003. "Commodity Currencies: Developing Countries Reliant on Commodity Exports See the Fate of Their Exchange Rates Tied to Fickle Commodity Markets." *Finance and Development* 40 (1): 45–48.

Cavoli, Tony, and Ramkishen S. Rajan. 2005. "Have Exchange Rate Regimes in Asia Become More Flexible Post Crisis? Revisiting the Evidence." CIES Discussion Paper 0503, Center for International Economic Studies, University of Adelaide.

Chen, Yu-chin, and Kenneth Rogoff. 2002. "Commodity Currencies and Empirical Exchange Rate Puzzles." IMF Working Paper 02/27, International Monetary Fund, Washington, DC.

Chinn, Menzie D., and Hiro Ito. 2002. "Capital Account Liberalization, Institutions and Financial Development: Cross Country Evidence." NBER Working Paper 8967, National Bureau of Economic Research, Cambridge, MA.

Clarke, George, and Scott Wallsten. 2004. "Do Remittances Protect Households in Developing Countries Against Shocks? Evidence from a Natural Disaster in Jamaica." Unpublished paper, World Bank, Washington, DC. November.

Cohen, Benjamin J. 2000. "Life at the Top: International Currencies in the Twenty-First Century." Princeton Essays in International Finance 221, Department of Economics, Princeton University. http://www.princeton.edu/~ies/old_series-win.htm.

Corsetti, Giancarlo, Paolo Pesenti, and Nouriel Roubini. 1998. "What Caused the Asian Currency and Financial Crisis? Part I: A Macroeconomic Overview." NBER Working Paper 6833, National Bureau of Economic Research, Cambridge, MA.

Courtis, N., and B. Mander, eds. 2003. *Accounting Standards for Central Banks*. London: Central Banking Publications.

Dailami, Mansoor. 2000. "Managing Risks of Global Financial Market Integration." *Managing Financial and Corporate Distress: Lessons from Asia*. Washington, DC: Brookings Institution Press.

Doidge and others 2004.

Edwards, Sebastian. 2001. "Capital Mobility and Economic Performance: Are Emerging Markets Different?" NBER Working Paper 8076, National Bureau of Economic Research, Cambridge, MA.

Edwards, Sebastian. 2005. "Capital Controls, Sudden Stops and Current Account Reversals." NBER Working Paper 11170, National Bureau of Economic Research, Cambridge, MA.

Eichengreen, Barry. 2001. "Capital Account Liberalization: What Do Cross-Country Studies Tell Us?" *The World Bank Economic Review* 15 (3): 341–65.

Eichengreen, Barry, and Ricardo Hausmann. 1999. "Exchange Rates and Financial Fragility." NBER Working Paper 7418, National Bureau of Economic Research, Cambridge, MA.

Frankel, Jeffrey, David Parsley, and Shang-Jin Wei. 2005. "Slow Pass-Through around the World: A New Import for Developing Countries?" NBER Working Paper 11199, National Bureau of Economic Research, Cambridge, MA.

Fischer, Stanley. 2001. "Exchange Rate Regimes: Is the Bipolar View Correct?" *Journal of Economic Perspectives* 15 (2): 3–24.

Fleming, J. Marcus. 1962. "Domestic Financial Policies under Fixed and under Floating Exchange Rates." *International Monetary Fund Staff Papers* 9 (November): 369–72.

Goldfajn, Ilan, and André Minella. 2005. "Capital Flows and Controls in Brazil: What Have We Learned?" NBER Working Paper 11640, National Bureau of Economic Research, Cambridge, MA.

Goldstein, Morris. 2002. "Managed Floating Plus." Policy Analyses in International Economics 66. Institute for International Economics, Washington, DC.

Hawkins, John, and Philip Turner. 2000. "Managing Foreign Debt and Liquidity Risks in Emerging Economies: An Overview." BIS Policy Paper 8, Bank for International Settlements, Basel.

Hawkins, Andrew. 2003. "Accounting for Financial Instruments." In *Accounting Standards for Central Banks*. London: Central Banking Publications.

Ho, Corrinne, and Robert McCauley. 2003 "Living with Flexible Exchange Rates: Issues and Recent Experience in Inflation-Targeting Emerging Market Economies." BIS Working Paper 130, Bank for International Settlements, Basel.

International Monetary Fund. Various years. *Annual Report on Exchange Arrangements and Exchange Restrictions*. Washington, DC: IMF.

———. 2006. "Inflation Targeting and the IMF." Monetary and Financial Systems Department, Policy and Development Review Department, and Research Department, International Monetary Fund, Washington, DC.

Johnson, Simon, Peter Boone, Alasdair Breach, and Eric Friedman. 2000. "Corporate Governance in the Asian Financial Crisis." *Journal of Financial Economics* 58 (1–2): 141–86.

Kapur, Devesh. 2004. "Remittances: The New Development Mantra?" G-24 Discussion Paper Series 29, UNCTAD/GDS/MDPB/G24/2004/5, United Nations

Conference on Trade and Development, New York. http://www.unctad.org/Templates/Page.asp?intItemID=2103&lang=1.

Kletzer, Kenneth, and Mark M. Spiegel. 2004. "Sterilization Costs and Exchange Rate Targeting." *Journal of International Money and Finance* 23 (6): 897–915.

Lane, Philip R. 2003. "Business Cycles and Macroeconomic Policies in Emerging Market Economies." *International Finance* 6 (1): 89–108.

Mendoza, Enrique G. 1995. "The Terms of Trade, the Real Exchange Rate, and Economic Fluctuations." *International Economic Review* 36 (1): 101–37.

Miniane, Jacques. 2004. "A New Set of Measures on Capital Account Restrictions." IMF Staff Papers 51 (2): 276–308.

Monetary Authority of Singapore. 2005. "Financial Stability Review." Monetary Authority of Singapore. December.

Mundell, Robert A. 1963. "Capital Mobility and Stabilization Policy under Fixed and Flexible Exchange Rates." *Canadian Journal of Economics and Political Science* 29 (November): 475–85.

Pinkowitz, Lee, Rene M. Stulz, and Rohan Williamson. 2003. "Do Firms in Countries with Poor Protection of Investor Rights Hold More Cash?" NBER Working Paper 10188, National Bureau of Economic Research, Cambridge, MA.

Quinn, Dennis P. 1997. "The Correlates of Changes in International Financial Regulation." *American Political Science Review* 91: 531–51.

Radelet, Steven, and Jeffrey Sachs. 1998. "The East Asian Financial Crisis: Diagnosis, Remedies, Prospects." Brookings Papers on Economic Activity 1, Brookings Institution, Washington, DC.

Razin, Assaf. 2003. "FDI Flows and Domestic Investment." *CESifo Overview Economic Studies* 49 (3): 415–28.

Rioja, Felix, and Neven Valev. "Does One Size Fit All? A Re-examination of the Finance and Growth Relationship." *Journal of Development Economics* 74 (2): 429–47.

Rodrik, Dani. 1999. *The New Global Economy and Developing Countries: Making Openness Work.* Washington, DC: Overseas Development Council.

Schneider, Martin, and Aaron Tornell. 2004. "Balance Sheet Effects, Bailout Guarantees, and Financial Crises." *Review of Economic Studies* 71 (3): 883–913.

Simmons, Beth A. 2000. "International Law and State Behavior: Commitment and Compliance in International Monetary Affairs." *American Political Science Review* 94 (4): 819–35.

Simmons, Beth A., and Zachary Elkins. 2004. "The Globalization of Liberalization: Policy Diffusion in the International Political Economy." *American Political Science Review* 98 (1): 171–89.

Stiglitz, Joseph. 2002. *Globalization and Its Discontents.* New York: W. W. Norton.

World Bank. 1997. *Private Capital Flows to Developing Countries: The Road to Financial Integration.* New York: Oxford University Press.

Yang, Dean. 2004. "International Migration, Human Capital, and Entrepreneurship: Evidence from Philippine Migrants' Exchange Rate Shocks." Policy Research Working Paper 3578, World Bank, Washington, DC.

Yang, Dean. 2005. "Coping with Disaster: The Impact of Hurricanes on International Financial Flows, 1970–2001." Unpublished paper. Gerald R. Ford School of Public Policy, University of Michigan.

Zellner, A., and H. Theil. 1962. "Three-Stage Least Squares: Simultaneous Estimation of Simultaneous Equations." *Econometrica* 30 (1): 54–78.

Statistical Appendix

The summary statistical tables have been significantly revised for this edition of Global Development Finance. The tables in this statistical appendix are now divided into three sets (see the list of tables on the next page for full details):

- **External financing.** These tables combine the IMF's current account, foreign exchange reserve, and net inward foreign direct investment data with the World Bank's portfolio equity and debtor reporting system (DRS) data to produce an overall tabulation of how regions finance themselves externally.
- **External liabilities and assets.** These tables provide a summary of the DRS debt data that is provided on a country-by-country basis in volume II.
- **Key external debt ratios and country classifications.** These tables provide a summary of indicators typically used by country risk analysts to monitor and classify countries. The two key ratios found in table A.29 are the present value

of each country's future debt-service streams (PV) to (a) gross national income (GNI) and (b) to exports of goods and services. These variables are especially important in the Heavily Indebted Poor Countries (HIPC) Initiative, where countries are classified based on the ratio of the present value of public and publicly guaranteed debt to exports of goods and services. These variables are averaged over three years, 2002–4.

These indicators do not represent an exhaustive set of useful indicators of external debt. They may not, for example, adequately capture the debt servicing capacity of countries in which government budget constraints are key to debt service difficulties. Moreover, rising external debt may not necessarily imply payment difficulties, especially if there is a commensurate increase in the country's debt servicing capacity. Thus these indicators should be used in the broader context of a country-specific analysis of debt sustainability.

Contents

Table A.1 External financing: all developing countries, 1998–2005

$ billions

	1998	1999	2000	2001	2002	2003	2004	2005e
Current account balance	−89.2	−3.5	47.8	20.5	72.0	123.8	158.3	245.8
as % GDP	−1.6	−0.1	0.8	0.4	1.2	1.8	2.0	2.6
Financial flows:								
Net equity flows	179.4	195.9	182.9	183.3	166.1	186.8	248.8	298.9
Net FDI inflows	172.4	183.3	168.8	176.9	160.3	161.6	211.5	237.5
Net portfolio equity inflows	6.9	12.6	14.1	6.4	5.8	25.2	37.3	61.4
Net debt flows	54.3	16.3	−1.0	−1.5	10.7	72.8	119.1	120.1
Official creditors	34.3	13.9	−5.7	27.4	5.2	−12.3	−28.7	−71.4
World Bank	8.7	8.8	7.9	7.5	−0.2	−0.9	1.3	0.7
IMF	14.1	−2.2	−10.7	19.5	14.0	2.4	−14.7	−41.1
Others	11.5	7.3	−2.9	0.4	−8.6	−13.8	−15.4	−31.0
Private creditors	19.9	2.5	4.7	−28.9	5.5	85.1	147.8	191.6
Net medium- and long-term								
debt flows	85.7	22.0	11.5	−6.2	1.2	30.2	77.8	122.3
Bonds	40.6	30.6	20.5	11.0	10.8	26.4	43.0	61.7
Banks	50.3	−7.1	−5.2	−10.8	−2.8	9.8	39.4	67.4
Others	−5.2	−1.5	−3.8	−6.3	−6.8	−5.9	−4.6	−6.7
Net short-term debt flows	−65.8	−19.6	−6.8	−22.7	4.2	54.9	70.0	69.3
Balancing item *	−128.1	−175.6	−184.4	−120.6	−76.9	−91.8	−121.4	−271.9
Change in reserves	−16.4	−33.2	−45.4	−81.7	−171.9	−291.6	−404.8	−393.0
(− = increase)								
Memo items:								
Bilateral aid grants	26.7	28.5	28.7	27.9	32.5	43.7	50.3	52.6
(ex technical cooperation grants)								
Net private flows (debt+equity)	199.3	198.3	187.7	154.4	171.5	271.9	396.6	490.5
Net official flows (aid+debt)	61.1	42.4	23.0	55.3	37.7	31.4	21.6	−18.8

Note: e = estimate.

* Combination of errors and omissions and net acquisition of foreign assets (including FDI) by developing countries.

Table A.2 External financing: East Asia and Pacific, 1998–2005
$ billions

	1998	1999	2000	2001	2002	2003	2004	2005e
Current account balance	59.8	60.3	53.7	39.8	61.2	74.9	93.6	143.4
as % GDP	4.5	4.2	3.4	2.4	3.2	3.5	3.8	4.9
Financial flows:								
Net equity flows	54.7	53.0	50.9	50.6	61.3	72.2	82.1	91.8
Net FDI inflows	57.8	50.8	44.3	48.5	57.2	59.8	64.6	65.3
Net portfolio equity inflows	−3.1	2.2	6.6	2.0	4.0	12.4	17.6	26.5
Net debt flows	−33.5	−11.7	−16.0	−8.2	−10.3	1.9	37.8	43.9
Official creditors	14.7	12.5	7.0	3.2	−7.9	−7.4	−5.5	−1.9
World Bank	2.8	2.4	1.8	0.9	−1.7	−1.5	−1.9	−1.2
IMF	7.0	1.9	1.2	−2.5	−2.7	−0.5	−1.6	−1.6
Others	4.8	8.2	3.9	4.8	−3.5	−5.4	−1.9	0.9
Private creditors	−48.2	−24.2	−22.9	−11.3	−2.4	9.3	43.3	45.8
Net medium- and long-term								
debt flows	−3.5	−10.9	−13.1	−13.0	−12.5	−9.2	9.1	15.8
Bonds	1.0	0.9	−0.7	0.4	0.1	2.5	9.7	12.3
Banks	−4.8	−12.0	−11.3	−11.8	−10.3	−8.6	1.4	8.1
Others	0.3	0.2	−1.0	−1.6	−2.3	−3.1	−2.0	−4.6
Net short-term debt flows	−44.7	−13.3	−9.9	1.7	10.1	18.5	34.2	30.0
Balancing item *	−60.3	−72.3	−78.5	−34.5	−24.1	−12.3	23.4	−61.2
Change in reserves	−20.7	−29.3	−10.1	−47.7	−88.0	−136.7	−237.0	−217.9
(− = increase)								
Memo items:								
Bilateral aid grants	2.5	2.5	2.5	2.2	2.2	2.5	2.8	2.7
(ex technical cooperation grants)								
Net private flows (debt+equity)	6.5	28.8	28.0	39.2	58.9	81.5	125.4	137.7
Net official flows (aid+debt)	17.1	15.0	9.5	5.3	−5.7	−4.9	−2.7	0.8

Note: e = estimate.
* Combination of errors and omissions and net acquisition of foreign assets (including FDI) by developing countries.

Table A.3 External financing: Europe and Central Asia, 1998–2005
$ billions

	1998	1999	2000	2001	2002	2003	2004	2005e
Current account balance	−24.5	−1.3	16.3	17.5	5.6	−2.0	4.2	24.8
as % GDP	−2.5	−0.2	1.8	1.8	0.5	−0.1	0.3	1.2
Financial flows:								
Net equity flows	31.4	31.7	31.5	33.0	34.8	36.4	66.5	77.9
Net FDI inflows	27.4	29.7	30.2	32.7	34.9	35.9	62.4	75.6
Net portfolio equity inflows	4.0	2.0	1.3	0.3	−0.1	0.5	4.2	2.3
Net debt flows	42.9	18.6	20.0	2.3	27.6	57.9	83.2	82.9
Official creditors	7.5	−0.6	0.0	2.2	2.7	−6.8	−10.5	−30.9
World Bank	1.5	1.9	2.1	2.1	1.0	−0.7	0.4	0.0
IMF	5.3	−3.1	−0.7	6.1	4.6	−2.0	−5.9	−9.7
Others	0.6	0.7	−1.4	−5.9	−2.9	−4.1	−5.0	−21.2
Private creditors	35.4	19.2	20.0	0.1	24.9	64.7	93.7	113.8
Net medium- and long-term								
debt flows	29.7	17.6	11.4	5.5	21.1	32.2	64.6	81.3
Bonds	16.0	8.2	5.3	1.6	3.9	10.4	25.7	34.6
Banks	14.6	10.1	7.7	6.1	18.7	23.4	40.6	48.5
Others	−1.0	−0.7	−1.6	−2.2	−1.5	−1.6	−1.7	−1.8
Net short-term debt flows	5.7	1.6	8.6	−5.3	3.8	32.5	29.0	32.4
Balancing item *	−44.7	−42.6	−51.1	−41.7	−24.2	−31.4	−74.6	−90.9
Change in reserves	−5.1	−6.4	−16.6	−11.1	−43.7	−60.9	−79.3	−94.7
(− = increase)								
Memo items:								
Bilateral aid grants	5.4	8.2	8.6	7.1	8.5	8.6	10.3	9.7
(ex technical cooperation grants)								
Net private flows (debt+equity)	66.7	50.9	51.5	33.1	59.7	101.1	160.2	191.7
Net official flows (aid+debt)	12.9	7.6	8.5	9.3	11.2	1.8	−0.2	−21.2

Note: e = estimate.
* Combination of errors and omissions and net acquisition of foreign assets (including FDI) by developing countries.

Table A.4 External financing: Latin America and the Carribean, 1998–2005
$ billions

	1998	1999	2000	2001	2002	2003	2004	2005e
Current account balance	−89.4	−55.4	−46.8	−51.9	−14.9	8.4	19.0	33.9
as % GDP	−4.5	−3.1	−2.4	−2.7	−0.9	0.5	0.9	1.5
Financial flows:								
Net equity flows	71.9	84.7	78.8	73.6	49.6	44.5	60.2	73.9
Net FDI inflows	74.1	88.3	79.3	71.1	48.2	41.1	60.8	61.4
Net portfolio equity inflows	−2.2	−3.6	−0.6	2.5	1.4	3.4	−0.6	12.5
Net debt flows	37.9	12.8	−4.7	6.2	−8.6	10.2	−11.4	−15.9
Official creditors	10.9	1.6	−11.1	20.4	12.8	4.9	−10.5	−36.5
World Bank	2.4	2.1	2.0	1.3	−0.3	−0.4	−1.0	−1.8
IMF	2.5	−0.9	−10.7	15.6	11.9	5.6	−6.3	−28.8
Others	6.0	0.4	−2.4	3.5	1.3	−0.3	−3.2	−5.9
Private creditors	27.0	11.2	6.4	−14.1	−21.4	5.4	−1.0	20.5
Net medium- and long-term								
debt flows	55.3	19.5	8.0	−0.6	−11.4	3.2	−3.9	18.5
Bonds	17.9	20.1	8.3	2.9	−0.4	11.3	−1.1	14.1
Banks	39.1	−1.4	0.5	−2.0	−9.1	−7.2	−2.8	4.4
Others	−1.7	0.8	−0.8	−1.4	−1.9	−0.9	0.0	0.0
Net short-term debt flows	−28.3	−8.3	−1.6	−13.6	−10.0	2.2	2.9	2.0
Balancing item *	−29.6	−49.7	−24.3	−25.1	−25.4	−29.9	−42.9	−59.7
Change in reserves	9.2	7.6	−3.0	−2.9	−0.8	−33.2	−24.9	−32.1
(− = increase)								
Memo items:								
Bilateral aid grants	3.2	2.9	2.5	3.2	2.8	3.0	4.9	3.2
(ex technical cooperation grants)								
Net private flows (debt+equity)	98.9	95.8	85.2	59.5	28.2	49.9	59.3	94.4
Net official flows (aid+debt)	14.1	4.5	−8.6	23.6	15.6	7.9	−5.5	−33.3

Note: e = estimate.
* Combination of errors and omissions and net acquisition of foreign assets (including FDI) by developing countries.

Table A.5 External financing: Middle East and North Africa, 1998–2005
$ billions

	1998	1999	2000	2001	2002	2003	2004	2005e
Current account balance	−9.7	6.2	25.3	15.4	12.0	28.3	43.8	67.2
as % GDP	−2.9	1.8	7.0	4.0	3.1	6.7	9.3	11.9
Financial flows:								
Net equity flows	2.9	3.1	4.4	3.3	3.5	5.7	6.0	10.0
Net FDI inflows	2.7	2.4	4.1	3.4	3.7	5.6	5.3	9.1
Net portfolio equity inflows	0.2	0.7	0.2	−0.1	−0.2	0.1	0.6	0.9
Net debt flows	3.6	−3.0	−3.8	0.3	2.3	−0.4	−1.8	2.2
Official creditors	−1.6	−2.5	−2.7	−1.2	−2.5	−2.5	−4.1	−2.4
World Bank	−0.2	0.2	−0.3	−0.1	−0.3	−0.3	−0.6	−0.2
IMF	0.0	0.0	−0.2	−0.1	−0.3	−0.6	−0.5	−0.4
Others	−1.4	−2.8	−2.2	−1.0	−1.9	−1.6	−3.0	−1.8
Private creditors	5.2	−0.5	−1.1	1.5	4.8	2.1	2.3	4.6
Net medium- and long-term debt flows	1.8	−1.4	0.8	3.8	4.5	0.2	2.3	3.7
Bonds	1.3	1.4	1.2	4.4	5.0	0.7	3.3	2.2
Banks	2.0	−1.6	0.4	−0.1	−0.3	−1.0	−0.8	1.6
Others	−1.5	−1.2	−0.9	−0.4	−0.2	0.6	−0.2	−0.1
Net short-term debt flows	3.3	1.0	−1.9	−2.3	0.3	1.9	0.0	0.9
Balancing item *	1.5	−7.4	−21.1	−9.5	−5.8	−11.6	−33.7	−58.2
Change in reserves (− = increase)	1.7	1.2	−4.8	−9.5	−12.0	−22.0	−14.3	−21.3
Memo items:								
Bilateral aid grants (ex technical cooperation grants)	3.5	2.7	3.1	2.2	2.4	3.6	4.5	4.1
Net private flows (debt+equity)	8.1	2.6	3.3	4.8	8.3	7.8	8.3	14.6
Net official flows (aid+debt)	1.8	0.2	0.3	1.1	−0.1	1.2	0.4	1.7

Note: e = estimate.
* Combination of errors and omissions and net acquisition of foreign assets (including FDI) by developing countries.

Table A.6 External financing: South Asia, 1998–2005

$ billions

	1998	1999	2000	2001	2002	2003	2004	2005e
Current account balance	−9.5	−5.3	−6.3	2.2	11.4	10.6	−4.6	−24.1
as % GDP	−1.8	−0.9	−1.1	0.4	1.8	1.4	−0.6	−2.6
Financial flows:								
Net equity flows	2.9	5.5	6.7	8.8	7.8	13.7	15.9	20.6
Net FDI inflows	3.5	3.1	4.4	6.1	6.7	5.6	7.2	8.4
Net portfolio equity inflows	−0.6	2.4	2.4	2.7	1.0	8.0	8.8	12.2
Net debt flows	4.7	0.5	3.5	−0.9	0.0	0.3	7.7	6.4
Official creditors	2.3	2.5	0.5	2.2	−2.4	−1.7	1.0	3.4
World Bank	0.8	1.0	0.7	1.5	−1.0	−0.2	2.0	1.6
IMF	−0.4	−0.1	−0.3	0.3	0.1	−0.1	−0.3	−0.1
Others	2.0	1.6	0.0	0.4	−1.5	−1.5	−0.7	1.9
Private creditors	2.4	−2.0	3.0	−3.1	2.4	2.1	6.7	3.0
Net medium- and long-term								
debt flows	3.7	−2.1	3.9	−2.0	0.6	1.3	3.9	0.6
Bonds	4.2	−1.2	5.4	−0.2	−0.5	−3.0	4.1	−1.6
Banks	0.7	−0.5	−2.0	−1.4	1.2	4.4	0.0	2.2
Others	−1.1	−0.4	0.5	−0.3	−0.1	0.0	−0.2	0.0
Net short-term debt flows	−1.3	0.1	−0.9	−1.1	1.8	0.7	2.9	2.4
Balancing item *	4.8	4.3	0.8	0.1	7.8	10.4	8.2	3.4
Change in reserves	−3.0	−5.0	−4.7	−10.2	−27.0	−35.0	−27.2	−6.3
(− = increase)								
Memo items:								
Bilateral aid grants	2.1	2.3	2.1	3.2	2.5	3.9	3.5	4.5
(ex technical cooperation grants)								
Net private flows (debt+equity)	5.3	3.5	9.7	5.8	10.1	15.8	22.7	23.6
Net official flows (aid+debt)	4.5	4.8	2.6	5.3	0.1	2.2	4.5	7.9

Note: e = estimate.

* Combination of errors and omissions and net acquisition of foreign assets (including FDI) by developing countries.

Table A.7 External financing: Sub-Saharan Africa, 1998–2005
$ billions

	1998	1999	2000	2001	2002	2003	2004	2005e
Current account balance	−15.9	−7.9	5.7	−2.4	−3.4	3.8	2.4	0.6
as % GDP	−5.1	−2.6	1.8	−0.8	−1.0	0.9	0.5	0.1
Financial flows:								
Net equity flows	15.5	18.0	10.7	14.0	9.1	14.3	18.0	24.7
Net FDI inflows	6.9	9.0	6.5	15.0	9.5	13.6	11.3	17.6
Net portfolio equity inflows	8.7	9.0	4.2	−1.0	−0.4	0.7	6.7	7.2
Net debt flows	−1.3	−0.9	0.0	−1.4	−0.2	2.8	3.6	0.6
Official creditors	0.5	0.4	0.7	0.6	2.6	1.2	0.8	−3.2
World Bank	1.3	1.1	1.5	1.8	2.2	2.2	2.5	2.2
IMF	−0.3	0.0	0.1	0.1	0.5	−0.1	−0.1	−0.4
Others	−0.5	−0.7	−0.8	−1.3	0.0	−0.9	−1.5	−5.0
Private creditors	−1.8	−1.3	−0.7	−2.0	−2.8	1.5	2.8	3.8
Net medium- and long-term debt flows	−1.3	−0.7	0.4	0.1	−1.0	2.5	1.7	2.3
Bonds	0.3	1.2	1.0	1.9	2.7	4.6	1.2	0.0
Banks	−1.3	−1.7	−0.6	−1.5	−3.0	−1.2	0.9	2.5
Others	−0.2	−0.2	0.0	−0.3	−0.7	−0.9	−0.4	−0.2
Net short-term debt flows	−0.5	−0.6	−1.1	−2.1	−1.8	−1.0	1.1	1.5
Balancing item *	0.2	−7.9	−10.2	−9.9	−5.2	−16.9	−1.7	−5.3
Change in reserves (− = increase)	1.5	−1.3	−6.2	−0.3	−0.3	−3.9	−22.2	−20.7
Memo items:								
Bilateral aid grants (ex technical cooperation grants)	10.1	9.9	10.0	10.0	14.0	22.0	24.2	28.4
Net private flows (debt+equity)	13.7	16.7	9.9	12.1	6.3	15.8	20.7	28.5
Net official flows (aid+debt)	10.6	10.3	10.7	10.7	16.6	23.3	25.1	25.2

Note: e = estimate.
* Combination of errors and omissions and net acquisition of foreign assets (including FDI) by developing countries.

179

Table A.8 Net inward foreign direct investment, 1997–2005
$ billions

	1997	1998	1999	2000	2001	2002	2003	2004	2005e
All developing countries	168.7	172.4	183.3	168.8	176.9	160.3	161.6	211.5	237.5
East Asia and Pacific	62.1	57.8	50.8	44.3	48.5	57.2	59.8	64.6	65.3
China	44.2	43.8	38.8	38.4	44.2	49.3	53.5	54.9	53.0
Indonesia	4.7	-0.2	-1.9	-4.6	-3.0	0.1	-0.6	1.0	2.3
Malaysia	5.1	2.2	3.9	3.8	0.6	3.2	2.5	4.6	4.2
Philippines	1.2	2.3	1.7	1.3	1.0	1.8	0.3	0.5	1.1
Thailand	3.9	7.3	6.1	3.4	3.9	1.0	1.9	1.4	3.1
Europe and Central Asia	24.6	27.4	29.8	30.2	32.7	34.9	35.9	62.4	75.6
Czech Rep.	1.3	3.7	6.3	5.0	5.6	8.5	2.0	4.5	11.0
Hungary	4.2	3.3	3.3	2.8	3.9	3.0	2.2	4.6	4.0
Poland	4.9	6.4	7.3	9.3	5.7	4.1	4.1	12.6	7.7
Russian Fed.	4.9	2.8	3.3	2.7	2.7	3.5	8.0	12.5	14.6
Ukraine	0.6	0.7	0.5	0.6	0.8	0.7	1.4	1.7	7.8
Turkey	0.8	0.9	0.8	1.0	3.3	1.1	1.8	2.7	7.2
Latin America and the Caribbean	66.7	74.1	88.3	79.3	71.1	48.2	41.1	60.8	61.4
Argentina	9.2	7.3	24.0	10.4	2.2	2.1	1.7	4.1	4.7
Brazil	19.7	31.9	28.6	32.8	22.5	16.6	10.1	18.2	15.2
Chile	5.3	4.6	8.8	4.9	4.2	2.6	4.4	7.6	7.2
Mexico	12.8	12.4	13.4	17.1	27.7	15.5	12.3	17.4	17.8
Venezuela, R. B. de	6.2	5.0	2.9	4.7	3.7	0.8	2.7	1.5	3.0
Middle East and North Africa	2.1	2.7	2.4	4.1	3.4	3.7	5.6	5.3	9.1
Algeria	0.3	0.5	0.5	0.4	1.2	1.1	0.6	0.9	1.4
Egypt, Arab Rep. of	0.9	1.1	1.1	1.2	0.5	0.6	0.2	1.3	3.1
Morocco	0.0	0.0	0.0	0.2	0.1	0.1	2.3	0.8	1.0
South Asia	4.9	3.5	3.1	4.4	6.1	6.7	5.6	7.2	8.4
India	3.6	2.6	2.2	3.6	5.5	5.6	4.6	5.3	5.6
Pakistan	0.7	0.5	0.5	0.3	0.4	0.8	0.5	1.1	2.2
Sub-Saharan Africa	8.3	6.9	9.0	6.5	15.0	9.5	13.6	11.3	17.6
Angola	0.4	1.1	2.5	0.9	2.1	1.7	3.5	1.4	1.5
South Africa	3.8	0.6	1.5	1.0	7.3	0.7	0.8	0.6	6.3

Note: e = estimate. The data do not match GDF Volume II because of revisions of the estimates.

Table A.9 Net inward portfolio equity flows, 1997–2005
$ billions

	1997	1998	1999	2000	2001	2002	2003	2004	2005e
All developing countries	30.6	6.9	12.6	14.1	6.4	5.8	25.2	37.3	61.4
East Asia and Pacific	4.1	−3.1	2.2	6.6	2.0	4.0	12.4	17.6	26.5
China	5.7	0.8	0.6	6.9	0.8	2.2	7.7	10.9	19.0
Indonesia	−5.0	−4.4	−0.8	−1.0	0.4	0.9	1.1	2.1	−0.2
Malaysia	0.0	0.0	0.0	0.0	0.0	−0.1	1.3	4.4	0.9
Philippines	−0.4	0.3	1.4	−0.2	0.4	0.4	0.5	0.4	1.5
Thailand	3.9	0.3	0.9	0.9	0.4	0.5	1.8	−0.3	5.3
Europe and Central Asia	4.0	4.0	2.0	1.3	0.3	−0.1	0.5	4.2	5.8
Czech Rep.	0.4	1.1	0.1	0.6	0.6	−0.3	1.1	0.7	−1.5
Hungary	1.0	0.6	1.2	−0.4	0.1	−0.1	0.3	1.5	0.0
Poland	0.6	1.7	0.0	0.4	−0.3	−0.5	−0.8	1.9	1.3
Russian Fed.	1.3	0.7	−0.3	0.2	0.5	2.6	0 4	0.2	−0.2
Turkey	0.0	−0.5	0.4	0.5	−0.1	0.0	0.9	1.4	5.7
Latin America and the Caribbean	13.3	−2.2	−3.6	−0.6	2.5	1.4	3.4	−0.6	8.5
Argentina	1.4	−0.2	−10.8	−3.2	0.0	−0.1	0.1	−0.1	0.0
Brazil	5.1	−1.8	2.6	3.1	2.5	2.0	3.0	2.1	6.5
Chile	1.7	0.6	0.5	−0.4	−0.2	−0.3	0.3	0.0	1.7
Mexico	3.2	−0.7	3.8	0.4	0.2	−0.1	−0.1	−2.5	3.4
Venezuela, R. B. de	1.4	0.2	0.4	−0.6	0.0	0.0	0.1	−0.2	0.1
Middle East and North Africa	0.7	0.2	0.7	0.2	−0.1	−0.2	0.1	0.6	0.9
Egypt, Arab Rep. of	0.5	−0.2	0.7	0.3	0.0	−0.2	0.0	0.0	0.7
South Asia	2.9	−0.6	2.4	2.4	2.7	1.0	8.0	8.8	12.2
India	2.6	−0.6	2.3	2.3	2.9	1.0	8.2	8.8	12.2
Sub-Saharan Africa	5.6	8.7	9.0	4.2	−1.0	−0.4	0.7	6.7	7.2
South Africa	5.5	8.6	9.0	4.2	−1.0	−0.4	0.7	6.7	7.1

Note: e = estimate. The data do not match GDF Volume II because of revisions of the estimates.

Table A.10 Net inward debt flows to developing countries, 1997–2005
$ billions

	1997	1998	1999	2000	2001	2002	2003	2004	2005[e]
All developing countries	107.2	54.3	16.3	−1.0	−1.5	10.7	72.8	119.1	120.1
East Asia and Pacific	44.9	−33.5	−11.7	−16.0	−8.2	−10.3	1.9	37.8	43.9
China	18.5	−14.2	−1.6	−5.2	0.0	4.0	13.5	37.3	—
Indonesia	10.1	−4.6	−3.8	−0.7	−6.0	−7.5	−5.5	−3.0	—
Malaysia	8.4	−3.6	−0.7	0.3	5.2	3.4	−1.5	3.5	—
Philippines	7.5	−4.1	3.7	2.6	2.1	−0.8	0.6	−0.7	—
Thailand	−1.3	−7.9	−9.4	−13.7	−10.0	−10.0	−7.5	−1.4	—
Europe and Central Asia	35.6	42.9	18.6	20.0	2.3	27.6	57.9	83.2	82.9
Bulgaria	1.0	0.2	0.3	0.5	−0.2	0.6	1.0	1.7	—
Czech Rep.	3.3	1.4	−0.2	−1.7	−0.5	1.0	3.5	5.2	—
Hungary	−1.4	2.7	2.0	0.4	1.7	0.5	4.4	14.6	—
Poland	3.8	5.1	4.8	0.8	2.5	1.2	7.0	−2.2	—
Russian Fed.	7.6	21.9	−4.2	−2.8	−3.9	−2.6	12.8	10.8	—
Turkey	4.2	5.5	10.9	18.2	−4.5	13.2	4.9	13.4	—
Latin America and the Caribbean	25.2	37.9	12.8	−4.7	6.2	−8.6	10.2	−11.4	−15.9
Argentina	17.1	11.7	6.4	4.3	−5.6	−1.8	−0.1	−4.1	—
Brazil	−1.3	6.7	−4.9	−1.0	5.5	−1.6	3.9	−11.2	—
Chile	1.8	4.0	1.7	2.9	0.5	1.6	1.9	0.5	—
Colombia	3.6	0.8	1.3	−0.2	2.8	−0.9	0.6	0.6	—
Mexico	−4.9	9.0	6.9	−15.8	−2.9	−8.2	−1.3	−2.9	—
Venezuela, R. B. de	2.6	1.7	0.2	0.9	−1.1	−3.2	0.1	0.4	—
Middle East and North Africa	−3.5	3.6	−3.0	−3.8	0.3	2.3	−0.4	−1.8	2.2
Algeria	−0.4	−1.7	−1.9	−1.6	−2.0	−1.4	−1.3	−2.5	—
Egypt, Arab Rep. of	0.6	1.1	−0.6	−0.7	0.1	−0.7	−1.1	−2.0	—
Lebanon	1.1	1.7	1.5	1.8	2.7	4.4	1.2	3.4	—
South Asia	0.7	4.7	0.5	3.5	−0.9	0.0	0.3	7.7	6.4
India	−1.6	3.0	−1.1	3.4	−1.9	−1.4	0.0	7.1	—
Pakistan	1.6	0.7	0.7	−0.3	0.3	0.6	−1.1	−0.8	—
Sub-Saharan Africa	4.4	−1.3	−0.9	0.0	−1.4	−0.2	2.8	3.6	0.6
South Africa	−0.4	−0.3	−0.7	1.2	−0.8	−0.5	2.7	1.2	—

Note: e = estimate; — = not available.

Table A.11 Net inward short-term debt flows to developing countries, 1997–2005
$ billions

	1997	1998	1999	2000	2001	2002	2003	2004	2005e
All developing countries	9.2	−65.8	−19.6	−6.8	−22.7	4.2	54.9	70.0	69.3
East Asia and Pacific	4.7	−44.7	−13.3	−9.9	1.7	10.1	18.5	34.2	30.0
China	6.1	−14.1	−2.2	−2.1	1.8	9.6	18.4	29.3	—
Indonesia	0.6	−9.7	−1.6	1.5	−1.0	0.2	−0.9	1.6	—
Malaysia	3.9	−6.5	−2.5	−1.4	2.2	1.6	0.3	2.8	—
Philippines	3.8	−5.9	−0.9	0.5	0.5	−0.4	0.6	−1.1	—
Thailand	−9.9	−8.2	−6.2	−8.5	−1.7	−1.3	−1.0	0.5	—
Europe and Central Asia	10.9	5.7	1.6	8.6	−5.3	3.8	32.5	29.0	32.4
Bulgaria	0.8	−0.2	−0.3	0.2	−0.2	0.6	0.6	0.6	—
Czech Rep.	2.4	−0.5	1.1	0.2	0.6	−0.3	1.6	3.2	—
Hungary	0.0	1.4	−1.2	0.6	0.5	1.0	2.5	3.3	—
Poland	2.5	3.3	2.8	−1.7	1.5	0.4	4.8	−2.7	—
Russian Fed.	−1.4	−0.5	−1.0	2.0	2.5	−1.6	9.6	5.0	—
Turkey	0.6	3.2	2.3	5.4	−12.6	0.1	4.4	8.9	—
Latin America and the Caribbean	−7.8	−28.3	−8.3	−1.6	−13.6	−10.0	2.2	2.9	2.0
Argentina	8.5	−1.0	−1.5	−1.1	−8.3	−0.4	0.7	−0.3	—
Brazil	−16.0	−24.0	0.7	1.8	−2.5	−4.9	1.2	0.7	—
Chile	−1.5	−0.4	−0.8	1.9	−0.9	0.5	1.7	0.2	—
Colombia	−0.1	0.5	−2.3	−1.1	0.4	0.4	−0.1	1.8	—
Mexico	−2.0	−1.5	−2.3	−5.1	−4.4	−4.7	−0.7	−0.1	—
Venezuela, R. B. de	1.5	−2.0	−0.1	2.0	0.7	−0.2	−0.2	0.0	—
Middle East and North Africa	0.0	3.3	1.0	−1.9	−2.3	0.3	1.9	0.0	0.9
Algeria	−0.2	0.0	0.0	0.0	0.0	−0.1	0.0	0.3	—
Egypt, Arab Rep. of	0.6	1.3	0.0	−0.2	−0.7	0.1	0.3	−0.9	—
Lebanon	0.1	0.2	0.2	0.3	0.1	−0.1	0.6	0.8	—
South Asia	−2.1	−1.3	0.1	−0.9	−1.1	1.8	0.7	2.9	2.4
India	−1.7	−0.7	−0.4	−0.5	−0.7	1.4	0.9	2.5	—
Pakistan	−0.3	−0.5	−0.1	−0.3	−0.2	0.2	−0.3	0.0	—
Sub-Saharan Africa	3.5	−0.5	−0.6	−1.1	−2.1	−1.8	−1.0	1.1	1.5
South Africa	0.1	0.5	−0.6	0.3	−1.2	−1.0	0.0	0.6	—

Note: e = estimate; — = not available.

Table A.12 Net inward debt flows to public sector and publicly guaranteed borrowers, 1997–2005
$ billions

	1997	1998	1999	2000	2001	2002	2003	2004	2005e
All developing countries	42.0	69.4	31.0	9.3	20.1	4.1	−11.2	−3.1	−36.5
East Asia and Pacific	29.0	19.1	11.1	4.7	−0.8	−11.7	−12.4	−2.5	2.5
China	11.1	2.5	1.6	−1.1	0.0	−5.3	−5.7	1.5	—
Indonesia	3.6	9.0	2.0	0.9	−2.2	−3.1	−0.9	−4.4	—
Malaysia	1.7	0.5	0.9	1.4	3.1	2.0	−2.1	0.0	—
Philippines	1.8	1.6	4.6	3.0	0.2	0.7	0.8	1.4	—
Thailand	9.4	4.6	1.9	−0.2	−2.7	−6.2	−5.4	−2.2	—
Europe and Central Asia	15.6	21.8	7.0	5.2	−1.5	3.6	−4.6	−0.2	−13.8
Bulgaria	0.2	0.3	0.4	0.2	−0.1	−0.3	0.0	−0.7	—
Czech Rep.	1.0	1.0	−1.0	−1.0	−0.9	0.2	0.5	1.7	—
Hungary	−1.8	−0.4	1.5	−1.4	−0.8	−0.8	0.5	3.2	—
Poland	0.5	−0.1	−0.3	−1.4	−3.3	0.1	1.7	0.5	—
Russian Fed.	7.1	16.2	−3.5	−3.9	−7.0	−4.1	−7.2	−7.1	—
Turkey	2.5	−1.0	4.6	11.3	9.2	7.5	−1.7	−2.1	—
Latin America and the Caribbean	−2.0	25.2	12.4	−2.9	19.4	9.5	9.3	−2.5	−20.0
Argentina	4.9	8.4	8.7	6.4	6.7	−1.5	−0.9	−2.3	—
Brazil	−0.3	12.7	1.5	−3.4	9.6	10.4	3.1	−5.2	—
Chile	−0.3	0.6	0.6	−0.4	0.4	1.1	1.1	1.3	—
Colombia	1.1	1.0	3.4	0.9	2.5	−1.3	1.7	0.4	—
Mexico	−9.9	0.7	−3.7	−9.1	−3.0	−1.9	−0.6	−1.4	—
Venezuela, R. B. de	0.4	0.2	−0.6	−0.5	−1.7	−2.6	0.3	1.0	—
Middle East and North Africa	−4.1	−1.9	−2.9	−2.6	2.3	2.2	−2.3	−1.8	−1.4
Algeria	−0.3	−1.7	−2.0	−1.6	−1.9	−1.4	−1.7	−2.8	—
Egypt, Arab Rep. of	−0.1	−0.5	−0.7	−0.6	0.8	−0.8	−1.1	−0.8	—
Lebanon	0.5	1.7	1.4	1.4	2.5	4.7	0.6	2.5	—
South Asia	0.8	5.5	1.4	4.5	0.5	−2.4	−2.8	0.8	−1.8
India	−1.5	3.6	−0.1	3.8	−1.2	−3.4	−3.7	0.5	—
Pakistan	1.6	0.9	1.2	0.3	0.9	0.4	−0.5	−0.8	—
Sub-Saharan Africa	2.8	−0.4	1.8	0.4	0.2	2.9	1.6	3.1	−2.1
South Africa	1.1	−1.0	1.6	0.0	−0.4	1.4	0.0	1.1	—

Note: e = estimate; — = not available.

Table A.13 Net inward debt flows to private sector borrowers, 1997–2005
$ billions

	1997	1998	1999	2000	2001	2002	2003	2004	2005e
All developing countries	65.2	−15.1	−14.6	−10.3	−21.6	6.6	84.0	122.2	156.7
East Asia and Pacific	15.9	−52.6	−22.8	−20.6	−7.4	1.4	14.3	40.3	41.4
China	7.4	−16.7	−3.2	−4.1	−0.1	9.2	19.4	35.8	—
Indonesia	6.5	−13.6	−5.8	−1.6	−3.8	−4.4	−4.6	1.3	—
Malaysia	6.7	−4.0	−1.6	−1.1	2.1	1.4	0.6	3.6	—
Philippines	5.8	−5.7	−0.9	−0.5	1.9	−1.5	−0.1	−2.1	—
Thailand	−10.7	−12.5	−11.3	−13.5	−7.3	−3.7	−2.0	0.8	—
Europe and Central Asia	20.0	21.0	11.6	14.8	3.8	24.0	62.4	83.3	96.7
Bulgaria	0.8	−0.1	−0.1	0.3	−0.1	0.9	1.0	2.4	—
Czech Rep.	2.3	0.4	0.8	−0.6	0.4	1.6	3.0	3.5	—
Hungary	0.5	3.1	0.5	1.8	2.5	1.3	5.8	11.4	—
Poland	3.3	5.2	5.1	2.2	5.8	1.0	5.3	−2.7	—
Russian Fed.	0.5	2.4	−0.7	1.1	3.1	1.5	20.0	17.8	—
Turkey	1.8	6.5	6.3	6.8	−13.7	5.7	4.7	15.5	—
Latin America and the Caribbean	27.2	12.7	0.4	−1.8	−13.2	−18.1	0.9	−8.9	4.1
Argentina	12.3	3.4	−2.4	−2.1	−12.3	−0.5	0.8	−1.8	—
Brazil	−1.0	−5.3	−6.4	2.4	−4.2	−11.9	0.8	−6.0	—
Chile	2.1	3.5	1.1	3.3	0.1	0.5	0.8	−0.9	—
Colombia	2.5	−0.2	−2.1	−1.1	0.3	0.4	−1.1	0.2	—
Mexico	5.0	8.3	10.5	−6.6	0.1	−6.2	−0.7	−1.5	—
Venezuela, R. B. de	2.2	1.5	0.7	1.4	0.6	−0.6	−0.2	−0.6	—
Middle East and North Africa	0.6	5.5	−0.1	−1.2	−1.9	0.1	2.0	0.0	3.6
Algeria	−0.2	0.0	0.0	0.0	0.0	−0.1	0.5	0.4	—
Egypt, Arab Rep. of	0.6	1.5	0.1	−0.1	−0.7	0.1	0.0	−1.2	—
Lebanon	0.6	0.1	0.1	0.4	0.2	−0.2	0.6	0.9	—
South Asia	−0.1	−0.8	−0.9	−1.1	−1.4	2.3	3.2	6.9	8.2
India	−0.1	−0.5	−1.0	−0.4	−0.7	2.0	3.7	6.6	—
Pakistan	0.0	−0.2	−0.5	−0.6	−0.5	0.1	−0.6	−0.1	—
Sub-Saharan Africa	1.6	−0.9	−2.7	−0.4	−1.6	−3.1	1.2	0.5	2.7
South Africa	−1.5	0.7	−2.3	1.3	−0.4	−1.9	2.6	0.1	—

Note: e = estimate; — = not available.

185

Table A.14 Net inward debt flows from public sector creditors, 1997–2005
$ billions

	1997	1998	1999	2000	2001	2002	2003	2004	2005e
All developing countries	13.1	34.3	13.9	−5.7	27.4	5.2	−12.3	−28.7	−71.4
East Asia and Pacific	17.3	14.7	12.5	7.0	3.2	−7.9	−7.4	−5.5	−1.9
China	4.3	2.3	3.4	1.5	2.2	−1.2	−3.2	0.0	—
Indonesia	3.6	8.5	4.8	2.9	−0.8	−1.4	−0.3	−3.7	—
Malaysia	−0.2	0.2	0.6	0.6	2.1	−0.2	−0.1	0.7	—
Philippines	0.6	0.7	0.2	0.3	−0.3	−0.5	−0.6	−1.1	—
Thailand	8.4	1.8	2.5	0.3	−1.5	−5.5	−4.5	−2.6	—
Europe and Central Asia	6.7	7.5	−0.6	0.0	2.2	2.7	−6.8	−10.5	−30.9
Bulgaria	0.3	0.4	0.3	0.2	−0.3	−0.3	0.1	0.1	—
Czech Rep.	−0.1	0.0	0.0	0.1	0.2	0.0	0.1	0.0	—
Hungary	−0.1	−1.1	0.2	−0.2	−0.2	0.0	−0.5	0.4	—
Poland	−0.1	−0.5	−0.4	−0.5	−4.1	−1.1	−1.7	−2.8	—
Russian Fed.	4.2	6.3	−3.0	−3.3	−4.8	−3.3	−4.3	−4.9	—
Turkey	−0.2	−0.4	−0.1	4.4	10.4	6.7	−1.3	−3.4	—
Latin America and the Caribbean	−8.7	10.9	1.6	−11.1	20.4	12.8	4.9	−10.5	−36.5
Argentina	−0.1	1.1	−0.1	0.9	10.3	−1.4	−0.9	−2.2	—
Brazil	−1.2	9.5	4.5	−8.5	9.5	12.1	3.0	−7.3	—
Chile	−0.4	−0.1	−0.1	−0.1	−0.1	−0.3	−0.1	−0.1	—
Colombia	−0.5	0.2	1.0	0.1	1.1	0.0	2.1	0.1	—
Mexico	−8.0	−1.9	−5.3	−4.8	−0.7	0.2	−0.3	−1.2	—
Venezuela, R. B. de	−0.3	1.0	−0.1	−0.3	−1.1	−0.6	−0.6	−0.4	—
Middle East and North Africa	−4.0	−1.6	−2.5	−2.7	−1.2	−2.5	−2.5	−4.1	−2.4
Algeria	0.3	−0.4	−0.4	−0.4	−1.0	−1.3	−1.3	−2.3	—
Egypt, Arab Rep. of	0.0	−0.2	−0.5	−0.6	−0.7	−0.8	−0.8	−0.9	—
Lebanon	0.1	0.2	0.1	0.1	0.1	0.0	0.6	0.0	—
South Asia	0.3	2.3	2.5	0.5	2.2	−2.4	−1.7	1.0	3.4
India	−1.0	0.6	0.8	−0.3	0.4	−3.8	−2.7	0.9	—
Pakistan	0.7	0.9	1.2	0.3	1.1	0.9	−0.3	−1.0	—
Sub-Saharan Africa	1.4	0.5	0.4	0.7	0.6	2.6	1.2	0.8	−3.2
South Africa	−0.4	−0.4	0.0	0.1	0.0	0.0	0.1	0.0	—

Note: e = estimate; — = not available.

Table A.15 Net inward debt flows from private sector creditors, 1997–2005
$ billions

	1997	1998	1999	2000	2001	2002	2003	2004	2005e
All developing countries	94.1	19.9	2.5	4.7	−28.9	5.5	85.1	147.8	191.6
East Asia and Pacific	27.6	−48.2	−24.2	−22.9	−11.3	−2.4	9.3	43.3	45.8
China	14.2	−16.5	−5.0	−6.8	−2.2	5.2	16.9	37.3	—
Indonesia	6.5	−13.0	−8.6	−3.6	−5.2	−6.1	−5.1	0.7	—
Malaysia	8.6	−3.8	−1.3	−0.3	3.1	3.6	−1.4	2.8	—
Philippines	7.0	−4.8	3.5	2.3	2.4	−0.3	1.2	0.4	—
Thailand	−9.7	−9.6	−11.9	−14.0	−8.5	−4.4	−3.0	1.2	—
Europe and Central Asia	28.8	35.3	19.2	20.0	0.1	24.9	64.7	93.7	113.8
Bulgaria	0.7	−0.2	−0.1	0.2	0.1	0.9	0.9	1.6	—
Czech Rep.	3.3	1.4	−0.2	−1.7	−0.7	1.7	3.3	5.2	—
Hungary	−1.3	3.8	1.8	0.7	1.9	0.6	6.8	14.2	—
Poland	3.9	5.6	5.2	1.3	6.6	2.2	8.7	0.6	—
Russian Fed.	3.4	12.3	−1.2	0.5	0.9	0.8	17.0	15.7	—
Turkey	4.4	5.9	11.0	13.8	−14.9	6.5	4.3	16.8	—
Latin America and the Caribbean	33.8	27.0	11.2	6.4	−14.1	−21.4	5.4	−1.0	20.5
Argentina	17.3	10.7	6.4	3.4	−16.0	−0.5	0.8	−1.8	—
Brazil	−0.1	−2.1	−9.4	7.5	−4.0	−13.6	0.9	−3.9	—
Chile	2.2	4.1	1.8	3.0	0.6	1.9	2.0	0.6	—
Colombia	4.1	0.6	0.2	−0.3	1.7	−0.9	−1.4	0.5	—
Mexico	3.1	10.8	12.2	−11.0	−2.3	−8.4	−1.0	−1.7	—
Venezuela, R. B. de	2.9	0.7	0.3	1.2	0.0	−2.6	0.7	0.8	—
Middle East and North Africa	0.5	5.2	−0.5	−1.1	1.5	4.8	2.1	2.3	4.6
Algeria	−0.7	−1.3	−1.5	−1.2	−1.0	−0.1	0.1	−0.2	—
Egypt, Arab Rep. of	0.6	1.3	−0.1	−0.1	0.8	0.1	−0.3	−1.1	—
Lebanon	1.0	1.6	1.4	1.7	2.6	4.4	0.6	3.4	—
South Asia	0.4	2.4	−2.0	3.0	−3.1	2.4	2.1	6.7	3.0
India	−0.6	2.5	−1.9	3.6	−2.3	2.4	2.8	6.2	—
Pakistan	0.9	−0.2	−0.6	−0.7	−0.7	−0.3	−0.8	0.2	—
Sub-Saharan Africa	3.0	−1.8	−1.3	−0.7	−2.0	−2.8	1.5	2.8	3.8
South Africa	0.0	0.1	−0.7	1.2	−0.8	−0.5	2.6	1.1	—

Note: e = estimate; — = not available.

Table A.16 Gross market-based capital flows to developing countries, 1998–2005
$ billions

	1998	1999	2000	2001	2002	2003	2004	2005e
All developing countries	160.4	149.7	201.8	135.9	131.6	186.0	249.4	385.2
East Asia and Pacific	25.5	27.0	48.5	19.6	41.1	50.6	55.8	84.8
China	9.2	8.3	29.1	7.5	15.8	24.8	31.9	50.1
Indonesia	0.7	2.4	1.1	1.0	1.6	6.5	4.1	7.2
Malaysia	3.4	7.4	6.8	5.1	12.8	7.3	10.5	8.2
Philippines	5.8	7.2	7.3	3.6	6.5	7.1	5.4	8.2
Thailand	6.4	1.5	4.2	2.5	3.6	4.3	3.6	8.4
Europe and Central Asia	35.3	29.4	40.4	24.9	32.3	50.0	81.4	142.3
Czech Rep.	3.0	1.4	1.4	0.8	0.7	2.5	4.6	3.4
Hungary	3.6	3.4	2.1	2.7	1.8	5.4	8.7	10.3
Poland	3.6	4.4	3.6	4.7	6.5	7.9	6.9	19.1
Russian Fed.	8.3	0.7	5.3	4.6	9.9	16.4	26.8	62.8
Turkey	9.9	12.8	22.3	6.8	7.3	7.5	14.9	24.1
Latin America and the Caribbean	81.8	72.5	87.7	71.9	40.8	60.6	68.2	94.9
Argentina	25.4	20.1	18.8	6.3	1.9	0.7	0.8	2.5
Brazil	17.8	15.1	27.9	23.7	13.2	17.8	23.4	30.5
Chile	4.2	9.6	7.7	6.1	3.6	5.2	8.0	10.2
Mexico	19.3	17.4	20.9	18.4	13.2	26.7	22.6	30.2
Venezuela, R. B. de	7.6	1.8	2.9	4.8	0.6	4.1	4.7	6.5
Middle East and North Africa	4.8	8.6	6.4	8.5	8.5	5.6	15.5	22.4
Egypt, Arab Rep. of	1.8	4.5	1.1	2.4	1.0	0.4	1.7	6.7
Lebanon	1.5	1.4	1.9	3.3	1.0	0.2	4.4	1.8
South Asia	5.3	4.1	5.8	3.0	2.1	5.8	16.7	25.8
India	4.3	3.7	5.4	2.6	1.6	4.1	15.1	24.1
Pakistan	0.9	0.0	0.0	0.2	0.4	1.5	1.3	1.3
Sub-Saharan Africa	7.7	8.1	13.0	7.9	6.9	13.6	11.9	15.2
South Africa	4.9	6.0	10.4	4.9	3.7	8.3	6.2	8.4

Note: e = estimate.

Table A.17 Gross international equity issuance by developing countries, 1998–2005
$ billions

	1998	1999	2000	2001	2002	2003	2004	2005e
All developing countries	8.0	10.1	35.5	5.6	10.7	17.1	35.2	56.2
East Asia and Pacific	4.3	6.0	21.5	3.5	7.2	12.1	20.6	30.0
China	1.4	3.6	21.1	2.9	5.4	8.8	17.7	26.6
Indonesia	0.0	0.8	0.0	0.3	0.3	0.9	0.7	0.8
Malaysia	0.2	0.1	0.2	0.0	1.3	0.6	0.9	1.4
Philippines	0.5	0.4	0.1	0.0	0.1	0.1	0.2	0.9
Thailand	2.3	0.8	0.0	0.2	0.1	1.5	1.1	0.3
Europe and Central Asia	2.4	1.1	3.3	0.3	1.6	1.3	5.5	10.0
Czech Rep.	0.1	0.3	0.2	0.0	0.0	0.0	0.2	0.3
Hungary	0.3	0.2	0.0	0.0	0.0	0.0	0.8	0.0
Poland	0.8	0.3	0.1	0.0	0.2	0.6	0.9	0.9
Russian Fed.	0.0	0.1	0.5	0.2	1.3	0.6	2.7	6.5
Turkey	0.8	0.0	2.4	0.0	0.1	0.1	0.8	1.5
Latin America and the Caribbean	0.2	0.7	6.5	0.7	1.2	1.2	2.4	5.5
Argentina	0.0	0.3	0.4	0.0	0.0	0.0	0.2	0.0
Brazil	0.0	0.2	2.7	0.7	1.1	0.6	1.9	3.0
Chile	0.1	0.0	1.7	0.0	0.0	0.1	0.2	0.3
Mexico	0.0	0.2	1.6	0.0	0.0	0.5	0.1	2.0
Middle East and North Africa	0.4	0.3	0.4	0.0	0.0	0.0	0.2	1.2
Egypt, Arab Rep. of	0.1	0.3	0.3	0.0	0.0	0.0	0.1	0.7
South Asia	0.1	0.9	1.8	0.5	0.3	1.3	4.6	8.3
India	0.1	0.9	1.8	0.5	0.3	1.3	4.6	8.3
Sub-Saharan Africa	0.7	1.2	2.0	0.7	0.5	1.2	2.0	1.0
South Africa	0.7	1.2	2.0	0.7	0.5	1.2	1.9	1.0

Note: e = estimate.

Table A.18 Gross international bond issuance in developing countries, 1998–2005
$ billions

	1998	1999	2000	2001	2002	2003	2004	2005e
All developing countries	57.2	61.5	60.5	60.9	51.7	82.2	102.4	130.9
East Asia and Pacific	4.2	8.2	5.1	7.1	12.5	11.6	15.7	20.3
China	1.9	1.4	1.3	2.6	0.9	3.3	6.2	4.9
Indonesia	0.0	0.0	0.0	0.1	0.8	1.5	1.4	5.0
Malaysia	0.1	2.6	1.4	2.4	6.0	1.4	3.5	3.2
Philippines	1.9	4.2	2.4	1.8	4.8	5.1	3.3	4.1
Thailand	0.3	0.0	0.0	0.3	0.0	0.3	1.4	2.2
Europe and Central Asia	15.3	12.9	14.4	10.3	13.8	26.5	38.2	54.7
Czech Rep.	0.6	0.4	0.0	0.1	0.4	0.3	2.6	1.7
Hungary	1.6	2.3	0.5	1.2	0.0	2.4	5.5	7.3
Poland	1.1	1.6	1.4	2.5	2.7	4.7	3.9	11.8
Russian Fed.	5.8	0.0	0.1	1.5	3.7	8.6	10.5	16.3
Turkey	3.4	5.7	8.6	2.2	3.5	5.5	6.4	9.8
Latin America and the Caribbean	34.7	36.8	36.3	36.7	21.1	38.8	35.9	43.0
Argentina	13.7	13.3	11.9	1.7	0.0	0.0	0.0	0.5
Brazil	6.4	7.8	11.4	12.8	7.4	13.6	11.6	14.6
Chile	0.5	2.4	0.5	3.0	1.7	2.8	1.3	2.7
Mexico	7.9	8.8	8.5	8.2	7.1	14.1	12.8	10.0
Venezuela, R. B. de	3.3	1.4	0.5	1.7	0.0	3.7	4.0	5.9
Middle East and North Africa	1.5	1.9	2.4	5.3	2.7	1.0	5.6	5.4
Egypt, Arab Rep. of	0.0	0.1	0.0	1.5	0.0	0.0	0.0	2.8
Lebanon	1.5	1.4	1.9	3.3	1.0	0.2	4.4	1.8
South Asia	0.4	0.0	0.6	0.1	0.2	0.5	5.1	5.3
India	0.4	0.0	0.6	0.1	0.2	0.5	4.5	4.7
Pakistan	0.0	0.0	0.0	0.0	0.0	0.0	0.5	0.6
Sub-Saharan Africa	1.0	1.8	1.7	1.5	1.5	3.9	2.0	2.3
South Africa	1.0	1.8	1.7	1.5	1.5	3.9	2.0	2.3

Note: e = estimate.

Table A.19 Gross international bank lending to developing countries, 1998–2005
$ billions

	1998	1999	2000	2001	2002	2003	2004	2005e
All developing countries	95.2	78.1	105.9	69.3	69.1	86.7	111.8	198.1
East Asia and Pacific	17.0	12.9	21.9	9.0	21.5	26.9	19.5	34.5
China	5.8	3.3	6.7	2.0	9.6	12.6	8.0	18.5
Indonesia	0.7	1.6	1.0	0.5	0.5	4.2	2.1	1.4
Malaysia	3.2	4.7	5.2	2.7	5.6	5.3	6.2	3.5
Philippines	3.4	2.6	4.8	1.8	1.7	1.9	2.0	3.2
Thailand	3.8	0.7	4.1	2.0	3.5	2.5	1.1	5.9
Europe and Central Asia	17.6	15.4	22.7	14.4	16.8	22.2	37.8	77.6
Czech Rep.	2.3	0.6	1.2	0.8	0.3	2.2	1.8	1.4
Hungary	1.7	0.9	1.5	1.5	1.8	3.0	2.3	3.0
Poland	1.6	2.6	2.1	2.2	3.5	2.6	2.1	6.4
Russian Fed.	2.6	0.6	4.7	2.9	4.9	7.2	13.6	40.1
Turkey	5.7	7.1	11.3	4.6	3.7	2.0	7.6	12.7
Latin America and the Caribbean	46.9	35.0	44.8	34.6	18.5	20.6	29.9	46.3
Argentina	11.7	6.5	6.6	4.5	1.9	0.7	0.7	2.0
Brazil	11.4	7.2	13.8	10.2	4.7	3.7	9.8	13.0
Chile	3.7	7.2	5.5	3.1	1.8	2.2	6.6	7.3
Mexico	11.4	8.4	10.9	10.2	6.1	12.1	9.6	18.2
Venezuela, R. B. de	4.3	0.4	2.4	3.0	0.6	0.4	0.7	0.5
Middle East and North Africa	2.9	6.5	3.6	3.2	5.8	4.6	9.7	15.7
Egypt, Arab Rep. of	1.6	4.2	0.8	0.9	1.0	0.4	1.6	3.2
South Asia	4.8	3.2	3.4	2.4	1.7	4.0	7.0	12.2
India	3.8	2.8	3.0	2.0	1.2	2.3	6.0	11.0
Pakistan	0.9	0.0	0.0	0.2	0.4	1.5	0.8	0.7
Sub-Saharan Africa	6.0	5.1	9.4	5.6	4.9	8.5	7.9	11.9
South Africa	3.2	3.1	6.8	2.7	1.7	3.2	2.4	5.1

Note: e = estimate.

Table A.20 Change in foreign exchange reserves, 1998–2005
$ billions (– = increase)

	1998	1999	2000	2001	2002	2003	2004	2005e
All developing countries	−16.4	−33.2	−45.4	−81.7	−171.9	−291.6	−404.8	−393.0
East Asia and Pacific	−20.7	−29.3	−10.1	−47.7	−88.0	−136.7	−237.0	−217.9
China	−5.1	−9.7	−10.9	−46.6	−74.2	−116.8	−206.7	−208.9
Indonesia	−6.3	−3.8	−2.0	1.2	−3.7	−4.0	0.0	2.0
Malaysia	−4.7	−4.9	1.0	−1.0	−3.7	−10.2	−21.9	−4.3
Philippines	−2.0	−4.0	0.2	−0.4	0.2	−0.3	0.5	−2.8
Thailand	−2.7	−5.4	1.9	−0.4	−5.7	−2.9	−7.5	−2.0
Europe and Central Asia	−5.1	−6.4	−16.6	−11.1	−43.7	−60.9	−79.3	−94.7
Czech Rep.	−2.8	−0.3	−0.2	−1.2	−9.1	−3.0	−1.6	−1.3
Hungary	−0.9	−1.5	−0.2	0.6	0.6	−2.3	−3.3	−3.0
Poland	−6.9	1.1	−0.2	1.2	−2.8	−3.8	−2.8	−5.9
Romania	0.8	1.4	−1.0	−1.4	−2.2	−1.9	−6.6	−5.3
Russian Fed.	5.0	−0.7	−15.8	−8.3	−11.5	−29.1	−47.6	−54.9
Turkey	−0.8	−3.7	0.9	3.6	−8.2	−6.9	−1.7	−14.9
Latin America and the Caribbean	9.2	7.6	−3.0	−2.9	−0.8	−33.2	−24.9	−32.1
Argentina	−2.3	−1.6	1.7	9.9	4.1	−2.7	−4.9	−4.7
Brazil	8.2	7.8	2.3	−3.2	−1.7	−11.7	−3.6	−0.8
Chile	2.0	1.1	−0.5	0.6	−0.8	−0.4	−0.3	−1.2
Mexico	−3.3	0.5	−4.2	−9.2	−5.5	−7.8	−5.0	−10.2
Venezuela, R. B. de	2.4	−0.1	−0.9	3.8	0.8	−7.5	−2.3	−5.6
Middle East and North Africa	1.7	1.2	−4.8	−9.5	−12.0	−22.0	−14.3	−21.3
Algeria	1.2	2.4	−7.5	−6.1	−5.1	−9.8	−10.2	−13.1
Egypt, Arab Rep. of	0.6	3.6	1.4	0.0	−0.3	−0.2	−0.7	−6.4
Lebanon	−0.6	−1.2	1.8	0.9	−2.2	−5.3	0.8	−0.2
South Asia	−3.0	−5.0	−4.7	−10.2	−27.0	−35.0	−27.2	−6.3
India	−2.6	−5.0	−5.3	−8.0	−21.7	−30.6	−27.5	−5.9
Pakistan	0.2	−0.5	0.0	−2.1	−4.4	−2.6	1.1	−0.3
Sub-Saharan Africa	1.5	−1.3	−6.2	−0.3	−0.3	−3.9	−22.2	−20.7
Angola	0.2	−0.3	−0.7	0.5	0.4	−0.3	−0.7	−1.8
Nigeria	0.5	1.7	−4.5	−0.5	3.1	0.2	−9.8	−11.3
South Africa	0.6	−1.9	0.3	0.0	0.2	−0.6	−6.6	−5.5

Note: e = estimate.

Table A.21 Total external debt of developing countries, 1997–2005
$ billions

	1997	1998	1999	2000	2001	2002	2003	2004	2005e
All developing countries	2,107.0	2,321.8	2,345.7	2,283.9	2,280.7	2,359.0	2,581.8	2,755.7	2,800.4
East Asia and Pacific	526.3	533.3	538.8	498.0	516.9	515.9	541.5	588.9	633.7
China	146.7	144.0	152.1	145.7	184.8	186.4	208.7	248.9	—
Indonesia	136.2	151.2	151.2	144.4	134.1	132.2	136.9	140.6	—
Malaysia	47.2	42.4	41.9	41.9	45.1	48.3	48.5	52.1	—
Philippines	50.7	53.6	58.3	58.3	58.3	59.9	62.5	60.6	—
Thailand	109.7	104.9	96.8	79.7	67.2	59.4	51.8	51.3	—
Europe and Central Asia	390.4	490.3	502.9	511.0	508.1	561.4	680.5	794.9	870.1
Bulgaria	11.1	11.4	11.0	11.2	10.5	11.5	13.4	15.7	—
Czech Rep.	23.2	24.3	22.8	21.6	22.8	27.7	34.8	45.6	—
Hungary	24.6	28.5	29.9	29.5	30.3	35.0	47.4	63.2	—
Poland	41.7	57.7	65.9	65.8	67.4	78.5	95.5	99.2	—
Russian Fed.	127.6	177.8	174.8	160.0	152.5	147.4	175.5	197.3	—
Turkey	84.8	97.1	102.2	117.3	113.4	131.2	145.4	161.6	—
Latin America and the Caribbean	669.5	752.1	772.3	758.7	753.0	750.0	785.9	779.0	723.7
Argentina	128.2	141.4	145.7	147.4	154.1	149.9	166.1	169.2	—
Brazil	198.0	241.7	245.2	243.4	231.1	233.1	236.6	222.0	—
Chile	27.0	33.7	34.8	37.3	38.6	41.2	43.3	44.1	—
Colombia	31.9	33.1	34.4	33.9	36.2	33.2	37.0	37.7	—
Mexico	147.6	159.0	166.5	150.3	145.7	140.2	141.6	138.7	—
Venezuela, R. B. de	35.7	37.8	37.6	38.2	36.0	34.0	34.8	35.6	—
Middle East and North Africa	151.2	160.9	155.7	145.2	143.0	151.4	161.2	163.9	162.5
Algeria	30.9	30.7	28.0	25.3	22.6	22.9	23.6	22.0	—
Egypt, Arab Rep. of	30.1	32.4	31.0	29.2	29.3	30.0	31.4	30.3	—
Lebanon	5.0	6.8	8.2	9.9	12.4	17.1	18.6	22.2	—
South Asia	149.6	157.6	162.0	160.0	156.2	168.7	181.5	193.9	194.8
India	94.3	97.6	98.3	99.1	97.5	104.8	112.6	122.7	—
Pakistan	30.1	32.3	33.9	32.8	31.7	33.7	35.9	35.7	—
Sub-Saharan Africa	219.9	227.7	214.0	211.0	203.6	211.7	231.2	235.1	215.6
South Africa	25.3	24.8	23.9	24.9	24.1	25.0	27.8	28.5	—

Note: e = estimate; — = not available.

Table A.22 Total external debt of developing countries: medium and long-term, 1997–2005
$ billions

	1997	1998	1999	2000	2001	2002	2003	2004	2005e
All developing countries	1,719.8	1,971.4	2,012.7	1,967.5	1,943.7	2,021.4	2,161.0	2,261.0	2,243.7
East Asia and Pacific	394.2	448.7	465.8	435.4	410.9	398.8	400.8	414.0	426.6
China	115.2	126.7	136.9	132.6	128.5	120.5	120.4	131.3	—
Indonesia	103.3	131.1	131.2	121.8	112.3	109.4	114.0	116.1	—
Malaysia	32.3	33.9	35.9	37.3	38.3	39.9	39.9	40.7	—
Philippines	38.9	47.8	53.4	52.8	52.3	54.4	56.3	55.5	—
Thailand	71.9	75.3	73.4	64.8	54.0	47.5	40.8	39.8	—
Europe and Central Asia	331.2	415.2	423.5	424.4	425.5	474.2	547.6	634.4	675.9
Bulgaria	9.1	9.6	9.7	9.8	9.3	9.6	10.8	12.4	—
Czech Rep.	15.1	16.6	14.0	12.6	13.2	16.9	20.8	28.5	—
Hungary	21.2	23.7	26.3	25.4	25.7	29.3	38.4	50.8	—
Poland	36.6	49.3	54.6	56.2	56.3	64.6	76.0	82.3	—
Russian Fed.	121.7	163.1	159.0	144.4	133.5	131.1	145.1	162.2	—
Turkey	66.8	75.9	78.8	88.4	97.0	114.8	122.4	129.7	—
Latin America and the Caribbean	541.2	633.0	662.9	651.0	659.2	670.8	697.3	682.6	632.7
Argentina	96.2	110.5	116.2	119.1	134.0	134.8	143.1	141.8	—
Brazil	163.2	211.8	216.0	212.5	202.8	209.7	212.0	196.8	—
Chile	21.5	28.6	30.5	31.1	33.3	35.4	35.8	36.4	—
Colombia	26.2	26.9	30.5	31.1	33.0	29.5	33.4	32.4	—
Mexico	119.8	132.7	142.4	131.4	131.1	130.3	132.5	129.6	—
Venezuela, R. B. de	31.5	35.5	35.5	34.1	31.2	29.4	30.5	31.2	—
Middle East and North Africa	132.7	138.8	132.5	123.7	123.8	131.8	139.7	142.4	140.1
Algeria	30.7	30.5	27.8	25.0	22.4	22.8	23.4	21.6	—
Egypt, Arab Rep. of	27.1	28.2	26.8	25.1	26.0	26.5	27.6	27.4	—
Lebanon	3.2	4.8	6.0	7.3	9.8	14.5	15.5	18.2	—
South Asia	141.4	150.5	155.0	154.0	151.3	161.9	174.1	183.6	181.9
India	89.3	93.3	94.4	95.6	94.8	100.7	107.6	115.2	—
Pakistan	27.6	30.1	32.1	31.3	30.4	32.1	34.6	34.4	—
Sub-Saharan Africa	179.1	185.2	173.1	179.1	173.0	183.9	201.5	203.8	186.6
South Africa	14.3	13.3	13.1	15.3	15.7	17.6	20.4	20.6	—

Note: e = estimate; — = not available.

Table A.23 Total external debt of developing countries: short-term, 1997–2005
$ billions

	1997	1998	1999	2000	2001	2002	2003	2004	2005e
All developing countries	387.2	350.4	333.0	316.4	337.0	337.6	420.8	494.8	556.7
East Asia and Pacific	132.1	84.6	73.0	62.6	105.9	117.0	140.6	174.8	207.2
China	31.5	17.3	15.2	13.1	56.3	65.9	88.3	117.6	—
Indonesia	32.9	20.1	20.0	22.6	21.8	22.8	22.9	24.5	—
Malaysia	14.9	8.5	6.0	4.6	6.8	8.4	8.6	11.4	—
Philippines	11.8	5.9	4.9	5.5	6.0	5.6	6.2	5.0	—
Thailand	37.8	29.7	23.4	14.9	13.2	11.9	11.0	11.5	—
Europe and Central Asia	59.1	75.1	79.4	86.7	82.6	87.1	133.0	160.5	194.2
Bulgaria	2.0	1.8	1.3	1.5	1.2	1.8	2.7	3.2	—
Czech Rep.	8.1	7.6	8.8	9.0	9.6	10.8	14.0	17.1	—
Hungary	3.4	4.8	3.5	4.2	4.6	5.7	9.0	12.3	—
Poland	5.1	8.4	11.3	9.7	11.1	13.9	19.5	16.8	—
Russian Fed.	5.9	14.7	15.7	15.6	19.0	16.3	30.5	35.1	—
Turkey	18.0	21.2	23.5	28.9	16.3	16.4	23.0	31.9	—
Latin America and the Caribbean	128.3	119.1	109.5	107.7	93.8	79.2	88.6	96.3	91.0
Argentina	32.0	31.0	29.4	28.3	20.0	15.1	23.0	27.5	—
Brazil	34.9	29.9	29.2	31.0	28.3	23.4	24.6	25.3	—
Chile	5.5	5.1	4.3	6.2	5.3	5.8	7.5	7.7	—
Colombia	5.8	6.2	4.0	2.9	3.3	3.7	3.6	5.3	—
Mexico	27.9	26.3	24.1	18.9	14.6	9.9	9.2	9.1	—
Venezuela, R. B. de	4.2	2.2	2.1	4.1	4.8	4.6	4.3	4.4	—
Middle East and North Africa	18.6	22.1	23.2	21.5	19.2	19.6	21.4	21.5	22.4
Algeria	0.2	0.2	0.2	0.2	0.2	0.1	0.1	0.4	—
Egypt, Arab Rep. of	3.0	4.3	4.3	4.1	3.4	3.5	3.8	2.9	—
Lebanon	1.8	2.0	2.2	2.5	2.7	2.5	3.1	4.0	—
South Asia	8.2	7.1	7.0	6.1	5.0	6.8	7.4	10.3	12.8
India	5.0	4.3	3.9	3.5	2.7	4.1	5.0	7.5	—
Pakistan	2.5	2.2	1.8	1.5	1.3	1.5	1.2	1.2	—
Sub-Saharan Africa	40.8	42.4	40.9	31.9	30.5	27.8	29.8	31.2	29.0
South Africa	10.9	11.4	10.8	9.6	8.4	7.4	7.4	7.9	—

Note: e = estimate; — = not available.

195

Table A.24 Total external debt of developing countries: owed by public and publicly guaranteed borrowers, 1997–2005

$ billions

	1997	1998	1999	2000	2001	2002	2003	2004	2005e
All developing countries	1,366.8	1,470.6	1,476.4	1,422.3	1,400.9	1,470.1	1,557.9	1,589.5	1,482.9
East Asia and Pacific	271.9	288.8	307.4	288.0	277.5	277.8	278.6	280.6	279.9
China	112.8	99.4	99.2	94.9	91.8	88.6	85.3	90.8	—
Indonesia	58.8	76.4	83.9	80.6	77.9	79.4	84.3	82.6	—
Malaysia	16.8	18.2	18.9	19.2	24.2	26.4	25.4	25.6	—
Philippines	27.2	30.7	36.6	35.8	31.2	34.0	37.2	36.3	—
Thailand	24.7	31.3	34.7	32.5	27.9	22.9	17.7	15.3	—
Europe and Central Asia	288.6	320.8	315.7	304.5	292.1	309.5	336.3	352.5	327.8
Bulgaria	8.7	9.1	9.0	9.0	8.5	8.5	8.9	8.6	—
Czech Rep.	12.9	11.6	7.7	6.6	5.7	7.1	8.7	12.0	—
Hungary	15.3	15.9	16.9	14.4	12.7	13.6	16.3	20.7	—
Poland	34.2	35.1	33.2	30.8	25.7	29.4	35.0	36.6	—
Russian Fed.	119.8	140.9	136.4	122.6	111.2	102.6	103.9	103.2	—
Turkey	48.1	50.6	51.6	60.6	68.4	82.3	88.6	89.7	—
Latin America and the Caribbean	378.6	412.8	420.5	409.5	420.7	445.0	474.1	476.6	426.4
Argentina	72.8	82.6	88.9	93.2	102.4	106.3	114.7	117.9	—
Brazil	87.4	103.6	102.4	99.8	106.5	122.3	129.9	122.9	—
Chile	4.4	5.0	5.7	5.3	5.6	6.8	8.0	9.4	—
Colombia	15.4	16.7	20.2	20.8	21.8	20.7	22.8	23.4	—
Mexico	92.4	95.4	92.4	81.5	77.0	76.3	77.5	77.2	—
Venezuela, R. B. de	29.0	29.6	28.7	28.0	25.2	23.4	24.5	25.9	—
Middle East and North Africa	127.7	131.8	125.5	117.2	117.2	125.3	132.8	135.2	129.8
Algeria	30.7	30.5	27.8	25.0	22.4	22.7	22.9	20.9	—
Egypt, Arab Rep. of	27.0	27.8	26.3	24.5	25.3	25.9	27.3	27.4	—
Lebanon	2.3	4.0	5.3	6.6	9.0	13.8	14.8	17.5	—
South Asia	129.7	139.3	144.6	135.4	132.8	141.1	150.2	155.3	147.7
India	80.1	84.9	86.4	80.1	78.8	82.3	85.6	88.7	—
Pakistan	25.3	27.5	29.8	28.7	28.3	30.1	33.0	32.9	—
Sub-Saharan Africa	170.3	177.0	162.7	167.7	160.6	171.4	186.0	189.2	171.3
South Africa	11.9	10.7	8.2	9.1	7.9	9.4	9.1	9.8	—

Note: e = estimate; — = not available.

Table A.25 Total external debt of developing countries: owed by private sector borrowers, 1997–2005

$ billions

	1997	1998	1999	2000	2001	2002	2003	2004	2005e
All developing countries	740.2	851.3	869.3	861.6	879.7	889.0	1,023.9	1,166.2	1,317.5
East Asia and Pacific	254.4	244.5	231.4	210.1	239.4	238.1	262.9	308.3	353.8
China	33.9	44.6	52.9	50.9	93.1	97.8	123.3	158.1	—
Indonesia	77.3	74.8	67.3	63.8	56.2	52.8	52.7	58.0	—
Malaysia	30.4	24.3	23.0	22.6	20.9	21.9	23.2	26.6	—
Philippines	23.5	22.9	21.7	22.5	27.1	25.9	25.2	24.2	—
Thailand	85.0	73.6	62.0	47.2	39.3	36.5	34.1	36.0	—
Europe and Central Asia	101.8	169.5	187.1	206.5	216.0	251.9	344.3	442.5	542.3
Bulgaria	2.4	2.3	2.0	2.2	2.0	2.9	4.5	7.0	—
Czech Rep.	10.2	12.7	15.1	15.0	17.1	20.6	26.1	33.5	—
Hungary	9.3	12.6	13.0	15.2	17.6	21.4	31.0	42.4	—
Poland	7.5	22.6	32.8	35.1	41.7	49.1	60.5	62.6	—
Russian Fed.	7.8	36.9	38.3	37.4	41.3	44.8	71.6	94.1	—
Turkey	36.7	46.6	50.6	56.7	45.0	48.9	56.8	71.9	—
Latin America and the Caribbean	290.9	339.3	351.9	349.2	332.3	305.0	311.8	302.3	297.3
Argentina	55.4	58.8	56.7	54.2	51.6	43.6	51.4	51.3	—
Brazil	110.7	138.0	142.8	143.7	124.6	110.8	106.7	99.1	—
Chile	22.7	28.7	29.2	32.0	33.0	34.4	35.3	34.6	—
Colombia	16.5	16.3	14.2	13.1	14.5	12.5	14.2	14.4	—
Mexico	55.2	63.5	74.1	68.8	68.6	63.8	64.1	61.5	—
Venezuela, R. B. de	6.7	8.2	8.9	10.2	10.8	10.6	10.4	9.7	—
Middle East and North Africa	23.6	29.1	30.2	28.0	25.8	26.0	28.4	28.7	32.7
Algeria	0.2	0.2	0.2	0.2	0.2	0.2	0.7	1.1	—
Egypt, Arab Rep. of	3.1	4.6	4.8	4.7	4.0	4.1	4.1	2.9	—
Lebanon	2.7	2.7	2.9	3.3	3.5	3.2	3.8	4.7	—
South Asia	19.9	18.3	17.4	24.6	23.4	27.6	31.3	38.6	47.0
India	14.3	12.7	11.9	19.0	18.7	22.6	27.1	34.0	—
Pakistan	4.8	4.8	4.1	4.1	3.4	3.5	2.9	2.8	—
Sub-Saharan Africa	49.7	50.7	51.3	43.3	43.0	40.3	45.2	45.8	44.3
South Africa	13.3	14.1	15.7	15.8	16.1	15.6	18.7	18.7	—

Note: e = estimate; — = not available.

Table A.26 Total external debt of developing countries: owed to public sector creditors, 1997–2005
$ billions

	1997	1998	1999	2000	2001	2002	2003	2004	2005e
All developing countries	790.1	865.6	880.0	839.5	827.1	875.7	926.3	924.1	820.8
East Asia and Pacific	152.5	179.1	200.2	188.1	180.4	183.7	190.1	193.6	190.1
China	39.8	45.1	50.4	50.4	50.6	50.8	51.4	57.2	—
Indonesia	45.5	58.2	66.4	66.0	62.1	65.7	71.0	69.5	—
Malaysia	4.0	4.5	4.8	5.0	5.9	5.8	6.2	7.0	—
Philippines	19.6	22.1	23.6	21.9	19.7	20.9	22.2	21.6	—
Thailand	17.8	21.4	25.3	23.9	20.8	16.6	13.1	10.7	—
Europe and Central Asia	156.3	172.5	170.9	166.8	159.3	166.0	169.8	168.5	131.0
Bulgaria	3.4	3.9	3.9	3.9	3.4	3.5	4.1	4.5	—
Czech Rep.	1.1	1.1	1.1	1.2	1.3	1.6	2.1	2.2	—
Hungary	3.3	2.3	2.3	1.9	1.7	1.9	1.7	2.3	—
Poland	26.6	27.1	25.1	23.7	17.8	19.7	20.4	18.6	—
Russian Fed.	76.8	88.3	86.7	82.5	71.7	62.2	58.2	58.0	—
Turkey	14.3	15.0	13.8	17.3	26.9	35.8	37.5	35.3	—
Latin America and the Caribbean	145.3	160.6	162.8	149.7	162.3	182.4	196.0	187.4	148.2
Argentina	24.0	25.8	25.4	25.5	35.2	35.6	36.9	35.6	—
Brazil	22.2	32.7	37.7	31.1	37.2	52.1	58.2	52.3	—
Chile	2.2	2.2	2.1	1.9	1.7	1.5	1.4	1.3	—
Colombia	5.6	6.0	7.8	7.7	8.6	8.9	11.3	11.5	—
Mexico	32.1	31.4	26.3	20.8	19.9	20.5	20.6	19.6	—
Venezuela, R. B. de	5.5	6.7	6.6	6.1	4.9	4.4	3.9	3.5	—
Middle East and North Africa	99.5	103.8	98.2	90.7	88.2	91.5	96.4	95.6	90.2
Algeria	20.3	21.5	20.4	19.2	17.7	17.7	17.9	16.2	—
Egypt, Arab Rep. of	25.9	26.9	25.7	24.0	23.4	24.7	26.4	26.4	—
Lebanon	0.7	0.9	0.9	0.9	1.0	1.0	1.7	1.8	—
South Asia	98.9	104.6	113.3	102.7	101.1	106.3	113.4	116.1	113.8
India	52.8	53.9	58.6	50.6	49.8	49.8	50.7	51.7	—
Pakistan	22.8	25.1	27.7	26.7	27.0	29.3	32.3	32.0	—
Sub-Saharan Africa	137.6	145.0	134.5	141.6	135.8	145.9	160.7	162.9	147.5
South Africa	0.4	0.0	0.0	0.1	0.1	0.1	0.2	0.3	—

Note: e = estimate; — = not available.

Table A.27 Total external debt of developing countries: owed to private sector creditors, 1997–2005
$ billions

	1997	1998	1999	2000	2001	2002	2003	2004	2005e
All developing countries	1,316.9	1,456.3	1,465.7	1,444.4	1,453.6	1,483.4	1,655.5	1,831.6	1,979.6
East Asia and Pacific	373.8	354.2	338.6	309.9	336.5	332.2	351.4	395.3	443.7
China	106.9	98.9	101.6	95.3	134.3	135.5	157.3	191.7	—
Indonesia	90.7	93.1	84.9	78.5	72.0	66.5	65.9	71.1	—
Malaysia	43.2	37.9	37.1	36.9	39.2	42.5	42.4	45.2	—
Philippines	31.1	31.5	34.7	36.4	38.5	39.1	40.3	39.0	—
Thailand	91.9	83.5	71.5	55.8	46.4	42.7	38.7	40.6	—
Europe and Central Asia	234.1	317.8	331.9	344.2	348.8	395.4	510.7	626.4	739.1
Bulgaria	7.7	7.5	7.1	7.3	7.1	8.0	9.3	11.2	—
Czech Rep.	22.1	23.1	21.7	20.4	21.5	26.1	32.7	43.4	—
Hungary	21.3	26.2	27.6	27.6	28.6	33.1	45.7	60.9	—
Poland	15.1	30.6	40.9	42.2	49.6	58.8	75.1	80.6	—
Russian Fed.	50.8	89.5	88.1	77.6	80.8	85.3	117.3	139.3	—
Turkey	70.5	82.2	88.4	100.0	86.5	95.4	107.9	126.2	—
Latin America and the Caribbean	524.2	591.5	609.5	608.9	590.7	567.6	589.9	591.6	575.5
Argentina	104.2	115.6	120.3	121.9	118.9	114.3	129.2	133.7	—
Brazil	175.8	209.0	207.5	212.3	193.9	181.0	178.4	169.7	—
Chile	24.9	31.5	32.7	35.4	36.9	39.7	41.9	42.7	—
Colombia	26.3	27.1	26.6	26.2	27.7	24.3	25.7	26.3	—
Mexico	115.6	127.5	140.2	129.5	125.8	119.6	121.1	119.1	—
Venezuela, R. B. de	30.2	31.0	31.0	32.0	31.1	29.6	30.9	32.1	—
Middle East and North Africa	51.7	57.1	57.5	54.6	54.8	59.9	64.8	68.3	72.3
Algeria	10.6	9.2	7.6	6.1	4.9	5.2	5.7	5.7	—
Egypt, Arab Rep. of	4.2	5.5	5.3	5.2	6.0	5.3	5.0	3.9	—
Lebanon	4.3	5.9	7.3	8.9	11.5	16.1	16.9	20.4	—
South Asia	50.7	53.0	48.7	57.3	55.1	62.5	68.1	77.8	80.9
India	41.5	43.7	39.7	48.5	47.7	55.0	61.9	71.1	—
Pakistan	7.2	7.2	6.2	6.1	4.7	4.4	3.5	3.7	—
Sub-Saharan Africa	82.4	82.7	79.5	69.4	67.8	65.8	70.6	72.2	68.1
South Africa	24.9	24.8	23.9	24.7	23.9	24.9	27.6	28.2	—

Note: e = estimate; — = not available.

199

Table A.28 Gross foreign exchange reserves of developing countries, 1997–2005
$ billions

	1997	1998	1999	2000	2001	2002	2003	2004	2005e
All developing countries	571.6	588.0	621.2	666.6	748.3	920.1	1,211.8	1,616.6	2,009.5
East Asia and Pacific	212.5	233.2	262.5	272.7	320.4	408.4	545.0	782.0	999.9
China	139.9	145.0	154.7	165.6	212.2	286.4	403.3	609.9	818.9
Indonesia	16.1	22.4	26.2	28.3	27.0	30.8	34.7	34.7	32.8
Malaysia	20.0	24.7	29.7	28.6	29.6	33.3	43.5	65.4	69.7
Philippines	7.2	9.1	13.1	13.0	13.4	13.2	13.5	13.0	15.8
Thailand	25.7	28.4	33.8	31.9	32.3	38.0	41.0	48.5	50.5
Europe and Central Asia	90.8	95.9	102.3	118.9	130.0	173.8	234.6	313.9	408.7
Czech Rep.	9.7	12.5	12.8	13.0	14.2	23.3	26.3	27.8	29.1
Hungary	8.3	9.2	10.7	10.9	10.3	9.7	12.0	15.3	18.3
Poland	20.3	27.2	26.1	26.3	25.2	28.0	31.7	34.6	40.5
Romania	3.7	2.9	1.5	2.5	3.9	6.1	8.0	14.6	19.9
Russian Fed.	12.8	7.8	8.5	24.3	32.5	44.1	73.2	120.8	175.7
Turkey	18.6	19.4	23.2	22.3	18.7	26.9	33.8	35.5	50.4
Latin America and the Caribbean	166.5	157.3	149.7	152.7	155.5	156.4	189.5	214.4	246.5
Argentina	22.2	24.5	26.1	24.4	14.5	10.4	13.1	18.0	22.7
Brazil	50.8	42.6	34.8	32.5	35.7	37.4	49.1	52.7	53.5
Chile	17.3	15.3	14.2	14.7	14.0	14.8	15.2	15.5	16.7
Mexico	28.1	31.5	31.0	35.1	44.4	49.9	57.7	62.8	73.0
Venezuela, R. B. de	14.0	11.6	11.7	12.6	8.8	8.0	15.5	17.9	23.5
Middle East and North Africa	43.7	42.0	40.8	45.6	55.1	67.1	89.1	103.3	124.6
Algeria	8.0	6.8	4.4	11.9	18.0	23.1	32.9	43.1	56.2
Egypt, Arab Rep. of	18.5	17.9	14.3	12.9	12.9	13.2	13.4	14.1	20.5
Lebanon	5.9	6.5	7.7	5.9	5.0	7.2	12.5	11.7	11.8
South Asia	30.0	32.9	37.9	42.6	52.8	79.8	114.8	142.0	148.3
India	24.3	27.0	32.0	37.3	45.3	67.0	97.6	125.2	131.0
Pakistan	1.2	1.0	1.5	1.5	3.6	8.1	10.7	9.6	9.8
Sub-Saharan Africa	28.1	26.6	27.9	34.1	34.4	34.7	38.6	60.9	81.6
Angola	0.4	0.2	0.5	1.2	0.7	0.4	0.6	1.4	3.2
Nigeria	7.6	7.1	5.5	9.9	10.5	7.3	7.1	17.0	28.3
South Africa	4.8	4.2	6.1	5.8	5.8	5.6	6.2	12.8	18.3

Note: e = estimate.

Table A.29 Key external debt ratios for developing countries
%, averages for 2002–4

Country	Total external debt (EDT) to exports of G&S (XGS)	Present Value (PV) of EDT as a % of XGS	EDT as a % of gross national income (GNI)	PV as % of GNI	Total Debt service as a % of XGS	Interest service as % of XGS
Albania	74	51	25	17	4	1
Algeria	82	80	33	32	22	4
Angola	89	82	74	68	19	2
Argentina	451	510	141	159	33	6
Armenia	113	130	43	50	10	1
Azerbaijan	56	45	29	23	7	1
Bangladesh	179	124	37	26	6	2
Barbados	44	48	27	29	6	3
Belarus	30	30	20	20	3	1
Belize	188	208	99	109	65	15
Benin	268	*113*	56	*24*	9	3
Bhutan	431	432	99	100	9	4
Bolivia	275	*136*	77	*38*	23	6
Bosnia and Herzegovina	80	63	44	34	4	1
Botswana	14	12	8	6	1	0
Brazil	239	258	44	47	58	16
Bulgaria	139	143	81	83	22	5
Burkina Faso	432	*203*	48	*23*	13	4
Burundi	3,069	*203*	227	*15*	195	37
Cambodia	117	99	80	68	1	0
Cameroon	296	*72*	81	*20*	20	8
Cape Verde	144	100	67	46	7	2
Central African Republic	730	*599*	91	*75*	12	2
Chad	172	*79*	73	*33*	5	1
Chile	145	141	58	57	32	5
China	48	46	15	15	5	1
Colombia	189	204	45	49	38	12
Comoros	389	*276*	99	*70*	4	1
Congo, Dem. Rep. of	765	*131*	208	*36*	8	4
Congo, Rep. of	230	*356*	214	*331*	14	5
Costa Rica	66	70	34	36	8	2
Côte d'Ivoire	172	*170*	91	*90*	8	1
Croatia	200	194	113	110	33	8
Czech Republic	73	71	53	51	13	2
Djibouti	—	—	65	45	—	—
Dominica	176	159	93	84	14	6
Dominican Republic	62	61	39	39	7	3
Ecuador	191	205	65	70	42	14
Egypt, Arab Rep. of	123	108	36	32	9	3
El Salvador	114	123	50	54	10	5
Equatorial Guinea	10	9	—	—	—	—
Eritrea	260	*154*	90	*53*	7	3
Estonia	138	132	116	111	20	5
Ethiopia	460	*144*	97	*30*	7	3
Fiji	16	16	9	9	1	0
Gabon	124	117	80	75	7	1
Gambia, The	398	*231*	186	*108*	20	5
Georgia	133	100	49	37	14	2
Ghana	222	*76*	95	*32*	8	3
Grenada	232	213	115	106	16	10
Guatemala	85	88	22	23	8	4
Guinea	416	*186*	100	*45*	20	5
Guinea-Bissau	791	*779*	331	*326*	46	10
Guyana	171	*65*	189	*72*	6	2
Haiti	98	*76*	37	*29*	11	4
Honduras	171	*68*	95	*38*	9	3
Hungary	115	108	80	76	31	3
India	106	95	21	18	16	3
Indonesia	181	175	63	61	26	6

(continued)

Table A.29 (continued)

%, averages for 2002–4

Country	Total external debt (EDT) to exports of G&S (XGS)	Present Value (PV) of EDT as a % of XGS	EDT as a % of gross national income (GNI)	PV as % of GNI	Total Debt service as a % of XGS	Interest service as % of XGS
Iran, Islamic Rep. of	33	31	10	9	5	1
Jamaica	126	141	79	89	16	7
Jordan	108	101	77	72	9	2
Kazakhstan	193	182	107	101	52	5
Kenya	185	136	47	34	10	2
Kyrgyz Republic	240	*173*	114	*82*	18	3
Lao PDR	365	*276*	101	*76*	9	2
Latvia	243	239	112	110	26	6
Lebanon	470	488	116	121	92	30
Lesotho	88	64	60	44	6	2
Liberia	1,891	*2,133*	674	*760*	0	0
Lithuania	95	96	53	53	18	3
Macedonia, FYR	107	94	45	39	13	3
Madagascar	330	*170*	74	*38*	8	3
Malawi	584	*186*	188	*60*	10	4
Malaysia	42	42	52	53	7	2
Maldives	58	46	52	42	5	1
Mali	251	*98*	83	*33*	8	2
Mauritania	526	*186*	161	*57*	13	5
Mauritius	70	69	44	43	8	3
Mexico	69	77	22	24	25	5
Moldova	117	108	81	75	15	4
Mongolia 1/	143	108	114	86	4	2
Morocco	96	91	41	39	16	3
Mozambique	310	*54*	98	*17*	6	2
Myanmar	233	176	—	—	4	1
Nepal	180	*119*	56	*37*	6	2
Nicaragua	283	*78*	127	*35*	7	3
Niger	452	*156*	74	*25*	12	3
Nigeria	141	140	72	71	9	4
Oman	30	29	18	18	8	2
Pakistan	194	156	44	35	23	4
Panama	106	129	77	94	16	7
Papua New Guinea	87	80	72	66	19	3
Paraguay	109	104	54	52	16	5
Peru	245	265	52	57	21	11
Philippines	120	124	71	73	23	7
Poland	126	121	47	45	44	4
Romania	138	136	52	51	22	5
Russian Federation	117	120	45	46	13	5
Rwanda	964	*150*	96	*15*	14	6
Samoa	451	400	177	158	17	13
São Tomé and Principe	1,655	*459*	666	*185*	44	14
Senegal	165	*61*	60	*22*	14	3
Serbia and Montenegro	216	209	80	77	13	5
Seychelles	101	104	94	96	9	2
Sierra Leone	903	*188*	177	*37*	14	7
Slovak Republic	87	86	68	67	20	4
Solomon Islands	169	129	76	58	16	6
Somalia	—	—	—	—	—	—
South Africa	58	54	18	17	8	3
Sri Lanka	134	111	61	50	9	3
St. Kitts and Nevis	217	212	96	94	32	15
St. Lucia	109	105	64	62	7	4
St. Vincent and the Grenadines	143	129	71	64	12	4
Sudan	478	*625*	116	*151*	8	2
Swaziland	24	25	26	27	2	1
Syrian Arab Rep.	250	249	102	101	4	2
Tajikistan	78	55	58	41	9	2

(continued)

Table A.29 (continued)
%, averages for 2002–4

Country	Total external debt (EDT) to exports of G&S (XGS)	Present Value (PV) of EDT as a % of XGS	EDT as a % of gross national income (GNI)	PV as % of GNI	Total Debt service as a % of XGS	Interest service as % of XGS
Tanzania	398	*115*	76	*22*	6	3
Thailand	52	50	36	35	12	2
Togo	242	*191*	106	*83*	3	0
Tonga	125	90	46	33	4	1
Trinidad and Tobago	49	53	29	31	7	3
Tunisia	148	147	79	79	16	6
Turkey	213	221	67	69	45	10
Uganda	379	*162*	78	*33*	8	3
Ukraine	70	71	42	42	14	2
Uruguay	338	351	104	108	42	16
Uzbekistan	130	123	48	45	22	4
Vanuatu	81	64	44	35	2	1
Venezuela, R. B. de	106	125	38	45	20	7
Vietnam	75	65	45	39	3	1
Yemen, Rep. of	95	66	53	37	4	1
Zambia	530	*112*	170	*36*	31	6
Zimbabwe	264	264	33	33	5	1

Note: For definition of indicators, see Sources and Definitions section. Numbers in italics include the effects of traditional relief and HIPC relief and are based on publicly guaranteed debt only. Under the Multilateral Debt Relief Initiative (MDRI), IDA, IMF and the African Development Fund are currently finalizing arrangements to provide debt stock cancellation to post-completion point HIPCs on debt owed to the three institutions. The IMF and ADF are providing 100 percent stock cancellation on debts outstanding as of year-end 2004, while IDA will provide 100 percent stock cancellation on debts owed as of year-end 2003. The present value of debt for HIPCs provided in the GDF does not incorporate debt reduction under the MDRI and may include penalty charges. Exports comprise the total value of goods and services exported, receipts of compensations of employees and investment income and worker's remittances. In the ratios, the numerator refers to the 2004 data and the denominator is an average of 2002 to 2004 data. For exports and GNI averages, staff estimates are used when necessary.
— = not available.

Table A.30 Classification of countries by region and level of income

Income group	Subgroup	Sub-Saharan Africa — East and Southern Africa	Sub-Saharan Africa — West Africa	Asia — East Asia and Pacific	Asia — South Asia	Europe and Central Asia — Eastern Europe and Central Asia	Europe and Central Asia — Rest of Europe	Middle East and North Africa — Middle East	Middle East and North Africa — North Africa	Americas
Low-income countries		Burundi Comoros Congo, Dem. Rep. of Eritrea Ethiopia Kenya Lesotho Madagascar Malawi Mozambique Rwanda Somalia Sudan Tanzania Uganda Zambia Zimbabwe	Benin Burkina Faso Cameroon Central African Republic Chad Congo, Rep. of Côte d'Ivoire Gambia, The Ghana Guinea Guinea-Bissau Liberia Mali Mauritania Niger Nigeria São Tomé and Principe Senegal Sierra Leone Togo	Cambodia Korea, Dem. People's Rep. of Lao PDR Mongolia Myanmar Papua New Guinea Solomon Islands Timor-Leste Vietnam	Afghanistan Bangladesh Bhutan India Nepal Pakistan	Kyrgyz Republic Moldova Tajikistan Uzbekistan		Yemen, Rep. of		Haiti Nicaragua
Middle-income countries	*Lower*	Angola Namibia Swaziland	Cape Verde	China Fiji Indonesia Kiribati Marshall Islands Micronesia, Fed. Sts. of Philippines Samoa Thailand Tonga Vanuatu	Maldives Sri Lanka	Albania Armenia Azerbaijan Belarus Bosnia and Herzegovina Bulgaria Georgia Kazakhstan Macedonia, FYR[a] Romania Serbia and Montenegro Turkmenistan Ukraine		Iran, Islamic Rep. of Iraq Jordan Syrian Arab Rep. West Bank and Gaza	Algeria Djibouti Egypt, Arab Rep. of Morocco Tunisia	Bolivia Brazil Colombia Cuba Dominican Republic Ecuador El Salvador Guatemala Guyana Honduras Jamaica Paraguay Peru Suriname
	Upper	Botswana Mauritius Mayotte Seychelles South Africa	Equatorial Guinea Gabon	American Samoa Malaysia N. Mariana Islands Palau		Croatia Czech Republic Estonia Hungary Latvia Lithuania Poland Russian Federation Slovak Republic	Turkey	Lebanon Oman	Libya	Antigua and Barbuda Argentina Barbados Belize Chile Costa Rica Dominica Grenada Mexico Panama St. Kitts and Nevis St. Lucia St. Vincent Trinidad and Tobago Uruguay Venezuela, R. B. de

(continued)

Table A.30 (continued)

Income group	Subgroup	Sub-Saharan Africa		Asia		Europe and Central Asia		Middle East and North Africa		Americas
		East and Southern Africa	West Africa	East Asia and Pacific	South Asia	Eastern Europe and Central Asia	Rest of Europe	Middle East	North Africa	
High-income countries	*OECD*			Australia Japan Korea, Rep. New Zealand			Austria Belgium Denmark Finland France[b] Germany Greece Iceland Ireland Italy Luxembourg Netherlands Norway Portugal Spain Sweden Switzerland United Kingdom			Canada United States
	Non-OECD			Brunei French Polynesia Guam Hong Kong, China[c] Macao, China[d] New Caledonia Singapore Taiwan, China		Slovenia	Andorra Channel Islands Cyprus Faeroe Islands Greenland Isle of Man Liechtenstein Monaco San Marino	Bahrain Israel Kuwait Qatar Saudi Arabia United Arab Emirates	Malta	Aruba Bahamas, The Bermuda Cayman Islands Netherlands Antilles Puerto Rico Virgin Islands (U.S.)
Total	209	25	23	36	8	27	28	14	7	41

Source: World Bank data.

Note: For operational and analytical purposes, the World Bank's main criterion for classifying economies is gross national income (GNI) per capita. Every economy is classified as low income, middle income (subdivided into lower middle and upper middle), or high income. Other analytical groups, based on geographic regions and levels of external debt, are also used. Low-income and middle-income economies are sometimes referred to as developing economies. The use of the term is convenient; it is not intended to imply that all economies in the group are experiencing similar development or that other economies have reached a preferred or final stage of development. Classification by income does not necessarily reflect development status. This table classifies all World Bank member economies, and all other economies with populations of more than 30,000. Economies are divided among income groups according to 2004 GNI per capita, calculated using the World Bank Atlas method. The groups are: low income, $825 or less; lower middle income, $826–3,255; upper middle income, $3,256–10,065; and high income, $10,066 or more.
a. Former Yugoslav Republic of Macedonia.
b. The French overseas departments French Guiana, Guadeloupe, Martinique, and Réunion are included in France.
c. On 1 July 1997 China resumed its exercise of sovereignty over Hong Kong.
d. On 20 December 1999 China resumed its exercise of sovereignty over Macao.